MAKERS OF THE ENVIRONMENT

MAKERS OF THE ENVIRONMENT
BUILDING RESILIENCE INTO OUR WORLD ONE MODEL AT A TIME.
BIM OF THE BOOK ABOUT INFORMATION!
FINITH E JERNIGAN II

MAKERS OF THE ENVIRONMENT
BUILDING RESILIENCE INTO OUR WORLD ONE MODEL AT A TIME.
BIM OF THE BOOK ABOUT INFORMATION!
FINITH E JERNIGAN II

All rights reserved. No part of this book may be reproduced or transmitted in any form or by any means, electronic or mechanical, including photocopying, recording or by any information storage and retrieval system, without written permission from the author, except for the inclusion of brief quotations in a review.

Copyright © 2011 by 4Site Press, Salisbury, MD

Jernigan, Finith E
Makers of the Environment: Building Resilience into Our World, One Model at a Time. BIM of the Book about Information!/(Finith E. Jernigan) — 1st ed.
p. cm.
Includes bibliographical references.

ISBN: 0-9795699-6-6
ISBN 13: 978-0-9795699-6-8
Library of Congress Control Number: 2011914951
4Site Press, Salisbury, MD
1. Creative Thinking. 2. Value Added.
3. Built Environment—Technology. 4. Healthcare Management.
5. Change Management.   I. Title. II. Title: Makers of the Environment.

Publisher: 4Site Press
Salisbury, MD 21801-5038, USA
publisher@4sitesystems.com
http://www.4sitesystems.com

Printed in the United States

USE CASE FOR THIS BOOK

> If people can't figure out what "enough" is, where the end lies, they may decide it's not worth starting. Sad but true. —Seth Godin

Dear Reader,

My goal is to advance new tools and processes into the mainstream, making complex ideas about the future of the built environment clear to the reader. I have long advocated for simplicity and clarity. The goal is to give readers a perspective that allows them to assess where we are today and where we can be tomorrow, in terms that everyone can understand.

The award winning *BIG BIM little bim* focused on implementing new technology and practices in architects' design offices. This book focuses on possibilities and design futures for where technology can lead culture and how each of us can prepare ourselves for tomorrow. We need to know where the power of an interconnected world will take society.

When I started this book, I intended to release a third addition of *BIG BIM little bim*, describing the new and exciting things that have happened since the release of the second edition in 2008. The goal was to help readers understand where these rapidly evolving technologies and processes are heading. As I began the research and planning, it soon became apparent that adding case studies and tweaking the original book to include the latest happenings could not accurately represent the change.

The ability to interact with everything in the built environment is the most compelling aspect of the information that surrounds us. Easily using the distributed, multidimensional tools and processes that connect data from multiple sources is not a dream… People are doing it today. Collaborative processes, rich data repositories and advanced graphics are the seeds of this information revolution. Properly applied, the tools that make this transformation possible are straightforward and accessible. Anyone can apply them to their benefit.

The information that connects the world is not linear nor is it simple. This complex information affects us all, every day in everything we do. It comes from anywhere and everywhere. It defies linear description, and the complexity can overwhelm. Few are actively working to address the complexity for those most affected.

Many talented people have been working to address this complexity for the professionals that design and build today. Building information modeling is the tool that they use to represent and connect to this complexity. This book is designed to help the rest of us understand and use the information.

Accurately representing this multidimensional tangle of information in a real book seems to be difficult or impossible. How does one write a book that accurately represents this complexity? This was the challenge.

The solution was to make this book an information model itself…a book that connects to external information that connects to the built environment. Writing a book that is itself an information model involves several structures.

Where additional data, or the wisdom of others might improve understanding, the book links to external information via your web-enabled device, using tags. Tags allow the reader to jump to more detailed and technical discussions about topics included in the book. Those reading the book on a web-enabled reader, such as an iPad, find links taking them to the same places.

I have chosen to use the Microsoft Tag format. The tags offer several benefits:

They establish direct links to more information and let one embed information into a printed book. Think of them as a glossary on steroids.

They allow the reader to examine the broad ideas and possibilities, or to use the book as a technical text for students or others learning the subject in more depth. Think of the book as a 3-D symbolic model with links to underlying data.

They allow updating of connected information as things change, and offer the possibility of direct communication with the reader. They allow one to add data in real-time after publication of the physical book. Think of them as a database connection that over time can access an ever-richer representation of information.

The second structure is a narrative table of contents. The table of contents allows the reader to move through the book's content in any order. Professionals approach their information modeling process from different viewpoints; the reader can experience this book the same way. I have organized the book in one logical order. Some readers will prefer to approach the order differently.

The Narrative Table of Contents creates the opportunity to map out your personal path through the book. Different people use information models differently. They approach them from differing viewpoints. They have different needs. A community leader evaluating new sidewalks needs different views of her information model than would a builder trying to schedule when to bring in the concrete finishers. Use the Narrative Table of Contents to read the book in the sequence that seems right. Feel free to explore elements that appeal, circling back to the story line as it suits your exploration.

Get your free mobile app at - http: //gettag.mobi or read more at - http://4sitesystems.com/iofthestorm/?page_id=814

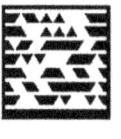

Finally, I designed the book around a series of interconnected near-future usage scenarios. I built the scenarios around technology and processes that exist today or that can credibly be projected from today's tools and environment. They are fictional projections, not case studies. Think of these design futures as individual an information model much like the Revit or ArchiCAD models that architects and contractors build.

The central design future that flows through this book describes technology that allows people to manage these issues in the built environment. This scenario shows how an organization in a small, depressed rural county can pull together to take advantage of short development cycles to become a world leader in the management of information to support the built environment. With systems and processes such as this design future describes, we for the first time in history can have a secure, verifiable, and accessible archive for the digital assets that help us to define and manage real-world assets. The central design future forms the backbone for the three scenarios that use the information to improve the world.

The design futures include rich information, show how to take advantage of existing tools, and allow just-in-time decision making, but they are not yet fully realized. The individuals in these scenarios are archetypes of the people that manage similar issues today.

I mention few real people in the book. Where real people are included, I believe them to be the originator of the idea or critical to the reader's understanding of the issue under discussion. The locations that serve as the stages for these scenarios are, for the most part, physical places that can be found on any map. I have modified them to communicate within the time lines and needs of this book. Woven within the scenarios are commentary, opinion, and facts from the world today. These historical and present day passages are shaded for clarity. Chapters that begin with dates and places are design fiction.

—Finith E. Jernigan

 *Introduction on the web at http://4sitesystems.com/iofthestorm/?page_id=1541*

TABLE OF CONTENTS

1: WICKED PROBLEMS IN OUR WORLD 1

Interconnected models that focus on people, organizations, and technology are among the data sets hosted by BIMSynergy. **Page 30** • The instant that you create data and save it to a static file system, the information is dated. **Page 31** • The Onuma System's ability to maintain data as a living resource and to interface with expert systems via web services made it one of the first, and most critical tools that enabled BIMSynergy to maintain live data at all times. **Page 55** • Schedule management, clash detection, financial management, value chain management, tagging and tracking, process automation, risk management, optimization, and logistics are all supported by BIMSynergy. **Page 69** • The SMART Connexion Server provides rules-based planning, real-life decision making, geographic analysis, and product life cycle coordination. **Page 48** • BIMSynergy is only one part of a global data modeling continuum. **Page 48** •

You can also follow the tag to Wicked Problems in Our World Chapter Narratives on the web at http://4sitesystems.com/iofthestorm/?page_id=467

2: INFORMATION AS FORCE MULTIPLIER 75

The system allows nontechnical users to work with computer-aided design, building information modeling, and geographic information system data. **Page 82** • Integrated systems, such as the Consequences Planning System and the Onuma System, used to develop the design for CGSysOps, allowed users to accelerate the decision-making process. **Page 102** • In the early years of the twenty-first century, the Coast Guard started the process of mapping out how to use existing data and how to move forward in a world where data was becoming critical. **Page 89** • The systems assist knowledgeable people by presenting data about the built environment and Coast Guard processes that were not readily accessible before. **Page 82** • Up-to-date, real-time information and just-in-time imagery translates into actionable plans and goals that can be implemented effectively and support routine operations. **Page 100** •

You can also follow the tag to Information as Force Multiplier Chapter Narratives on the web at http://4sitesystems.com/iofthestorm/?page_id=471

3: EDUCATION FOR TOMORROW 115

Professionals are finding that geographic information, facility information, utility information, operations information, business information, political information, sustainability information, and virtually every other form of information are intertwining. **Page 143** • The line between information producers and information users is vanishing. Yet, rather than using scientific methods and looking at the underlying structure and systems, we have fallen back on tradition and legacy systems to drive educational decision making. **Page 138** • Most of the jobs that people will hold twenty years from now have not yet been invented. **Page 121** • Today's collaborations need people who can synthesize information and problem solve within the collaborative framework. **Page 136** • People must synthesize new things from what usually look to be unrelated things. **Page 126** • The willingness to innovate backed up by deep knowledge and broad interests are the keys to making the changes required in an integrated world. **Page 124** •

You can also follow the tag to Education for Tomorrow Chapter Narratives on the web at http://4sitesystems.com/iofthestorm/?page_id=475

4: THE STORM 151

Social networking systems, tightly integrated web conference systems, BIMSynergy, and rules-based decision-making tools work together to engage decision makers, wherever they are at the time. **Page 158** • In this fictional case study, we explore how fact-based decision-making tools can improve public trust and compliance, simplifying emergency management. **Page 152** •

You can also follow the tag to The Storm Chapter Narratives on the web at http://4sitesystems.com/iofthestorm/?page_id=479

5: THE ART OF CHANGE 165

Design and construction delivery methods, such as design-bid-build, design-build, construction management at risk, agency construction management, and integrated project delivery, are someone's idea of how to achieve a perfect project. **Page 209** • The Virtual Enterprise Network is an alliance of individuals and companies coming together to share their knowledge and resources to respond to the needs of Cork Point and the community. **Page 201** • With a construction manager acting as a trusted advisor to the owner and a design team contractually obligated to share and collaborate, agency construction management offers a significant step toward integrated project delivery. **Page 213** • Capital planning is connected to facility planning, is connected to architectural design, is connected to construction, is connected to business planning, is connected to health-care planning, is connected to facilities management, is connected to operations, is connected to staffing, is connected to medical equipment, is connected to... **Page 169** • As design and construction professionals convinced people of the value of information modeling, some people started to see the disconnect between the file-based information models and the life cycle benefits that should happen. **Page 226** •

You can also follow the tag to Art of Change Chapter Narratives on the web at http://4sitesystems.com/iofthestorm/?page_id=483

6: COMMON SENSE MULTIPLIED BY TECHNOLOGY 241

In this fictional case study, we explore how geographic information systems, sensor networks, information models, model servers, and many other technologies enable the Network for Sustainable Decisions to bring the information to people. **Page 253** • Sandy officially kicks off BIMStorm Chesapeake Agriculture. **Page 263** • A consensus was reached that data is essential and the creator of that data should be the ultimate owner. **Page 263** • The group's processes encourage just-in-time decision making, eliminate duplication, and make the appropriate information available. **Page 250** • Strident, polarized groups spent so much time fighting and arguing that they had no time or energy left for fixing the problems. **Page 237** • As design and planning teams create solutions and the area adapts to the changes required by the bay recovery, BIMStorm Chesapeake works to manage the ebb and flow of support needs. **Page 270** •

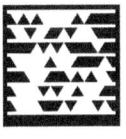

You can also follow the tag to Common Sense Multiplied by Technolgy Chapter Narratives on the web at http://4sitesystems.com/iofthestorm/?page_id=487

7: END GAME...297

You can also follow the tag to End Game Chapter Narratives on the web at http://4sitesystems.com/iofthestorm/?page_id=491

Information models, geographic information systems, sensors, devices, financial systems, and much more are linked. **Page 297** • Every system is connected. **Page 301** • The focus of the tools and processes are the larger world issues that will sustain the world for our children. **Page 295** • The core design future that flows through this book describes technology that allows people to manage complex information in the built environment. **Page 305** •

APPENDIX...315

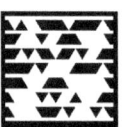

You can also follow the tag to the Glossary, Character Sketches, the Bibliography and other information on the web at - http://4sitesystems.com/iofthestorm/?page_id=495

Manage the process of exchanging data through the built environment value network. Information modeling makes processes available to the right person at the right time. It focuses on buildings (building information models), business processes, software engineering, data, semantics, and many other things. **Page 318** •

GLOSSARY..317

You can follow the tag to the Glossary on the web at http://4sitesystems.com/iofthestorm/?page_id=1000

Definitions and explanations of the terms and concepts included in Makers of the Environment. **Page 324** •

TIMELINE...330

You can follow the tag to the Interactive Timeline at - http://4sitesyste iofthestorm/?page_id=709

INTRODUCTION

 **POWER OF INFORMATON**

> Man built most nobly when limitations were at their greatest.
> —Frank Lloyd Wright

This book is an information model. Some might call it a building information model, but book information model is probably more accurate. The goal is to represent the complexity and power of information modeling technologies and processes within what has up to now been a linear media.

Information models have structure and represent one's vision and data about the world. They connect bits of data to create frameworks for managing the complexity so that we can make better decisions with facts. They make information accessible; they create order, from what is often chaos.

Your home has context in the real world. It is part of a nation, a state, a city, a neighborhood, and a street. It has a foundation, walls, floors, ceilings, heating, lighting, a roof, and many other parts. So do information models in the virtual world. These models create connections to the world. They connect with data about the things in the model and about the things that influence the model.

Your model knows that you have (or plan to have) bamboo flooring in your family room. It also knows how strong the flooring is, how long it will last, how to care for it, where it came from, who installed it, and how much it cost. That is just the start. Your model also knows where they grew the bamboo, who cut it, and how it impacts on your country's foreign trade balance and gives three-dimensional views of any of this information.

Your model brings all of this information any time a decision about your flooring is needed. It lets you look at the data, massage it, and use it to make better decisions. What type of rug would be best? Where can I buy the right rug? How can I fix the scratches that Buster made? Who can do this work? How much will it cost? Consult your model and get the facts that you need to decide.

This book does much the same thing. This book has a structure that puts information into context and builds a framework to represent a future vision of where information modeling is heading.

Today, information modeling is taking hold in the built environment, the man-made part of the world. The built environment provides the setting for human activity; ranging from buildings to neighborhoods to cities, and including infrastructure, such as transportation, water and energy networks, and other things that relate to humans over time.

Many specializations built around information are rapidly folding together as experts realize the power and possibilities that information modeling brings to the built environment. This is happening in a context that increases public access and makes data more democratic and useful. As in the best of today's building information models, this book approaches the data from many viewpoints, with different media and many levels of detail, all intended to amuse and educate about the power of information to improve the world.

PROLOGUE

GRACE'S GREEN THUMB
DEVOL, OKLAHOMA
JULY 17, 1999

Grace had a green thumb and could grow anything, even in the dry and desolate environment of southern Oklahoma. To her, gardening was essential to the family's survival. Her garden was the centerpiece of her pink and white prairie bungalow, and a showplace in Cotton County, Oklahoma. She grew vegetables, fruit, and the prettiest flowers in the county. Her neighbors suspected that Grace's windbreak had a lot to do with the strawberries that she grew every spring.

That farming is a struggle to balance the things that affect success or failure was never more true than in Oklahoma's hot and dry conditions. Floyd and Grace farmed wheat and barley and raised four daughters in the times of recovery after the Dust Bowl. In those days, it was a constant struggle to survive. Soil conservation and water management were not luxuries. They were necessities of life. One of President Roosevelt's windbreaks, forty feet deep, protected Floyd and Grace's house and garden.

The Eastern Red Cedar windbreak protected the north and west exposures. To Floyd and Grace, the windbreak was not a bunch of trees; it was a vital part of their life. The windbreak was part of the Great Plains Shelterbelt program, one of the first "green" mandates designed to reduce wind velocity and slow evaporation of moisture. By the 1990s, their trees were thirty feet tall and formed an almost impenetrable barrier. Damaging the windbreak was taboo.

Young kids are natural explorers. They explore their environment guided by their natural curiosity. Their imagination can lead them to entertaining and sometimes unexpected consequences. Sandy was like that. She poked her nose into everything. She built tree houses and snow forts. When bored, even a blanket over a couple of chairs made for a magical place. Who knew what mysteries the impenetrable interior of the windbreak held?

It was a sunny, hot, and still Oklahoma Saturday. The adults were doing adult things, leaving the kids to keep themselves occupied... A perfect opportunity to explore the dark and impenetrable depths of the windbreak. After a trip to the barn, with clippers and limb loppers in hand, Sandy and her brother headed for the windbreak. Snip...lop...snip...snip.... Branches fell. Soon they found themselves in the shady interior of the windbreak. It was perfect and dry, with a blanket of soft needles. It was the best fort that they could imagine. For a couple of hours, they let their imagination roam.

As usually happened after an absence of a couple of hours and when they had fun, they heard their mom calling. When she found them and discovered their work on the windbreak, things stopped being fun...fast. They had trouble sitting down for a couple of days. They learned the true value of conservation, in an intensely personal way.

Grace and the Devol, OK Gardening Club among her garden backed by her Red Cedar windbreak, circa 1960. 34° 11' 26 N 98° 35' 6" W

People have remarkably short memories when it comes to environmental disaster. To Sandy, the Dust Bowl was a superb example of the problems we bring on ourselves and how hard it is to recover. Growing up in north Texas and Oklahoma, conservation programs were part of life. Her experience in her grandmother's windbreak directly affected how she related to the land. Even as a young child, she was a fast learner, especially with the proper reinforcement.

The Dust Bowl spawned severe drought. Intense farming with little regard for erosion control and indiscriminate cutting of trees and prairie grasses combined to form enormous dust storms that wiped out farms, forced over 2.5 million people from their homes, and scoured earth from millions of acres of land. Only when the dust storms reached the eastern seaboard in the mid-1930s did the catastrophe begin to be taken seriously by the rest of the country. The area started to heal as mandated soil conservation took hold. The programs encouraged farmers to restore and improve soil fertility, to minimize wind and water erosion, to preserve resources and wildlife. Recovery and stabilization required cooperation and active participation from many people over decades.

Environmental practices have changed since the days of windbreaks. Scientific research has given us a better understanding of the natural forces that drive the environment. We have learned more about what works and what does not work. Today we consider the Eastern Red Cedars, which Floyd and Grace planted to survive, to be invasive plants. As a monoculture, Red Cedars cause a loss of biodiversity, contribute to loss of endangered species, degrade air quality, and are a threat to water resources. New data and better science gave us a new view of a plant once valued for its rapid growth and dense vegetation.

The lessons that Sandy took away from the Dust Bowl and the Red Cedars is that we must find ways to fix those problems that affect us today, all the while keeping in mind that we may have to be flexible and change when more accurate information and new facts become available. The process can take decades.

> **The very process of the restoring the land to health is the process through which we become attuned to Nature and, through Nature, with ourselves.**
> **—Chris Maser, Forest Primeval**

THE SUNSET THREW LONG SHADOWS
NORFOLK, VIRGINIA
SEPTEMBER 3, 2022

The sunset threw long shadows from the woods. Pete Jarvi looked out the kitchen's sliding glass door of his Virginia Beach house. The deer were back! A doe and four almost grown fawns. Two deer hopped a few feet at the sound of the door opening. He walked out on the deck. Then they stopped and looked at him. Friend or foe? He did not like deer, at least, not in his back yard. He had put deer repellent around just a month ago. It was incongruous, his feelings about deer. He was sympathetic to the environment, and while not a tree-hugger, he did not like the idea of offshore oil drilling in Florida or more drilling in Alaskan wilderness. He liked spotted owls more than big lumber companies. He liked wildlife. He taught his kids to respect nature. They were Friends of the National Zoo—just no deer in his backyard!

Pete Jarvi's house backs up on woods and a creek in Virginia Beach, VA. 36° 51' 25" N 76° 02' 02" W. Google Earth Imagery copyright Google 2011

He worried about the kids, Thomas and Cindy, getting Lyme disease or something worse. He was thinking about picking up more tick repellant, when the phone rang. It was probably one of Cindy's friends calling about soccer. She would pick it up.

"Dad, it's Mr. Boyle."

"Pete, I need you to get in here as fast as you can." It was Gary Boyle, his boss at CGSysOPs.

"Can you tell me anything?"

"No. Just hurry!"

Jarvi poured the remainder of his bourbon and water down the sink. He yelled down the basement steps, "Mel, I've gotta go to the office. I don't know whether I'll be back tonight. I'll call you later, if I can."

Melanie, Pete's wife and mother of their kids, was in the basement supervising—make that refereeing—air hockey, and booting up the computer for Thomas to play games. The thing had been buggy lately.

"Call me when you can. Your overnight bag's in the hall closet," she called up the steps. "Paul's supposed to come up tomorrow and stay over. Call me if you aren't going to be back in time."

Jarvi cranked the Toyota Camry and WNIS was broadcasting the news of an explosion in Portsmouth, a probable air attack. He figured that was why Gary called. The details were sketchy. It was probably serious, because Fred Boyd was on call for the weekend. If they called them both in, it was probably a disaster. Worse, they were probably expecting multiple attacks, like 9/11.

THUMP... THUMP... THUMP...
CRISFIELD, MARYLAND
APRIL 17, 2026

Every time the pile driver hammer dropped, the whole hospital jumped. Barring further problems, they would finish the piles today.

Yesterday, a hydraulic blowout shut down the operation. For a while, it looked like everything would stop for the rest of the week. Elle was beside herself; they certainly could not afford downtime this early on the new surgical wing, but Joe's team jumped on the problem and they only lost three hours, just like they said, everyone working like a team this time.

In her head, she knew that they could do it, but in her heart she still had a hard time believing in this new integrated project technology. This information modeling stuff was just too much like magic. If the contractor at her last hospital had the same problem, he would take a day to figure out what was wrong. Then he would take four days to get the part, even if it were in stock right down the street. Joe's crew did it in three hours! She truly did need to let her team handle things like this, and stop micromanaging.

Thump…thump…thump…. Elle's immaculate desk jumped. Already focused on the reimbursement spreadsheet on her laptop, she did not notice.

Traditional shanties and blue crab shedding floats near Cedar Island Marsh, Somerset County, MD. 37° 57' 52" N 75° 50' 51" W

Dr. Elaina Bagayoko-Smith (Elle to everyone that knew her) led Cork Point with the finesse of a symphony maestro—or, some would say, with the fire of a drill instructor. Her friends said that she was not a Type A personality; she was an A++. Elle had mastered the chess game played by all health-care CEOs, always looking five steps ahead to find strategies with significant payoffs. She was obsessive about managing risk.

Most healthcare CEOs just did not have time to focus on facilities. Their priorities were on keeping the medical staff happy, getting paid, and raising money. Elle was different. Her architects said that she was the best of clients, one who thought that design was essential. She truly got into the process... Some would say too much. It was not that she did not handle those other priorities. It was just that she saw things a lot more holistically. She had bet her career on the fact that she could create a people-centered, sustainable life care system by integrating everything.

Cork Point could no longer exist by focusing only on sick care. The system had to change. Elle knew that she needed to heal people when they were sick, but that could no longer be the only focus. Cork Point must become a real health-care system. The system must focus on personal health through prevention and education. Her priorities must become community integration and collaboration.

Cork Point must become an integrated enterprise. Otherwise, they would be living in a world where they would be the last holdout. Every day Elle saw and used products created by others who had already gone down this path. Her grocery store was integrated. Her local car care shop was integrated. Her bank was integrated. Integrated processes affected everything she did, every day. Cork Point must become the same.

She knew that the first task was to move away from command and control; the culture must adjust to allow collaboration, if they were to prosper.

MAKERS OF THE ENVIRONMENT

WICKED PROBLEMS IN OUR WORLD

1.

The Chesapeake Bay is in crisis. The Network for Sustainable Decisions is creating systems that let everyone actively participate in the revival, while managing the interests of all. Sandy Kim, a virtual enterprise manager, manages environmental recovery using live data, collaborative systems, and rule-based controls.

The United States Coast Guard has a mission of keeping us safe and secure. Information enables them to fulfill this mission in a world of ever-increasing complexity and threat. Meet Pete Jarvi, a BIM manager. He is your guide to using information to get certainty of outcomes.

A forward-thinking health-care enterprise faces all of today's issues. They are using technology and new ways of working to capitalize on peoples' passions. They let people use their art to create a better world. Dr. Elle Smith, hospital administrator, shows how a health-care organization can use information to grow and support the community in a world of fiscal and regulatory constraints.

In each case, Somerset County's BIMSynergy Corporation, led by your narrator George Thomas, the county development manager, provides the backbone to maintain the consistent, shared and authoritative data to get the job done. The corporation is just one of the public utility businesses that fulfill this need across the world.

SOMERSET COUNTY, MARYLAND
JUNE 1, 2030

> Imagination is more important than knowledge. For while knowledge defines all we currently know and understand, imagination points to all we might yet discover and create.
>
> —Albert Einstein

Since 1666, the county has seen a lot of ups and downs. We are pretty good at working through them...even if it takes a while. My name is George Thomas. I am the county development manager. The county has always had a farm- and seafood-based economy. My job has been to help the area become a player in the new world of information.

The changes required us to look deep inside of the way things operate around here. We had to be willing to make adjustments to just about anything and everything. We started out with a couple of dead-serious questions:

- Can a small group bring the resources to bear to support certainty for all?
- Can we handle information to make the world better for the future?

The seafood industry is dying. MSX has decimated the oysters. This year the crab population is okay. Last year crabs were scarce. Rockfish have rebounded, but rockfish do not keep the fishing fleet alive. It costs more to haul your boat and paint the bottom than a waterman can earn in a good season, these days. It is even hard to keep a few skipjacks sailing for the annual races on Labor Day. This year only four skipjacks filed their oyster-dredging certificates. We are a hardheaded bunch, known for patience, perseverance, and, most importantly, the ability to change when we must. Commerce and competition had changed from the day where a poor county was beholden to the urban areas.

A couple of years ago, the leadership in Princess Anne got together with the county and the university and decided that they would do whatever it took to turn the county into a haven for new technology. The members of the Somerset Intelligence Initiative figured that we could make this small, rural area into the showplace for the flat world described by Tom Friedman. The county took advantage of a level playing field, where perception and will opened up opportunities across the world. The Somerset Intelligence Initiative's first big step in that direction was to install fiber-optic cabling and WiMAX everywhere, accessible to everyone. Photovoltaics, sustainability, net zero, smart grid, building information modeling, and model servers are the new names in the game, just as Friedman hinted.

The people who live and work in Somerset County and local leaders rebuilt the tax system from the bottom up. Local people did such a good job of making changes to the systems that people from all over the world asked us to help them with their change initiatives. We became the go-to for enlightened political change in rural communities and for integrating data to manage government better. New people are moving here to fill the new jobs. Not twenty years ago, there were only 5,444 families in the county. Last year the commissioners calculated that there were 12,000 families, a 120 percent increase! They think that it will double again in the next five years. We are busting at the seams. We are building new schools, new sewerage plants, and just about everything else that it takes to handle the growth.

The hospital down in Crisfield is one of the county's greatest successes. They were among the first that embraced the integration idea. Their programs took off. It has become something that most have never seen—a place where young, old, and everyone in between can live, work, and play.

The hospital has a rich history. The leadership down there capitalized on tradition. They are keeping the hospital connected with the community. They did extensive research and marketing studies to make sure that the changes they proposed would work to better the community. The hospital even changed the name back to the original Cork Point to emphasize the long-standing connection to Crisfield and Somerset County.

Edward McCready, a Crisfield native, ran his family's cork business from Chicago. On September 13, 1919, Edward, his daughter, and the young girl's nurse embarked on the long drive home after visiting relatives in his native Crisfield. That fateful Saturday morning, they collided with a train near Westover. Both adults died at the scene. Rescuers rushed the girl to the hospital in downtown Crisfield, but the child succumbed to her injuries en route. When the heartbroken Caroline McCready reached Crisfield after the accident, she endowed Edward W. McCready Memorial Hospital with money and property, in memory of her husband and daughter.

Built on a peninsula flanked by Daugherty's Creek and Hospital Cove known as "Cork Point," the hospital opened May 6, 1923, with nearly three dozen beds, becoming one of Delmarva's largest hospitals at the time. In 1961, the hospital added a small addition. They built a nursing home in 1968 in memory of Alice Byrd Tawes, the mother of Governor J. Millard Tawes. The nursing home put McCready Memorial in rare company since even now few nursing homes in the area directly connect to a hospital.

Accessible by land, sea, and air, the hospital ministers to the residents of Crisfield and the surrounding Somerset County. In 1980, a $3.9 million replacement hospital connected the nursing home to the 1920s-era building. Now, they use the old hospital for clinics and administrative offices. In 2010, the hospital opened the Tawes Nursing &

Rehabilitation Center. The four-story, $12.5 million design included a skilled nursing unit and assisted-living apartments on the top floor.

Using cloud-based computing, integrated project delivery systems, and information modeling, the hospital's leadership has committed to creating new ways of doing business and supporting the community to help us all. They are wise and have an ability to deal with ambiguity and uncertainty. They believe in the notion that while things are uncertain now, further investigation will reduce ambiguity. They have faith in the future.

In the first part of the twenty-first century, they started to see opportunities for aligning technology and people. They saw new tools and new ways of working popping up every day. Significant numbers of people were using information tools. The hospital knew that they needed live, reliable information that would be available whenever people needed it for whatever reason. Few believed that it was possible. Many were so wedded to the old ways that they passively or actively undermined progress in the early days.

By creating and managing information models with second-order leadership tools, they created a system that defines how projects ought to happen. Their approach requires defined working practices, methodologies, and behaviors. Their process overlays multi-stage prototypes and cost management onto the five-phase process that has been the traditional approach to projects. Cork Point projects are truly collaborative, reward exemplary work, and are flexible enough to respond to change and new ways of doing business.

The changes have taken a willingness to modify how the hospital does business and how it manages its projects. The changes took a commitment to embrace new technology. Most of all, they required a high level of personal and corporate responsibility. The hospital's leaders use systems thinking to prepare for an uncertain future in the global economy. Their systems approach lets them understand things on a larger scale than we normally see around here.

The benefits to the community come from consistently applying and reinforcing the concepts that are the foundation of the Cork Point system. They use the best available tools for the job at hand. However, the tools are secondary. The goal is improved projects with positive outcomes, every time.

At Cork Point, they focus on providing sustained value for the community. They eliminate or reduce inefficiencies in the process. They eliminate tedious and repetitive tasks. They put in place systems that let them play what-if games. They test outcomes by changing variables and running their models at high speed. They use a comprehensive systems thinking process. The Cork Point Planning Team know that most people do not think particularly strategically… Not about their own lives, or the lives of future generations. So they created a system that lets them think about thinking about the future.

By doing this, they have become stewards of their resources. Their approach creates an archive of information in interoperable databases. They use this information to maintain and operate the facility, allowing others to benefit from it for many years to come.

Often it seems like people believe that we can solve environmental and facilities problems with traditional methods. They act like the problems can be handled by purchasing a new piece of software, training people more, or learning some new tricks. It is just not so. Treating these issues with the traditional approach has led to waste and declining productivity. We need to understand the subtleties that drive the changes to the world today.

That is what the county and Cork Point are doing every day.

SUBTLETIES

> Insanity is doing the same thing over and over again and expecting different results.
>
> —Albert Einstein

First-order tools and techniques simply follow the rules and focus on doing-things-the-right-way. They are the foundation for expertise and process compliance.

Second-order techniques use first-order tools and higher-level skills to adapt, modify, and improvise to focus on doing-the-right-thing. They are targeted on achieving the end goal.

Complicated tasks can be difficult to understand as a whole, but they have an understood set of rules. If you follow the rules, step by step, you can solve complicated problems. Quadratic equations and building Boeing 747s are complicated tasks, but if you know the rules they can be completed successfully.

Tame problems are well defined with a straightforward problem statement. The ability to solve tame problems is a part of professional development and is a step toward mastery. They can be complicated, but you know when you have reached a solution. The solution is either right or wrong. You solve most tame problems using similar methods, and the result can be tested to determine whether it works or not. Most of the project management tools that we use in the early twenty-first century are designed for tame problems. Tools for managing tame problems can be called first-order tools.

Complexity does not follow the same pattern. The lacrosse coach cannot lay out every action in advance. Today a weak member of the opposing team could have her best game ever and score a hat trick. How can you plan for that? You cannot know where things are heading until other things happen. Things are likely to happen about which you have no knowledge or control over. The unknowns and uncertainties that characterize complex tasks make them difficult to solve with traditional tools.

With real-world experience, you can prepare for some of the known unknowns that happen in complex situations. Other things are outside of your control. It is the things you don't know that you don't know that make complex tasks so difficult to resolve. Farming is an example of a complex task. Many things can be planned; the farmer can choose the right time to plant and can use the land properly, but weather, pests, and all of the other things that cannot be controlled make the difference between success and failure.

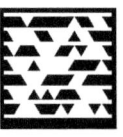

Follow this tag to learn more about complicated and complex at http://4sitesystems.com/iofthestorm/?page_id=870

Wicked problems are complex. Wicked problems usually involve significant numbers of people changing their behavior and mindsets. A wicked problem is a moving target. When you think you have solved a wicked problem, usually all that you have done is to identify a new problem. Even defining a wicked problem is in itself a wicked problem. Wicked problems do not have a stopping point. There is no test of solutions to wicked problems. Rather than "right or wrong," a wicked problem can usually only be described by "better or worse." Every wicked problem is essentially unique and can be considered a manifestation of another problem.

The ability to work with wicked problems and their complexity requires the leadership and expertise of a master. Tools for managing wicked problems can be called second-order tools. Second-order tools focus on systems thinking, appropriate leadership, and flexibility to respond appropriately to complex situations, and not to process compliance. Community planning, the environment, energy, sustainability, integrated practice, and most of the other issues that affect our future can be said to be wicked problems.

If a problem is wicked, the traditional approach doesn't work. No proscribed linear approach will solve a wicked problem. The linear approach must develop solutions just to see the hidden issues and flush out the hidden stakeholders. As the unknowns and uncertainties form and you add more resources, the situation becomes worse. Approaches that use first-order management tools alone often do not perform as expected, even when used by trained professionals who have worked all their lives to gain expertise.

A significant percentage of built environment projects that have used traditional tools and processes can be considered failures. Traditional project management is usually unable to respond effectively to unknown situations. Wasted resources, cost overruns, missed schedules, litigation, lack of support, and many other problems are the result.

Some things do not change. Deeply buried within the traditional approach is an orientation to a linear process. Many of today's projects involve wicked problems. Viewed from this perspective, it becomes clear that the failures are not simply due to incompetence and mismanagement. They are mainly due to an organizational adherence to using a linear, scientific process. The tendency is to cling to step-by-step linear thinking in the belief that first-order tools such as project management will lead to a solution to the problem. Problem projects and failures are the result.

Solving wicked problems requires more interaction than any linear sequence of steps provides. You do not "solve" a wicked problem as much as broker shared understanding and shared meaning about the problem and the possible solutions. Communication and collaboration, more even than creativity, are critical to success on wicked problems.

Designers are driven to look for linear solutions that speak to how they personally understand problems. Yet, a wicked problem is more like a chess game than a game of dominos. Each action that is made initiates a new although interconnected set of possible actions and outcomes. The second-order approach refocuses the design process toward communication, systems thinking, and collaboration in a context of human interests, concerns, and meaning making. Creativity, insight, and innovation emerge spontaneously as the consequence of shared knowledge and shared responsibility.

HUB OF THE MESH

The Internet is everywhere. Everyone uses it. The complexities of the technology and the standards supporting it do not need to be understood by the user. Users log into Expedia and make reservations in real-time without needing to know about databases, HTML, web services, XML, or anything else. Emerging technology can read and manipulate the information in this world. This is the beauty of the Internet: simple-to-use interfaces and minimal or no training required for beneficial use.

Dependable and readily accessible data are essential to modern society. Economic prosperity, national security, and public health and safety can no longer be achieved without data. Communities that lack such information even for short periods have trouble satisfying basic needs for food, water, shelter, and law and order.

Over the past thirty years, building owners have spent a lot of money to implement new technologies. Typically, they threw away old systems and started over every time a new approach became the standard. Each time this happened, they had to bear the costs to resurvey, re-input, and replace their entire system. The costs to do the work over have been significant. The costs from lost inertia, resources, and knowledge have been incalculable.

These costs pushed owners to accept low bids. Owners cut corners and accepted halfway implementations with ongoing usability problems. Often, the data was accessible and usable by a limited group of people. Project outcomes suffered. The rework squandered limited resources. Building owners spent too much money, with little value in return. The built environment suffered.

How often have you tried to open a file from one version of your current software, only to find that you cannot open it with the latest version? How many times have you needed to open a floppy disk used five years ago, to find that your machines have no floppy drives? How many times have you tried to access a CD-ROM burned six years ago and found that it was unreadable?

Information managed in systems that make the data accessible, keep it up-to-date, and allow the data to be added to over time begin to solve these issues. The successes of the Internet have focused people on finding long-term solutions. Many are moving away from the cycle of lost information and starting over each time a new technology develops.

The ability to capture knowledge that can be added to and shared over time has been elusive for those that design and build the world. The problems in the built environment would not go away if tomorrow we woke up and every software product on the market could magically "talk to and understand" every other product. There are other issues.

The Internet thrives on shared information and is highly productive. The Internet moves from success to success, based on sharing information. Construction professionals continue to resist the need for archived interoperable data that could do the same for the built environment. Traditional construction industry approaches stymie innovation. Productivity is in decline.

Data can be standardized, shareable and usable by any software tool. The Internet relies on this "usable" interoperability—and not just for viewing data. Merely viewing data is of little value. It is the ability to access the data in ways that allow work to get done that is the foundation of most of the things that we find of benefit on the Internet, including maps, travel sites, social networks, and most other systems.

You can follow the tag to explore more about Interoperability on the web at http://4sitesystems.com/iofthestorm/?page_id=839

The Internet depends on consistent archives of data. These systems organize data in consistent and safe ways that make it so that we can find the information that we need. The information is shareable. We rely on it coming to us in consistent ways. The information is georeferenced (located in its correct place in the world), quality checked, and version controlled. When others check out the information, it is compliant with international standards, tied to a location on the earth and the latest version.

Today, we can do the same thing for the built environment, rather than recreating information every time a decision must be made. As the benefits of reusable information become better understood, those that work in the built environment will hopefully embrace sharing and interoperability to benefit us all. Accessible, shared information that lets us manage without becoming mired in the details may be the ultimate step in moving away from the "throw it away and start over" approach that has been a hallmark of the construction industry.

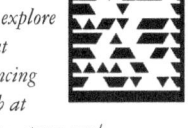

You can follow the tag to explore more about Georeferencing on the web at http://4sitesystems.com/iofthestorm/?page_id=863

PRINCIPLES

> It is impossible for anyone to begin to learn what he thinks that he already knows.
>
> —Epictetus

Complexity and ambiguity are everywhere. Information overload has become a way of life. Reliable systems are needed to help us to adapt. We must move beyond the bias for specialization, linear processes, and rote knowledge that most have learned in the twentieth-century education system. Systems-focused processes that enable people to interconnect complex information and respond to new issues are a key to the future.

By organizing around principles that allow people to learn new things that often have little to do with their current career specializations, we become more flexible and collaborative in our approach to the environment. We learn to adapt to new situations rather than becoming mired in detail and complexity. We begin to find the optimal approach to managing the wicked problems that beset the built environment.

Focusing on five broad areas helps to guide one toward a more collaborative approach and the flexibility to respond appropriately to complex situations. Integrated processes in the built environment need to focus on:

Use communication and technology to provide immediate access to all. Clear and open communication is the first priority. Without this, little else is possible.

Integrate and optimize working practices, methods, and behaviors to deliver maximum value for the least effort. Create a society where everyone is able to work together efficiently and effectively.

Interoperability and the ability to build structures that capture everything in shared and reliable ways that encourage collaboration. Use the simplest way to do what needs to be done. Do not get mired in detail. Focus on relationships and solutions. Share information and eliminate redundancy. Do something once and use the information for many purposes…forever.

Build knowledge and capture information about anything and everything in, and related to the built environment in stable archives. Use real-world rules about how things relate to each other to improve efficiency. Use information to eliminate the mundane and speed critical decisions. Pay attention to the details. Use technology to supplement the knowledge and understanding of those that must decide.

Fixate on certainty of outcomes. With informed knowledge, one can consider the options and arrive at the optimal solution. Yet nothing can guarantee that the solution will be the right global decision. We can use technology and systems thinking to help us to find the optimal "big-picture" solution. Use everything at your disposal to make things clear. Reuse data to get the right information, at the right time, to those who must decide.

Today, we are confronted with issues that have consequences far beyond what was the case even ten years ago. We are asked to make decisions that are outside of our areas of education and specialization. Our personal knowledge and experience is not sufficient to inform our judgment. We must focus on creating the most efficient and effective ways to support informed decision making. We must become more agile and more efficient; become a leader and adapt to change; flexibly manage uncertainty; and embrace new tools and thought processes to establish the wisdom needed in tomorrow's world.

FLUENCY

> He who rejects change is the architect of decay. The only human institution which rejects progress is the cemetery.
> —British Prime Minister Harold Wilson

Technology that was once specific to industry is no longer about designers, builders, or any other group; it is about the information that is transforming our world. The first principles behind this transformation remain the same today as they were when *BIG BIM little bim* was released, though the direction that technology is taking is decidedly different today. Today, the issues revolve around the intersection of cloud computing, geographical information, integrated business processes, and improving our world. Technology is moving toward a world that is participatory and inclusive, rather than hierarchical and expert-driven.

The built environment is becoming increasingly complex, confusing, and difficult to tie into neat packages. Forty-six percent of global resources are consumed in the built environment. Historically we as individuals had little say about the decisions that affect this situation. Technology is poised to redefine how we interact with people from beginning to end. Today's technology gives each of us the ability to interact and positively affect society. Technology and new ways of working affect us all.

Most people are not achieving mashable software fluency that would allow them to participate in the wider conversation about the built environment. Significant numbers of people have been shown the technology and experienced the tools, without a theoretical understanding of how to reach the long-term benefits. They attend a seminar, purchase a software package, and get to work, doing the same things that they did before. They install the software and start, working with the technology in isolation, often without knowing how to engage in the collaborative, open, and distributed world around them. The long-term possibilities and opportunities generally fall by the wayside as collaborative tools are used much like last year's deskbound software.

Industry is having a problem making intelligent decisions about how to embrace the technology, even when presented with facts, evidence, proof, and successful case studies. Changing the minds of many in industry is difficult. It is not so much about "Show me the facts, and I will get with the program," as "Nothing that you show me will ever change my mind." Evidence seems to have no power for some people.

Changing the minds and habits of those who must help society achieve the benefits that integration brings may need to be underpinned with evidence, but approaches that rely on evidence to change people may not be the best approach. Testimonials from friends, storytelling, peer pressure, and the sheer power of money may be more powerful change tools. Only when the majority embraces a system approach, collaboration, and free exchange of information will some come around. Only by educating everyone to the opportunities will society truly benefit.

Markets are shifting. Technology and integrated processes are rapidly becoming de facto standards in design and construction. Usually these shifts are a part of individual organizations' business decisions. As isolated business decisions, they cause little concern. But where the shifts intentionally misrepresent the processes, they lead others down the wrong path. Misrepresenting the shifts, whether due to selfishness or ignorance, forms a barrier to development and implementation of the system and increases the likelihood that we, as a society, will never reach the potential benefits. Too often, a focus on short-term benefit leaves the long-term advantages out of the process, even when they cost no more or take no more effort.

We must identify and define the barriers that are keeping us from using information technology to improve the built world. Many of the barriers are the result of inertia and existing processes. Others are barriers of knowledge and understanding. All need to be managed.

CRISFIELD, MARYLAND
JULY 1, 2019

> New ways are needed for a new age. Large contractors and well-known architects are unlocking value using building information modeling. Their brands are still limited by the legacy of an outdated process.
>
> —Anonymous

It was quite a task to figure out what we needed to do to make these principles work for everyone. From Somerset County, we made an extensive search, looking for systems that could support these principles.

Some of the questions that we asked helped us to understand the directions that the technology needed to develop. Questions such as "Is it practical in today's economy to continue to replace drafting by hand with drafting by the computer? How will integrated practice improve projects? Will regular people find benefit from readily accessible information?"

We learned that one of the things holding the entire information modeling process back was that there was no way to manage consistent archives of information. We learned that any system for organizing data needed to allow us to save and find information in consistent and safe ways. The biggest secret seemed to be to keep this information up to date after it was stored. The data needed to be stored so they could be shared and reused. But reusing the data wasn't enough. The data had to remain fresh. Whatever the system looked like, it had to let people start small and then build complexity over time.

Do you remember floppy disks? If you do, have you ever tried to open the file from a five-year-old floppy, only to find that the disk is unreadable? Have you ever tried to use a file you created in version 2 of your software only to find that you cannot open it in version 4? Has someone ever given you a SyQuest disk only to find that none of your machines has a SyQuest drive any longer? Have you ever tried to open the file from a six-year-old CD-ROM to find that it was unrecognized by your current computer? These are some of the day-to-day issues that we found we needed to manage.

One of our first goals became to find a long-term solution that handles this type of problem. Information modeling loses much of its value if you can't even get to the information when you want it. Even if when you need it is several years later. When you look at this problem in the context of the many situations where people have had to start over every time a new software or technology comes along, it becomes even more critical. An information model without well-maintained data in standardized formats that are software neutral and interoperable is just 3-D modeling. It makes pretty pictures and maybe lets you see things better, but it certainly doesn't solve many problems.

Agreed-upon standards such as Industry Foundation Classes (IFC) are necessary. Rather than starting over, IFCs let many people work with the same information using any software product they wish. Data interoperability does not solve all the problems by itself. If tomorrow you woke up and every software product on the market could magically talk to and understand every other software product, many of the problems would not go away. We learned that we had to have standards, but people and archiving of information are more critical yet.

Today much of the energy associated with information modeling goes toward developing standards for the future. Some ask, "Who really follows complex standards?" There is a strong case for simple and concise standards. Without such standards, information modeling might always be marginal technology and might never reach its potential. We found that data interchange standards need to become more widely adopted than they are today.

The National Institute of Building Sciences (NIBS) created the buildingSMART alliance (bSa) to figure out how to make this happen. The buildingSMART alliance initiatives produced Part 1 of the National Building Information Model Standard (NBIMS) in 2007. In 2011, and several times since, the standard has been added to, improved, and refined. Many of the systems that make up BIMSynergy and other model servers in the utility grid are based on the work of the buildingSMART alliance. They are a key influence in how information modeling has affected the built environment.

Without standards, the model server utility business would collapse. This was one of the most difficult issues that we faced as we created BIMSynergy. Traditionally, standards were often not enforced. When standards are not enforced, they become impediments to productive and focused effort.

More than a few people told us about their attempts to follow standards in the past. It seemed as though those doing large complex projects, usually with high fees and high-production costs for the federal government, were the only ones that even attempted to follow standards. High-visibility, high-value projects were not seen as being the key issue. We felt that finding a way to transparently overlay standards for the thousands and thousands of other projects that make up the bread and butter of the built environment was certainly more fundamental.

Our solution was to create a system that could be used by anyone with little expertise and minimal training. In fact, our goal was to make it so that with thirty minutes of exposure to the system one could begin to produce usable results. By doing this, we could make the value to real people obvious. We could make the system ubiquitous.

In a paper-based world, management of information created libraries. In the information modeling world, model servers are the equivalent. In the paper and desktop computer-based world, almost every area had a public library. Every area also had an electric utility, a telephone utility, and a cable television franchise. In the information modeling world, distributed model servers are a mash-up of these public services.

Model server utilities provide communities the opportunity to create unique and tailored approaches to managing information for property owners, the design and construction community, and everyone else. They support better decision making, better collaborations, and easily shared data that communities can build into long-term knowledge bases. Community leaders and the public can use these long-term knowledge bases to inform decision making.

We live in a complex world and must deal with ever-increasing ambiguity and uncertainty. Systems that capture and build knowledge over time let us reduce uncertainty. People need to have faith that the world will become clearer over time.

It took a lot of soul-searching, research, and energy coupled with some pretty slick front-end development for us to create BIMSynergy. Now we connect people with information, foster zero energy and other sustainable technology, and let people work from anywhere at any time.

WHY WASTE ENERGY?

About twelve years ago, we realized that we had a real problem. For some time, we felt that we were fighting everyone. No matter what we did, it seemed like our projects were always over budget and late. Contractors seemed to be fighting us at every step. Our architects and engineers seemed to have stopped coordinating their work, and every project was a battle. We realized we needed to do something else, but we didn't know what that something else was.

We tried adding our own people to monitor the process, and that seemed to make things worse. We learned the hard way that you cannot add inspectors, especially when they do not know the contract, in the middle of projects. It became clear that throwing people at the problems wasn't the solution. We needed to make bigger changes.

Most of the people in the county didn't care or understand what was causing the problem; they were just fed up with the outcomes. It was easier to shoot the messenger than to find a fix. The commissioners saw how exposed to scrutiny they were every time they approved a plan. Being politicians, finding a fix became really important to them.

In many cases, we created situations where our leaders could only hope to be brilliant, or to apply rational logic using experiential knowledge, or to get lucky and guess the correct solution. We asked for wisdom from those whose lack of judgment often did not override their urge to decide, even when they had no real knowledge from which to form their opinions.

We decided to tackle the problem just like we would have approached any other significant disaster. We got everyone together in the same room to talk about it. We started a public dialogue that got everyone excited. And we did our research, looking for new ways of doing things and new tools that would allow us overcome the problems.

We found that if we could figure out a way to understand our projects earlier in the process, we could make much better decisions. We could become more confident of the outcomes. And we could get the community involved so that our projects were bought into by the community. We also found that in most cases, people just like the benefits. They need to know that their money is being spent wisely and that we are getting value for their money. They do not genuinely care how things happen.

We also found that when we talked about technology, people's eyes glazed over. The details are just too complex. The details are not relevant to most people; they just want to make sure that things happen correctly. They want to open the browser on their computer, click on an icon, and participate in the decision-making process with straightforward, easy-to-use tools. The public actually wanted something like Facebook or Expedia. They did not want to learn how to use a desktop tool.

So why waste energy trying to get people to do things they don't want to do? We knew that systems thinking was natural to everyone, but a lot of people never really develop their abilities. Our schools do not seem to teach people about how they relate to the rest of the world. The systems are working on teaching things like critical thinking, but don't seem to draw connections between the subjects. Our first job was to get people talking about how we relate to the rest of the world. We started conversations about siloed knowledge and people who know a lot about their jobs and little about how their professions connect to today's integrated global society.

We had people talking, we had a lot of public input about what people want, and we knew some of the things that were creating problems in our projects. We had a hunch that we were not alone in our quest, but at that time we did not understand how widespread the problem truly was. We did not know that the problems we were experiencing were affecting everyone who interacts with the construction industry at any level.

Sometimes when people focus on their own little slice of our world, they are focusing on a more global problem. I guess that's what happened to us. Since we didn't know better, we just jumped in and started to develop solutions that made sense to us.

We tested hundreds of software and hardware tools, both individually and as part of systems. We created an environment that focused on trying anything and everything that popped up on the Internet. All testing had the goal of finding the "best" and most beneficial solutions. Some we kept and apply today. Some we discarded for a variety of reasons. Some never worked, some worked for a while, and some are wonderful.

We performed these explorations in the real-world setting of Somerset County. Ours were not "ivory-tower" tests. Rather, we used the tools on real projects. If they worked, great, if not, we moved on and looked for the next possibility. This was a ten-year exploration. In those years we learned volumes about how systems for managing technology and systems for managing people differed. We learned that we needed to change how we educate people to create adaptable, lifelong learners. We learned about interoperability and model servers. We learned about the Toyota Production System and management by constraints. We learned that little bim tools might help us perform better, but **BIG BIM** integrated processes tied to the larger world were actually what it would take to solve our problems.

We came to the realization that we needed to drive the process, even at the education and technology levels. We could not wait for others to show us how to get it done. We had to take responsibility for the built environment and we had to devise ways that everyone could participate and benefit. We found that we needed to create a system that embodied sound judgment, high moral standards, a strategic perspective, and systems thinking.

We found that there are some things that people genuinely want. People want things to be under control. They want to know where things are going. They want to understand how things relate to each other in ways that improve decisions.

Properly organized technology and systems thinking gives us the tools to make this happen.

The design and construction process seemed to be broken with no fix in sight. People complained about the problems. Electing new politicians every time there was an election was not solving the problem. No one seemed to be stepping up to create an environment that would provide the solution. That's what led to BIMSynergy.

INFINITE SOLUTIONS

> An undefined problem has an infinite number of solutions.
> —Robert A. Humphrey

Dreams are good. We all need dreams. When we stop dreaming, we stagnate. We lock into doing things the same way repeatedly, even when we do not see the results that we want and expect.

Have you ever dreamed about a time when you could call up the details for your house in real time? Without hiring an engineer or fussing with the utility company? Without leaving your chair? Have you ever dreamed about a time when you could start a browser and receive details for all your appliances, including how much power they are using and how old they are? Have you ever wished that you could truly know how your new air conditioning system works, without doing weeks of head scratching and fact finding? Well, now you can.

Information modeling is as a concept so universal and so wide reaching that it can (and probably does) include almost anything that you can think of. If it touches on the built environment, the modeling processes can make it better and more efficient.

Figuring out how to integrate technology into the built environment is a monumental task. The built environment is so widespread and includes so many players that it is hard to wrap it into a tidy package. It is so diverse that it touches everything in our lives. It is hard to define, and when a problem is hard to define, it is hard to solve.

Finding solutions to problems within this complex system has always been difficult. Professionals have made incremental changes, trying to solve individual problems. Their improvements have tended to focus on one group or one situation. At times, these solutions filtered through the industry and sometimes became public. Before information modeling technology became available, few groups attempted to find real solutions to the larger problems that need wide public interaction. It was business as usual. Hire an architect…design a building…get a bid…build the facility and move in, usually with token public involvement and always with a linear process that has been shown to waste nearly 30 percent of our resources each step of the way.

The construction industry is a mess today. We have made many unwise decisions. We fail to learn from past mistakes. Without changes, we will make more serious errors in the future.

Information modeling addresses a group of problems that are integral to how we live, work, and play. These problems fit the definition of wicked problems. Dealing with them is both complex and difficult. They require many to change how they look at the built world.

In the broadest sense, people are taking a narrow view of models. They focus on models as "things" used for visualizing and managing projects. This view is not surprising, as most people use information tools for current profit-making tasks. In the long run, a worldview that is focused only on "What's in it for me?" will likely sub-optimize the benefits and may well be the factor that keeps information models from truly achieving the productivity benefits that are possible.

There is a place for guiding and measuring quality and capabilities within that limited framework. Project-focused information models must be managed within a much larger conceptual framework that integrates with geographic information, non-project business processes, and other areas that both gain value and create value for the entire information model value proposition.

Software vendors, university faculty, think tank teams, progressive wings of national institutes, and other experts throughout industry are working to create new tools to handle the information that is needed to help others understand specific needs from the expert's perspective. The Internet does not require each website to reinvent the way text, graphics, and data are displayed. Why should cloud-based tools for the built environment be any different? Experts in this area are able to build upon existing standards and add their expertise to create unique approaches to fostering ubiquitous communications, decision-making content, and new ways of collaboration.

Every day it seems as if information models are easier to use. They will be universally accessible. Just as the Internet makes complex technology easy to use, these models will simplify the complexities of industry. The complexity will still exist, only now the data that you need (and only the data that you need) will be readily accessible.

Communication and collaboration must happen directly through information models. Knowledge, decisions, costs, people, predictions, and everything else must be integrated. The use of first-order tools such as project management and e-mail cannot achieve the benefits. These tools continue processes that are fragmented or siloed, fostering a false belief in their ability to further the evolution to integrated processes. All these bits of data must be interrelated in order to achieve the productivity gains that will overcome the industry's continued slide. Finding ways to solve these wicked problems is a work in progress. Trying to solve them using traditional approaches is much like a coach trying to lay out the whole sequence of plays before the game starts. Solutions demand efficient and effective conversations with those affected by an issue in order to create shared understanding and commitment.

This book is a work of design-fiction. It is like science-fiction, bringing into focus matters of concern with how we manage our environment. The goal is to question how we now use technology and speculate about future possibilities to incite imagination filling conversations about the future of the built world.

Scattered through the book is text within grey boxes like that above. Text shown this way is either opinion or fact. All else is design fiction.

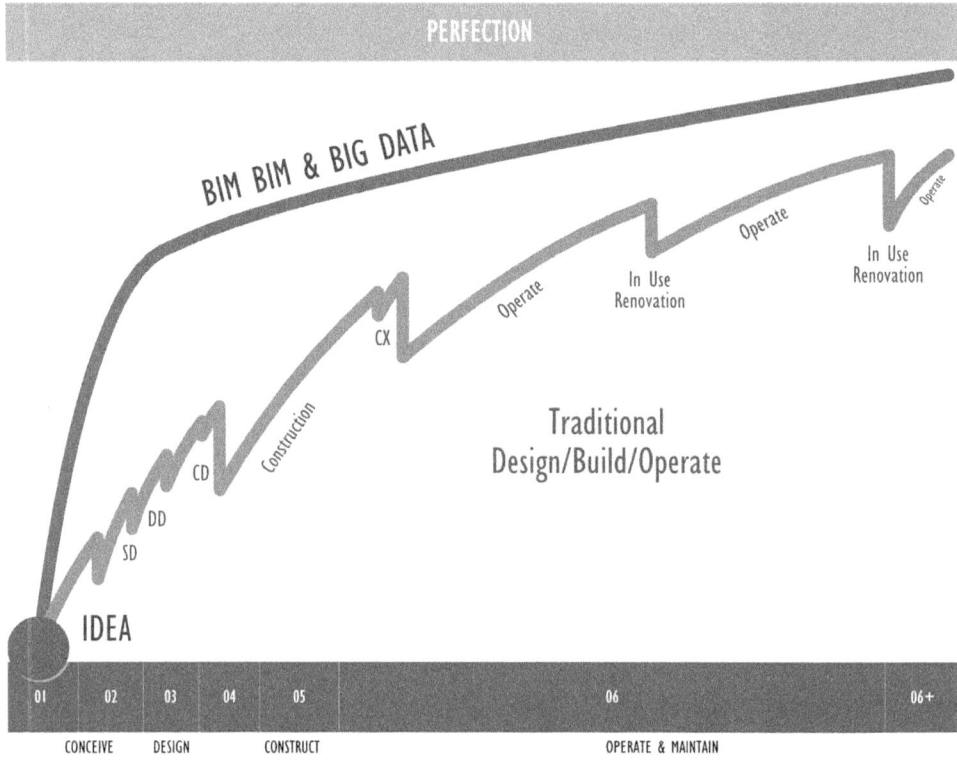

The move to information modeling supports users as they strive to higher levels of perfection over the lifetime of projects. Using BIG BIM and BIG Data within a framework that enables distributed use of the information, people are able to reduce the inefficiencies and errors that plaque traditional approaches.

The decision was made to headquarter BIMSynergy in Princess Anne, home of the University of Maryland Eastern Shore and the historic county seat of Somerset County, Maryland.

A WELL THOUGHT OUT PROCESS
PRINCESS ANNE, MARYLAND
SEPTEMBER 7, 2020

When we look back it is easy to forget that much of what we now take for granted was revolutionary when we started our journey. The way that we operate today did not happen by accident. Today's approach came about because a bunch of creative people in Somerset County applied creative ideas to solve problems. They took risks to achieve results and make the world a better place.

When people did most of the work by hand, it was relatively easy to fix problems. As society adopted increasingly technological innovations, it became harder and harder to make systemic repairs. Creating an efficient and sustainable built environment is hampered by problems of poor execution and poor cost controls. Traditional processes are deteriorating.

Technology has increased the speed and extent of change. Some people thrive on change, while others seem to be stuck in the past. Resources to respond to these changes are limited. People who can adapt and make change a part of their everyday lives are valuable. Unfortunately, too often these change agents are impeded by the status quo.

It becomes increasingly difficult to build and benefit from one's knowledge and experience with these new tools and processes. Every day it becomes more difficult to respond to new needs. When traditional business practices intersect with new technology, the issues multiply. In many cases, information management tools used while holding onto traditional ways of doing business produce sub-optimal results.

The issue is especially severe in those who hold nominal leadership positions in society. Their self-image and the expectations of their followers put pressure on them to have the answers…even when they do not have the knowledge. They give in to the pressures to have the answers, without having a frame of reference and sufficient information. The variables they are being asked to address are too numerous to work out with pure logic. The more complex the social or built environment problems, the greater the chances of serious errors in judgment.

The number and complexity of information systems has reached a level such that multiple experts are required to deliver workable solutions, much less the optimal solution. Nearly anything can be compared to anything else to create relationships, patterns, and possibilities, in real-time. Experts need the ability to view and manipulate the data, all at the same time, to achieve optimal results. The sheer number of new options quickly overwhelms traditional systems and processes.

How you do business and how you adopt new technology contributes to your success or failure. Technology is only a fraction of the equation. A well-thought-out process that pulls everything together is needed. You need to manage the details to be successful with information models. Managing these details becomes synonymous with using technology to improve processes to relieve the stresses on society and to become sustainable.

Because of the complexity of the built environment, systems that provide free exchange of information and transparent processes are the future. The days where we had to work with highly complex desktop applications requiring significant computing power are rapidly falling behind us. No single software product offers a magic information button, since the built environment is too complex. Cloud-based BIG BIM systems that provide data from all sources to be visualized, analyzed, and accessed from anywhere are the future of information modeling. You become more relevant and more valuable as you move into this new world.

Built environment tools and processes exist to support our efforts. The challenges in adopting cloud-based modeling systems are recognized. These systems are similar to the social networking and e-commerce systems that have become a part of your everyday life. Standards to support these tools and processes have been in the works for years. Some of the standards are extremely complex, require significant global investment, and are slowly becoming available. Others are extensions to the same kind of standards that have proven themselves to be effective in Web 2.0 applications.

People want their projects to be done better, but few care to become immersed in the process. Creating systems that are effective and give people greater certainty of outcomes will be the winning combination. You can actually explain these benefits to people. It is easy for them to understand that they benefit if we use technology to deliver greater certainty of outcomes and better decision-making information earlier in any process.

Somerset County saw this as a potential competitive advantage. We could use an information archive through the life cycle of our projects to level the cyclical nature of built environment business. We believed that, by managing data, we would create opportunities for residual income streams. We could also use technology to reduce peoples' concerns. When we thought about it, who could better manage the range of variables and complexity that affect our society? We could!

WEDDING OF TECHNOLOGIES

> Describing a "strategy of social futurism," where "you can't run the society on data and computers alone," Alvin Toffler, author of Future Shock, wrote that, "Attempts to bring this knowledge together would constitute one of the crowning intellectual efforts in history—and one of the most worthwhile."

Information modeling, geographic information systems (GIS), relational databases, argumentation theory, ontology, socio-technical systems modeling, web services, Semantic Web, and the Internet are all coming together to achieve Toffler's vision. Building on these concepts, you can now use rules-based dialectic planning systems to capture and integrate knowledge at all levels. If you can describe something, it can be captured. If it can be captured, you can determine its relationship to other knowledge. By applying the rules that govern how these bits of data interact, you can determine options more quickly and more accurately than ever before. Where planning once relied on vague generalities and "rules of thumb," you can now simulate "real life" using readily annotated and qualified available tools.

Today information modeling often does not link business decision making directly to projects. We undervalue the use of models. But this is the place where society receives high value through strategies that reduce wasted time, money, and resources. These benefits allow people to create tactical solutions with the highest chance of success and long-term sustainability. Communities and organizations now have unprecedented abilities to create world-class solutions to complex problems, using information modeling technologies and local professionals.

Complexity has changed the nature of the planning game. Innovative owners, progressive communities, and ambitious developers realize that they need new ways of doing business. They need new tools to thrive in today's fast-changing and often unpredictable markets. People have learned that information modeling can help them to make planning decisions with irrefutable facts, allowing them to mitigate risk in today's fast-paced environment. They are learning how to use cloud-based models to improve decision making and business planning. They are becoming more valuable to their communities and the world.

DEPLOYMENT

The enterprise model of business that for so long ruled industry was turned on its head by new single-purpose and loosely coupled tools. Suddenly, individuals became their own technology services, with resources to challenge the largest corporations. Individuals using apps and readily available specialized tools, ideas, and collaboration services could respond so quickly that top-down corporations couldn't keep up. In one generation, the focal point for innovation and expertise moved out of the corporation and into the hands of millions of consumers.

We were trying to capitalize on the power of consumers, which had become so strong with the communications revolution led by Google+, Twitter, and Facebook. Apple Computer's App Store provided a place where the lines between developers and consumers became blurred. All interconnected with rapidly developing tools that solved individual problems. The ecosystem that was created changed the way that people used technology, and had sweeping impacts on our world.

When we built BIMSynergy, we focused on creating a system that would support individual innovation. We focused our efforts, time, and resources to achieve the highest possible return for as many as possible. We created a system that will flourish in a fast-paced and loosely coupled world where individuals' innovation is at the forefront.

Our motto was: do it fast, do it right, and do it ethically. The system was deployed in a planned and sequential manner. We did not do everything at once. We focused on deploying the mission-critical systems first in the most complete and user-friendly manner possible. When these systems were fully running and validated by users, other tools were deployed in a step-by-step manner. The system supports one user or millions of users.

One of the issues that we wrestled with in designing BIMSynergy was the fact that the construction industry was not properly aligned with this world of cloud computing, service-oriented architectures, and fifth-generation technologies. We needed agreed-upon definitions for how people would use models and exchange information. There was a strong case for using a system that would allow us to determine whether BIMSynergy would perform as required. We determined that capability maturity models (CMM) would serve this purpose. Fortunately, several industry organizations were already on the path to developing maturity models for the built environment.

The construction industry had a significant problem in coming to a consensus on how to manage change. Agreeing on incremental steps to correcting business inefficiencies and waste took many years. Some groups were developing ad hoc approaches to underpin their own certification systems. Disguising images to make them seem to be information models, bim-washing, happened too often. Awards programs featured winning entries that were made to look like peoples' concept of information modeling. Few users of information model authoring software knew or cared that software developers were creating products to satisfy their large clients rather than to satisfy built environment needs. Software developers were getting mixed messages. Developers concentrated on maximizing their profits. Their users did not seem to care about the long-term issues. Most people in the industry focused on a small fraction of the built environment—design and construction.

Once industry leaders realized that capability maturity models could become the vehicle to help people realize that the built environment is larger than design and construction, things began to change. Before, a significant number of architects and contractors engaged in self-limiting behaviors that retarded development. Now, those same architects and contractors found themselves faced with a much larger market, with many more opportunities. The industry always suffered from drastic swings in activity. Now, the up and down cycles were much smaller and less harmful.

An industry-wide effort created a series of capability models that align the people, organizations, and technology needs of the built environment. These models allow us to evaluate how individuals use BIMSynergy based on an agreed-upon standard. Organizations can assess the maturity of their processes using our tools. They focus on capitalizing on their strengths and correcting their weak points. Developers use the models to develop products, knowing where they fit into the system, based on a clear definition of a minimum information model. Interconnected capability maturity models that focus on people, organizations, and technology are among the data sets hosted by BIMSynergy.

The instant that you create information model data and save it to a static file system, the information is dated. Degradation has already started. When this fact became apparent, it became clear that the only solution was to create a system that would keep the information up to date and accessible. We needed to create a server continuum that would allow people to hold knowledge, update their data at will, and access the information at any time from any place. In addition, the server would need to have the capacity to keep information fresh with little or no human intervention.

Follow this tag to learn more about integration maturity at http://4sitesystems.com/iofthestorm/?page_id=833

FIFTH GENERATION

We do not believe in long development cycles. Innovation must be continuous and rapid. The speed of development of the Internet requires us to move quickly. Moving from a static World Wide Web with hyperlinks to information sharing and user-centered design toward the personalized web of data where machines understand and connect meaning has happened in what could be considered the blink of an eye. Cloud computing, mash-ups of information from many sources, and the integration of specializations make it imperative that we respond quickly.

When we go through long cycles of diagramming and research, how much knowledge passes us by? When we assign decision making to committees, how much expertise and experience do we lose? When everything must be perfect, do we miss out on opportunities? Are we better as a society when we quickly adapt and respond, even though imperfections creep in? Can we learn to fail fast and move along, rather than punishing imperfection?

Technology has developed to a point that allows us to set rules for how we wish things to happen. From these rules, we can create systems that leverage our knowledge to allow us to make better decisions. From these rules, we can clear the tedious and mundane to allow us to focus on the critical items.

First-generation technology can be described as machine language. At this level, technology was difficult to learn and even more difficult to edit when errors occurred. In the second generation, assembly languages for programming made it easier to manage imperfections. The third-generation languages enabled the computer to take care of nonessential tasks. Fourth-generation technology enabled the development of commercial solutions that could access data with near-human language. With fifth-generation technology, we have the ability to solve problems using constraints given to the program. These constraints, or rules, can simulate human thinking and behavior. They can simulate intelligence to supplement and improve how we reach solutions and how we make decisions.

In order for us to take advantage of these fifth-generation technologies, we need to encourage a structured approach to information sharing. As we develop systems and integrate the parts of the built environment, we need to build upon flexible design principles. Systems must be able to talk to each other. They must be able to be used by anyone and everyone. Users must be able to combine and reuse services and systems to better understand and coordinate their lives. Whether a company needs to manage their facility assets within their business, or an individual needs to understand which appliances in their home are using the most energy, the system needs to accommodate their needs. Ideally our solution will become the glue that lets people adjust to new needs and new situations, reusing data and tools within the system.

PRESSURE

> There is nothing more difficult to carry out, nor more doubtful of success, nor more dangerous to handle, than to initiate a new order of things. For the reformer has enemies in all those who profit from the old order, and only lukewarm defenders in those who would profit from the new order—the lukewarmness arising partly from fear of adversaries who have the laws in their favor, and partly from the incredulity of mankind who do not believe in anything new unless they have had actual experience of it.
> —Niccolò Machiavelli, The Prince

The construction industry wastes almost five times more than other industries. Traditional project delivery processes are fraught with lack of cooperation and imperfect information sharing. Traditional checks and balances have failed. Building owners have found that they can no longer rely on their industry partners to ensure outcomes. The industry is too disruptive and undependable. Studies suggest that owners experience schedule problems and cost overruns on 85 percent of all projects.

The problems have been building for many years. As other industries have improved productivity, the construction industry is in continuous decline. As a society we need to be better stewards of our scarce resources. Waste in construction continues to be substantially higher than in any other industry. Many of the pioneers in such areas as information modeling have had as a goal the improvement of these conditions. Many of the systems that have been created in the last twenty years have been intended to help professionals do a better job and be less wasteful. In some cases, they have been successful; in many others, not so much.

The tools and processes that have made other industries more productive have not been adopted in the built environment sector for a number of reasons. The industry is highly fragmented. Thousands and thousands of small, independent organizations make up much of the industry. Even the largest organizations within the industry tend to rely on this system of disconnected and independent production. Approaches based on systems thinking that integrates just-in-time delivery and other similar approaches that have become common in other industries are difficult to achieve in the built environment.

Because of the industry's fragmentation, it is difficult to make sweeping changes. New tools that benefit some are often either ignored or not considered to be relevant to other groups. Where in other industries a small number of technology creators can develop software tools that support well-defined processes industry-wide, in the construction industry each group and subgroup seems to have different requirements.

When you factor in open competition, the highly self-actuated nature of entrepreneurs in this area, and the highly cyclical nature of the industry, the difficulties of implementing systems that are sustainable begins to be understandable. Traditionally, those that become most successful tend to have a "What's in it for me?" approach. They have fought for projects, fought to respond to errors, and fought to make a profit in a highly competitive world that often rewards the appearance of success rather than success measured by clear evidence and metrics. Often appearances are more influential than outcomes.

Traditional systems have allowed this situation to occur. Traditional systems have allowed anecdotal approaches to problem solving. Decisions happen too late in the process to affect outcomes in positive and sustainable ways. The complexity is making solutions difficult. It makes understanding the underlying processes both difficult to control and hard to explain. Projects take too long, too many bids come in well over budget, too many conflicts arise, and too little truth results from the traditional process.

For the most part, computer software and hardware vendors and large corporations have, in this environment, worked to develop systems that will help to handle these problems. Unfortunately, most of these systems have been extensions to processes that are the basis for the industry's fragmentation, poor communications practices, and lack of integration. In effect, most of the tools do little more than computerize processes that likely will never be able to handle the complexity that characterizes our built environment. Software developers need to focus on developing integrated standards and sustainability to deliver open tools that improve our ability to make in-context decisions that will have a positive impact on the future.

Computers are constrained to work on one small bit of information at a time. They can build storehouses of local and global knowledge that, properly interconnected, can guide intelligence in making decisions. They can do this very fast and can be quite comprehensive. With the right type of knowledge captured in these comprehensive, interrelated data storehouses, computers can supplement the human brain's ability to analyze and find patterns in order to make good decisions in a complex and fast-changing world. With wisdom, intelligence, and creativity, people can supplement the things that they have learned with computer-based knowledge to maximize the chances of making good decisions.

The continuing downward productivity trend cannot be solved by simply computerizing traditional processes. Without fully integrated tools, based upon agreed-upon standards, the fragmentation and waste will remain. Today, we live in a world that can no longer afford such waste. We must become better stewards of the built environment. To make this change, we all must change.

Software vendors must begin to deliver second-order tools, rather than just building upon the traditional approach. Companies (and their supply chains) must embrace integration and become truly collaborative, rather than merely paying lip service to the trends while continuing their normal business practices. Communities must become truly centers of open data and transparent government, no longer managing the environment as rigid, siloed fiefdoms. Utility companies and their regulators must deploy standards-compliant smart technologies such as the smart grid to provide their customers a way to manage their personal use of energy data. Individuals must embrace the change, must participate in the change, and must become active stewards of their world.

We can attribute part of the problem to retiring baby boomers causing a brain drain. Many organizations are losing experienced staff at a rapid pace. When you include the layoffs, lost jobs, and widespread damage done by the recession, the brain drain has been tremendous.

Throughout the built environment, knowledge resources are being lost as experienced people retire or are forced into unemployment. Although many people are out of work, every year it becomes more difficult to recruit experienced and knowledgeable senior staff. Yet, many of these workers represent old paradigms. The knowledge they take with them is old-fashioned and often obsolete.

Meanwhile, systems such as IBM's Watson and other unstructured data tools extract and organize knowledge. These systems are having significant impacts in both the legal and medical domains. Knowledge bases in these domains go far beyond simple search engines to enable new-era workers to leverage their knowledge. Competing programs include open source and free applications in bioinformatics and medical decision making. Those using these new knowledge flow analysis and modeling tools work in health-care institutions such as Cork Point. In these situations, knowledge flow happens, even without the pool of experienced workers.

The loss of knowledgeable workers, inefficiency, and lack of coordinated work flows can be seen as a plague, or a boon to the entire industry. As firms lose experienced people, the trend has been to automate traditional tasks, rather than finding real solutions. Task-based automation is a first-order solution. It may mask the problem, but does not handle the essence of the problem. The problem is to capture real knowledge and to continuously test and improve. This knowledge can then be used to achieve dynamic real-world goals.

The errors caused by the absence of senior staff and other problems worsen as society cannot find effective ways to capture knowledge and make it available to the next generation. As little as thirty years ago, the training of even the most highly educated professionals included a significant amount of time in transferring knowledge from the previous generation, in the form of internships and mentoring. Although in theory such knowledge transfer programs still exist, in practice they rarely work, due to the pace of change, the extent of job displacement, and generational issues.

Information models, properly integrated, are proven tools for capturing the knowledge base that is so crucial to our modern world. We cannot afford to re-create knowledge every time a new person steps into a new role. Things change too fast. We have the tools to capture the knowledge that underpins much of the decision making in the built environment. Today, there is little reason to spend scarce resources on fact-finding missions, production of as-built documents, and research into solutions that have worked before. We have little excuse, when those new to a task make the same mistakes that others made before. We are in an age where technology creates an environment, where "bad" history does not have to repeat itself.

Some surveys predict that 50 percent of all senior managers will retire in the next ten years. When you add the layoffs due to the recession, the situation is not just a concern; it is a crisis. If a solution to these issues is not implemented, we are likely to find ourselves in a world where the catastrophic errors of judgment and flawed decision-making collapse the old system.

BARRIERS

Late in the twentieth century, information modeling seemed fresh and new. The early adopters were achieving extraordinary results using the tools that were then available. Software developers and pundits positioned and argued about what to call the technology. Virtual building, virtual design and construction, and building information modeling were all terms under consideration. A consortium of enterprises created the International Alliance for Interoperability(IAI). IAI later became buildingSMART International and promoted new business processes and interoperability throughout the international community. The focus was on new technology, standards, and reaching a critical mass of users that understood and embraced this better way of doing things. The fact that building information modeling has become the next new thing in the industry speaks to the success of these efforts.

As the World Wide Web became ubiquitous, there were other efforts underway to standardize information. These efforts resulted in an Internet that allows users and developers to interact and share information to support social networking, e-commerce, and the other tools that now seem essential in our everyday lives. These standards exist behind the scenes and usually do not affect the lives of everyday users. Users do not see the complexity and depth that underpins their purchase of an airline ticket or their dealings with their circle of friends on Facebook. Developers and programmers create these systems knowing that they can interact with information in agreed-upon and predictable ways.

Most of today's systems that we interact with are now moving entirely to the cloud. This distributed network of hardware and software is accessible from anywhere at any time. The system is rapidly moving away from the need for desktop computers and fixed bases of operation toward agile connections such as iPads, iPhones, and Android devices. We are fast approaching a time where these cloud-based services will eliminate the need for a powerful desktop computer. This evolution in computing and human relations is poised to revolutionize how we work. The day of the professional designing off-line and telling others of the outcomes is waning. were mainly related to technology and computer power, now the barriers have shifted toward people and learning. These new barriers to progress fall into the following seven flawed thought processes:

1. Approaching the change as technology, not people. Information modeling is about interaction and collaboration enhanced by technology. We have the technology. It has been proven to work well when used properly. People have to master the technology, not the other way around.

Follow this tag to learn more about the barriers to effective information modeling and integrated practices at http://4sitesystems.com/iofthestorm/?page_id=827

2. Lack of holistic thinking and strategic vision. Linear processes are needed, but they can only take you so far. Today our world is beset with "wicked problems" that defy linear solution. We must change our educational systems to teach systems thinking.

3. Focusing on projects as an end goal. This is a subset of the need for systems thinking. Legacy systems and yesterday's processes make us focus on projects. We must begin to focus from the beginning on long-term solutions. As we focus on individual projects, we tend to make local decisions that all too often are globally wrong.

4. Focusing on "What's in it for me?" As information modeling took hold in the late twentieth century, it seemed to be essential for people get instant personal benefit from making the change. This focus on "me" has often become the endgame, slowing progress. There is no doubt that we all need to be rewarded for our efforts, but this cannot be the primary focus.

5. Focusing on the wrong social structures. Working in a collaborative environment requires that we form teams designed to bring the appropriate skills to bear on issues. Hierarchical command-and-control organizations are falling by the wayside. They are being replaced by distributed sharing and collaborative process organizational structures. This change leverages personal knowledge.

Soon, professionals who are able to be active participants and moderators of highly interactive and information-rich processes that involve entire communities will be the norm. Technology is rapidly becoming a powerful tool for increasing interaction. The use of technology to streamline routine tasks and process compliance will still be with us. We still need to write books, but they will happen faster than ever. We still need to manage projects. Technology will enable us to manage them better.

Using technology for first-order tasks is only the beginning. Doing the right thing and achieving the optimal goal is the real value of this technology. Making decisions and improving the built environment are such priceless benefits that even against resistance these technologies continue to grow. However, there are significant barriers that restrict the public from understanding and using information technology to improve the built world.

The construction industry is significantly behind the curve when we discuss interoperability, collaboration, and transparent operations. Where the World Wide Web capitalized on new technology, the computer, with little historical precedent, the construction industry is different. Hundreds of years of inertia and existing processes must be changed. As the twenty-first century unfolds, much work remains to be done.

Today the focus is on using information modeling to make improvements to traditional design and construction processes. Too often information modeling tools are seen as nothing more than advanced software systems. In many cases, this focus improves visualization, identifies conflicts between construction trades, and improves coordination. In most cases, these items involved improvements to processes that are already the responsibility of the designers and constructors. They deliver value to owners and society. They cause fewer problems, create less friction, and save time and money. Unfortunately, it is rare that these improvements produce long-term value to society. Long-term gain and improved decision making before the traditional design process and after construction are where the greatest benefits lie.

The inertia that comes from traditional processes is impeding progress. An object, or a process, at rest tends to remain at rest. Lack of systems thinking, proscribed linear processes, and lack of general knowledge are slowing implementation. Where the barriers to progress once

6. Confusing process with product. Integrated project delivery is not the end goal of information modeling. Integrated project delivery is a process. The end goal of information modeling is better collaboration, enterprise integration, integrated decision making, and a better world.
7. Focusing on systems that are too complex, too finished, and too difficult to master. It is easy to be trapped by the complexity that has characterized most of the software tools up to this point. Functional information modeling that has real value can be simple and easy to use. There may always be the need for highly specialized systems requiring highly trained experts. Fortunately, most of what must be done with information modeling is best done with simple information models.

STANDARDS

In 2004, FIATECH helped fund a National Institute of Science and Technology (NIST) report entitled, "Cost Analysis of Inadequate Interoperability in the U.S. Capital Facilities Industry." The report documented the fact that the current system is wasteful and perhaps not sustainable. By correcting disordered processes, NIST predicted savings of over $15.8 billion annually (1 to 2 percent of total industry revenue). Obviously, owners would receive the greatest part of these savings. NIST estimated that the owners' part of the savings is $10.6 billion. Constructors' part of the savings is an estimated $1.8 billion, with fabricators and suppliers saving an additional $2.2 billion. Architects and engineers' part of the savings is an estimated $1.2 billion. Since 2004, the problems, the costs, the waste, and the savings have all increased dramatically.

Groups continue to work to find solutions to these problems. One active owner group is the Construction Users Roundtable (CURT). CURT's goal is to "create strategic advantage for construction users." Soon after the 2004 NIST report, CURT issued a wake-up appeal to many in the built environment, offering a strategy for owner leadership in enabling change. One could argue that they were responsible for much of the recent focus on building information modeling and integrated practice. Their call-to-action white paper entitled "Collaboration, Integrated Information and the Project Life Cycle in Building Design, Construction and Operation" issued a strong and clear message: stop the finger-pointing, litigation, and lack of accountability that seem to be business as usual. In 2005, CURT followed up with a second white paper, titled "Optimizing the Construction Process: An Implementation Strategy."

Leadership by owners, contractors, and architects working in tandem has been seen as essential to the future. In 2006, the American Institute of Architects (AIA), CURT, and the Associated General Contractors of America (AGC) began a collaborative effort to transform the industry. This joint effort is one of the many initiatives looking at interoperability, collaboration, risk management, and integrated processes.

Many such initiatives exist, sometimes overlapping with the programs of other organizations. Often it seems as though each subspecialty organization has to define its own path. The work of many of these groups is redundant, but some is disconnected and adds to the confusion.

NIST identified losses due to lack of interoperability. There is much the same problem with implementation, as many organizations work to understand integration and modeling. The complexity and fragmentation of the U.S. construction industry makes interoperability, even at a basic level, a major challenge.

Even with these challenges and the new processes represented by integrated practice, building information modeling, and rules-based systems, many professionals still seem to be paying lip service to society's broader concerns. This complexity has led many of the pioneers to be bogged down in an endless loop of adding detail upon detail. They have distinguished goals—to develop fully functional and user-friendly systems that everyone in the built world can use to interact with each other. They work to engage all of the information that our world revolves around. We cannot wait for them to finish.

Building information modeling is the next new thing. Right now it's hot. People approach modeling in a number of different ways. Some are sowing the long-term seeds for the future, some are little more than ways to pick the "low-hanging fruit" to capitalize on "What's in it for me?" and some are little more than clouds of fog obscuring traditional processes to make people think that they are getting the benefits of information modeling and integrated processes.

Those few that work toward long-term success spend much of their time developing standards, studying how data is exchanged between the different players, and attempting to negotiate the highly fragmented professional associations that all seem to want to write their own standards. A few are also actively deploying systems that lead the way into a cloud-based, fully integrated, and collaborative environment. As their work individually, in teams, and in professional associations evolves and is implemented, tested in practice, discussed in conferences, videos, and the Web, and synthesized into the industry, we will all benefit.

Those that take advantage of the "low-hanging fruit" still add value in the world, as their work forms the basis for proofs of concept and case studies. To the extent that these companies clearly define what they are doing and use commercially available tools to make their work better for their clients, they provide immediate benefit. To the extent that they confuse others about what they are actually doing, through either implication or hype, they sometimes undermine progress. Rarely do they achieve benefit beyond their projects, for that is their goal.

Those that use the vocabulary to confuse the uninitiated, and focus on information as software with little or no process change, offer few benefits. They do not understand the basic principles, the logic behind the change, or the potential benefit, to themselves or to society. For this group, modeling and integrated processes are often nothing more than checking off an owner requirement in order to get the job. Since they are committing to do things that they do not know and cannot truly deliver, they stimulate the same types of conflict and confusion that characterize processes in the traditional process. They often impede and undermine the future benefits.

Align yourself with those systems, processes, and people that are working toward the long-term success of information modeling in the built environment. Work with those capitalizing on the "low-hanging fruit," realizing that they are focusing on projects, rather than on the greater good for the built environment. Work to eliminate those that "blow smoke" and confuse the issue in order to keep doing what they have always done. Sometimes it is difficult to tell the difference, but if you look carefully and examine the options knowing what is possible, you can sort it out and make our world a better place.

THE OPEN MODEL SERVER CONTINUUM
WESTOVER, MARYLAND
NOVEMBER 7, 2020

People in Somerset County did the research to understand how to overcome these barriers. We decided to create a system that could take information from anywhere and let anyone use the data easily. The system would need to be capable of scaling to allow massive amounts of information to be managed. It would have to be flexible enough to respond to people with widely variable knowledge and abilities.

Some people would use the system as a cloud-based file storage. Others could need a building information model or green building analysis capability. Some could be interfaced with geographic information systems, proprietary software, and information model authoring tools. The system must allow for collaboration, financial system integration, and connection with many other servers. At least part of the system would need to be an open-standard Industry Foundation Class (IFC) model server fully configured with industry-standard data interchange, dictionaries, and delivery manuals. In short, the system will need to handle just about any information that relates to the built environment.

We figured we needed to create a system that would tie together information being held and created in thousands and thousands of different places, for thousands and thousands of different organizations, by millions and millions of people. The system needed to form a continuum that would work with anyone and everyone to make data available to all. Figuring out the system and then making it real was a major undertaking.

We quickly realized that no one central organization could hope to create or manage the system. Just figuring out how to bring technology into the building industry was a big task. The industry is so widespread and includes so many different players that it's hard to wrap up in a tidy package. The built environment is so diverse that it touches upon everything in our lives. It's hard to define, and when something is hard to define, it's hard to solve. Only by embracing the concepts of wicked problems and systems thinking could we possibly envision how the system would work. Ideally, it would at heart be a simple system that would grow and adjust naturally as the organization matures.

Our research started by looking at systems that could handle this complexity. We found that international groups had been working for years to define standards and create usable model servers. Their efforts seemed to have regularly run into funding issues and a lack of focus since most of their work was done with volunteers. Too often, it seemed as though these groups were merely adding complexity in a very complex and hard to understand segment of our world. In fact, some of the groups were tacitly delivering the message that in order to play in their sandbox you had to use their version of standards-compliant tools. Even with the best of intentions, they seemed to be limiting progress.

Most of the systems that resulted from these groups could only be operated by specialists. They required too much effort, too much training, and normal for-profit companies were slow to accept them. On top of that, none of the systems that we found were capable of handling the extensive data required for effective communications, existing systems, and other high-level needs. We found some groups that had started to look at mash-ups of model servers and property life cycle servers to act as collaboration hubs. These groups were focused on the fact that building information modeling and product life cycle management are very similar processes. These groups' work led us to a number of conclusions:

No single software product could possibly manage all the necessary information. No single server product could manage all of the required tools. Allowing this need to be taken over by proprietary solutions from one or more of the thousand-pound gorillas that drive software markets in the industry would not be beneficial to society's long-term needs. If the large software developers were to come together to create open standards solutions for this need, that would be wonderful. It seems as though the business case for this type of collaboration has never been clear to these developers. This lack of clarity has resulted in a worldwide movement that relies on the volunteer efforts of individuals and corporations.

In Europe and other parts of the world, government resources have supported development. A more comprehensive mechanism for research and development of built environment information systems seemed to be needed. Without dependable funding mechanisms that recognize the benefits to society, development of these systems will always be slowed. We needed to find ways to monetize a comprehensive system that people could get behind.

Open standards are the only way to go. The built environment is complex and conceptually the Industry Foundation Class (IFC) schema reflects it in a comprehensive way. IFC is the interoperable standard for sharing building information model data. IFC handles geometry, topology, elements, relationships, spaces, terrain, structure, systems, furniture, time, constraints, analysis, people, work plans, costs, and external data. IFC had limited ability to manage versioning and model exchanges between disciplines. Access control and change tracking were also limited.

Integrating IFC model server technology with Product Life Cycle Support (PLCS) seemed to be well suited to compensate for the limitations of IFC by adding the business support required for real-world integration. Change management, requirements documentation, maintenance and communication capabilities with PLCS filled the gaps.

Groups successfully prototyped the connection of IFC with PLCS. IFC plus PLCS achieved superior integration. From a design and construction project focus, there was progress. It was difficult to see a path that would lead to life cycle management of built environment assets.

Requiring people to understand the complexity of the IFCs before they could start connecting to built environment data looked a lot like a proprietary format. It certainly made the data difficult to work with. We needed ways to support the complexity while at the same time providing for simple ways for people to jump in. IFC may well be the format for managing built environment data over the long term. Because of IFC's complexity, it may not be well suited to handle current needs. We need to encourage simple solutions while continuously developing standards and tools behind the scenes.

Model servers in isolation were not ready for prime time. In a continuum that is designed to support the larger need of society, model servers could play a critical role. IFC model servers focus on managing and defining all of the components of project-oriented construction. Other model servers could handle small subsets of this information, connecting others to everything else. As the world moves toward managing assets and life cycle management of the built environment, IFC model servers will need to be supported by other systems.

Successful prototypes in Europe added to our belief that it is possible to create a system that weaves servers, databases, and many other tools together into a unified whole that will support better decisions and improved planning. Although there were barriers to achieving this goal, we decided to move forward with creating a system that is a hybrid of the generation and power systems that Edison invented for public utilities and neural networks. The Internet, wide area networks, and mobile networks would act as the distribution system for our new model server public utility.

> The Onuma System was arguably one of the first systems that credibly accomplished many of these tasks. By focusing on a subset of IFC, the system works to support early stage planning, business decision making, and management of life cycle information. Data connects from anywhere and everywhere via web services. The system is entirely cloud-based. End users follow the same rules that they have come to expect with other Internet systems. One cannot send a fax to Expedia to book an airline seat. It is not possible to use pencil and paper to send an e-mail. The same tools that allow one to collaborate on the Internet allow one to plan, create, and manage the built environment.

The Onuma Model Server was the first that allowed a wide range of people with little or no technology experience to experience the enhanced decision making possibilities model servers offer. Other model servers were not readily accessible and too complex for the majority of users. Without experiencing the power and opportunities that come from open-source, cloud-based model servers, few could understand the need for such systems. By exposing people to the model server in ways that got results for the non-expert, the logic and need began to become clear to people throughout the built environment.

CONNECTIONS

Our goal is to manage the data of the built environment to promote integrated decisions and collaboration. We call ourselves BIMSynergy. We are working to make information modeling ubiquitous and significant. The information that we host is present in a controlled and secure manner that is also easy to connect to and accessible from any direction. Homes can connect to the Internet. Companies can connect through wide-area networks, the Internet, or through mobile devices. Government agencies can reproduce our resources within their firewalls. Schools can join in. Businesses tie in. Anyone can connect.

The system acts as a central point for utility demand response, live sensor data, and a lot of analysis tools. Environmental monitoring, energy management, agricultural control systems, and any type of automation connected to a network can interface with the system. By embracing open systems and tools with open protocols that make it easy for developers to connect, all of this is possible.

The goal is to give everyone that uses the system a personalized experience. As people use the tools, their contributions to the data are a high percentage of the value in the system. Both positive and negative feedback loops let us participate in dialogue with users, so the corrections can occur almost instantaneously.

Easy to use model servers, that keep the complexity transparent to users became key components of the SMART Connexion Server that provides rules-based planning, real-life decision making, geographic analysis, and product life cycle coordination within BIMSynergy.

BIMSynergy is only one part of a global data modeling continuum. There will eventually be many information modeling server-based utilities that tie into this continuum of information. Some will be publicly owned and operated. Some will be stockholder owned. Some will be shared enterprises. And others will be independently owned. The model server utility continuum will support all built environment information. It will also support the retail building information modeling business. Each utility will require domestic or international support to ensure reliability, consistent planning, and coordination of services.

Without consistent ways to share information at all levels across the built environment, information modeling and integrated decision-making would remain much like off-the-grid housing is today… Isolated and disconnected.

INVESTMENT

One can think of BIMSynergy much the same way that one would think of electric utility companies.

Thomas Edison's vision for electricity touches almost every place that humans occupy. Scarce resources are taken in to generate power. The power is then sent on and used to heat our homes, cook our food, run our computers, and many other things. Companies buy and sell the charged particles that we call electricity.

The electric network is made up of power generation facilities such as dams and power plants. Transmission lines, substations, and power lines distribute power across states, regions, and the nation. Underground and overhead lines carry electricity to homes and offices. Overloads and shortages are balanced. Wind power, photovoltaic power, and other point sources provide off-the-grid power generation. With these point sources, one can also generate power and sell it back to electric companies.

Some electric utility companies are regional behemoths. Some are cooperatives. Some communities have their own electric company. The system is widely distributed, monetized, and regulated to serve society. We all benefit, and we all pay the costs.

The model server grid is the same type of thing. The Internet and cloud-computing are the power lines and substations to extend the model server grid across the world. Model server utility companies such as BIMSynergy act much like the power generation facilities. The buildingSMART alliance and the International Organization for Standardization regulate the system and control standards.

Electric utilities are based on mature technology. They plan and budget for repair and replacement, new production facilities, and technology upgrades within a well-known system. The model server utility plans and budgets for many of the same things within a highly volatile and evolving framework that is likely to see black swan events on a regular basis. Because of this, model server utilities are agile. Their systems are designed to be flexible and planned for future change.

Individuals and companies connect their local model servers to the grid much like one would add a photovoltaic field or wind turbine to the electric grid. Some model server utility companies are behemoths, but the vast majority are small, relying on the grid for support and resources.

A regional utility such as BIMSynergy is the heart of the Infrastructure as a Service (IaaS) environment that connects and brokers the needs of millions of servers doing different jobs. Users are freed from the complexities and use basic hardware and software to access the vast resources of the model server grid. Sharing resources reduces the cost for all. As with electric utility pricing, cost for these services varies based on local regulatory costs, infrastructure costs, personnel, and the customer mix.

Follow this tag to learn more about black swan events at http://4sitesystems.com/iofthestorm/?page_id=883

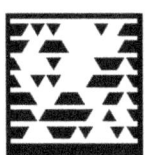

It has long been considered a fact that people do not easily pay for future savings. Belief in this theory may be the reason that people focus on the "low-hanging fruit" of information modeling, to the exclusion of the greater benefits. The improved processes, reduced waste, and savings in costs and time build real and lasting value. Recognizing the importance to individuals and society, the BIMSynergy revenue model is designed to make people want and need to use the services.

Too often, Software-as-a-Service and Infrastructure-as-a-Service organizations have created terrific products and then created revenue models that undermined their value. Creating a product with the end goal of fostering collaboration and then charging per user is just one example. The numbers of individuals that are signed up for collaborations monetized this way is always smaller than those that reward for participation. Because of this factor, most of the fees are built around information flow and storage capacity.

The necessary tools are available for the taking. At the low end, part of the income results from pay-per-click and other online advertising. For most people, the system's value comes from making reliable information available when and where they need want and need it. Much of the revenue is earned from millions of people that participate in the ebb and flow of information through the system. For this, we use an approach that is a combination of those used by the most successful Amazon Web Services and by 37signals LLC, the creators of Basecamp, Highrise, and Backpack.

The balance of revenues comes from leading innovation and support for a wide variety of user groups. Traditional infrastructure providers, such as water, sewerage, and electrical utility companies, may have had a small, specialized group that provided ongoing services to their customers. We realized early in the development process that that approach was no longer viable. After the profound changes that happened in the newspaper industry, publishing, the steel industry, the automotive industry, the music industry, and many others, people's lives were turned upside down. People and organizations needed to change faster. They needed to innovate more. People could no longer rely on the company telling them what to do and paying them well for it. One had to learn how to succeed in the new age. We help them with that.

We have staff whose mission is to make sure that the technology works perfectly. Most of our staff is dedicated to helping people manage information. To a person, everyone in this group can be called "T-shaped." They have deep knowledge and broad interests because those are the characteristics that make one best able to work in the world of tomorrow. We make their deep expertise in one skill set, their passion, and their ability to interconnect what to some may look like isolated concepts, available to people that need their help.

Follow this tag to learn more about the concept of T-Shaped people at http://4sitesystems.com/iofthestorm/?page_id=330

Supporting people to improve the built environment is a vital part of our mission. Supporting those who make it happen is essential, as well. T-shaped people are hard to find. Bringing their skills and passions to bear at the right time is even harder. We faced a dilemma. We solved it by creating a decentralized system of virtual enterprise networks across the world. Where BIMSynergy is a distributed grid, tying millions of model servers together, BIMSynergy Support is made up of hundreds of virtual enterprise networks that link to the network. They turn their attention to a specific geographic area or specialty service.

Some of these virtual enterprise networks are focused on users who require information to support local issues. They are typically represented by small firms and casual users who require data to support personal decision making, for example, "Where is the as-built operating data for my local elementary school?" or, "In what flood zone is my home?" or, "What do I have to do to get historic district permission to paint my house?"

Follow this tag to learn more about the concept of Virtual Enterprise Networks at http://4sitesystems.com/iofthestorm/?page_id=820

We also work with top-secret organizations that require model servers. Often they require dedicated model servers housed in hardened facilities that are mirrored to other hardened facilities. These users have extensive and mission-critical needs that demand skills and expertise tailored to their world.

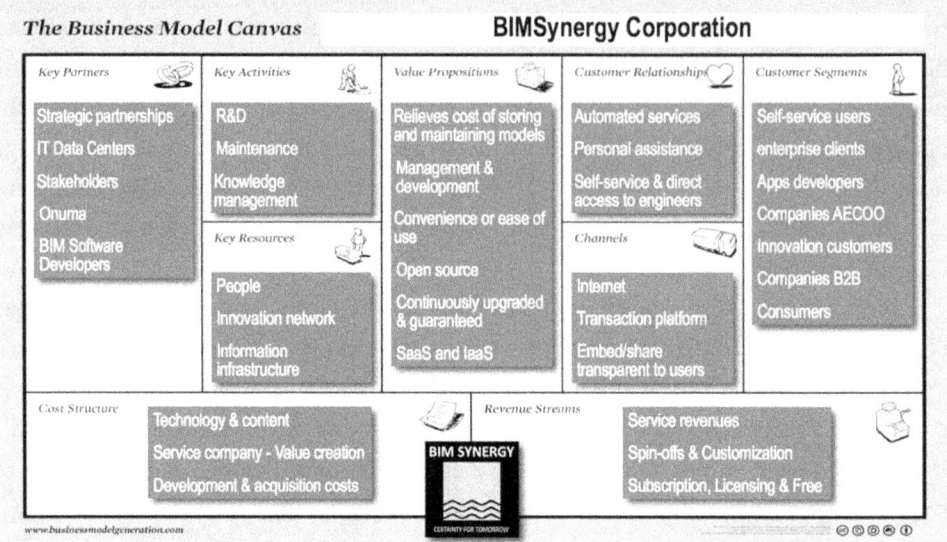

For some of their clients, these small firms combine their talents to help. In most cases, one or two of them provide services. In this one building, we can usually find the expert that is needed to solve any problem. Best of all, they can connect us to virtually any expert we need, anywhere in the world, almost instantaneously. Their system is driven by connecting people. They have learned that they cannot manage modeling and integrated processes with halfway measures. This image is subject to the terms of a Creative Commons, Attribution-Share Alike license from Business Model Canvas, www. businessmodelgeneration.com

BIMSynergy creates a rare and tailored approach that encourages owners, the design community, constructors, and everyone else to adopt collaboration and decision making using reliable and readily available shared data. We accommodate all users. At heart, we provide a straightforward schema that grows and adjusts naturally as the information model market matures.

RULES BASED SYSTEMS

> Consumers, by definition, include us all. They are the largest economic group in the economy, affecting and affected by almost every public and private economic decision. Two-thirds of all spending in the economy is by consumers. But they are the only important group in the economy who are not effectively organized, whose views are often not heard.
>
> —John F. Kennedy

In the 1980s, rules-based systems began to become available to help experts make decisions about complex things, such as investments. These systems were expensive and limited to special cases. In the 1990s through early in the twenty-first century, rules-based systems began to be more accessible. The Onuma System was one of the first rules-based systems in the built environment. Few understood the possibilities and power that came from rules-based systems tied to information models.

In the late part of the twentieth century, much of the development effort toward interoperable formats seem to be focused on highly complex and confusing definitions of how to exchange information between the different disciplines. The complex nature of IFC development was even more complicated than similar projects that led to the Internet, because much of the work was done on a volunteer basis. Development was ad hoc and consensus-based. When one is developing standards for an entire industry, consensus is vital.

Consensus is essential, but if one is not careful, groupthink can cause you to miss the larger picture. In this case, much of the development effort became so mired in the complexities that it would have stalled, were it not for individuals such as Kimon Onuma. His BIMXML and BIMStorm programs were the first to achieve rules-based design systems and BIG BIM functionality in the built environment. Not until about 2012 did things actually start to change in the development of industry-wide systems.

In 1987, Carnegie Mellon University developed a model for improving the software development process, called the Capability Maturity Model (CMM). Over the years, CMM began to be applied to improving business processes and personal development as well as software development. CMM could be staged, allowing one to determine areas that needed improving and focusing on them. CMM could also be continuous, allowing one to determine a future ideal and then move to achieve that goal. People used continuous CMM to further their education and training. Organizations used staged CMM to evaluate their process maturity level and to work toward improving specific areas where they fell short. Technology developers used staged CMM to determine needs and outcomes for their tools.

After much discussion, some in the industry realized that rather than continuing the somewhat ad hoc approach that had been the norm for the past twenty years, the industry needed to embrace CMM. Using CMM as a high-level planning tool that can determine, check, and improve over time, the development of information models accelerated.

Previously software developers often found themselves responding to meet individual large clients' desires. Now the developers could create tools that delivered at a known level of maturity, knowing that their tools would satisfy the majority of users.

Previously most architects and contractors focused their information modeling efforts on design and construction, the "'sweet spots" of their businesses. Now these professionals could move to a life cycle view of the built environment that took into account all of the other things that go together to make our world.

Previously building owners and employers found themselves in a position of wanting information modeling services and products, only to find themselves unable to describe what building information modeling truly meant. They faced "bim-washing" and images dummied up to look like people's idea of information models. Graphic representations of information model data are easy to fake. It is difficult to separate the image view of an information model from the flat imagery. Now they have measurable standards for certifying work products and testing of employees.

Where at the turn of the century many saw information modeling as an opportunity, they now understood the big-picture issues and knew how to determine where they stood.

EXPERT SYSTEMS

In the early days of the twenty-first century, there was a groundswell of new users having their first experience in working with information modeling systems. These modeling systems offered significant improvements in visualizing and documenting projects. There were a number of obvious benefits to the process, and that is where most advanced users focused their attention. That is where they could be immediately productive.

The information modeling programs worked on desktop computers. Valuable work could be done with these programs using relatively low-powered desktop computers. Large projects and detailed information models required significant hardware investments. In most cases, the files produced by these desktop applications were stored in proprietary file formats on the local file server.

In the first decade of the twenty-first century, Kimon Onuma was already giving people a peek at some of the magic that has made the Onuma System so attractive to large, multi-facility clients, especially in the federal arena. At this stage, Mr. Onuma was unique in the fact that he was able to show his creation live. Canned presentations tend to obscure flaws and shortcomings. We have found that live demonstrations and hands-on tests are the only ways to be sure that technology works. The Onuma System was one of an exceedingly small handful of systems that could actively maintain links to live information across the built environment life cycle. The system's ability to maintain data as a living resource and to interface with expert systems via web services made it one of the first, and most critical, components of BIMSynergy.

The Onuma System demonstrated a number of key parts that BIMSynergy needed to address. First, the system did not impose hardware or software restrictions on users. Users were fully functional without dedicated server hardware. Work took place using Internet-accessible, non-dedicated virtual servers, or cloud computing. Second, the system fostered rules-based planning so that smart codes, smart costing systems, and rules-based planning, analysis, and simulation take place quickly.

The system worked with not only Industry Foundation Class (IFC) frameworks, but with many other flat and simplified structures that allow spatial data to be used by all. Without these critical capabilities, the model server would not deliver the things that people needed.

Model servers, IFC, XML, building information model, bim, BIMSynergy, web services, COBie2, Onuma System, BIMStorm, GBXML, BIMXML, and hundreds of others: this is a world of jargon and acronyms. The new language is difficult for normal people to understand. The Internet does not actually expect you to know as much jargon. Maybe this is because the Internet focuses on helping millions of people to interact. Many of these social interactions happen without fee or investment from most users. On the other hand, most users just don't see the costs or the investment, because the advertisers and vendors bury them in the transactions.

Perhaps the reason that jargon is so prevalent in the built environment is that many professionals have not made the effort to learn to communicate with the rest of the world. They are only talking to other construction professionals. They focus on details, even when knowing the details is counterproductive. Most people would find themselves mired in jargon should Google share the details behind their systems. If Facebook required that their users understand and speak the language of programmers, how many ordinary people would actually sign up? How many friends would you have? Is it truly necessary for everyone to talk the language of model servers, any more than they talk the language of Google?

People need to be heard. People want to connect with their friends. People want things to be predictable and straightforward. When we understood these facts, we decided that most people would see BIMSynergy the same way they see Google or Facebook. It would become the main focus of built environment information and no one would have to learn new words or to be a programmer in order to use it. For most people, BIMSynergy just works, period.

SIMPLE INFORMATION
SALISBURY, MARYLAND
JUNE 15, 2022

We were following some intriguing things happening just north of us in Wicomico County. That is where most of the architects and engineers around here live. BIMSynergy Corporation is shaking up things all over the place.

BIM Delivery Company is typical of the medium and small firms that have designed most of the schools and hospitals around here. They are led by a couple of well-connected and well-thought-of architects and have a staff of about fifteen. Like many architects, they have been closely following the success of building information modeling, integrated project delivery, and interoperability. The last few years, they have tried a lot of different things and used a number of different tools to improve their processes. From what they tell me, they believe that it's vital to give their clients the singularly best projects, on time and under budget.

About twelve years ago, the BIM Delivery Company was one of the first to adopt collocation. Their office building is now more of a hub for change than it is a standard architect's office. Within that one building, there are architects, managers, lawyers, planners, software developers, engineers, and all kinds of design professionals. Each of the professionals that move here is independent. They remain in the building because they are collaborators and excellent at what they do. Those that cannot collaborate effectively or are driven by ego and self-interest are quickly weeded out.

It seems like they tried every option out there, and found that automating the old ways of doing things just didn't work. Now that BIMSynergy is available, they find that it becomes much easier to share their knowledge with everyone involved in the design process. The BIM Delivery Company and the others co-located with them are moving forward to be part of the grassroots program that is making information models happen with a life cycle worldview.

The last time I visited their office it looked like they were using information modeling every day on everything they do. I liked the fact that they used the simplest form of model suitable for the situation they were trying to get done. They know about standards. With that in mind, it looks like they always opt for standards that are simple. They told me that they found that if one wants people to follow your standards, the standards must be simple. So they've created internal standards that are as uncomplicated as possible. Much of what they do also revolves around BIMXML, rather than IFC, in order to get the most work done in the simplest way possible.

When we were doing the research for BIMSynergy, we found that too many of the highly developed standards were at heart controls for flat CAD productivity. Others focused solely on specific applications. Neither approach actually added anything to the modeling work flow. We found that most standards don't help one to do better work in this fast-paced technology. When we encoded the integrated processes using information models that form the core of BIMSynergy, we found that we could abandon most of the old standards without hurting our users' work product whatsoever.

There seemed to be an awful lot of interim documents leading to many of the standards that we found. They contained so much jargon that most of us couldn't understand them. They spent so much time debating the minutiae of information exchanges between domains that they were more confusing than anything else we found. We knew that these documents were a step in the process and necessary. But we resolved not to let them get in our way. Because we knew that, even with interim standards and evolving tools, information modeling had been proven to be a more effective delivery system.

I think that it is interesting that the BIM Delivery Company and most of the other firms I know have attended a lot of seminars and conferences. I was amazed to learn how many people in all segments of industry have gotten involved in this change. Some of them embrace the process and do real projects. Others are more theoretical and focus on standards in the future. I have learned to love the theorists and to embrace the doers. The focus on standards and interoperability is clearly necessary and admirable, but it doesn't actually help us to get things done.

The folks at BIM Delivery Company used to have complicated CAD standards and office manuals, written with noble goals in mind. They tended toward extremely rigid and complex controls with hundreds of layers, pen tables, and standard layouts that are almost always automated in an information modeling process. Their controls made navigation and understanding difficult, and they did nothing to improve document coordination. These CAD-based standards needed a specific rule for every specific instance of every specific task. They were just too inflexible. By their nature, they were impediments to change. So, they got rid of them.

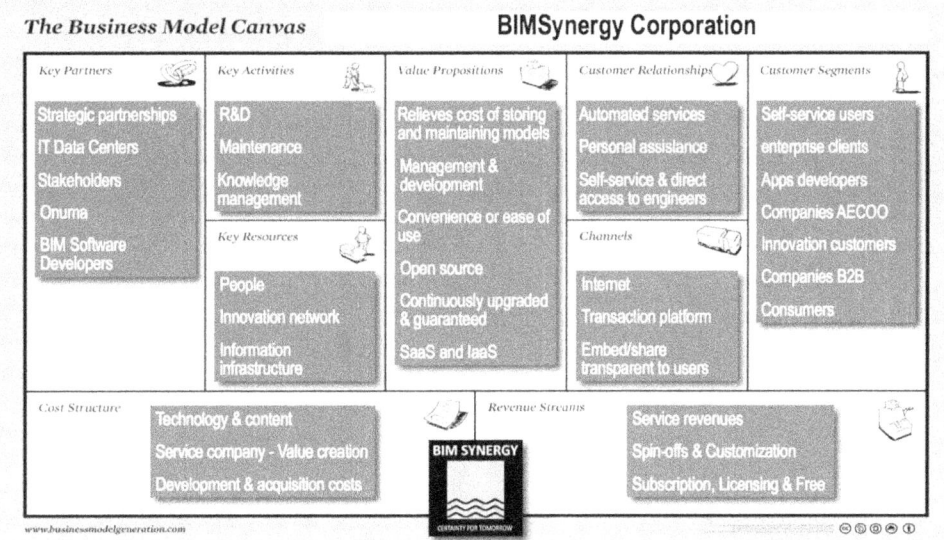

Those responsible for organizational information know that their data must be normalized to system standards before their databases will be connected. Many organizations faced an enormous task cleaning up the messes that their programmers created. The ad hoc approach that allowed anyone and everyone to create databases to accommodate seat-of-the-pants enterprise operations has been recognized as counterproductive and a drain on corporate resources. Few organizations allow this any longer. This image is subject to the terms of a Creative Commons, Attribution-Share Alike license from Business Model Canvas, www.businessmodelgeneration.com

They have learned that integrated processes using information models must be flexible and allow for easy transitions between projects, tasks, and people. Everyone needs to understand what needs to happen, without a data table or rule book. They need accepted and logical names. Like others, they started by defining only a small handful of attributes. After they completed several projects, they looked at them and threw away everything that was not necessary. What was left turned out to be a pretty decent information modeling standard for their office.

We found that our clients are more than a little concerned that without clean, affordable, and reliable ways to manage and exchange information, they might not see long-term rewards for their investments. The BIMSynergy Corporation seems to be just the ticket to let us actually help people to control their data. Since everything that goes into the server is based on standards, it opens up an altogether different world of residual income possibilities for people. Their data is now valuable long after their projects are completed. It creates a situation where people no longer have to be tied to projects. They can now work with their clients to help them manage their assets. They become stewards of the built environment.

For many years, groups such as the International Organization for Standardization (ISO) and buildingSMART International focused their efforts on creating consensus standards to enable IFC model server technology. Fifteen years into the twenty-first century their efforts appeared to be lagging behind the explosive growth of the Internet. Arguably this was because of the complexity of IFC and the complications that came from consensus-making volunteer operations.

In European tests, IFC was shown to have limitations. Since BIG BIM is best defined as collaborative processes that enable integrated and optimized built environment operations, IFC alone was not the final solution. Version management, partial model exchanges, access controls, and change history limited IFC's ability to support BIG BIM. The European testing found that with the addition of Product Life Cycle Support (PLCS) services that it was possible to achieve superior integration. PLCS added built environment business objects such as change management, versioning, consolidation controls, requirements management, as-built documentation, and maintenance to the mix.

We realize that the technology is changing every day. New ways to use the technology and new opportunities pop up in the journals every month. The name of the game is change. We do not let this intimidate us or slow us down. We are learning to thrive and adapt to the rapidly evolving environment.

We learned some valuable lessons as we created BIMSynergy. The first and hardest lesson may be that we cannot be all things to all people. Nor do we know the answer to every question. We have embraced the concepts of sapience and systems thinking.

As we have come to understand what sapience means, we have learned to have the wisdom to recognize our own limitations and to override the need to give opinions even when we have no real facts from which to form our opinions. We know when to engage others. We embrace cloud-based tools that inform our knowledge base to enhance our ability to make sound judgments. In a complex world, our decisions have consequences. We often find ourselves needing to make significant judgments under unfamiliar circumstances.

Fortunately, we found systems such as the EPM Technology model server, BIMserver.org, and the Onuma System that archive and build knowledge to promote better decision making. In these systems, information plus advanced graphics equal certainty. We take advantage of them and realize that we do not have to do everything at once. But with the proper tools, a strong orientation toward systems thinking, and a strategic approach, we think that we have created a distributed solution that has a high probability of being correct.

To become adept systems thinkers we had to embrace change, learn to be more flexible, and value lifelong learning. We knew that our clients could not wait for someone else to figure out all the complex systems and standards for us. We found that, with the resources and tools readily available, we could do BIMSynergy. As we learned to use our resources and tools in new and more sophisticated ways, we have been able to produce a system that makes built environment information available to anyone, anytime that they need the data.

There are many issues that we had to overcome before we could create this system. We had a lot of personal and industry inertia to overcome. When we looked at information models as a hardheaded business decision geared to deliver a superior way to manage and maintain data, the change became a no-brainer. As the BIMSynergy solution has matured, the decision made even more sense.

We're doing more things in more areas than we would have believed to be possible several years ago. Embracing information to improve the environment creates new opportunities every day. We now focus on helping others to make better decisions. We're now leading the development of the technology, connecting to data everywhere, and continuing to change to get better and better.

BIMSYNERGY CORPORATION

Here are some of the things that BIMSynergy provides (apologies for the jargon):

1. The first is what we call the SMART Connexion Server. This server's mission is to connect to rules-based planning system data to help people to make decisions in real-life situations. Included as part of the SMART Connexion Server are linkages to a variety of open geospatial information servers. These servers manage geographic data in earth browsers such as Google Earth, Google Maps, and mobile mapping devices. They also interface in open formats for geographic transactions. They allow sharing of remote sensor data from sources such as agricultural tracts and marine environments.

2. Surrounding the SMART Connexion Server are a series of servers that focus on life cycle management services. They include:

    Enterprise Asset Management (Facilities Management) Servers designed to optimize and manage physical assets to maximize their value.

    Product Life Cycle Support (PLCS) Servers designed to connect people, information, processes, and business systems to manage communications and resources. Most of the systems that people associate with business operations, such as financial management, mailing lists, and procurement, are built into the Product Life Cycle Support Servers. These servers are required to optimize the value of the IFC model server backbone.

    Smart Grid Servers designed to manage and control electric grid demand response, by enabling direct sensor connections to homes, schools, hospitals, and all other energy users.

3. Communications servers form the next ring. These servers allow real-time video, audio, and text. They focus on collaboration and social networking while embedding all communications within the information model environment. E-mail is not supported within BIMSynergy, since e-mail is not well suited to virtual, collaborative environments. Too many communications fall through the cracks and too many passive aggressive, I-didn't-get-your-e-mail issues happen with normal

e-mail. Only when communications are clear and available for all to see does true collaboration begin to happen.

Traditional e-mail is still available outside of the system for those personal, one-on-one communications that continue to take place, but communications within the BIMSynergy communications servers are the definitive source for facts about the built environment.

4. Supporting these servers is a shareable database system. This system is a hybrid that uses a consistent, logical model of information combined with natural language, concepts, and roles. The system is based on relational and object-oriented data models. End users can directly transfer information into and out of the databases. Usually the code is embedded, so that end users do not know it is there. The underlying principles are that the databases are transparent to most users and are intentionally designed to handle information that no one has anticipated. They recognize that it is impossible to predict the information that will be required over the generations.

To enable the databases to evolve as information needs evolve, there were strict requirements for how the information was named and structured. In the past, databases were created ad hoc, often resulting in data that was defined and named based on the whims of individuals. This resulted in one database storing "door1," the next storing "DOOR1," another storing "Door One," and yet another storing "D1001." As a single instance of a door, this would be easily fixed; with millions of doors, and all of the other items that are part of the built environment, consistently naming things became critical.

Making existing, or legacy, databases consistent is called normalizing. One of the major hurdles that we overcame in creating BIMSynergy was to manage this issue. Today, there are still millions of databases, and all of them are moving toward interconnection in our distributed computer environment, for that is how we are able to leverage the value of information.

Information stored in nonstandard ways or in proprietary formats has become irrelevant. Those that understand this are thriving. The others are going the way of the dinosaur. Open standards and normalized data are the new gold standard.

5. BIMSynergy is a mash-up of many server technologies, interconnected to optimize the built environment life cycle operations. At the most complex level, the system uses Industry Foundation Class (IFC) model servers. Supporting the servers are a comprehensive set of Model View Definitions (MVD) that describe processes and relationships. An MVD is a clear description that guides how information is exchanged in the built environment processes defined by the system's Information Delivery Manual (IDM). A dictionary layer, called the International

Framework for Dictionaries (IFD), also catalogs what objects are called to allow data to be linked from many sources. The IFD is an open, shared, and internationally agreed-upon terminology library that supports the exchange of object-oriented information.

6. Because of all of these factors, BIMSynergy embraced simplified data formats that allow developers and users to work using data exchanges that are similar to those used across the Internet. In some cases, the data exchanges are not drawn from IFC alone, and may not be derived from an IFC model view definition. Allowing these "incompatible" structures allows for many simple exchanges of information. These exchanges deal with a lot of data and allow for flexibility that does not come from rigid structures. In many cases, these exchanges are straightforward enough to be opened and understood by a 12-year-old with reasonable computer skills.

   These simplified formats open the connections to BIG BIM and use open standards. They move information modeling into the mainstream rather than reserving the technology for a handful of users who understand IFC. Many more users can make the connection, and the power of social networks becomes available to improve the inefficient and wasteful processes that have so long characterized the industry.

   Using the simplified formats allows such innovations as real-time connection of the room-by-room temperature data directly into building information models. Using "plain vanilla" XML, it is now possible to create live connections from sensor data with minimal effort. Updates are visualized in real time, rather than requiring remote manipulation or adjustment.

   The adoption of these simplified formats was a small step, requiring minimal complexity for all levels of users. These formats are the catalyst that enabled rapid mass adoption of BIMSynergy.

7. We faced a number of security challenges as we developed BIMSynergy. Security has to be strong enough to keep out the bad stuff and good enough to let the good stuff in. The goal was to convince people to use the system. Because of this, we could little afford to be seen as too restrictive. Nor could we come off as being the least bit lax. It was a delicate balancing act. The ability to tag each piece of data with a creation data and ownership information and then to protect the data set so that no one could change it, was a core process in the system's data assurance program. Resolving the questions of ownership, time and versioning were the baseline steps as we moved away from merely archiving data. The PLCS server was critical to our current objective of creating a responsive and fine-grained security system that fit the bill.

The databases in the system are mirrored for safety, security, and for clients with dedicated BIMSynergy installations. The ability to connect and mirror our services was another critical component. The system was first deployed in a virtual environment that allows the system to grow exponentially as people adapt to the new processes. There were also organizations that needed government-grade security, near 100 percent uptime, full off-site backup, and expandable storage area networks to handle the massive amounts of information that they created.

For the first time, people and organizations knew where the data resided. They knew that it was IFC compliant, to the extent necessary. They knew how to access data for the purposes that they needed the information. This knowledge has always been key to BIG BIM. Without this level of certainty and data security, information modeling is just another technology that will be replaced when something better comes along…just like CADD.

8. We provided users with a series of programs and apps that simplified input and output to the server. The goals are to make sending and synchronizing data as simple for the user as possible. Data is georeferenced, quality checked, and version controlled. When others work with the data, they receive information that is IFC compliant, tied to a specific location on earth, and the latest version.

   When the system first went online, much of the data that was delivered was incomplete, poorly formatted, and needed to be localized. To spur adoption, in the early days, we hosted IFC data in whatever form and of whatever quality was submitted. A large portion of our early technical support offerings focused on assisting people in improving their data. It did not take long for that to change, moving toward the goal of validated data.

9. There are several services and management systems that operate behind the scenes. These devices and high-level programs are the glue that holds the system together. The Object Request Broker is one of these systems. The Object Request Broker uses artificial intelligence and a neural network to referee web services and allow programs to talk to each other, regardless of language or operating system. It manages the web services layer, rules-based routing, and all flavors of XML to make information accessible, independent of platforms and program languages.

Most events are handled with automated reactions. The Request Broker also provides for greater interoperability and some protection from proprietary software lock-ins. A transaction monitor makes sure that each transaction is processed correctly and, should an error occur, it takes the appropriate action, based on a set of predefined rules. Open standards are the glue that holds everything together.

KNOWLEDGE AND TOOLS

The built environment is a big part of our world. There's not much in our world that we don't touch, at one time or another. If a human touches something, it is part of the built environment. Those that reason that the process is only about design and construction are missing the point. It's a much bigger place than that. It is so immense that prior to computers, we could not hope to visualize large parts of the built environment—especially not in ways that would make us better stewards of the environment.

Many of society's achievements were completed without the computing power that is commonplace today. The technology that enabled our greatest achievements, such as NASA's moon missions, can be replicated today with a handheld device. By today's standards, they happened at a snail's pace and required unprecedented resources from leading governments and corporations. Entire nations focused on solving the problems. The solutions came from experts. Only with society's best and brightest were they possible.

Focus and commitment drove these achievements. They occurred in a top-down, hierarchical world that brought the skills and knowledge of nations to bear to solve problems. They did it without massive computing power, the Internet, or 24x7 media. They saw an emergency or global issue and stepped up to solve the problem.

We can do the same. We can step up to optimize our systems to reduce waste. We can create sustainable communities. We can overcome today's challenges. We have the technology. Systems such as BIMSynergy allow us to communicate, evaluate options, and work together like never before. We can find the focus and commitment.

We have new challenges of training and communication. We live in a flat world where command and control no longer works like it once did. This new, more collaborative world requires that we create new and better ways of working with each other.

We still need the knowledge that comes from education. We also need the expertise that comes from experience. Without deep knowledge, passion, and curiosity, it is difficult to achieve greatness. Technology and shifts in how things work are changing society. No longer can we depend on processes and values that have been with us since the industrial revolution started.

Today we have tools that allow everyone to participate. Much of the specialized knowledge that yesterday's experts spent years in school and work perfecting, today is available with the click of a mouse in a rules-based system. There is no longer an excuse for not evaluating the options before we decide. When we decide to create a new school rather than renovating the old school without considering all aspects of the situation, we do the community a disservice. Society can no longer afford this level of egotism.

BIMSynergy and the distributed model server network are designed to make the knowledge and tools available to everyone. There is no longer an excuse for proceeding without data. Information modeling interconnected with collaborative systems brings the knowledge of the many to bear on problems of society. It has been said that many eyes find all problems in any situation.

We can now create and share geographic information directly linked to the process. We now know that we have a stable and repeatable way to communicate and assemble information. And it is entirely due to an open standard that makes an unusually cool product even cooler.

The opportunities and tasks that the model server grid let one handle are enormous. A small sampling includes:

- Many work on a problem without relocating. People leverage the knowledge of others without the financial and energy costs. They make use of the power of time zones to get things done quickly.
- People select tools that suit their needs. They communicate with everyone else involved.
- Simple interfaces focus on clear, easy-to-understand and easy-to-use processes.
- Users see lightweight products that engage large number of people. All emphasis is away from large complex products that do too much.
- Teams model their work within files maintained to eliminate redundancy and waste.
- Documents of all kinds (architectural and engineering views, specifications, correspondence, project management data, etc.) are linked to those things that they reference. No longer must one sort through real or virtual file cabinets to find the information that one needs.
- One visualizes data to see what will happen. Static and dynamic views come from the same data so that any view is a reliable visualization, not merely an artist's sketch. With minimal effort, one visualizes and understands airflow, heating/cooling, life cycle, lighting, acoustics, energy, life safety, force protection, environmental issues, life expectancy, and almost any other thing that one needs to know.
- Building and zoning codes, regulations, standards, and reviews are largely automated. Rules guide designers to ensure safety, accessibility, and other key issues. Real-time model checkers generate code reviews quickly and completely. The days where people waited months for code officials to evaluate their work are behind us. All submittals, reviews, and monitoring occur within the model server, directly connected to the project model and georeferenced.
- Specifications, bills of materials, quantity takeoffs, standards, and estimates are generated as a part of the model. Product manufacturers include everything relevant about an item. When a designer selects a product and places it into his or her model, the

product interacts with everything else just as it will in the real world. Models develop incrementally. Early models rely heavily on rules-based systems. Later models rely on the creation of a virtual representation of the final product. Yet, early models and their later incarnations all are highly accurate, generating quantities and costs that can be relied upon.

- Reliable models allow procurement and bid tendering at almost any point in the sequence.
- Schedules are managed within the model server environment, and happen continuously. Since much of the classic design and documentation effort occurs early in the process, scheduling, time management, logistics planning, and coordination efforts also begin early. Time is coordinated within the framework of the enterprise, making design, procurement, construction, operations, and management all part of the larger environment.
- Everything occurs within a life cycle view of the built environment. No longer are facility management, operations, real estate, and property management separated from other building industry functions. Portfolio planning and management, post-occupancy monitoring, and investment analysis are all supported.
- Demolition, reuse, and reconstruction are now another part of the life cycle continuum. Management of the embedded energy and recyclable resources is essential to the built environment.
- Planning is integrated into everything that one does in the model server environment. Perhaps Kimon Onuma said it best when he described this new world as "finding the train wrecks early, well before they happen."
- Everything that can be captured is collected in the model server. This vast amount of data is assessed by rules-based systems, filtered, and managed to make the knowledge available to all. The system classifies and organizes the information. Formal groups review for the best practices and next practices knowledge base. Reference libraries, rules-based systems dictionaries, and action checklists are created and available within the system. Proprietary knowledge is maintained so that the owner has control at all times.
- Real-time sensors feed data from constructed projects for operation within the model server. These sensors rely on open standards and report sustainability, usage, energy, controls, environmental conditions, growth conditions, water quality, security, lighting, and anything else that can be monitored and measured. Since these sensors provide real-time feedback and control, their data can be visualized in several ways through the model server. Traditional graphs, visualizations that change colors as sensors vary from setpoints, and alerts through mobile devices are all possible.

- All procedures and controls are supported by the model server. Schedule management, clash detection, financial management, value chain management, tagging and tracking, process automation, risk management, optimization, and logistics are all supported. Work site safety, traffic control, and large venue command and control also take place within the model server environment. Significantly more work is now done off-site in factory environments. Management and control of modular and plant production systems for functions such as scheduling coordination tied to fabrication, shipping, and installation are also a function of the model server.
- Metrics and naming conventions, or semantics, occur as the models develop. Information from multiple sources is available to support marketing, product sales, and information visualization.
- Extensive sensor networks and the ability to track them within the models allows for a high level of emergency services command and control. Incident commanders are able to visualize scenes, follow their people while on site, and plan for changes to response patterns on the fly. Scenario planning and model analysis allow emergency services planners to determine response times, to identify evacuation sites, and to preplan for shelters. Emergency services operation is tied directly to a department's mission to prepare for assessing equipment needs, resources, and funding.
- Communities use the system to improve their planning processes. Advanced visualization tied to real-time data has been shown to improve citizen participation. Strategic and master planning benefit enormously from the ability to see options quickly. Most of the narrative aspects of traditional planning have fallen by the wayside. When citizens see information from the model server, they are beginning to realize that they are seeing the facts.

This is only a sample of the things that BIMSynergy makes possible. If something is part of the built environment, or something is being added to the natural environment, the model server will allow you to see it better, organize it better, build it better, and make it more sustainable.

A LIKELY FUTURE

Industry Foundation Class (IFC) was probably the long-term future of interoperability. IFCs were important since they represented an approved international standard (ISO 16739). Yet, for many reasons, IFCs were difficult for both developers and users to implement, well into the twenty-first century. Even after almost twenty years of development, they were still not ready for prime time as BIMSynergy went to production. IFCs were sufficiently developed to allow for the interchange of data between authoring tools and analysis tools. A few IFC model servers were in place and functioning. For most users, these model servers required too much technical knowledge and were rarely used.

Because of the complexities surrounding IFCs, Onuma, Inc. created BIMXML, a simplified structure, for collaboration. BIMXML describes building information such as sites, buildings, floors, spaces, resources, and attributes. It is intended to simplify the exchange of information and to link data models to other information through web services. BIMXML continues to be used by the Onuma System (Onuma, Inc.), DDS Viewer (Data Design System), vROC (Lavelle Energy LLC), Tokmo (EcoDomus, Inc.), and to support other authoring applications such as Revit and ArchiCAD. BIMXML also underpins the award-winning BIMStorm programs.

Follow this tag to learn more about BIMXML at http://bimxml.com

BIMStorms occur in close to real time and use a number of knowledge-modeling tools and processes. They demonstrate the power of unified communications and decision making. In the BIMStorm, people make mistakes early. They test-fit possible solutions to reduce the chances of serious errors. They focus on solutions with greater confidence that they are making the right decision. BIMStorms help communities engage citizens. They help organizations prepare for the future. They stimulate the design process.

Participants visualize solutions in an environment where they can clearly see problems and make changes that affect outcomes. Their work is integrated with information about costs, sustainability, and other information. Their communications and research are also integrated. Since all of this data is clear and collaborative, participants are able to make fast, fact-based decisions, well before the traditional design process. Finding solutions may not be the most striking part of a BIMStorm. Often, the most meaningful answers come not from finding solutions, but from finding constraints and the things that will affect outcomes.

BIMXML, IFCs, and the other structures are making BIMStorms possible. Hundreds of people can and have participated in BIMStorms in order to learn about BIG BIM technologies and the future of the built environment. Key to the process is collaborative, open-standard exchanges of information that allow people to use many different software products. In a BIMStorm, the first information might be created by hand on paper, followed by a spreadsheet on Google Docs, and then imported as a georeferenced building information model. The model, now imbued with areas, volumes, costs, and sustainability, can then be adjusted and visualized in context. The model can be exported in a number of formats to many other tools for refining and analysis. When the refinements and the necessary analyses are completed, the models return to the Onuma System. Information is exchanged in the BIMStorm system using a number of different structures.

One of the structures is Green Building eXtensible Markup Language (GBXML). GBXML is an open-source schema that facilitates the transfer of information from data to analysis tools. It is a de facto standard, especially for energy and sustainability analysis.

Excel XML offers another way to share data from spreadsheets, databases, and applications. The Onuma System uses Excel XML to move spreadsheet data into and out of information models to simplify spatial programming and analysis. The Construction Operations Building Information Exchange (COBie) uses Excel XML to convey data between authoring tools and operations and maintenance tools and processes.

COBie is important because it is the first tool available that encourages information flow between construction and facilities management. Because of COBie's spreadsheet oriented structure, it allows for data to be added throughout the design and construction processes. A higher level model specification called the Life Cycle Information Exchange (LCie) underpins COBie and most other Architecture/Engineering/Construction/Operate/Own (AECOO) information exchanges.

Simple and well-thought-out Extensible Markup Language (XML) allows people to exchange information. It fosters the ability to link data from multiple sources. Mash-ups of different tools and systems are what make the Internet work so well.

There are hundreds of variations of XML available. They provide the ability to interconnect information quickly. They allow people to communicate and use information from everywhere to achieve their goals.

The world of the geographer and the world of the constructor are converging. This is one area with tremendous opportunity for improving how we live, work, and play in the built environment. Today, when you hike, bike, or drive, you are as often as not guided by geospatial information. This information is defined using latitude, longitude, and altitude to place you anywhere on the earth. You can see your path, select from the restaurants that are close to you, and companies can advertise products from nearby stores right to your cell phone. In the past, buildings and other structures were seen as either blobs or photographs in this geospatial world.

By adding detailed building information to geospatial information, one has the complete code of everything about the built environment. Together they form a continuum with enormous benefit to the built environment. This convergence of technologies has been building since early in the twenty-first century. Arguably one could say it began with Keyhole Markup Language (KML). For the first time, people could actually visualize geographic data without the baggage that came with Geographic Information Systems (GIS). They could zoom into a site and get a real-world view, without knowing much of anything about GIS.

The only limitations revolved around the fact that one pretty much had to be part of the federal government to use it. Then along came Google.

Google bought Keyhole in 2004. Keyhole then became Google Earth, and all was well. It looked like geography and architecture were finally coming together to allow BIG BIM. Yet buried deep in this fantastic development was a deep, dark secret that might have stopped progress in its tracks.

The secret revolved around a simple question: "Who owns the data?"

Proprietary information could scuttle the whole system. There needed to be a way to make sure that the information would remain free and usable. There needed to be standards…not Google standards, but standards that were public and shared with everyone.

Without such standards, Google Earth would continue to be a truly refreshing tool. With such standards, it could become the basis for new ways to do business that allow us achieve true sustainability. On April 14, 2008, Ron Lake, chairman and chief executive officer of Galdos Systems, Inc. announced that the Open Geospatial Consortium (OGC) had adopted Keyhole Markup Language (KML) as an OGC standard. This announcement created the basis for moving forward with confidence.

USE CASES

Technology coupled with demands for better, faster, less costly projects and processes that are more effective are driving change globally. One captures and integrates knowledge at all levels. If one can describe something, it can be captured. If it can be captured, one can define its relationship to other knowledge.

By applying the rules that govern how these bits of information interact, one assesses options more quickly and more accurately than ever before. Where planning once relied on vague generalities and "rules of thumb," we can now simulate "real-life" built design futures. Decision-making facts are now available in close to real time.

It has been said that "all the big problems happen on the first day." Never before was this more true. Decision makers need dependable fact-based information; anecdotes and past precedents are no longer reliable. Facts are supported by imagery and presented clearly using tools that maximize understanding. Delays to "study the issue" and "go/no go" decisions that take months are not appropriate responses in this fast-paced environment.

Today, the most widely used systems are driven by building design and construction needs. They accelerate processes. They reduce conflicts, improve scheduling, and increase the efficiency of architects and builders. These systems focus on the middle of the built environment. Planning, forecasting, development, portfolio management, property management, operation, real estate, and a lot of other areas are often ignored. Information models offer virtually unlimited opportunities.

INFORMATION AS FORCE MULTIPLIER

2.
Five years make a difference. In 2008, BIMStorms were novelties. Three years of back-to-back information modeling in the cloud demonstrations finally started to change how people related to the built environment. By 2011, people were starting to realize that the information about the environment is a precious commodity. Command-and-control organizations were finally beginning to believe that they live in a flat world. Those with legacy systems were learning that their investments could no longer be sustained, unless they embraced collaborative ways of working and open sharing of information.

In January of 2015, the newly formed BIMSynergy Corporation held their organizational meeting. The Somerset Intelligence Initiative leadership charged the corporation with becoming a leader in the management of information. The effort took off and things happened quickly.

By early 2019, BIMSynergy was at the forefront of the global campaign designed to engage millions of people in the decision-making process. The movement was making information available to all. The days of closely held intelligence, stovepipes of information and processes, and top-down controls were the reasons that many things in the built environment had been so sloppy and ineffective. BIMSynergy was helping to change that situation.

Aerial view of CGSysOps on Craney Island Creek off the Elizabeth River, VA. 36° 52' 55" N 76° 21' 19" W Image from Bing.com courtesy USGS, Navteq and Microsoft

Optimized Assets for a Resilient World

COAST GUARD SYSTEMS OPERATIONS CENTER
PRINCESS ANNE, MARYLAND, AND PORTSMOUTH, VIRGINIA
JULY 1, 2019

It was a hot and sunny day in Portsmouth. Hot, humid, and hazy, just like most days in the summer in Tidewater Virginia.

Today was Pete Jarvi's first day on the job. Last month, when Adm. Kosinski made the offer, Pete snapped it up, realizing that the admiral was offering the opportunity of a lifetime. Pete had been assigned to help establish the new Coast Guard System Operations (CGSysOps) from bare earth. His new boss, Gary Boyle, had spent the last six months getting the funding in place. Today planning and design would start.

Pete was one of those people who knows what he knows, and more importantly, he knows what he doesn't know. He was an advocate for "fail fast and move on." He quickly discarded theories that could not be made to work. Pete was able to tell you almost immediately whether he could help you, and if so, how. Everything was negotiable. Anything was possible, and Pete could hardly rest until he had things settled, decided, and set. He was open-minded and had a seemingly limitless capacity for improving upon anything that took his interest.

In his last job, Pete used an automated design process to facilitate mission support. His group prototyped highly accelerated planning, design, documentation, and procurement processes using integrated technology to deliver mission-critical facilities. They proved that it was possible to constrain the design process directly to business objectives. Their projects used automated processes to create building information models at the building, space, and furniture levels directly from end-user programming requirements. Pete's group created customized systems that were built on sets of rules that defined parameters that allowed rapid assessment of many solutions to complex design problems. By linking legacy knowledge through web services, the group captured the knowledge that makes the Coast Guard special.

CGSysOps made working with others a snap. Since internal information, interagency information, and feeds from multinational resources flowed through the system, the Coast Guard could handle operations and their assets from the time that planning began until an asset was decommissioned. This was true enterprise-wide life cycle asset management. Property acquisition, analysis, planning, performance monitoring, utilization, budgeting, and recapitalization data flowed into the system and could be accessed when and where it was needed to make decisions. No longer was facility design done in isolation from other business processes.

Cloud computing integration made network access possible throughout the areas served by the Coast Guard, on both land and at sea, visually and in real time. Users saw live data at the proper level for their need and security level. Security will always be a concern. Classified and unclassified networks will always require physical separation. Issues of co-location of classified and unclassified information were resolved as Coast Guard systems were mirrored through high-security servers tied into BIMSynergy.

CGSysOps was possible because BIMSynergy gave the Coast Guard the ability to capture and use their legacy data. Where Pete and Gary found missing information or poorly named data, they knew that BIMSynergy would make the corrections automatically. The system audited the data and allowed them to prioritize and build upon the legacy data. Since the model server acted to connect data, no matter the source, Pete and Gary were able to integrate the information that was required and ignore the information that was out of date or incorrect.

Planning for the new CGSysOps facility started by engaging Coast Guard experts and subject-matter experts in all the areas that the system would affect. Using mind maps and process flow diagrams, the group quickly reached agreement about those things that must be included. The resulting program document identified spaces, room sizes, and other needs in a well-organized spreadsheet. From the first meeting to leadership sign-off of the program spreadsheet required a total of two weeks. Fifteen minutes later the spaces were imported onto the site as building information model elements. Immediately the system reported that the building would be three stories and 67,666 gross square feet. It would handle an occupant load of between 70 and 90 staff. It would cost $7,452,759 to build and $814,019 per year for operations and maintenance. CGSysOps could expect to use 1,278,883 kWh per year of electricity and 6,089,917,645 BTUs per year. Pete focused on the building elements for an hour, and Admiral Kosinski could visualize the first option's massing on location in 3-D and click to see the size, consumption, and cost. By the end of the day, Pete completed six more options. He understood what would work on the site.

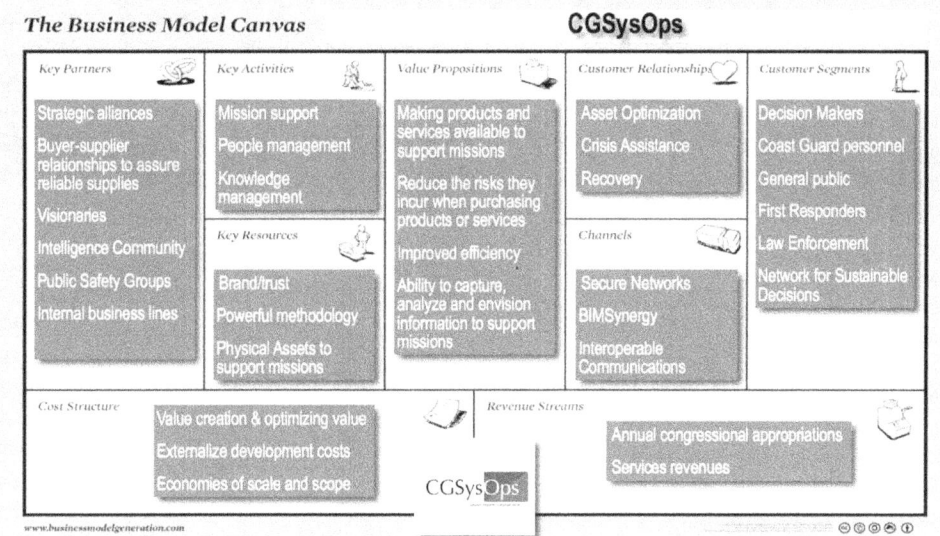

Combining automated design with formal knowledge, the Coast Guard created a way to remove tedious work and make strategic and tactical decisions easier. With this system, users provided actionable intelligence. They responded to requests for information that they received from other agencies. They watched maritime traffic round the clock. They evaluated trends, provided analysis, monitored areas of concern, followed vessels of interest, and tracked events that might impact on Coast Guard operations. CGSysOps was the collection and distribution point for the information that people needed in order to do their jobs. They provided the tactical information that was critical to integrated decision making.. This image is subject to the terms of a Creative Commons, Attribution-Share Alike license from Business Model Canvas, www.businessmodelgeneration.com

The spaces in Pete's options included the furniture and equipment that Coast Guard rules identified should be included. In the Enterprise Control Center, affectionately called the "BIG BIM Room," large video monitors filled one wall to show tracking maps, station locations, CNN, radar, and any other information managed by CGSysOps. Tables, chairs, coffee machines, desks, mechanical equipment, flooring, computers, and everything else that years of experience said should be included, was included.

Peter could pull side-by-side reports and analyses that let him compare details of his seven options. Everything in these reports came directly from system data and could be exported in open-standard formats for further development.

The rich information that Pete and the experts created in their two-week planning process would be used to control the detailed design process, as the architects and engineers began their work. The information would also serve as a check on the remainder of the process. Pete's work defined "the box" that encompassed the project that would contain CGSysOps when it was done. Everyone on the team now had a defined measure of success for their work. Rather than creating a design solution that was measured by the whims of the review committee, the designer now could prove significant compliance, without resorting to anecdote or approximations. Aesthetics, human needs, and other aspects retained their power, but now reviews were more holistic and fact-based.

The designer would pull the programmatic data from Pete's models, create her solution, and send it back to Pete's model for validation. Variances from program requirements and Coast Guard needs would now be highlighted. Improvements would also be reflected. Significant variations would require a real-time conversation between Pete and the architect. Both would see the situation and could reach a solution together.

THE SMALL PLANE DIVES...
PORTSMOUTH, VIRGINIA
SEPTEMBER 3, 2022

At precisely 9:54 a.m. eastern time, a single-engine Piper Comanche entered the airspace above the Coast Guard facility known as Base Support Unit Portsmouth in Virginia, as their four new offshore patrol cutters prepared to leave ahead of the approaching hurricane. Twenty minutes ago USCGC Nestor was first to get underway and was now clearing Hampton Roads. The small plane dove steeply to three hundred feet toward the three remaining cutters and ascended immediately in a north-northeast direction that would take it to Crisfield, Maryland, in about fifteen minutes.

Rear Admiral Elmo Kosinski was tucking in his uniform blouse as he left his private bathroom, when the window behind him shattered, and the building rocked—three times. His life and his job were usually pretty predictable. He was planning to go out and catch some rockfish this weekend with his wife, Marian, who was a better fisherman. He liked to cook and eat them, and he liked relaxing on the boat. He was pretty sure their plans had suddenly changed. Then he thought about the blasts. Either there was a catastrophic failure on one of the new cutters, or terrorists had bombed his base. Next he thought about casualties. At 1000, there were about 400 sworn personnel and civilians on station, battening down and departing ahead of the storm that looked to be heading straight up the Chesapeake Bay....

At 9:55 a.m., there was an explosion that destroyed the bridge of USCGC Maxfield as she pushed away from Dock One. Seconds later, another explosion near the stern of USCGC Kerwin shook the entire base. The final explosion ignited Dock Two's fueling system and holed the USCGC Dexter.

CHAMPION

The Coast Guard had long been under significant funding pressure. Most funding went directly to mission-critical needs. Support for other functions such as buildings was cut to the bone. The role of facilities engineering was rapidly being phased out. The Coast Guard needed a new approach. They focused on integrated operations.

The fact that something was done one way for the last twenty (or two hundred) years was not going to work anymore as a rationale. "We did it that way for twenty years, why should we change now?" However, it had become evident that we could not rely on anecdote and history. The pace of change, politics, and economic complexity increased the opportunities for catastrophic errors of judgment. The risk of making decisions without facts was too great.

We needed teams and tools that enabled us to make more informed, fact-based decisions…well before we expended significant resources. We needed to make "go/no go" decisions early in the process. We had to minimize the chances of being over budget, late, or buried in problems. We needed to manage our assets, not just our projects.

Making these goals a reality in the Coast Guard required a champion. Admiral Kosinski became the advocate for using information to overcome the inertia and legacy mindset. Since taking on the task, he fought an uphill battle, for too many depended on things being the way they always had been. Too many learned one thing in school or their first job, and now although things had changed, they had trouble adapting to the new circumstances and needs. The mindset could be directly linked to many of the failures that the organization saw early in the twenty-first century. The organization seemed to spend more time on answering questions and addressing issues such as "Who will own the information in our database?" and "You are not cleared to use my data" than on actually finding resolution and concrete ways forward.

Admiral Kosinski headed up the organization that the Coast Guard developed to go beyond these issues. Coast Guard System Operations (CGSysOps) capitalized on the opportunity to start over without the prejudice of legacy systems. Where appropriate, CGSysOps integrated legacy data. Where the best way forward was to innovate using new technologies and new systems, that was what they did. CGSysOps were built around an integrated web-based decision process called the Consequence Planning System (CPS). The system directly interfaced with the national model server distributed network. In fact, CPS was a high-security, mirrored section of BIMSynergy.

CPS offered a rules-based framework and a visual interface that used system data to support scenario planning and "what-if?" analysis. The system was designed to allow nontechnical users to work with computer-aided design, building information modeling and geographic information system data. The system allowed those with second-order knowledge and wisdom to leverage their abilities to plan and control fluid and complex situations. Much of the domain knowledge (or content) that was embedded in legacy systems formed the core of the rules-based system in CPS. The intent of CPS was to create a visually based platform for integrated decision making. CPS automated assessment tasks that were done manually or were not possible before. It was not an "easy button" automated solution. CPS assisted knowledgeable people in the integrated decision-making process by presenting data about the built environment and Coast Guard processes that were not readily accessible before. Using the Consequence Planning System, people connected knowledge from many sources to make more informed decisions.

LEGACY SYSTEMS

> You may be disappointed if you fail, but you are doomed if you don't try.
> —Beverly Sills

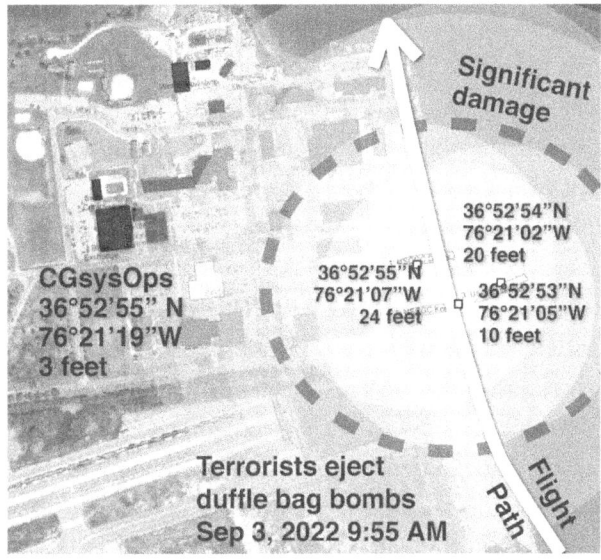

A cutter was adrift, blocking navigation. Other cutters were in danger of sinking at dock. There was extensive damage to infrastructure. People were injured and killed, and a significant hurricane was bearing down on the victims. Terrorists had exploited a "soft target" in a time of crisis to maximize their impact and media attention.

It was a "perfect storm," where all the wrong things fell into place at one time. This design future offers an opportunity to explore the complexities and difficulties that organizations such as the U.S. Coast Guard must prepare for, as they protect the homeland. After September 11, 2001, the U.S. Coast Guard became a crucial part of the Department of Homeland Security. The Coast Guard's new and expanded mission required that they optimize their capabilities to save lives, protect the environment, defend the homeland, and remain ready to handle any crisis. To fulfill these missions, the Coast Guard embraced interoperability and the use of shared information to improve decision making throughout the enterprise.

Like any large, highly dispersed organization, a major constraint on the change was legacy systems. Over the years, a combination of purpose-built databases (and spreadsheets used much like databases) had grown to fill the need for tools to respond to problems. One database managed a portion of the financial system. Another tracked deferred maintenance. Yet another tracked capital budgets. Spreadsheets tracked assignments and work orders. These were the tip of the iceberg.

Over time, the systems became more complex and difficult to use and manage. The systems became corrupted with non-normalized data. In one place, one found "WIN–1066." In another place, the data showed "window–b." WINDOW2-76, w12-458, DH-Win2, and many other designations, in the same database, might refer to a window. When one considered all of the databases that might contain information about windows, this non-normalized data created significant disruption. Whenever someone searched the databases, they could not depend on getting reliable or credible results. Because these systems involved the personal time and expertise of individuals, the organization met resistance in consolidating or replacing them, even though many would have admitted that these legacy systems undermined collaboration, created negative competition among internal teams, and were inherently stovepipes.

For many, the first reaction to any crisis was to abandon new tools. They reverted to tried and true, "legacy" systems. The perception was that internal experts created the systems. These experts tailored the systems to the problems that Coast Guard units face. The old way had to be better than new systems, right? The result was that competing internal factions, influenced by embedded investments, existing vendors, and inertia, fought bureaucratic battles to maintain their individual systems. Others bought into assurances from vendors that they could exploit legacy systems to create an interoperable, consolidated system.

Competing factions that pushed for the continuation of legacy systems, even though they were not working in a changed environment, could no longer be tolerated. The new world of data required fast and accurate responses, both day-to-day and in a crisis. When legacy systems were not managed to ensure consistency, they became the enemy of sharing and interoperability. Locating the information that one needed fast was hampered by inconsistent data. Legacy systems did not have the flexibility and scalability to manage complex, enterprise-wide information or large-scale crises.

The Support Unit Portsmouth design future illustrates how critical it is to be able to access reliable information quickly, especially in a crisis. When the first responder incident commander arrives on the site, he or she needs to create an accurate picture of the situation. Non-normalized data in databases disconnected from each other might well be the difference between life and death.

The Coast Guard proactively looked for a better way. They realized that complex information required new ways of working. Better analysis and real-time intelligence resulted from normalized data. They increased collaboration and communication with other agencies. They continue to work to be a more flexible, agile, and responsive organization.

SEPTEMBER 3, 2022—PORTSMOUTH, VIRGINIA

> Vision without action is merely a dream. Action without vision just passes the time. Vision with action can change the world!   —Joel Arthur Barker

After fighting the chaos at the main gate for thirty minutes, Pete got to his station at CGSysOps. Traffic was backed up all the way to the truck exit at the Marine Terminal. Between the extra security, fire trucks, ambulances, and television crews, getting on base, even for essential staff, was trying. Everyone was in shock. Fortunately, CGSysOps only had minor damage. Since the building was designed after 9/11, it was reinforced and blastproof, unlike most of the rest of the base buildings. The rumblings said that there were almost 200 injured and that the damages could be a quarter billion dollars and three of our new cutters lost…. Surely not.

Pete found CGSysOps hard at work on coordinating response to the bombing. For the first time since 9/11 the terrorists had managed to launch a strike on the Coast Guard. How could this have slipped through the cracks?

Gary Boyle was hard at work coordinating the rescue operations. He was at his station when the three bombs went off. He spent the first hour after the attack helping the wounded, until the first responders finally asked him to get out of the way so that they could do their jobs. Although Gary was a bit put out by the brusque handling, he was mad enough to head back to CGSysOps and start using the systems to figure out how this could have happened.

Fred Boyd had just posted the initial casualty report. Twenty-seven dead and over a hundred injured in the harbor area alone. Ten killed and forty injured elsewhere on the base. The USCGC Nestor sailed at 0935, sparing an additional eighty-eight personnel. Personnel on the two small cutters and two buoy tenders tied up on the bulkhead were not scheduled to arrive until 1130, since they were moving to hurricane holes up the Elizabeth River, or there would have been more casualties.

Gary and Fred were mobilizing assessment teams. Pete planned to start by analyzing the sensor network to get a clear idea of the extent of damages. He knew that soon they would be asked for a situation report. The brass would require complete information about casualties, site conditions, and recovery options. Pete would let Gary and Fred handle the present crisis while he focused his attention on making sure that nothing was missed. Plans needed to get underway to repair the damages to both people and property fast.

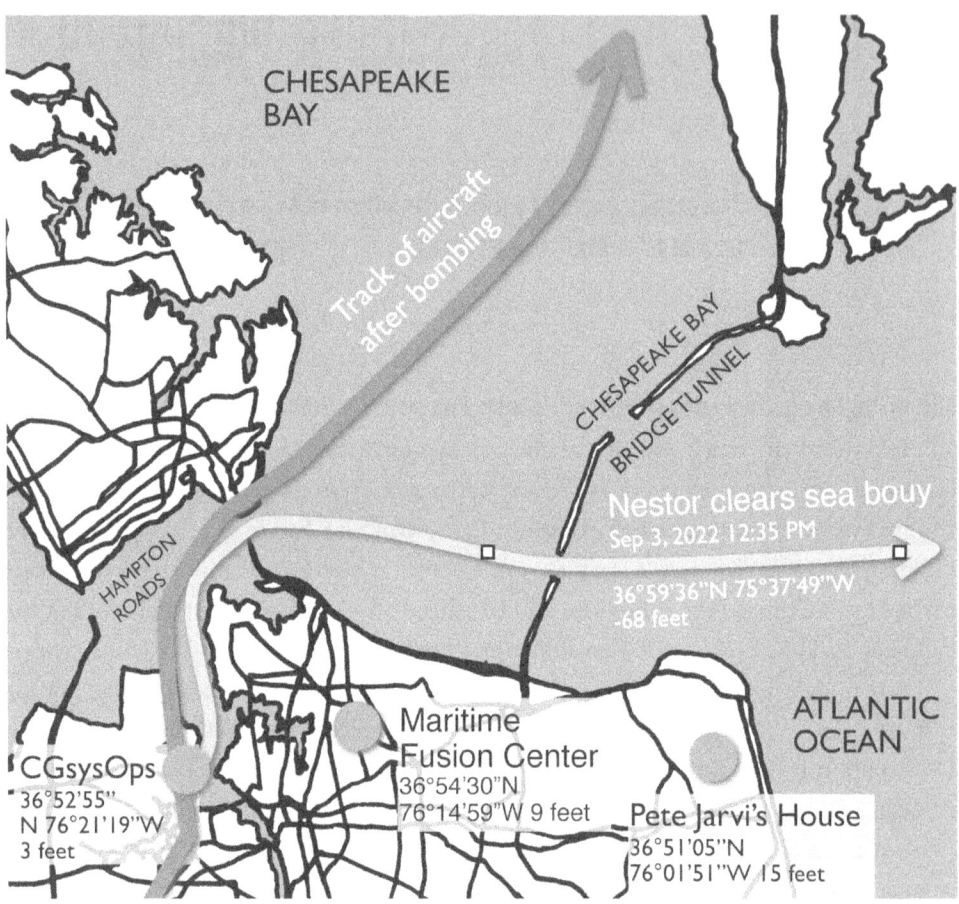

In 2020, much of the Tidewater area was converted to a system of open-source sensors and controls tied into the Consequence Planning System. Built into the process were automated emergency response actions that reacted automatically when the explosions occurred. First responders and hospitals were called out across the region. First response teams were handling the pressure. The system had automatically triaged events and assigned assets where they were most needed. Years of coordinated training and system integration that informed and managed fire services, emergency medicine, local law enforcement, and federal assets was working.

The rules that governed this system likely prevented more extensive damage. One of the explosions seemed to have happened right on top of Dock Two's fueling port. Sensors were set to activate a shutdown onshore in this type of event. That minimized the fuel that might have fed the fires after the explosions. Similar things happened all over the base. Sensors integrated into the new cutters also took over and closed watertight doors and deployed fire suppression systems automatically. The Maxfield went aground, blocking the channel. Her systems deployed the ground tackle and automatically stabilized the ship in place. Tugs were en route to get her off and get her in tow to the navy yard before Hurricane Edgar closed things down.

Two hours had elapsed since the explosions. Everyone was working against a critical time schedule. In six hours, the brunt of the storm would be crossing into the bay. It looked like the base would not feel the worst of the storm, since Portsmouth would be in the storm's left quadrant. Yet three wrecked cutters, two badly damaged small cutters, two severely damaged buoy tenders, buildings with substantial damage, and bomb debris made quick response key. Even eighty-mile-per-hour winds and a five-foot storm surge would make a terrible situation much worse.

On top of this, there remained the issue of responding to the damage that was expected to occur on the Delmarva Peninsula. The storm's path appeared to be taking the worst of the winds and storm surge up the length of the peninsula. The communities in the storm's path could see devastation that rivaled the worst storms ever. The Bay's topography funnels surges into the many inlets causing what might be a six to eight foot surge, to become much greater. Past hurricanes that directly hit the Chesapeake Bay caused excessively high tidal surges. At Category 2, with winds of around one hundred miles per hour, Hurricane Edgar would likely overwhelm Crisfield and other bayside communities with a twelve- to fifteen-foot storm surge.

Pete and his associates dug in and worked to handle the response to the devastation, both from the bombs and from the weather.

BUCKETS OF INFORMATION

> It is a capital mistake to theorize before one has data.
> —Sir Arthur Conan Doyle

An organization that has been in continuous service since 1790 with over 85,000 employees creates much information. Some of the information describes people, places, and things. Some of the information tracks costs, projections, and analysis. Procurement requirements, mission details, environmental cleanups, crisis management, education, and many other forms of information are in the system. The Coast Guard has buildings, bases, ships and boats, aircraft, cars and trucks, and all the other things required to maintain a current enterprise. Managing and integrating this "legacy data" was the key undertaking that faced the Coast Guard as they moved toward integrated decision making. Without the ability to build upon this institutional knowledge, much of the richness built over the years would have been lost.

In the early years of the twenty-first century, the Coast Guard started the process of mapping out how to use existing data and how to move forward in a world where data was becoming critical. Visionaries within the organization saw a future where information would allow the organization to become highly optimized. Business and mission decisions would be backed up by accurate and timely information. Information at the granularity level required would flow up and down the organization to support integrated decision making.

At one end, a carpenter needing woodscrews would be able to see how many screws were available, at what locations, and what sizes. If the appropriate screws are not in stock, the carpenter could order them at the best current price with the push of a button, knowing when they would be delivered and how the time delay would affect his overall schedule. At the opposite extreme, the commandant would open a window on her computer and see the current status of every asset in the Coast Guard in real time. Current status would be summarized to a level that directly responded to the commandant's current need, and if she wished she could drill down and see the carpenter's request for screws. The system would reflect current reality, with minimal conjecture or anecdote. Real, credible, and repeatable information is vital.

The Coast Guard's mapping exercise identified several issues. One of the most notable was that much of information about real assets was not in the system. Buildings were documented on paper, often as isolated renovations and additions over many years. Some of these paper documents were antiquated blueprints. Vellum, Mylar, tracing paper, diazo prints, photographs of historic prints, and hand sketches could all be found about many of the buildings. Older buildings with recent renovations were somewhat documented in computerized drawings. New buildings were sometimes documented in CAD and sometimes by hand drawings. There was no appreciable documentation standard that had prevailed over the generations. Building documentation was chaos.

Campus-scale documentation was not much better. Waterfront facilities, parking, and auxiliary structures were documented much like buildings. Little or no geographic reference was available. Tying individual buildings and other structures together on the site was hit or miss. As often as not buildings could be placed in their exact position only by resurvey or mash-up of disconnected documents.

Regional-scale documentation, when it existed at all, was not much better. First-generation space technology made viewing of facilities distributed across several states possible. In most cases satellite views offered little data. They were photographic views with minimal computational value. Even measuring the distance between two bases required workarounds.

At national or global scale, the same was true. One could use a satellite view, or put pushpins in a map or globe. Decision-making data was limited to these visual representations and large-scale approximations. Few projects included accurate and geographically referenced as-constructed documents. Only a small fraction included information models, and those were created in the last year by a specialist consulting group. Information models, and ultimately model servers, respond to these issues.

In many circles, this concept has been minimized and used primarily to mandate the items that architects, engineers, and constructors must include in each step of the process. Levels of Detail definitions intended to be prescriptive requirements to control document creation may be effective as a stick to enforce contracts, but Levels of Detail are actually much more.

The vast majority of the built environment is already built. High-performance building experts believe that 86 percent of funds for U.S. buildings go to renovation. Obviously, the remaining 14 percent is significant. The fact remains that the majority of facilities remain to be renovated, added to, restored, repurposed, maintained, and operated. In the Coast Guard, the percentages were even more skewed toward an existing building stock.

Every renovation project must begin with knowledge of the existing conditions. Historically, this effort takes place several times over a facility's life cycle. Each time, the property must be re-measured, existing documentation must be recorded, and significant resources are expended to get to the project starting line. This is a serious waste of resources. Information models, maintained in a model server, allow the process to begin with as-exists information. With information models, an owner spends the money once and reuses the information for the life of the building.

With 21,000 buildings on 66,000 acres of land, the Coast Guard will see significant savings once all of these assets are properly documented in information models. The challenge was with that 21,000 buildings and millions of square feet, it would cost several million dollars to create this documentation at one time.

That's where the idea came into play. In the first conception, there were four "levels of detail." When implemented, there were two additional levels, plus four separate views of the built environment information.

Using an incremental approach to model development, one can economically transition to information model-based systems. There is no reason that any owner should not start the process. Even with an information bucket holding one's legacy information, there are significant benefits. Making fact-based decisions is the only way to reduce the risk of catastrophic errors in today's highly volatile world.

The descriptions above show only a tiny fraction of the possibilities that come with understanding Levels of Detail. There is significant discussion, angst and passion surrounding how people view LOD. Is it Levels of Detail or Levels of Development? Is LOD an appropriate proscriptive requirement to control delivery of information models? Or, is LOD a misunderstood and misused concept that creates barriers to acceptance and forward progress?

LEVELS OF DETAIL (LOD)

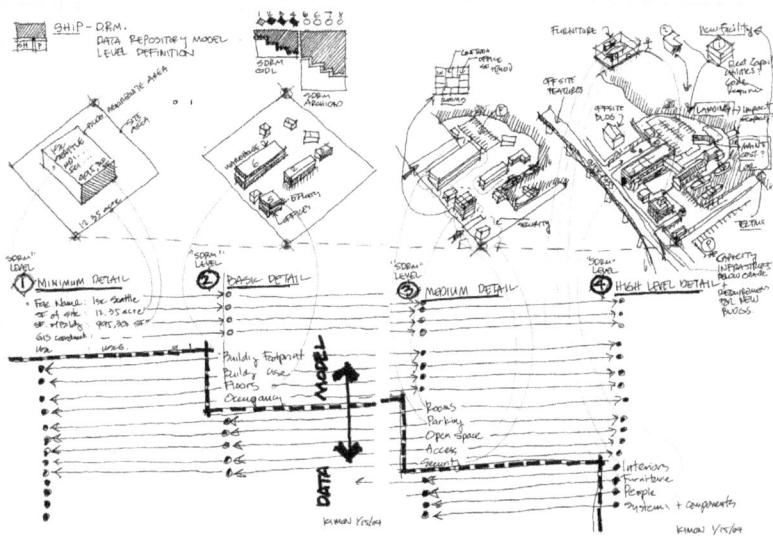

Information buckets turned out to be the solution. On the morning of January 15, 2004, on an airplane headed to Cleveland, Ohio, Kimon Onuma sketched out what was to become known as the concept of Levels of Detail (LOD). In the sketch, he referred to the concept as Data Repository Model, Level Definition. Information models can be created in steps over time with little or no data loss in the transitions. By creating a concept that defines a long-range plan for data, information models can be implemented much like one might implement a contacts database: over time. Many exceptional people worked to define the framework upon which the LOD concept builds. Image courtesy of Onuma Inc

The first two Levels of Detail focus on viewing a complete portfolio, campus, or area. At these levels, one views all sites on a world map. Everything down to the furniture in rooms is tagged with latitude, longitude, and altitude. Clicking on an icon opens a site plan and building footprints that show property information. They allow the tracking of information across entire portfolios and deliver tangible links between geographic information systems and information models.

A Level of Detail One (LOD1) model is, in fact, an information bucket. The bucket holds legacy and planning information. Anything that is in the current database can, after cleaning up the data, be placed in this bucket. Using geographic views, location information can be included. With the introduction of rules-based design, models at this level suddenly become significant decision-making tools. With these models, one flies in from a global view, zooming in on regions, campuses, and groups of buildings. Parametric operations and construction costs, sustainability checklists, clearances, areas and volumes, and many other planning measures are generated at this level. Models at this level have been used for master planning, community planning, and what-if analysis. A Level of Detail One model is as good as the information that is added to the bucket, and often that is exceptionally good indeed.

A Level of Detail Two model builds upon LOD1, adding massing and context details. At this level, one begins to see space and shapes. Metrics are more tailored. Sensors are added. One can begin to visualize temperature changes, water usage, webcams, and other events in real time. With minimal effort, a LOD2 model can be used for energy conservation study. For many situations, this level is all that is required to connect to the built environment. Level of Detail Two models enable visualization and control of significant amounts of data. Many find that they can operate at this level until the time that renovations or repurposing takes place.

At the third level, one begins to focus on floor plans that were traditionally managed in static CAD or PDF files. At this level, floor plans are live data objects that change the system as one makes changes in the floor plan, and vice versa. Manual coordination of changes is no longer required; since the data is live, the information remains accurate over time throughout the system. Layouts for spaces, furniture, and equipment are connected the same way. One can add these items, tracking them through the system, or otherwise the system can know that they are there using rules-based controls.

A Level of Detail Three model can be called a design model. Where LOD1 and 2 models tend to reside in a system that relies on planning-level visualization, at this stage the model begins to reflect reality. These models, usually prepared by the architect or other designers, include materials, doors, and windows. The information in the model continues to grow richer. Since this version includes more of the elements that one will find in the building when it is completed, a wide range of analysis tools work on this data. At this stage, the model begins to become a virtual representation of the real world. Imagery from these models can easily be confused as photographs of completed buildings.

Level of Detail Four and Five models are generally used for construction purposes. The LOD4 model focuses on construction planning. One example would be in a situation where the architect or constructor shows structural systems. The beams he or she shows include material properties and are virtual copies of the steel support that they represent. The W36X160 beam knows that it is 36.01 inches deep with a flange of 12 inches wide. It will hold a load of 1,780 kips per square inch. This information is then shared with the structural engineer, who has the capacity to use these properties to determine solutions that can be re-injected into the information model. Every construction component operates essentially the same. As this model grows in complexity, it can be used for detailed analysis, quantity surveys and costing, clash detection, scheduling, and more.

The Level of Detail Five model focuses on building operations and production. These models allow the constructor to organize and manage all of the things that must go together in the proper order at the proper time to reach the optimal construction outcomes. Using this level of model, a significant percentage of any project can be prefabricated off-site. Materials are then tagged with radio-frequency identification devices or other methods. They are then tracked, from the first cut, to hoisting into place, to final installation. At this level, the model enables the commissioning of systems and coordination of the information that will help the operations and maintenance processes after construction.

A Level of Detail Six model includes all of the information added in Levels One through Five. At this stage, the model is exceptionally rich and extremely valuable…arguably more valuable than the building itself. Assuming that the planning, design, and construction activity occurred over a two-year period, this model will continue to grow, perhaps for fifty years or more.

Few buildings go through their life without renovations and additions. This model accumulates all of these changes to truly become a virtual representation of the building at any time. Over time, the model will contain ever-increasing amounts of details about the facilities operation. These details form the basis of highly accurate and fact-supported decision making. With this model, decision makers no longer must rely on seat of the pants and inference; they have the facts about what is happening within their environment.

INTEGRATE TECHNOLOGY

Levels of Detail were conceived to enable integrated decision making. By bringing data together over time, information modeling allows us to manage the routine tasks that often make up a large part of any work effort. When a capital budget proposal was put together, more time was spent organizing the backup material than in analyzing and planning for the future. The promise of information modeling has long been to reduce repetitive tasks, so that people can turn their attention on critical issues. Re-creating backup information every time one begins the task is not only wasteful; it leads to mistakes.

With a long-range plan that looks at an organization's assets with a Levels of Detail view, leaders are better able to determine where to apply limited funds. Rather than investing large amounts of money in the creation of highly detailed information models, the development can build incrementally. Development of information model technology has been rapidly evolving for many years. Software tools are becoming more sophisticated than they were. Networks are changing. People's understanding of how to proceed is changing. In this highly volatile situation, incremental development becomes both cost effective and an organizational survival strategy.

With the purpose of using technology and new business processes to improve early decisions, Levels of Detail enable organizations to better withstand public scrutiny, no matter the political climate. The organization can identify errors before the errors cost serious money, time, or trouble. They ensure the required quality at the lowest reasonable cost.

Constructors evaluate projects before building—resulting in fewer misunderstandings, faster bidding processes, and reduced surprises, disputes, and legal claims. Over time, they make decisions that make them more efficient.

Architects and designers have information that is so clear that they can understand the effects of a design choice as it cascades through the built environment. They are able to access rich sets of real-time facilities information and use rules-based systems to remove most of the repetitive work. Their systems tie into the business decision-making systems of their clients to inform their design decisions.

Homeowners learn how they are using energy. They see the impacts that their actions have on their energy use. They turn down the thermostat and begin to see their fuel bills start to go down. They turn on the air conditioning at a time of peak use and see their demand charges spike. They look for replacement windows, and rules-based systems guide them through the decision-making process.

Rules-based systems can be described as rules of thumb on steroids. They work with the things that are known about any subject. By defining what we know, and defining the relationships between things, we can automate many assessments and planning tasks. If we know that for every twenty square feet of space we need ten square feet of carpet and ten square feet of tile, the rules-based logic would tell us that the hundred-square-foot space needs fifty square feet of carpet and fifty square feet of tile.

There are extensive listings of all the bits and parts that make up most of the things that exist in the built environment. Whether a school, a park, a Coast Guard office building, or a hospital, someone created the rules of thumb that defined what the facility includes. Rules of thumb are approximations, and only as reliable as the facts upon which they are created. Rules-based systems have the same limitations. They get you close—and sometimes remarkably close—but they still require the involvement of thinking humans.

Pete used such a system as he conceived the CGSysOps facility.

Extensive lists of everything that makes up a command center exist. These lists cover every desk, chair, floor, monitor, partition, light fixture, toilet, door, ceiling, wall covering, and computer. Each record includes facts about that item, such as size, weight, cost, and much more. Each item is assigned based on how many of them exist in a specific amount of space. They also are assigned by how many of them exist for each staff member and other factors. The quantities and requirements have been researched and time tested.

Databases exist for the costs of materials and labor, by location codes, for much of the world. The same is true for structural loads, accessibility requirements, life safety requirements, and most other codes. Standards also exist for numbers and types of employees, operations and maintenance costs. Planners, architects, and engineers have expertise in this project type.

From this knowledge base, one can define the items that must come together to create a command center. One can make a basic parameter list. One can define the measures that control the size, shape, and quantities for a command center in almost any environment and of virtually any type. One can develop metrics to assist the planner in understanding the costs and other parameters that will be incurred. One can program an intelligent planning system. One can make a system to remove the mundane from the design process.

For example, Pete knows that he must create a command center to be the focus of the Coast Guard's capital asset decision-making process. He knows how many people will be assigned, in what categories. He knows where the command center will be located. He knows the tasks that the command center must perform. The rules-based system knows that, for each information modeler, they will require X amount of carpet, Y amount of general lighting, and Z amount of furniture.

Pete inputs the items that he knows to define the constraints that will drive the rules-based system. From these inputs, the system computes the size and quantities of spaces and all of the items that would normally be found in these spaces (floors, walls, ceilings, furniture, systems, equipment, and people). The system computes costs, operations and maintenance, sustainability and energy. The system assigns factors such as space relationships and mission requirements that are specific to the Coast Guard.

Pete reorganizes the spaces and creates multiple options. He focuses on organizing the spaces to resolve the design. He finds the "train wrecks" in the rules-based system, rather than having to wait until concrete is poured. As he creates options, he is able to see how they work in context, in three dimensions. The rules-based process and tools that Pete used may seem incredible to some people. Some may not understand how tightly integrated many processes are in our world today.

When you bought your last airplane ticket, did you get it on the Internet? If so, you interacted with a rules-based, highly integrated system. Reservation systems such as Expedia are tightly integrated. Users go to a website and type in a few parameters—when, where, and how long— and hit enter. The system searches all the available flights to your selected location and gives you tailored choices to refine your search. The system quotes the price, takes your money, and books your flight. Your needs were met, quickly and efficiently.

Behind the scenes, many systems are tied together (integrated) to make this happen. You do not see the complexities of systems that track the thousands of planes. You do not see the systems that maintain the engines to keep the aircraft safe. You do not see the personnel tracking system that makes sure that the right pilot is on the right plane in the right airport at the right time. All you see are the items crucial to your current requirement. Thousands of systems combine to let you book your ticket from the comfort of your home. When you buy from online stores or communicate on the web, you are using the skills necessary for success in this environment. These skills, added to top-level problem-solving abilities, make you uniquely qualified in integrated processes.

The process is similar to the rules-based system that Pete used to enhance his command center. Such systems have become so widespread that it makes you question how the rest of the built environment fits into this world. What stops people from embracing the system when it comes to buildings? What stops them from using the tools to do a better job of managing time and costs for projects in the built environment?

There is value in certainty. We know it and are willing to pay for it. We are pleased to pay for better decision-making information delivered at the optimum time. This is how we can produce superior results and become more productive. When we know where we are going, we reduce our risk. Having the information to make decisions early in any process allows us to engage others earlier in a more collaborative way. Having the information to make timely decisions results in better, or at least more understandable, outcomes.

Little is totally new. As obvious as it may seem, simply providing people with better information makes it easier for them to see what lies ahead in our world. Rules-based systems are a way toward systems that we can operate effectively to supply complete information models. With rules-based systems, we improve control—we can better record decisions, consistently. We get more time and energy for other things, since the mundane tasks are handled by the rules and there are fewer issues to "work out." We spend less time on the things that are already known. We deliver high-quality outcomes while investing fewer hours. We work with up-to-date, real-time information and just-in-time imagery.

Cloud-based model servers such BIMSynergy help us manage the entire life cycle of our world. From the first ideas, to advance planning and schematic design, to design development and automated document production, and into use, BIMSynergy provides an intuitive user interface that allows us to build complex, shared information models across a wide segment of our society.

Large-scale facility programs, individual projects, and other implementations all use the system. Enterprise clients such as the United States Coast Guard (USCG) use BIMSynergy to manage and maintain their facilities and infrastructure systems. They use the system to connect their facilities to their mission execution. The result has been improved building life cycle management and better allocation of resources. Each of us can use BIMSynergy to plan our world, schools, homes, and offices. BIMSynergy users gain immediate benefits as they produce information models that automatically connect with other information in distributed systems on the Internet.

TIE SYSTEMS TOGETHER

The Coast Guard and local emergency responders use information models in many ways. Proving the value of the models was easy. Once a firefighter, EMT, or law enforcement officer saw live images tied directly to geographic information, the question was not "Should we do this?" but "How soon can it happen?" Once the situation was modeled and deployed on the model server, new possibilities popped up every day.

In a fire, what usually happens is that a single fire engine arrives on the scene. Before the engine's firefighters are allowed to enter the building, they need four people. Two firefighters remain outside to operate the equipment. Two firefighters enter the building to fight the fire. This standard is called "two in/two out." In many situations "two in/two out" can be difficult to achieve early in a response. When the incident commander arrives at the scene, he or she needs to be aware of where all of his or her people are, in relation to hose connections, the actual fire, and many other contextual issues. With BIMSynergy, the commander is able to visualize the situation on a web-connected device while on the way to the fire. Each firefighter is tagged and located in space. Every stairway, hose connection, and exit is shown. Where systems in the building are connected to the sensor grid, the commander can clearly visualize conditions on every floor, in every area. The sensor network also allows mechanical system fans to be shut down. Smoke removal systems can be engaged. Elevators can be controlled and fire barriers can be verified, even when the automated responses from these controls may not have worked properly.

The same level of visualization, situational awareness, and incident management occur when police respond to a call, when the Coast Guard responds to a boater in trouble, and when a natural disaster occurs. Geographic information connected to built environment information connected to sensors accessible through the Internet of Things make the information available when and where it is needed to handle the situation and protect victims and responders.

Crime Prevention Through Environmental Design (CPTED) principles, enhanced by comprehensive response scenario planning, are the basis for these rules-based systems. Since these systems are now used from the beginning of projects and even before events occur, they are reducing costs and improving outcomes.

Knowledge from various sources integrates to simulate events. The planner sets parameters. The system creates a simulation of what could happen. Major strides in simulating security issues took place because of the pressures after 9/11. By integrating CPTED principles, properties of destructive devices, and facilities information, systems predict outcomes at a high level, before a terrorist strike or disaster occurs. The security planner, using these systems, can make high-level assessments, even if it is not possible to visit the site. Geographically accurate visual representations automatically display critical information. Mission dependency, asset condition, and standoff distances are presented. It is easier for the planner to offer suggestions for how to proceed. Knowledgeable security professionals trained to work this way are achieving results as reliable as or better than that achievable from site visits. The results are available in highly accelerated time frames.

Information models give the security planner the ability to influence behavior and improve performance and security. Safety and security depends on both physical and operational issues. Operational changes alone, in a "target-rich environment" may have minimal results. By integrating operations with physical changes, one gets a more complete view of conditions and threats. Adding the ability to make detailed assessments early in the planning process allows the security planner to envision solutions before a project progresses to a point where changes are difficult. The goal is to make the safest environments possible while supporting and enhancing the organization's mission.

Planning is not able to stop every event. The terrorists were able to attack the cutters at Portsmouth by capitalizing on the holes in the system and an unusually short time between the start and end of their actions. Overlaying response-enhanced design considerations on Crime Prevention Through Environmental Design principles positions the facility's staff and the first responders to know what has to happen as the recovery begins. They know where to deploy to protect the victims from further harm. They know the locations of supplies and who is to do what action. They have rehearsed what needs to be done and role-played possible scenarios. Information modeling tied to security planning lets them respond effectively and quickly.

Knowledgeable security planners integrate security and emergency response considerations into the plan as early in the process as possible. This assures the selection of appropriate tactics that fit with the overall safety goals and existing facility use, before other decisions "lock in" a direction. When included as part of the initial planning process, integrating safety and security reduces costs.

A successful strategy requires an assessment that will identify and prioritize the assets to be protected and establish the set of threats the organization and the facility may face. The plan also determines the vulnerability to threats and evaluates risks to the organization's mission. The emergency response plan then translates the analysis into actionable plans and goals that can be implemented effectively and support routine operations.

The major advantage of information modeling in this environment is that options are modeled and visualized before the design is completed. By front-loading these considerations, security is easier to optimize and integrate into the solution. Early decision making saves time and money.

SEPTEMBER 3, 2022—PORTSMOUTH, VIRGINIA

> It has long been an axiom of mine that the little things are infinitely the most important.
> —Sir Arthur Conan Doyle

How often have you heard the lament, "That changes everything"? How often have you been totally sure that you had the right answer about something, and then a new piece of information came along and forced you to admit your mistake? We make decisions based on the facts that we have. It is not surprising that we make decisions without having all of the facts. Much of the time we don't even know that we don't have all of the facts.

The integrated systems that Pete uses to develop the design for CGSysOps, allow users to carry more of these small bits of "fact" into play in the decision-making process. They don't exclude the fact that information continues to flow into the system. They organize the information that is currently available and present the facts in ways that lead to better decisions. They do not replace the hard-won wisdom that comes with age and experience. They supplement the information that you have acquired over the years, with reference knowledge and background to provide greater wisdom.

We make too many decisions at the wrong time, with too little information. The ability to make early, informed decisions is a significant advantage of information models. No longer must we make decisions on the "spur of the moment" or "by the seat of the pants." Now we make decisions with facts and a clear understanding of needs and relationships.

Fact-based decisions require clear and open communications to be a first priority. Without good communications, the information model rarely reflects the complexity and richness of the world. Individuals, groups, companies, cities, states, and nations contribute to the knowledge that is linked to the model server. The same people contribute to the decision-making process based on their knowledge. Little about information models and integrated processes is a solo operation. Technology gives direct access to the many. Without this access, the system is isolated and sub-optimized.

When the wisdom of the many is captured through the model server, we begin to leverage resources within the organization. We integrate with business processes. A decision about plant relocation takes into account the effects the decision would have on the company's bottom line and the company's employees. The system enables you to use information to get the facts. It serves up the facts in forms that you can understand and use. As the data sources expand, the system becomes more intelligent. This knowledge allows us to integrate with the physical world.

We combine resources so that society achieves the benefits. The special abilities of one group link to the special abilities of another to focus the resources of a third group to deliver solutions that none of the three could achieve alone. Geographic information system practitioners do a terrific job of documenting "what is" in the environment; they do not do much with "what's to be." Architects and planners are fluent in synthesizing the "what is" into "what could be." Engineers armed with sensors and motes show us what we consume. The combination creates a highly sustainable, zero energy EcoDistrict that is a walkable, fun place to live, minimizing a city's use of scarce resources.

The model server is a web-based connection to share data between many people and many specialists. With this link, information models share information and integrate information, in context. By connecting geographic, facility, and resource information, we make decisions in context. We make our world a better and more sustainable place.

CAPTURE

By 10:08 a.m., the Maritime Intelligence Fusion Center in Dam Neck, Virginia, picked up on the attack and was coordinating the effort to find and capture the terrorists. The Air Force, the Navy, local law enforcement, and Coast Guard units up the Chesapeake Bay were all mobilized. The center scrambled guard aircraft from Langley Air Force Base and Norfolk Naval Air Station. They brought satellite resources to bear to find the terrorists. They initiated a national alert to shift all resources toward the response.

The Coast Guard learned from the 9/11 attacks. One of the first things they did was to make sure that this was an isolated incident. Homeland Security's new systems were pretty strong at checking that sort of thing, these days. At 10:40 a.m., they learned that the terrorist plane had just landed at the tiny airport near Crisfield, Maryland. By 10:45 a.m., the call was out. The chase was on.

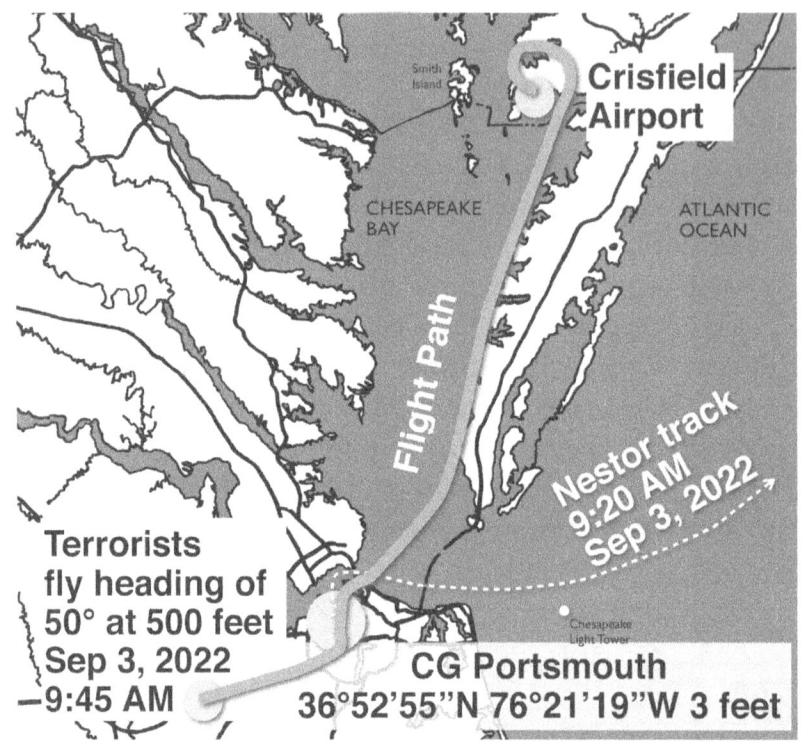

The operations center did not so much miss this attack as they just could not react fast enough. It is next to impossible to catch a single-engine plane that takes off from a small airport and is dropping improvised explosive devices before the plane gets to altitude. Four minutes from departure until bombs start exploding is not much time. The terrorists' timing was impeccable.

The initial assessment pointed toward the terrorists looking for an easy target where they could get many casualties and dramatic results. They found a symbol of the best of the United States, saw an opportunity for media exposure, and slipped through the cracks in the system. Using a mixture of ammonium nitrate and fuel oil in plastic jugs, military surplus duffel bags with solid bottoms, and blasting caps tied together with pressure switches, they created three devices, each with the equivalent of 100 pounds of TNT. They set up at a small airport with a runway that allowed them to take off head to gale force winds. The pilot never turned on his transponder and flew low and slow right over the cutters, while his partner kicked out the explosive devices.

The hurricane tracking to hit the bay gave the terrorists perfect cover. To the fixed-base operator down at Hampton Roads Executive Airport, it looked like the plane's owner was simply moving his Piper Comanche inland to protect it from the storm. They took advantage of the airport's confusion, then they used the fact that the cutters were in the process of preparing for sea ahead of the storm to achieve their goals. They did serious damage to people and property to get media attention for their cause.

The storm made the attack successful for the terrorists. The concrete docks at the base were felt to be insufficient protection for the four new offshore patrol cutters. When the National Weather Service issued a hurricane warning, the decision was made to deploy the cutters to sea, ahead of the storm. The Weather Service predicted that the storm would make landfall at Kiptopeke, Virginia, at about 6:00 p.m. All four cutters needed to leave port by 11:00 a.m. so that they would have time to clear the sea buoy. The crews received their recall and deployment orders at midnight.

Each cutter was manned by twelve officers and seventy-six crewmembers. That meant that about 260 staff were on the docks and the cutters when the bombs dropped. Added to that are the quartermasters, maintenance personnel, food service truck drivers, and others that were scrambled to get the ships ready to sail. It was Saturday morning. There was a lot of activity in the small area surrounding the concrete docks.

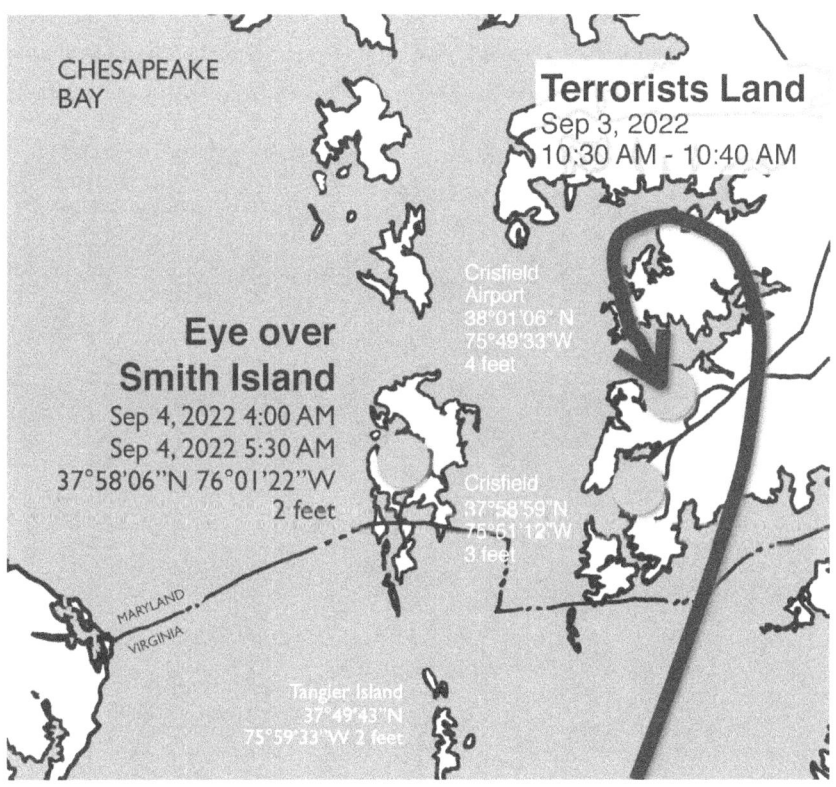

At 10:40 a.m. the terrorist airplane circled and landed at the Crisfield-Somerset County Airport. Since it was Saturday, no one was around. Two more terrorists were waiting with two cars. One car drove off to the southwest, heading for the work boat harbor in Crisfield. The other fled northeast toward U.S. Route 13 and points north.

At 10:45, the call went out from the maritime desk at the Fusion Center to notify the Coast Guard Station in Crisfield and local law enforcement about the terrorists' current position. The Maryland State Police Barracks in Princess Anne, Maryland, dispatched four cars to set up roadblocks, one north of Maryland Route 667 East and one south of Maryland Route 667 West near Marion Station. The terrorists passed Route 667 West before the roadblock was established and at 11:08 were intercepted and captured without gunfire at the Route 667 East roadblock.

Meanwhile, the Coast Guard station in Crisfield deployed their forty-five foot Response Boat-Medium into the Little Annemessex River just south of the Crisfield Harbor entrance. They were in constant communications with the Somerset County sheriff and Crisfield police as they set up roadblocks in town. The station's twenty-six foot defender class response boat also deployed near the mouth of Back Creek, near the town's work boat harbor. A boat from the local contingent of the Maryland Natural Resources Police was backing them up with two officers. At eleven forty-five, as the last of the terrorists worked to cast off the Chesapeake Bay dead rise work boat that they bought from Captain Tyler last week, they were intercepted and captured. Crisfield police officers prevented their flight to land and the Coast Guard's response boat blocked their escape by water, from the mouth of the harbor.

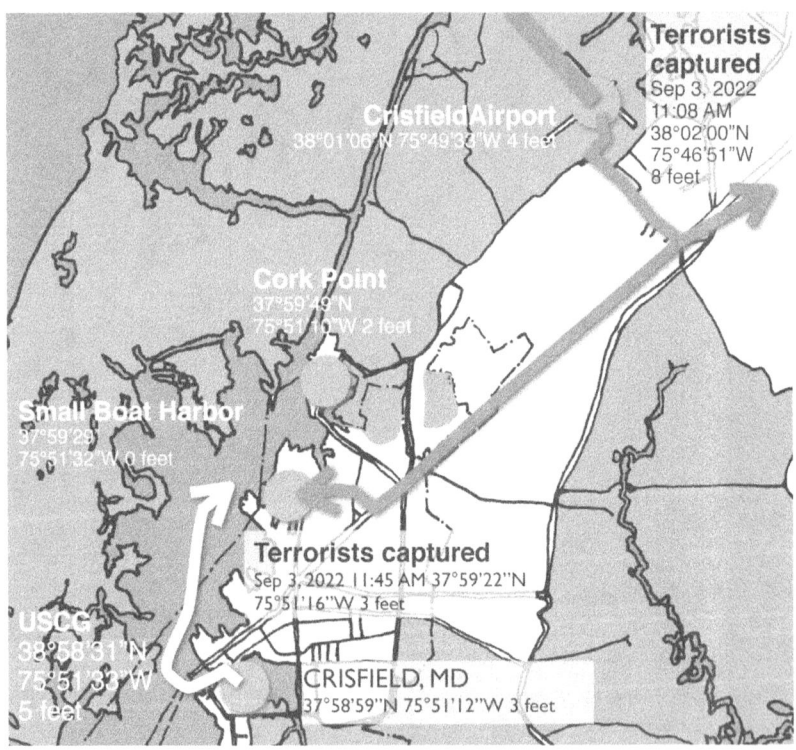

The system could not stop the attack, but once the response was engaged, the holistic response plans coupled with a system that was integrated and interoperable reacted swiftly and decisively. The system brought the right resources to bear to identify, locate, and catch the terrorists in less than two hours from the first bomb exploding.

Since all systems were interconnected and interoperable using BIMSynergy resources, the information flowed to all who needed access. Those gathering information to locate and identify the terrorists, those conducting the intercept operations, those responding to the casualties, and those managing the recovery efforts all benefited from the information. Since the information flowed from many sources and was used by all, duplication was minimized. Decisions were expedited. Accurate, timely, and reliable information, presented at the accuracy level required for each use, underpinned the decision-making process throughout.

MARCH 17, 2023—ANCHORAGE, ALASKA

> Information about money has become almost as important as money itself.
> —Walter Wriston, CEO of Citicorp

Jim pulled up the status and metrics for the base facilities he managed. Yesterday he was surfing in Hawaii. Now he was back in Anchorage. His capital improvement request had to be submitted to headquarters today; otherwise, all hell would break loose.

In the good old days, Lt. Commander Jim Krauss had a month to get this done. Now he only got a day. Before all these new management and analysis tools, working up the capital budget was a nightmare. Jim spent months and months pulling together information that people wrote down and misfiled. He spent more time tracking down the information he needed than he did filling out the paperwork.

When it came down to it, the capital improvement plan could usually be called the "my boss's opinion of how much money we need to scrape by next year" plan. The plan was riddled with opinions, wishes, guesses, and Scientific Wild Ass Guesses, or SWAGs. About two months after the capital plan went in, Jim and his boss got to spend two days negotiating with the guys at headquarters about how much of their request would move forward in the system.

Jim was always pretty adept at defending his positions, but he often had few facts to sell. It was pretty hard to explain something when it was based on speculation and everyone knew it. Jim's boss knew it. His boss's bosses knew it. Congress knew it. The newspapers suspected it. The public did not see it and would have been mad if they ever found out.

Every year, at every step, Jim's requests got bounced around. Some things went up. Some things went down. The station never got enough money to do the job. Every year, more and more things went onto the deferred maintenance list. Jim was only able to keep up with the maintenance that his boss thought was essential.

Things worked pretty well as long as the boss had been around a while and knew the base. For the year or so after Jim got a new boss, budgeting got pretty weird. Someday, someone was going to make a critical mistake. Something vital would not be maintained. Something seriously awful was going to happen.

Around the turn of the century, things got tense. Budgets had always been tight. Now they were worse. The Coast Guard needed new boats and aircraft to do the job. Everything else had to be lower priority. Everyone knew that budget requests were not based on facts—though who would admit it? Budgets went into survival mode. It got so severe that even people were eliminated. Facility engineers were rapidly becoming a thing of the past.

People were walking around in a daze, wondering why others could not see that shore facilities were still relevant. Without boats and aircraft, the Coast Guard could not do its job. Obviously, after people, ships, planes, and helicopters are the first priority; but none of them can succeed over time without a place to tie up, a hangar or housing. Facilities and the built environment are also critical to the mission. All those years of seat-of-the-pants budgets and facility conditions assessment by anecdote were coming back to haunt them.

Jim and his coworkers needed a way to get their case understood. They needed to move toward fact-based decision making. They all knew that when Jim told his boss that they needed money to fix the roof on Building 4-603, his boss must know that it was so. When Jim's boss told his chief, and the chief's boss told the commandant, and the commandant told Congress, they all needed to know they were getting the straight facts.

The pressure and uncertainty got too strong. Jim started to focus on information modeling and integrated decision making on his own time. He went back to school to find a fix that might work.

"So…do I re-roof the data center that has a Facilities Condition Index of 0.05 and a Mission Dependency Index of 94, or repair the paint storage building that has a FCI of 0.30 and a MDI of 5?"

Metrics measure and quantify results. Metrics fall into a number of categories, such as performance metrics, project metrics, security metrics, and business metrics. Constant data collection and assessment support metrics. Metrics tied to data models and the other information hosted by BIMSynergy allow the Coast Guard to understand the interactions and relationships between assets. By measuring specific conditions and determining how they relate to other conditions, the organization can define a set of agreed outcomes. Metrics allow decision makers to automate "what-if?" analysis and scarce resource allocation using agreed-upon standards. Money to improve the data center roof that is in superb condition but critical to the mission may be spent before replacing the failed roof on the storage building that is extremely insignificant to the mission.

Using agreed-upon metrics, agreed-upon trigger points, and information models linked to capital asset management, the Coast Guard can quickly and accurately assess their complete list of assets. With this assessment, they can then prioritize spending and ensure the flow of resources to the places that are most critical to the organization's success. They decide where to spend limited funds based on facts. One of the highest forms of data integration is an intuitive user interface that allows your employees to teach themselves how to use your system. As they interact with the tools, the system adapts to their needs for information.

Performance, project, and business metrics can be linked to produce outputs that would solve part of the equation. The information model is what makes use of metrics truly remarkable. The organization's Condition Index can be displayed for individual buildings, bases, or the entire Coast Guard. This enables pattern recognition to let one see the current status of assets. A Replacement Requirement metric lets one see the timeline for when assets will require significant repair or replacement. The Mission Dependency Index metric lets one realize how valuable an asset is to the Coast Guard's mission. Overlaying the three metrics lets one optimize the decision-making process. By balancing condition and mission import, one can choose, "Where is the best place to spend my money?" The Coast Guard focuses on the condition and importance of their assets rather than on cost alone.

The process captures knowledge and stores it in BIMSynergy. The Coast Guard retains this corporate knowledge to support new staff with reliable historical data that would otherwise be lost as experienced staff retires or moves to other assignments.

This corporate information is also used to allow rapid planning. Modules of intelligent objects based on metrics, proven equipment, and room layouts allow planners to tailor existing spaces for new uses or to establish new facilities. Pete's work on the new CGSysOps facility: this is the information that made it possible.

As Jim has used these tools, he has seen an 8 to 15 percent savings on new projects and up to 35 percent savings in design costs for repeat projects. The savings accrue to both the Coast Guard and their consultants. The savings are the result of reusing information, better decision-making information earlier in the process, and better early-stage study, leading to on time, on budget projects with minimal problems.

The modules for rules-based systems include the definition of all components, volumes, and materials. Modules for furniture and other things are there from the start. As the process proceeds, the planner adjusts to create "the box" that defines the concept. Three-dimensional room layouts allow the planner to configure the facility while including clear information that has been captured and validated over time. The team visualizes solutions in two dimensions, three dimensions, and tabular formats, all generated from the same data. How the information is viewed is a personal preference or project requirement, rather than a constraint on the viewer. After assembling the modules and adjusting them as appropriate, the result is forwarded for further development and validation.

MAY 20, 2023—WASHINGTON, DISTRICT OF COLUMBIA

> The data about our facilities are more valuable than the physical facility itself.
> —Adm. Thad Allen

The imprint of the U.S. Coast Guard grew over more than two hundred years of service and dedication. The Coast Guard is not like a private organization. Moving from command and control to a flat structure was not practical for an organization that is a part of the United States Armed Forces. New ways of working had to be found to achieve the free-flowing information and activity streams that represent the most successful of today's businesses. Openness and sharing of pertinent, sensitive information on a regular basis is harder to achieve in an organization that has law enforcement, regulatory, and military missions. The Coast Guard's brand was (and is) well respected and valued.

One could describe some Coast Guard employees as obsessed with the nuance behind their way of working. The way they worked made sense to them. The system belonged to them. They understood it. At a deep level, the system did everything right, or was the best that could be expected under the circumstances. From their perspective, if others knew the situation, they would understand.

When there was a disaster and outsiders thought that the organization had failed, insiders said, "It's not fair." "It is not expected." "We did the best we could have under the circumstances." This pride in self and pride in the group was necessary. But it had a downside. This pride made it almost impossible for the organization to innovate. The perception was that the organization must be right. If the organization were exceptional, why would one need to innovate? If failures were not tolerated, or better yet embraced, transformation was impossible. Innovation requires that we risk failure.

Legacy systems and old ways of working were creating significant barriers to innovation. Outside of the Coast Guard, new tools were enabling people to do things that were thought to be impossible only five years before. The systems and processes that people learned in school and early in their careers could no longer do the job. The world was changing…fast.

Usually individual leaders steered the organization toward innovation, even though the culture did not tolerate failure at any level. Tight budgets, exceptional people, and high levels of personal responsibility all worked to keep the group humble. Individuals and small groups worked with severe constraints, yet they were able to innovate and overcome organizational challenges. Until late in the twentieth century, the system worked. Then, the pressures became too strong, and the pace of change and competition for resources started to overwhelm the organization's ability to embrace innovation.

Early in the twenty-first century, a push by farsighted individuals in the organization began to hone in on systems that would allow the Coast Guard to adapt to a new, fast-paced, and flat world, while retaining the things that made the organization great. Integrated decision making, information modeling, and model servers were all part of the solution. By eliminating stovepipes of information, accurately measuring those things that can be measured, integrating legacy information, and connecting their data, the Coast Guard changed to work flows and a culture that embraced innovation.

One of the outcomes of this change was that now the Coast Guard had a tool for everything. Having the right tool for the job makes one's job easier; Coast Guard tools do much the same from an information point of view. Much as a carpenter would not use a crosscut saw when he needs a rip saw, the facility engineers manage their jobs using many different tools, but none in isolation. Other people can join in to collaborate and review tasks or answer questions. The tools tell everyone of the things that others are working on and need. The status of any project is always clear. Everyone knows when things are expected.

The Coast Guard retains a military structure, yet employees are empowered to achieve the organization's goals. They are encouraged to move fast and efficiently. Sign-offs by those higher in the organization slow down processes. As much as possible, these sign-offs are eliminated. Everyone in the organization knows that doing things this way leaves the possibility of mistakes and failure. Sophisticated monitors and a comprehensive reporting system catch flaws quickly. When an error is identified, the system immediately notifies the right people, who act collaboratively to address the issue quickly.

The system builds on everyone's knowledge and efficiency. Standards, exceptional people, and integrated tools backed up by effective monitoring systems eliminate the need for top-down approval. The Coast Guard believes in strategic decentralization. Where flat structures are possible and innovation is crucial, that is what they do. For military and rescue missions, command and control take over. The system is highly effective. Milestones and queries are broadcast to notify team members. These streams of activity enable them to get involved globally. The system gives people a clear understanding of their roles and accumulates data that can be processed and refined in near real time. The Coast Guard's system cuts down on tedious and difficult-to-manage tasks such as e-mail, photocopying, meetings, finding answers, and problem solving. The system is in a constant state of evolution. Information is power.

BIMSynergy hosts the activity streams. Connecting these activity streams with information models and planning systems, Coast Guard personnel at all levels are able to see what is happening in the organization in near real time. They are able to present capital requests to decision makers, and the presenter can drill down to any level of detail, live.

The system automates the creation of capital budget plans. Every year, the commandant must justify the funding required to support the Coast Guard. Facts do not always win in the world of politics. Yet, information that is easy to understand and obviously supported by facts positions the Coast Guard for the best outcomes when she faces Congressional reviewers. Using information modeling, she quickly drills down into any facility or mission area to get the details that support her requests. She no longer relies on memorization and narrative. The commandant goes into meetings with facts at her fingertips.

She can access information to present all activities, events, and trends within any domain touched by the Coast Guard, whether air, land, sea, space, or cyberspace. She can present the conditions that could jeopardize safety, security, the economy, the environment, or people. Knowledge of capabilities, intentions, methods, objectives, goals, ideology, and organizational structure, plus factors that influence behavior, strengths, vulnerabilities, and centers of gravity are all fair game.

This information is essential to supporting decision making for planning, identifying requirements, prioritizing resource allocation, and implementing operations. Information enables the Coast Guard to identify potential threats and enhances appropriate responses. The system enhances information sharing and supports a consistent risk management strategy.

The commandant opens her BlackBerry and gets a real-time update on the status of all facilities in CONUS, seconds before she sits at the table in the Senate Briefing Room, and…

EDUCATION FOR TOMORROW

3. Few things are certain in our fast-paced world. Change is one of them. Predicting what you will do for a living in ten years is not certain; you cannot be certain that your current career will even exist in ten years. You may think you can predict where you will be and what you will be doing, but you are most likely wrong.

Considering those aging out of the system, plus those laid-off and those now entering the system, we need to pay attention to how best to educate for the future. We can no longer afford a system that trains for disconnected specialization.

In the first half of the twentieth century, our education systems focused on teaching people thinking skills. The goal was to understand the world in context. In the last half of the twentieth century, most people focused on specialization, and professions became compartmentalized. Information disconnects began to have a major negative impact on the world. In the twenty-first century, we need to reinvent education to emphasize systems thinking. Without such a change in focus we will not be able to create a workforce that is adaptable to rapid change. The technology may be available to handle the pace, but there may be no one to work with the technology.

Cloud-based model servers, rules-based systems, and modeling tools enable any of us to deliver high-performance outcomes in many areas that have long been considered the province of professionals. Much as happens on the Internet with e-commerce, travel services, and social networking, these tools in the built environment allow for just-in-time decision making, crowd sourcing, polling, and a host of other distributed processes. One can argue that allowing the public to solve problems this way may miss the subtleties and level of care that professionals provide. In most cases, it would seem that society is willing to accept the loss in order to avoid the problems they are experiencing in the traditional process.

The fact is that the role of professionals must change. Processes that allow professionals to retreat to the ivory tower, or the glass office building, are no longer viable. Accountability and transparency suffer when professionals work in isolation. Fannie Mae and other big financial meltdowns would have been detected and responded to much earlier in a true open environment. Rather than openness, the entire financial meltdown illustrated behind-closed-doors programs that enabled processes to proceed without investigation and criminal proceedings.

Professionals must become more flexible. They must become brokers and aggregators of data, helping people to find their own solutions in the complexity. Although the master builder, the arbitrageur, and the architect may as archetypes continue to exist, these roles are not likely to be the model for professionals in the future.

THE WRONG CODE

> The code that is the hardest to debug is the code that you know cannot possibly be wrong.
>
> —Anonymous

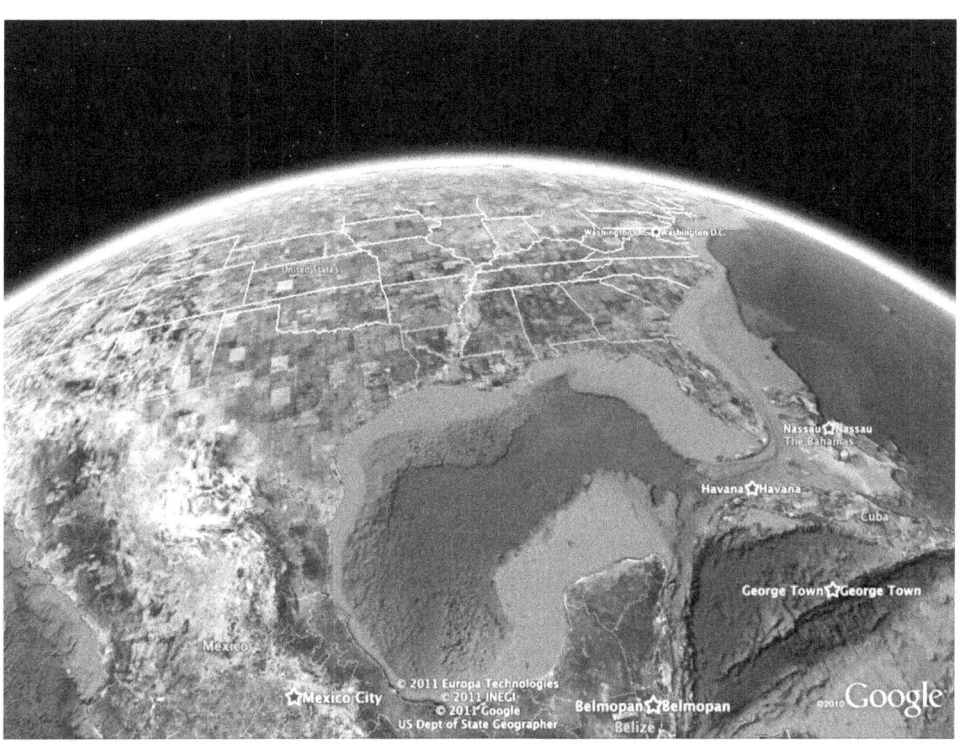

Done correctly, integrated processes change how everyone looks at our world. Can education be changed to keep up? For too long, industry has relied on processes that are inefficient. The focus has been on task automation, resulting in an industry that is less productive today than it was before computers. Automating inefficient processes has not worked.

Finding solutions to problems within this complex industry has always been difficult. Professionals have made incremental changes, trying to solve individual problems. Their improvements have tended to focus on one group or one client area. At times, these solutions filtered through the industry.

Before building information modeling, it was extremely difficult to access and use real-time data for planning and design. Although theoretically possible, connecting costs, energy, and other metrics was only possible on the largest projects for the largest firms.

Deke Smith, executive director of the buildingSMART alliance—the leadership association for building information in the United States—recently sent a letter saying, "There are 10 million professionals we need to educate." These professionals find themselves in a market where they see tremendous benefit to themselves and their clients. Yet they have trouble sorting through the hype and misinformation to achieve the larger benefits. Getting clarity for these professionals is only part of the need. Of greater importance is the need to enable and empower everyone else. Everyone will have greater impact and participation in tomorrow's built environment.

Owners have strongly asserted a need for better integration of processes. They see building information modeling technology as the way to streamline the built environment. They are exploring how to fix the industry's problems. Modeling and integrated practice are making it possible to expand into areas where few have gone before. Step up to the plate and embrace information!

If you are not using integrated processes, you may be one of the last holdouts. Every day you see and use products of others who have already gone down this path. Your grocery store is integrated. Your local car care repair shop is integrated. Your bank is integrated. Integrated processes affect everything you do.

When will you make the change? How much longer can the construction industry be the last holdout?

EARLY DECISIONS

Every day you use e-mail. Texting, tweeting, and social networking are essential. You probably get your news from the web. When you buy something, more often than not you use a credit or debit card. When you travel, you make your plans with Expedia or one of the other travel sites. Your TV programs come into your home through the Internet. They are integrated with other online entertainment scheduling systems. When you watch a movie, you rent it on the Internet, and it is streamed into your living room. You interact with integrated systems every day.

Most of us have seen the tremendous value that comes from integrated systems on the Internet. Can you remember how complicated it used to be just to a plan a flight from your home airport to Cleveland, Ohio? The paper that it would take to print all of the schedules for the flights leaving one airport on one day would fill a room. Many phone calls to hotels and car rental agencies would be required. After several days of coordinating several people and reading hundreds of pages of printed text, you would accomplish the same thing that you can do now in five minutes on your laptop.

For most, returning to the days of travel agents, print newspapers, paper billing, and the other common technologies from before the Internet is out of the question. Yet when we design and create a new house, or interact with the city's building department, we act like the Internet doesn't even exist. Certainly, we use computers for drawing lines and taking information, but most things in the built environment stop right there. Why do built environment processes lag so far behind?

People change at different rates. Some can accept broad, sweeping, and almost instantaneous change. Most require a transition period. Some prepare better. Some have more money, more support, and can handle faster transitions. Some like to go fast. Some like slow and consistent change.

Leading change requires that we build on two key leadership skills: knowing and using your resources, and understanding the group. Both leadership skills revolve around finding ways to adjust change to the rate that people need, in order to move forward. Both tailor change to people's ability to manage the change.

No longer is it about "What's in it for me?" Today the questions are "Does it work for us all?" and "Does it seem fair?" Encourage everyone to achieve his or her full potential to generate innovative ideas. Get a handle on what everyone has to offer. Know every member of your group and see how they fit together to support the overall team. In an integrated framework, our approach must be that it is not possible for anyone to succeed if one member of the team fails. Collaboration is an essential, not a luxury.

How do we move to this new way of living? How do we make this change?

For many of us, the change comes from learning new ways of working, becoming more collaborative, and being lifelong learners. We must actively evaluate each new venture and be sure that we do not apply the isolated processes that we were taught in school. We must learn how to use new collaborative tools and how to change how we work, even though at times it seems counterintuitive.

Others of us are new to the workforce. We have finished our formal education and are now learning on the job. For us, the change requires constant reevaluation of what we have been taught. Often our education taught us the wrong things. Our storehouse of knowledge is built on shifting sands, because much of what we learned in school is no more true than what our elders learned in school twenty or thirty years ago. We embrace the Internet and social networking. That is a terrific place to start. Now we need to figure out ways to bring collaborative and integrated processes into the built environment to make our careers more significant.

Some are still in the process of formal education. We are in elementary school, high school, junior college, and university. We are searching for how to proceed. We look for what we need to know. We are planning for a future, often with little or no data upon which to judge. Our guidance counselors assuredly don't get it. Our schools still teach subjects that are irrelevant now and will be even more irrelevant in the future. We fear that we are being taught to do things that will not exist when we become adults. We are not being taught how to work with the things that don't even exist yet. We don't even remember a time without the Internet. Social networking, gaming, and three-dimensional geographic representation are no significant deal. Figuring out what to do, figuring out what to study, and planning for the future are serious issues.

The last group has not been born yet. They need our help. There is little justification for not correcting the learning and systemic issues that the other groups are experiencing today.

BROKEN EDUCATION

> There is nothing permanent except change. —Heraclitus

In the post-World War II period, there was a flood of students seeking college degrees. Universities and colleges expanded into many areas of skills that were traditionally blue-collar, turning them into professions that required four years of in-depth education. As these technician-level trades became degree programs, different departments opened to accommodate growth in demand.

As society became more complex, it was believed that a common curriculum should be applied to high school education, to prepare all graduates for lives in a complex industrial society. The knowledge considered necessary and relevant grew. A four-year high school education no longer provided the knowledge needed for even blue-collar jobs. College-level education was the only model filling the gap. Trade schools were looked down on as not worthy.

No Child Left Behind and Race to the Top did the opposite of what they promised. Their primary method for measuring success was the standardized test on standardized curriculum. Test-taking abilities and memorization seemed to be the result.

Competition for students forced institutions of higher education to spend money on nonessential services and facilities such as sports teams and stadiums. These ancillary services often did not improve the core mission of educating people.

Grade inflation became endemic in the system as colleges focused on retention. Misuse of assessment systems and online ratings by students pushed teachers and administrators to bend when it came to issues of quality and rigor. The only sustainable model for funding classes was to have large course sections. These classes, often taught by teaching assistants, generated revenue to support smaller advanced subject classes.

The modern university tried to be all things to all people and ended up becoming useless to most. Turning education into a commodity caused the quality of education to decline. The common wisdom that college was an almost guaranteed path to success was no longer true.

As standards failed to hold volumes up, incompetent or uncaring people filled jobs that should have gone to those with higher levels of understanding and better preparation. There was a general slackening of the emphasis on professionalism, ethical considerations, and responsibility to society. Competency of graduates declined.

Curricula often targeted the lowest common denominator of the class—the average student. Since coursework was focused on those of average intelligence, the rigor of subjects was reduced so that the average student could handle it. Lowered standards in high school and undergraduate programs migrated to higher levels as well. This created PhDs who went into teaching unable to handle the rigorous content themselves.

Our society relied on several premises when considering the problems:

First, we ignored the possibility that not all people have similar general intelligence levels. We then assumed that all children and young adults could learn the same things if we organized education and delivered it in such a way that they could absorb the concepts. No longer was the student responsible for learning.

Second, we assumed that higher education would lead to higher pay. The belief was that "if you want a better job, you need more education." Although educated individuals may on average have higher incomes, that does not support the hypothesis that all people with higher education will have higher incomes. Even smart people occasionally lack wisdom and miss this subtlety. They are sometimes surprised to find that many blue-collar workers earn more money than lower-level white-collar workers with business degrees.

Finally, society generally accepted that we could teach people most effectively by using the assembly line or linear model to move people though the system in lockstep. When we assumed that all children at a given age could learn the same things, at the same rate, we had to have effective methods to push them through the system. As a result, the belief in a standardized curriculum for professional and science degrees became strong. The search for knowledge and scholarship went by the wayside.

The higher education system was ready to implode and needed radical redesign as revenues continued to deteriorate and legislatures continued to reduce budgets. Institutions reached the point where fees and expenses could no longer maintain core needs. Peripheral revenue sources could not support the system. Administrators responded by cutting programs and downsizing, simultaneously protecting their own jobs, as the number of students drastically declined and tuition skyrocketed to raise revenue. Some administrators began to focus on the quality of students they admitted, instead of selling seats to the highest bidders, but this tiny compromise could not fix the problem.

Fortunately, we found another way forward.

Universities began by radically cutting the costs of ancillary activities, especially related to the executive bloat that came with the assembly line model. They began to refocus on the core mission of higher education…which was not to be "all things to all people."

Departments secondary to the core mission, with their associated administrators, had been the main cost drivers. They were eliminated. Growing enrollments and programs had become the model, and to expand, institutions had to out-compete their rivals in terms of athletic facilities and other amenities of student life. Each of these took too many resources, cost too much money, and detracted from the core mission. These amenities were also eliminated.

The commodity approach had changed the governance of universities from the traditional faculty deliberation and consensus model into a business management model. As institutions became nominally nonprofit capitalist enterprises, they required professional management and the fiefdoms that bred.

In the traditional higher education governance model, senior faculty rotated through the department chair, dean, and provost positions. Few had the need or the desire to create fiefdoms. As this model of governance fell apart, administrators morphed into professional chairs, deans, and provosts.

The faculty senate, president, and regents working in unison was no longer functional. Faculty senates became advisory bodies to the president and regents as they became more like business executives and boards of directors. Fewer boards of regents' members came from the ranks of emeritus professors and civic leaders. Universities became training facilities for workers rather than places to allow higher thinkers.

By returning to earlier models, governance improved. Faculty took on the roles of deans and provosts, often for no other reason than to reverse the upward cost spiral. Education went back to the core mission of exploration, understanding, and scholarship. Society re-imagined the university in its early form to provide places for growing minds, not training for jobs.

People realized that most of the jobs that people will hold twenty years from now have not yet been invented. Training students for jobs that are likely to be discontinued or end does not make sense. We now teach people to embrace new paradigms.

We educate for deep skills that can be applied to solve problems and maximize collaborative processes. As a society, we now realize that we need people with intellectual engagement and values-driven thinking. We need strategic thinkers that are able to recognize patterns and have a problem-solving mindset.

We teach for broad scope and knowledge that embraces the possibilities and pitfalls represented by an interconnected world. An ability to connect the dots, a tolerance for ambiguity, and a willingness to accept shared risks and rewards are essential traits we value. The measure of our educational future is people who recognize and can thrive in a team-based process, using trust, communication, and an ability to manage change.

JULY 4, 2019—NORFOLK, VIRGINIA

> Even if you're on the right track, you'll get run over if you just sit there.
> —Will Rogers

The first three days at CGSysOps were crazy. Pete had never experienced anything like that before. He walked into his office at eight o'clock and at five o'clock he wondered where the day had gone. It was so intense and required so much concentration that he found himself in "the zone" for three days straight. If things continued this way, he would never get tired of this job.

The new job was a challenge; Pete was ready for a break. A Fourth of July crab feast in his backyard with his friends and Mel and the kids was just what he needed. Time to kick back with a St. Pauli Girl until the gang showed up.

On any other holiday, Pete would be on his J/24 on the bay near Deale, Maryland. He genuinely did need to get the boat moved down to a marina a little closer to home. He was going to lose his crew from the DC office when he moved the boat. They liked racing on Saturdays out of Deale, but Mel was pushing hard for him to start taking Thomas and Cindy on the boat more. The kids would have a real gap in their education if they grew up without experiencing the Chesapeake Bay.

"Pete! Gary and Fred are at the front door. Will you let them in? I'm getting the kids into their swimsuits," Mel called down from the second floor.

Gary Boyle and Fred Boyd were two of Pete's best friends. They had both been at CGSysOps for about four months. Gary was an old guy…he had to be every bit of fifty, but he was pretty savvy and got to CGSysOps the hard way.

Pete and Fred were exactly the same age. They'd had a tremendous party on their birthday, about three weeks ago, when they'd turned thirty-seven. They could not be more different from each other. Fred had dropped out of community college and gone into the Army, where he'd worked as a GIS technician. When he got out of the service, he'd worked for an architect as a drafter. He finally got a job with the Coast Guard about four years ago.

Pete got to CGSysOps the traditional way. He'd leveraged his Eagle Scout to get a full ride at Penn State. After he'd finished his architecture degree, he'd gone to work for a series of firms that eventually led to his being hired at CGSysOps. Underneath his veneer of conformism, he was rather unconventional. He could not accept the fact that most of his peers did not seem to have a problem with the waste and mistakes that architects and contractors routinely made. They seemed to accept business as usual even though many of the projects that they worked on cost too much and gave too little value for the money. To Pete, there was not much excuse for not trying to fix the mess.

The three friends were as different as could be in most things. At heart, they had similar values and attitudes that made them successful in the rapid-paced, integrated, and collaborative environment that was CGSysOps. Experience had shown them the things that were critical to success in that environment.

They had expert-level capabilities in various software tools. That expertise did not overlook the fact that they were each fluent and fluid in many other applications. None of the three focused on only one application. They had learned that the ability to adapt to new technology was much more valuable than individual product expertise. When they heard bragging about how great someone was in one software solution, to the exclusion of all others, they knew that person was not suited to work in their world. They understood the value of expertise, but flexibility was the new standard.

At times in their careers, they had each been tagged as "not a team player." Some people saw focus and single-mindedness as coldness, aloofness, and lack of team engagement. Not much could save a truly abrasive personality. Sometimes ego was just ego without actual knowledge. Pete, Gary, and Fred saw the flip side of that equation.

To them, focus and single-mindedness were characteristic of deep knowledge and confidence. Brilliant people often had these traits. If you were going to do work in high-energy environments that required people to be fast on their feet, you wanted people who were focused and could "get in the zone." They always opted for broad knowledge and deep skills. If that meant working through other issues, so be it.

For these three, success came from how they used their beliefs and values; by applying them consistently, they made their own way of doing things. They had learned that the willingness to innovate backed up by deep knowledge and broad interests were the key to making the changes required in an integrated world.

When they were asked to speak at schools, they offered the same advice. They asked the students to determine who they were and where they were now. Do I have the temperament to be successful? They explained that the skills that drive social networking and relationship management were survival skills for the future. Most important of all, they told the students that they must become lifelong learners.

No one can learn everything. The world is just too big and too complicated. By necessity, you can only become expert in a limited range of issues. This makes collaboration with many other people a necessity, not a luxury. The sheer volume of data that affects you every day can be a blessing or a curse. By developing strategies for managing this data, you maximize its value in your life. You can either embrace the changes that come with new processes or let the information inundate you.

It is essential to become a systems thinker. Orchestras need a conductor to get the best from a group of musicians. Future leaders need inspiration and teamwork skills to get the best from people in an integrated world. We must engage others in collaborative ways. Clear communication ensures that we find common objectives. By sharing information and developing open and honest standards that protect us all, we thrive. We live and work in a world of highly interconnected processes. Because of these interconnections, we all have an impact on things far into the future.

We must realize that no one can refuse leadership. Everyone needs to adopt new technology and high levels of responsibility for our world. Experts have been trying to force business as usual on the built environment. Too often, market forces and self-interests underpin their message. Without changing how we react to our world and to others, we may never see the benefits of technology in the built environment. We can no longer afford the waste and inefficiency that has gone before. We all have to change. Otherwise, we are bound to fail.

Today's leaders must engage people in the process. As a nation we can learn to take the long view, and together we will be successful. Talk is cheap; action is priceless. As leaders, we must stop arguing about the political minutiae and lead the way.

Become fluent in technology and embrace a long view of our planet and the built environment. Use your knowledge and experience to become effective in leading this change. People with a life cycle view and personal experience are invaluable. Assessing, deciding, and acting are key traits in future leaders. Others will come to know and buy into the vision.

WIDE AND DEEP

> In the long history of humankind... Those who learned to collaborate and improvise most effectively have prevailed. —Charles Darwin

Pete, Gary, and Fred share some common traits. To a large extent, these traits are the basis for their success in an interconnected and fast-paced world. In some cases, they chose paths that built on underlying values. More often, the route taken was the result of reacting to the choices offered as they progressed. Some of their choices could be said to have been wrong. Yet, like all of us, they made what they felt to be the correct decision at the time, always moving forward.

Each is a unique character who brings broad interests and deep knowledge to the mix. Pundits would say that they are all T-shaped personalities. Pete is a master at looking at seemingly unrelated data, detecting the patterns and interactions, and synthesizing innovative solutions to connect the dots. He doesn't merely analyze things, he synthesizes new things from what usually look to be unrelated things. When you add this to his ability to fluently mash up technology to manage the process, he is invaluable to the team.

In his downtime, Gary is a master mechanic. He can fix just about any engine. His confidence around motors is sometimes mistaken for arrogance. He brings attention to detail and his mastery of the interactions between things to everything he does. His ability to see patterns and opportunities comes in handy every day.

Fred is a musician. He plays the sax. He is not just a middling sax player...he is professional. Fred gets offers to play in professional jazz groups all the time. He is a master of the sax. He doesn't just read music; he understands the composition and structure right down to his toes. You should hear him when he jams with a group at the Cellar Door in Georgetown. His music translates to a passion for organization and structure. He is a master at figuring out how to pull teams together and how to build the relationships.

The three worked for years to master their art—the deep part of the T-shaped person. None of the three limits his interests to his specialties. You can find Pete sailing on the Chesapeake Bay, hunting with his Chesapeake Bay retriever near Cambridge, coaching his daughter Cindy's soccer team, and reading every book he can get. Gary travels, a lot. He just got back from Estonia and next month he is heading to Taiwan. Fred delivers Meals on Wheels, attends Rotary every week, and takes classes in Oriental cooking.

They have broad interests. They are insatiably curious about life and unrelenting in their quest for learning. They test their knowledge through experience and trial and error, and are willing to learn from their mistakes. This curiosity led them to information modeling and integrated systems. The knowledge they have mastered, tempered by insatiable curiosity and interests, is the model for the future.

They have the skills that allow them to recognize and appreciate the interconnectedness of all things. They are systems thinkers. They are willing to accept ambiguity, inconsistency, and uncertainty in the pursuit of purpose and meaning. They embrace shared risks and rewards. They are resilient, adaptable, and perseverant. Each of the three has developed a passion for knowledge. They are curious about our world. They have learned how to be flexible and quick on their feet. They know that nothing is permanent except change. By embracing change, they have learned to look at things from many different perspectives.

They are empathetic. They have found a balance between science, art, and imagination in their lives. They are whole-brain thinkers. They understand the subtleties of how people interact with each other. Values drive their thinking. They value their ability to work in teams using integrated processes. Trust and communication are among their first priorities. Collaborative thinking, working, and doing are critical.

They focus on the question, not only answers. They have the ability to craft a narrative about their work that is enjoyable and informative. They have problem-solving mindsets. They do things so well that they go right through professional and cross over into obsessive. They know what they know. More importantly, they know what they do not know. They are so utterly into CGSysOps' business that they are perfectly poised to exploit information modeling and integrated decision making to their full potential.

Pete, Gary, and Fred exemplify the traits and beliefs that will make people successful in the fast-paced world of tomorrow. Many paths lead to becoming T-shaped. The beauty of the concept is that, with forethought and hard work, most people can become T-shaped. Becoming T-shaped does not revolve around capability lists that proscribe a series of tasks that theoretically create a worker. One becomes T-shaped by mastering something of value and nurturing the curiosity and intellectual naïveté that we had when children. With this mindset, one prepares for new paradigms and jobs that have not yet been invented.

The beliefs that guide Pete, Gary, and Fred are the culmination of years of experience and training. These beliefs are based on what they have been taught and learned as they worked their way through life. Their beliefs guide their actions and can change the way they proceed, for the better. Their beliefs could also stall their advancement so that they never reach their full potential.

The three have come to understand their strengths and weaknesses. They understand how they relate to others and how others relate to them. They have created their personal narratives of the future. Their personal guidebooks define the steps they need to take to make their personal narrative a reality. Pete, Gary, and Fred's personal guidebooks are used like road maps.

One learns how to become obsessive and to apply that passion to make something meaningful happen. One embraces the world with open eyes and a curiosity to question everything, to learn anything, and to adapt to change. One moves from workforce development for the industrial age to worker development for an integrated world.

COMPETENCY

In times of rapid change, we need to understand our current situation and an idealized future vision that we can work toward. The design futures in this book are intended to give you clues to opportunities. Use them to create your personal, idealized view of your future. First understand your skills, attitudes, and capabilities. With your assessment in hand, it is then possible to see how you compare with others and where you stand compared to the idealized future state, and create a personalized action plan. With a personalized plan, focus your development program to fill gaps that exist in your skills and capabilities. As you progress through your program, you should regularly reassess and refocus to build on your positives and to manage negative issues.

We live in a knowledge economy. The explosion of information is becoming overwhelming to many. The line between information producers and information users is vanishing. We can have a significant impact on the world, without a large staff. We can work with information ourselves. We may need help to organize data feeds, but we no longer need to be information technology experts. Technology levels all playing fields.

Companies are dependent on knowledge workers. Yet many of their work flows, tools, and skills remain grounded in industrial age thinking. Many companies need to change to adapt to the new reality. Their tools are too complex and too expensive. They take too much time and bottleneck other processes. Their data became more complex and interconnected, almost without their knowing. What could once be done with a spreadsheet now requires extensive databases and integrated decision-making tools. Their belief is that the correction "is too hard" or "costs too much money" or "takes too much time." They feel overwhelmed and revert to business as usual.

Companies can hire people to create databases and domain knowledge; both require easily taught and learned skills. They have a much harder time hiring people with process knowledge and expertise. They need people who are intuitive about managing processes and can envision success. They need people with the capacity to persuade others to their point of view. They need people capable of dealing with multiple priorities. These skills are insanely valuable and hard to learn. They are challenging to evaluate and nearly impossible to include in a database.

They need your unique capacity to create value. They need you to "connect the dots" between their products and services and their customers. This is the situation across all industries, business types, and places. In the built environment, it is often even worse. In the built environment, there are still architects drafting by hand. Contractors return to technology that the master builder of the cathedral in the thirteenth century would recognize. Planners favor systems that worked well during the Kennedy administration. Facility managers manage to crisis.

We are in the midst of a systemic and comprehensive change to how things work. The change requires new competencies—competencies that usually do not fit the checklist or database; competencies that are difficult to measure; competencies that are critical to the future.

A competency is a pattern of behavior that sticks. A competency comes from a combination of knowledge, skills, abilities, and motivations. It is not only about technical knowledge, experience, or age. The competencies that determine a person who will thrive in an interconnected future look something like this:

Creative competencies

- Knowing and understanding a range of problem solving techniques.
- Ability to use logic to identify different approaches and judgment to analyze their strength and weakness.
- Ability to synthesize and reorganize information to find better ways of doing things.
- Ability to use fresh ideas to solve problems and lead groups.

Mashable competencies

- Ability to identify the nature and cause of problems and the dynamics that define them.
- Constant desire to improve.
- Ability to identify, collect, and use only the information that is necessary.
- Ability to think outside the box, even when it is not popular.
- Understanding the underlying principles that are the foundations of technology and using them to improve outcomes.

Emotional competencies

- Willingness to listen to others and to try new ideas.
- Curiosity and an open mind to the ideas and solutions of others.
- Being observant and understanding of others' behavior.
- Voracious study to find innovations and trends in various fields.
- Well-rounded personality that seeks information from all areas of life.
- Ability to relate seemingly unconnected ideas to find novel approaches to situations.
- Ability to predict the likely outcomes that will result from changes.
- Willingness to acknowledge changes that have occurred.
- Ability to create a narrative of an ideal working condition.
- Ability to plan strategically.

Futurist competencies

- Ability to predict the likely outcomes that will result from changes.
- Willingness to acknowledge changes that have occurred.
- Ability to create a narrative of an ideal working condition.
- Ability to plan strategically.

Change competencies

- Understanding of the phases of change and the barriers to change.
- Ability to evaluate and identify those things that promote and inhibit change.
- Willingness to act against traditional ways of working when they impede development.
- Willingness and ability to take calculated risks.
- Ability to know when to stop and figure out the right way before doing something.
- Ability to encourage and reward others for initiative and creative work.
- Ability to facilitate change initiatives.

HOW CAN I ACQUIRE THE SKILLS?

> Don't let yesterday use up too much of today. —Will Rogers

It can be difficult to find the best way to prepare yourself for the world of the future, especially if you do not clearly understand the scope of the changes that are taking place. Reliable advisors are hard to find. Few realize that by imposing industrial revolution era concepts onto a knowledge ecology, they are pushing systems and processes that are rapidly becoming extinct. There is a serious lack of reliable advice and support to help you to focus your personal development within an information-rich world.

Knowledge has long been transferred from one generation to the next by methods that changed little since the days of medieval guilds. Things are changing too fast for that to work any longer. You want to be useful to society quickly. Employers expect the same. Preparing for the transformation requires you to look at yourself in the context of a vision of the future.

Few focus on the people side of the change equation. Training, development, planning, and discussions focus on the organization. Seminars and books on information modeling and integrated ways of working focus on using technology, case studies, and standards. They describe how their organization uses information modeling. They communicate the results and outline the metrics from business operations. Most gloss over the fact that we are seeing the demise of collocation and command and control. Most ignore the fact that the world is changing to become more open with more complex social structures. The impact on individuals is rarely discussed. One key aspect of business is usually missing: people.

One of Bill Caudill's (founder of Caudill, Rowlett & Scott Architects) favorite lines perhaps says it best: "People are more important than organizational structures. Structures we can design if we have any administrative creativity."

The future will be messy, because the future depends on people. Technology and business are merely tools and structures to enable and manage people. This is the age of the individual. Suddenly a single person, properly interconnected, out-produces the company. The individual becomes a linchpin.

This is what change in our society is all about. You need to get a handle on what everyone has to offer. You want to learn how social networks operate and how they fit together to support the overall team. You need to build your skills at working with people—all kinds of people, in all kinds of places, from all kinds of cultures. You want to learn how to get the best results from teams made up of consultants, internal staff, constructors, subject matter experts, and a lot of others to get things done. You want to become an expert at the social side of the changes in our world.

Whether you have grown up with the Internet or are in mid-career, you cannot afford to focus on technology or organizational change. You are the key driver in this change. You know the world is changing and becoming more collaborative. You know that we want to become sustainable. You need to change how people relate to the built environment. Information modeling creates the opportunity to respond at the pace of today's world. By capturing the knowledge of today's leaders and engaging the new "You" Generation in the change, we all benefit. We can create a more efficient and sustainable world for those that follow in our footsteps.

EMBRACE THE FUTURE

Knowing yourself and understanding how the others you connect with work is one step toward success. Realize how interconnected you are with others. Do not wait for others to delegate authority; make yourself a leader. Provide value in our collaborative world. Expand your vision of your role in the built environment and plan your way into the future.

The world needs new programs that demonstrate new ways of working and thinking; new ways that are more collaborative, innovative, and integrated. There is a need for new patterns that allow people to "fail fast and move on." Without risk, there is little change. Without innovation, there is little growth. Without failure, there is little progress.

We obviously cannot accept failure in some highly developed and key systems. None of us want to be on the aircraft, with the pilot in change mode, risking failure. These systems need to be foolproof. In today's world, that means enabling the failures early, so that when the systems become critical, failure is no longer an option. This is why the Level of Detail concept of information modeling is crucial. One takes the risks and makes the mistakes early, and well before the plane is built or flown. Virtual failures are easy to fix. Plane crashes are not. Making the distinction is one of the critical issues in information modeling and integrated decision-making.

When are failures okay? When are failures unacceptable?

In most situations, innovation stops when a system can tolerate zero failure. In a zero failure situation, everyone becomes fearful. People become obsessed with trying to be perfect and there is little forward movement. No one takes a chance and nothing changes. There is no innovation.

At the other extreme is chaos. Many ideas emerge, but little gets done. Progress stops when there is no need to be responsible for outcomes. When failure is always acceptable, at any time in any process, it can be catastrophic.

A balance must be reached between taking risks to enable innovation and dependable performance.

For most, the line is drawn when the contract is signed, or the concrete is poured. When serious capital, time, or resources will be required to correct a failure, most demand that failure should be minimized. All would say failure should be eliminated when lives are at stake. In today's world of cloud computing, information modeling, and model servers, these definitions allow a lot of flexibility, if we use the technology correctly. It all depends on collaboration and integrated processes that move systematically from concept through documentation into realization.

Collaboration in this new world will not look like anything in use today. E-mail will not be the primary form of communication. Information will be attached to the model. Each user will have access to the interconnected data.

In some arenas collaboration has become an avoidance tool. In these environments, teams become punitive and petty, placing value on the collaboration above outcomes and work products. Working as a team becomes the end goal. Those who do not seem to be team players are exorcised or shunned. Much is subjective. Team member productivity is rated not by successfully moving projects forward, but by standards that value team play above scoring goals and winning the game. The team is the end goal.

This view of collaboration can be found in many parts of modern society. We see it in government and businesses. This approach sometimes seems to be the standard approach. When collaboration becomes the end goal, the work becomes secondary. Fortunately, there are other approaches.

Unless a group is focusing on understanding, spiritual harmony, closeness, and empathy, collaboration is not about sitting in a circle and singing "Kumbaya." Collaboration should focus on leveraging the expertise of each team member to get one's job done so well that others' work is better.

We all need to do excellent work. Each of us values recognition and personal satisfaction. Each of us has unique skills and knowledge. Each of us comes to a team with different levels of expertise and experience. We come to the group from various disciplines. Each of us is different, valuable, and indispensable. Because of these differences, successful collaborative processes can be hierarchical, as long as everyone is respected and valued. Within successful collaborations, professional differences serve a practical purpose. Team members are interdependent, value other members, and acknowledge others' expertise and standing in the hierarchy to learn and advance the work. As a rule, team members with more diverse skill sets are the most valuable.

One of the major concerns of any collaboration is to get the appropriate people on the team. Different types of people are critical to success in this environment. Today's collaborations need people that can synthesize information and problem solve within the collaborative framework. Collaborations go far when filling this need.

Collaborations revolve around processes that allow team members to develop their craft. Members gain expertise step by step as they see what worked and what did not. They "fail fast and move on," rather than being corrected through punitive means. Failures are handled by doing tasks again, and doing them right. Team members become more valuable by learning to work collaboratively. They use education and natural skills to complete tasks in ways that allow others to do better work. They develop their ability to create and manage complex processes.

Positive collaborations use objective standards that value frankness and open communication. Clarity and directness are the goal, not vagueness and narrative. Collaborations should foster trust, openness, and reliable information. Because of the relationships that effective collaborations create, they can be decentralized and tapped into resources and expertise in loosely connected or distributed networks.

Collaborations must be agile to function properly under time and transactional pressures. They must be able to respond to changing conditions and new information. Trust is their currency. It is not what they say but what they do that counts. Agile and distributed collaborations cut across bureaucratic controls.

Managing people is a rapidly evolving process. It requires a different skill set and different ways of looking at people. It does not lend itself to the support hierarchy that most businesses now have in place. In a collaborative environment, the organization is flat—even senior team members participate at all levels. Collaborations are extremely flexible.

Managing distributed collaborations is difficult or impossible with traditional command-and-control structures. It is difficult to create organizational charts for distributed collaborations, as the team members' functions change frequently, and behind-the-scenes interactions are the norm. The organizational chart completed today will probably be decidedly different tomorrow. When the goal is to get the best people involved to get the work done, organizational charts have little real value. Distributed collaborations thrive on constant reorganization of the highly creative people who deliver the work.

PASSIONS

> The painter who has no doubts will achieve little.   —Leonardo da Vinci

We all have passions. Some have been fortunate enough to pursue their passions. Many have not. Our education system destroys the passion of most. We have created a system that requires learners to be lucky or exceptionally focused to survive the process, passions intact. We teach to the lowest common denominator, we honor and support the top 5 percent, and we do harm to the majority in the middle. Without malice, with the best of intentions, but we do it anyway.

According to the Deloitte Center for the Edge's 2009 Shift Index survey, only one out of every five workers in the United States is genuinely passionate about his or her work. A recent Gallup Poll indicated that one out of five employees is so disengaged that he or she actively seeks to undermine colleagues at work. Of course, most of us are in the middle of these two extremes.

The education system that evolved following World War II is under attack from many directions, and rightly so. People are tired of constantly escalating costs, wasted effort, and ineffective teaching. The news media focuses on athletic programs and largely ignores the core mission of our schools. Educators struggle with tight budgets. Standards and evaluations reward and punish educators for the wrong things. Politicians and unions drive too many decisions. These attacks sprang from an educational system that has not adapted to changes in our society.

Our education system is being pushed harder and faster than ever before. Rather than using scientific methods and looking at the underlying structure and systems that have been violated in the current system, we have fallen back on tradition and legacy systems to drive educational decision making.

We can do better. We can make changes using the same problem-solving skills and training that drive other successful programs in our world. We can fix the problem. We have the luxury of deciding how we want to continue. But we do not have much time, for we are currently in failure mode, and the system is primed to implode.

No two situations are exactly alike. Trying to tackle the educational system as a single reality is no longer viable. Technology is enabling the individual to work bigger and to compete globally. Education faces the same issues. We must adjust the system to each individual situation. We must remember that this, or any other type of system, will always be in a constant state of flux. This is a time that requires systems that are flexible and responsive.

A grand and global policy may not be the right approach to solving our educational problems. Has No Child Left Behind solved the education problem? Probably not. We have created an environment that frowns on individual competitive spirit. As a society, maybe there is some good that comes from leaving failing children behind and finding other ways to move them forward.

Changing education could be revolutionary—discarding all that went before, starting from scratch and inventing an entirely new approach. Alternatively, the change could be evolutionary—building on the good parts of the process that were considered normal before the war years and replacing those that no longer work, walking away from the mistakes of the last fifty years, and integrating the old with the new. In either case, a different way of educating people is the result.

Today's young learners are open and fluid in their use of technology. They use technology much differently than those who found technology later in life. Those of us born before 1970 may not understand how those born after 1990 use technology. To us, technology was an acquired skill. To them, technology is ubiquitous and a way of life. Few students wear wristwatches, and if they do it is a fashion statement, not a timepiece.

Using the model that was created to train workers for Henry Ford's assembly line is not valid with today's students. We are no longer educating for industrial age workers. The system needs to turn away from teaching tools and toward teaching technology as a way of thinking.

Education today values cooperation above collaboration. Cooperation is a procedure that can do harm, but rarely innovates. Cooperation says, "Don't get in each other's way." Given enough time and resources, cooperative tasks can be accomplished by a single person.

We need to develop academic standards that value collaboration as a core competency. Collaboration amplifies the value of many individuals and articulates ways to create opportunities. Collaboration is a high-fidelity notion that bridges the disconnect between education and the rest of the world. We must reconnect curriculum and reintegrate education with a new future vision. Collaborative processes and integrated tools are the mechanisms that make this possible.

If we do not change how we teach, we will not see the benefits of technology. We will continue, "business as usual." Educators must reassess their beliefs and knowledge. The skills that they have learned in the current system need to be reevaluated and refocused toward new ways of teaching. We need to rethink many of our closely held beliefs.

Today's educators face a variety of challenges. Educators take too long to learn about technology. Then they take too long to incorporate innovations into the classroom. Educators need to learn ways to reduce the gap between the entry of a new technology and its effective use in the classroom. Most lack the will or incentives to change. This is especially true in relation to the environment and the built world.

As an example, community colleges still teach things like computer-aided drafting. They continue to train people for jobs that are in decline or extinct. They take too long to see where things are headed, too long to prepare once they know, and too long to apply the appropriate learning processes. Is it a surprise that students leave school unprepared for the future and jaded about learning in general?

Educators need to create their own narratives about the future. They need to figure out what technology and systems will help them to train the next generation how to achieve these futures.

Educators must begin to look at new ways of teaching, new ways to use technology that will probably seem foreign. Educators must learn new methods to reflect the ways of working that will be common in the future. They need to stop teaching to an industrial era paradigm. Educators need to determine how technology can be used. Teaching someone how to operate a mouse or to draw a line in AutoCAD is no longer appropriate. Instead, educators should be asking their students to answer the question: "What technology would you use to solve this problem?"

BUILD

Nearly all discussions about technology in the built environment focus on tools, processes, and organizations. These are the "hard" face of information modeling and integration. One would find it difficult to identify a training program, seminar, or forum related to the built environment that focuses on people. This focus on the hard side of the equation, almost to the exclusion of the "soft" side—the people side—might not be surprising to you, but does it make sense?

My answer would be no. People matter as never before. By investing our energy in people, we build more robust, vigorous solutions. When one adds the fact that the Internet allows individuals to leverage their abilities and resources to be direct competitors with the largest organizations, something else must be happening. Perhaps the focus on the hard side of the equation is simply because it is easy: easier to understand, easier to quantify, and easier to sell. Perhaps it is because of legacy thinking and inaction. Whatever the reason, the focus on software, processes, and organizational change is not enough.

You and I and everyone we know, our children and their children, are part of this change. We need to learn and adapt. The tools exist. The processes are available. We need the will and knowledge to understand that each of us has the ability and resources to be important to the future. We are no longer a station on an assembly line. We need not be assessed and categorized in kindergarten and then pushed in lockstep through the education system. This is the age of the technology-empowered individual.

We need to lead the change. The change makes strategic thinkers, collaborators, and orchestrators more vital than ever before. Leadership at this level requires an understanding of the historic context, tied to how our planet works today. Leadership requires a strategic understanding of how we could, and should, work. We need a clear vision and ability to find positive solutions to difficult situations.

Key to managing this change is the ability to bring people from all perspectives together to achieve significantly more. Leaders need creativity and collaboration skills to get the best from complex teams.

Industry pundits have estimated that more than 10 million construction professionals need training to integrate technology issues and practices into their work. These professionals find it difficult to get answers from the sales hype and disinformation. Close behind them are millions of young people that must find innovative and compelling ways to combine technology into their lives to build a better tomorrow. We then need to add to that group homeowners, tenants, shopkeepers, doctors, lawyers, and everyone else in our world. Educating and changing the way that people look at the built environment is a daunting task, yet it must be done, because right now the built environment is too expensive and too extravagant to be sustainable.

If the built environment only included design and construction of projects, perhaps the traditional approach to education could be refined to improve quality and value. But the project-focused use of information modeling is only a small slice of the whole; the built environment is significantly larger. Technology is pushing society toward integrating all parts of our world. The realization is growing that, without this integration, much of the discussion about sustainability, zero energy, and conservation is moot. People see, use, and understand integrated processes on the Internet. They buy things, they make reservations, they interact with their friends and colleagues, and they do a myriad of other things. The built environment can be handled much the same way. We are beginning to feel the pressure.

We need to figure out how to involve everyone in the process. To handle the pressures now developing, research organizations and academia must be become more integrated with the rest of the world. We urgently need theoretical research to clarify how both professionals and the public will use and interact with new tools and processes. Applied research that models how groups and large-scale collaborations will use the tools, processes, and systems is essential. We also need case studies, test cases, and real-world trials to convince the skeptics.

We need to close the gap between innovation and education delivery. Finding ways to move the innovations taking place in industry, into the classroom needs to occur at what may seem like the speed of light. Slow adoption and linear, tradition bound educational delivery systems must be replaced with systems that reward those that more closely connect what is being taught with what is happening in the real-world.

The scale of the crisis creates tremendous opportunities. High-performing teams, emotional intelligence, information models, model servers, and integrated systems are the essence of the solution. People using their emotions effectively leverage the power of teams. Teaching people to use their cognitive abilities is well entrenched in our educational system. Analytic thinking, conceptual thinking, and information seeking are the subject of various educational programs. Education for emotional intelligence skills is far behind. Emotional intelligence helps people to engage others. Emotional intelligence is what builds influence, drives proactive behaviors, fosters concern for others, and builds enduring relationships. Emotional intelligence is the basis for success in the built environment of the future. Without the motivation, influence, self-confidence, teamwork, awareness, empathy, and flexibility that defines emotional awareness, information models and collaborative decision-making systems will always be sub-optimized.

For many years, specialists have basically worked in isolation. Their domains are now beginning to intersect in the larger conceptual framework of the built environment. Professionals are finding that geographic information, facility information, utility information, operations information, business information, political information, sustainability information, and virtually every other form of information are intertwining. The domains that each of these professionals "controlled" are becoming blended. The rise of new professions has started. The barriers between disciplines are slipping away.

In a perfect world, school systems would quickly adapt to this new reality. Course content and delivery mechanisms would change. Interdisciplinary, collaborative skills focused on society's narrative of the future would be the norm. Unfortunately, legacy mindsets and accreditation systems are unlikely to be able change at the pace required to keep up with the revolution that is upon us. Likely, the changes will only take place when we reach the point that the old way seems naive to the general public. Only when most people see that the current system is inefficient and ineffective will the change happen. By then, it will be too late. It is essential that each of us takes responsibility for his or her personal development in this environment. Understanding yourself and planning your journey through the system is more urgent than ever before. People with deep knowledge and broad interests must lead this revolution. You can thrive and succeed in this environment; success comes from planning and producing. Wait for no one. Just do it.

Pete Jarvi, Gary Boyle, and Fred Boyd illustrate the fact that people can develop competence and become "T-shaped" individuals through multiple routes. There is no single, "best" way to learn about information modeling and interconnected systems. There is no "magic potion" that will change everyone's way of looking at the world. Each of us must prepare our own way. That is why this book focuses on design futures detailing how things may look from many different perspectives. The built environment is all-encompassing and touches everything that people do. The complexity can be overwhelming. Fortunately, there are threads that tie everything together. When you see the power and possibilities, you can begin to prepare for what to do.

COMMUNICATE

> The man who insists on seeing with perfect clearness before he decides, never decides.
> —Henri-Frédéric Amiel

The more people struggle to maintain the status quo, the more problems they cause. Business as usual may defer the pain, but at what cost? Too many mistakes have been made by well-intentioned people cloaking themselves in the mantle of sustainability. They spend too many resources in attempts to make warped systems work for the future—usually for systems that never achieved their original goals, for systems that will not work in the future no matter how much time and money is spent trying to fix the flaws. Patchwork solutions designed to enhance outmoded and faulty systems rarely work. They cost too much and give too little.

As a society, we need to look at our world with a fresh set of eyes. We must begin to transcend the artificial limitations that surround us. We must move beyond those things and places that we find most comfortable to become lifelong learners. The built environment is a system made up of systems. Remarkable things happen when we learn to embrace the unique dynamics of these systems. We must find new solutions, ones that achieve the desired results economically and efficiently.

The world has shifted. No longer is "take what we make," a viable strategy. Now we must understand and respond, delighting others with our solutions. We are no longer in a world of semiskilled workers on the assembly line. Knowledge creation and flat organizations enable our talents and energies. We coordinate by dynamically linking our expertise to the requirements of others. Our values foster innovation and growth. Economic value and efficiency are byproducts. Top-down communications are replaced by conversations and problem solving. The shift focused us on the fact that no single, painless fix will solve today's economic, social, or political problems.

The world is complex and chaotic. The complexity of systems has reached a stage where individual action is not enough. The sheer volume of data and interrelationships is hard to understand. It is a mammoth task to find global solutions to the problems. Every day it becomes more difficult to respond to new needs. Proven technology exists to enable people to respond to this complexity, yet nearly everyone responds to this situation the same way, using last generation approaches.

They find complex and difficult solutions. The complex tools they produce are not always the best way to solve complex problems. Complex solutions marginalize people. People do not have the time, the interest, or the resources to understand the complexity. Most people want the tools and processes to be simple. Easy, clear, and straightforward-to-use technology is one way to remove people's fears and objections and to enable them to change.

This is one of the key reasons sites such as Google+, Facebook, and Expedia became popular. They are easy to understand, simple to use, and mask the complexity. They are better ways to succeed in the world of tomorrow than trying to force complexity on people. They overcome the resistance to change, and they are sustainable because they allow the range of communication paradigms. One-to-one, one-to-many, and many-to-many are available to those using the systems.

Tools in the built environment can use a similar approach. Using easy-to-understand-and -master tools, we can create, manage, and integrate high-performance and uncomplicated technology in the built environment. We can develop collaboration tools that reflect the best of social networking. We can make everyone part of the team and promote active participation. We know that it is possible because it has been done in BIMStorms.

Detailed design and construction make up a small percentage of the built environment, yet they receive the lion's share of the attention. Design and construction are the subject of media and politicians. They represent much of the sex appeal and romance in the system. They are essential. They need feature-rich tools and expert applications. Yet most people are not directly involved in design and construction.

In order to reduce the issues in the built environment, we cannot focus on design and construction. A much larger percentage of the built world involves real estate, planning, operations and maintenance, and other functions. These are the places where the vast majority of people interact with the built environment. These people need easy-to-use solutions to complex problems.

Continuing as usual is not a solution. The speed and extent of change has accelerated to the point that traditional approaches no longer suffice. Creating ever-more-complex and feature-rich tools does not solve the problem for most people. There are better and more efficient ways to succeed in the world of tomorrow.

THE STORM

4. Next we look at Cork Point, a unique undertaking that can be accessed via water, air, and road. At Cork Point, a group of savvy individuals have decided to use their passion to develop new and better ways to manage facilities to be sustainable. This design future revolves around a forward-thinking health-care organization that is faced with all of today's issues. They are using technology and new ways of working that show how people can use information to nurture and support the community, in a world of economic and regulatory constraints.

A few details to set the stage:

Cork Point sits on a low-lying peninsula that is becoming intensively developed, with thousands of residents. They also manage remote cottages for those who want to live elsewhere, but want to be served by Cork Point's systems.

Cork Point is located in Crisfield, on Maryland's Eastern Shore. Crisfield once had the second largest population of any city in the entire state of Maryland. Cork Point is the largest employer in Crisfield. Known as the "Seafood Capital of the World," Crisfield is famous for its skipjacks, soft crabs, and oysters. The oyster population decreased significantly as water quality in the Chesapeake Bay deteriorated. Crisfield slipped into decline. The town's famed watermen could no longer support themselves by fishing alone.

Crisfield's downtown is literally built atop oyster shells. It is, therefore, extremely small. Built in a floodplain, the town covers only three square miles, 53 percent dry and 47 percent underwater. The town is surrounded by salt marshes; the areas flood during times of high tides, storms, and hurricanes.

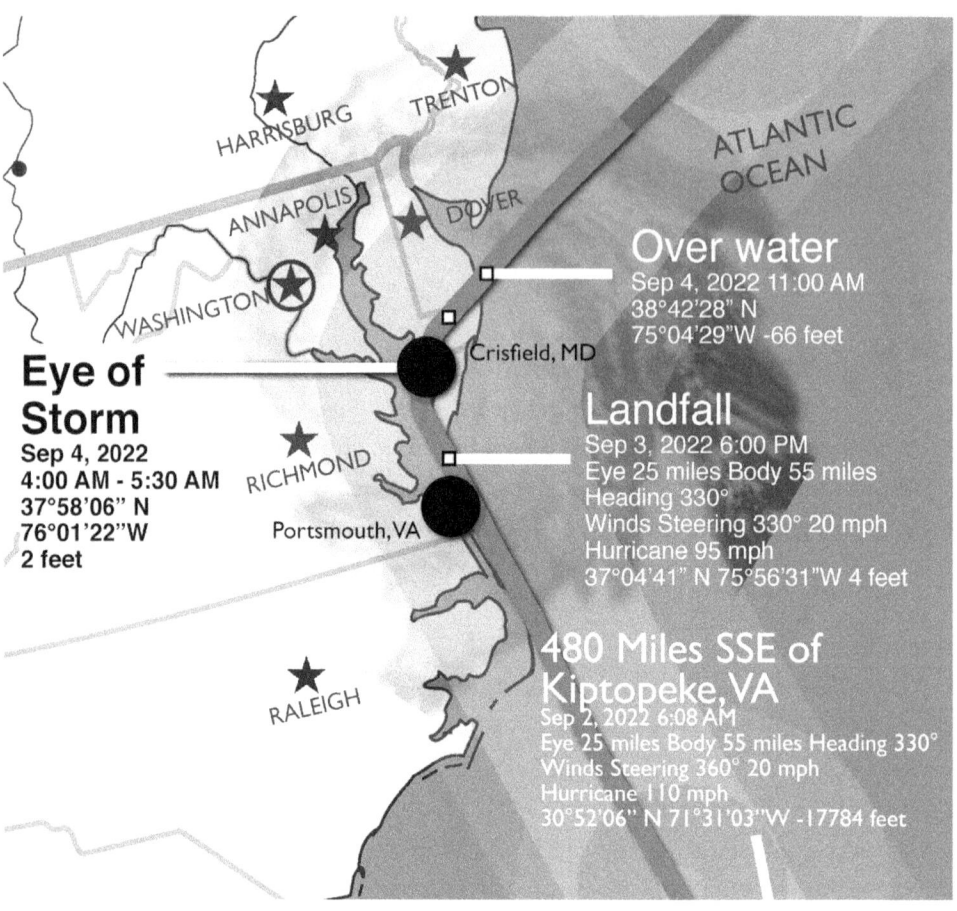

Hurricane Edgar tracks over Norfolk, VA and heads directly up the center of the Chesapeake Bay, turning abruptly northeast near Smith Island, MD. 37° 58' 06" N 76° 1' 22"

EDGAR IS COMING
KIPTOPEKE, VIRGINIA, TO OCEAN CITY, MARYLAND
AUGUST 31 to SEPTEMBER 4, 2022

At 6:00 p.m. eastern standard time on Wednesday, August 31, the National Hurricane Center issued a watch for Hurricane Edgar. The storm was twelve hundred miles southeast of Virginia Beach, Virginia.

At 6:02 p.m. eastern standard time on Thursday, September 1, the National Hurricane Center issued a hurricane warning. The storm was eight hundred miles south-southeast of the Eastern Shore of Virginia. The storm's body radiated sixty miles from the eye and was approaching on a heading of 330° at about eighteen miles per hour. Winds in the Class 3 hurricane were currently at 115 miles per hour, and the eye was thirty-five miles in diameter. The storm was picking up energy from the Gulf Stream.

At 6:08 p.m., September 2, soon after the start of the Labor Day weekend, Edgar was 480 miles southeast of Kiptopeke, Virginia, with winds of 110 miles per hour.

The storm that Eastern Shore residents had feared for so long was upon them. It could not have come at a worse time. Two days before Edgar had been predicted to go well offshore. The storm had suddenly veered. Now, there was an 80 percent chance that the eye would go over Kiptopeke in about forty-eight hours. On its current path, the Eastern Shore of Virginia and Maryland would suffer the worst effects. The right quadrant of the storm was predicted to track right up the Delmarva Peninsula; the additive effects of the hurricane's winds and the storm's steering winds made this the most dangerous place. Adding this to the storm's surge and the increased opportunity for tornadoes, the Eastern Shore faced a disaster.

Not since the Chesapeake Bay Hurricane of 1933 had a major hurricane tracked right up the Chesapeake Bay. The Category 4 Cape Verde storm of August 23, 1933, caused over one billion dollars in damages in today's dollars. The storm killed eighteen and had a record storm surge of 9.8 feet in an area where a five-foot surge was considered a once-in-a-hundred-year event. The damages from the eight-foot surge caused by Hurricane Isabel in 2003 might seem almost trivial in comparison to the damage Edgar would cause. The area was spared the worst of Isabel. Edgar could be a direct hit.

Across the Chesapeake region, the evacuation from low-lying areas had begun. Although much of the area remained rural, focused on agriculture and fishing, things had changed since 1933. Forecasting had improved, and that was a plus. The population had grown steadily. The tourist industry was in full swing. Today there were almost 300,000 visitors in Ocean City, Maryland, alone. The Labor Day celebrations were this weekend.

Rehoboth Beach, Cape Charles, Crisfield, Chincoteague, Ocean City, and other waterfront towns were packed.

Local emergency management decision makers were faced with difficult choices. For these resort communities, Labor Day made up a significant part of the local economy's annual income. Balancing public safety and the economic losses was not the kind of decision that politicians liked to make. These areas were tied into BIMSynergy and actively used the system's decision-making tools. Using geographic and weather information, crowd and traffic management data, and modeling tools, local decision makers were better able to understand their options. Once the choice became clear, they could then use the system to inform the public and guide the evacuation process. Fact-based decision-making tools improved public trust and compliance, simplifying emergency management.

Nowhere on the Delmarva Peninsula did the land rise more than one hundred feet above mean low water. Most areas were much lower. On Virginia's Eastern Shore, much of the land was at an elevation of one to eight feet, with only the backbone of the peninsula reaching into the teens and twenties. The Crisfield, Maryland, area was even lower, with much of the land in the two- to five-foot range. Only when one moved inland toward Princess Anne could one find land above an elevation of ten feet. The Atlantic Ocean beach resorts were little better. The land near the beaches ranged from two to ten feet above mean low water. It was easy to understand the impact of a hurricane storm surge on such low areas.

Most of these areas had only one way in and out. They bottled up at the Chesapeake Bay Bridge and Delaware Route 1. Because of the storm's path, anyone that wanted to escape to the south was already too late. The Chesapeake Bay Bridge Tunnel to Norfolk was closed due to high winds. Even on a tranquil holiday weekend, the Bay Bridge and Route 1 had been known to have twenty-five-mile backups. Moving five hundred thousand visitors and several hundred thousand residents through these choke points would be a nightmare. Even now it was almost too late to leave if you lived, worked, or played in any of the coastal communities.

The old-timers told stories of historic floods and high tides. To them, the bay was ever changing. They had learned to roll with the punches. Those who lived in towns such as Crisfield for their entire lives knew that things would flood regularly. They also knew that just as quickly the water would go away. They felt sympathy for those living in low-lying areas along the Mississippi River. To them, the Mississippi was much more of a problem. When the Mississippi flooded, people were covered up with water for weeks at a time. On the Chesapeake, the water came, but soon enough things always dried out.

The questions were: "What happens when the storm surge covers everything with eight feet of water, even if only for one day? How bad will hurricane-force winds make the problem?"

USCGC NESTOR (WMSM 301)
HAMPTON ROADS, VIRGINIA
SEPTEMBER 3, 2022

At 9:35 a.m. eastern standard time, the USCG Cutter Nestor pushed away from the dock in Portsmouth. Her crew of twelve officers and seventy-six seamen had been recalled at midnight. They were ordered to move the cutter to sea ahead of Hurricane Edgar. At 9:55 a.m., as the first bombs exploded in Portsmouth, the cutter was underway at the mouth of the Elizabeth River, sailing into Hampton Roads en route for the sea buoy outside of the Chesapeake Bay Bridge Tunnel. Upon learning of the bombings, her captain's first instinct was to return to the base to help. His request to return was disapproved by the Maritime Intelligence Fusion Center. Based on the storm's path, the Nestor had to stay on track. The cutter needed to make a quick transit; otherwise they would find themselves stuck in the eye of the hurricane. Three cutters were disabled or worse. The Nestor was a vital asset. Others must handle the on site disaster response.

The storm's path was shaping up to make this storm one of the worst disasters to hit the Chesapeake Bay in almost eighty-nine years. A lot of people needed to be evacuated or sheltered in an extremely short period of time. In the midst of the evacuation, they needed to catch the terrorists. While in transit, the Nestor's crew was helping both to find the terrorists and in storm preparation. They provided weather forecasters with real-time condition information. At the same time, they were scanning to find the aircraft used by the terrorists. Both efforts were essential.

By including information modeling technologies into the cutter's systems, the Coast Guard had taken one more step toward a fully integrated decision-making system. Personnel on the cutter monitored and managed all systems, while directly interfacing with systems both inside and outside of the Coast Guard. Their sensors were tied into the Coast Guard's decision-making system. Accurate information would help law enforcement catch the terrorists. It would also strengthen the emergency response to the hurricane.

Many of the systems reflected the processes that everyone had become familiar with on the Internet of Things. Where a procedure or process could be defined, systems had been created to handle them to guide decision making. Finding a port within cruising range with water that was sufficiently deep and dockage configured to handle the cutter's needs resulted from a single query. Maintenance, repair, and other support services were automatically engaged as systems deteriorated. The system assessed whether the port had sufficient hotel space to accommodate the crew when they arrived. Provisions were ordered based not only upon what had been used, but upon crew preferences. The menu adjusted to accommodate changing personnel and preferences. The system did not eliminate the need for people to interact and decide, but it minimized the tedious and repetitive tasks, allowing personnel to focus on key mission issues.

At 10:28 a.m. eastern standard time, the cutter's radar system picked up an unidentified small aircraft flying low and slow near Tangier Island, Virginia. The information was automatically patched into the operations center's network. Could this be the Piper Comanche used by the terrorists? It looked like a single-engine, low-wing aircraft. The plane was vectoring toward the Salisbury-Wicomico County Regional Airport and would over fly the Crisfield-Somerset County Airport in twelve minutes.

At 10:43 a.m. the plane vanished from radar. It looked like the aircraft had either landed at the tiny Crisfield Airport or crashed somewhere in Somerset County, Maryland.

RESPONSE

Since 9/11, security forces have become more visible, vigilant, and effective. They are well trained, well equipped, and have learned how to respond to new situations. Police officers, firefighters, emergency medical personnel, public works staff, and emergency management leaders are the backbone of the first-responder community.

Effective emergency response requires everyone to work together in real time. As a group, first responders are versatile and trained to adapt to new situations. Traditional first responders often have limited experience in handling significant events in the maritime domain. Bombs exploding on vessels in a key port area are a significant departure from the set of events the usual first responders are trained to handle. Clear communications and the ability to share real-time data are essential.

Leadership is about knowing and using resources. Terrorists who exploit the nature of the maritime environment make it difficult to bring the appropriate resources to bear on the problem. First responders trained to fight fires on land find themselves fighting fires on ships adrift. Emergency medical technicians with experience in helping heart attack victims must manage those with severe burns and chemical exposure. Police officers trained to handle offenders in the urban environment must now identify and capture a much different type of culprit. Where calling for tow trucks is a normal response, now tugboats and marine environmental services must be engaged.

Gaming and disaster simulation are time-tested approaches to preparing emergency responders for new and unexpected conditions. Emergency response leaders must understand all of the factors that surround an event to be able to mobilize the correct response. Some emergency responses can be preplanned and tested. Terrorist threats create unique situations that need the support of those who are not usually first responders.

Defining the scope of the problem, matching needs to available expertise, and engaging the right people to manage the emergency is critical. The system must accommodate and integrate new experts without requiring everyone to be in the same room. Collaborative, highly responsive, and open systems are needed to ensure success in this environment. In the fast-paced and chaotic world of emergency response, data and information rule.

Using data from a central repository that archives everything, emergency response leaders link information that once could not be linked to better understand and leverage available resources. Using the same information that supports building, business operations, maritime conditions, and other things that influence the built environment, they reach high levels of situational awareness, fostering real-time, fact-based decisions.

SITUATIONAL AWARENESS

At noon, Pete Jarvi logged into CGSysOps and learned that the terrorists were captured in two separate actions. Two suspects were captured by the Maryland State Police at 11:08 a.m. The second set of suspects were captured by Coast Guard personnel and the Maryland Natural Resources Police at 11:45 a.m. Reports said that the terrorists were scared out of their wits after landing at the Crisfield airport. They had no idea how isolated it truly was. When they scouted the scene they did not imagine how dangerous it would be to land there with a hurricane nearby.

That part of the reaction was complete. Pete could now turn his attention to helping to organize the first responders near the harbor and on the hurricane. CGSysOps itself sustained only minor damage from the bombs. All systems appeared to be functioning, with the exception of sensors and cameras around the dock area. Other buildings, the docks, and three cutters were not so lucky.

Pete's system managed continuous live data feeds. The rules-based processes showed live data maps for critical issues. With his system set to watch recovery operations and the storm, most of the facts that he was seeing related to those activities. On one monitor, Pete saw a 3-D representation of the areas expected to be over-washed as the hurricane headed up the bay. He had a hard time believing how much land area would be fully covered in water in the next few hours.

The system was set to answer questions like, "How will the hospital in Crisfield be affected by the hurricane? What damage can we expect to the hospital, if the hurricane's winds are ninety-five miles per hour and the storm surge is eight feet? What will change if the winds are 120 miles per hour, and the surge is ten feet? What will be the impact on Calvert Cliffs Nuclear Power Plant?"

By changing the triggering parameters for the analysis, he was able to evaluate different scenarios. Even the best case looked to be unusually severe. Pete told the system to format the five most likely futures. The weather service would get Pete's scenarios out to decision makers, as part of the evacuation and emergency planning process. Local emergency management systems were keeping track of residents and visitors alike as they got out of the way of the hurricane. When Pete's scenarios were overlaid on the evacuation maps, the areas of greatest concern would clearly pop up.

Live camera feeds filled most of the screen. Fortunately, most of the monitoring cameras had survived the blast. In the upper right-hand corner of Pete's second screen, he saw a real-time assessment of the bomb damage, overlaid by the BIM-Bomb tool. Based on the debris field and damage to structures, the system estimated that each of the improvised devices was the equivalent of about a hundred pounds of TNT. In the lower right-hand corner, Pete could see the current location of every response vehicle and first responder. As the first responders treated and identified the victims, they were popping up, as well. Thirty-two dead and one hundred twenty injured were showing on the system now, and the numbers continued to grow.

One of the first things that came from the BIMSynergy installation was the ability to achieve a high level of situational awareness, even before personnel arrival on site. The incident command-view was mirrored in the lower-left portion of Pete's screen. Each of the commanders could see the same information as Pete. Without the ability to keep track of their personnel and quickly identify shutoffs and other essential items, their jobs would be much more difficult. Good old-fashioned command and control and the new integrated systems had meshed to make significant improvements in this area. Commanders knew where their people were located. They knew where and how to use them to solve problems while minimizing risk.

At 12:35 p.m. eastern standard time, the Nestor cleared the sea buoy and continued eastward on a course of 87° magnetic. Four hours on this heading would put the cutter a hundred miles east of the storm's outer rain bands. The cutter's information systems showed a two-hour contingency. They would be dealing with tropical storm force winds the entire time, but this new cutter could handle that and a lot more.

Hurricane Edgar was now predicted to make landfall at Kiptopeke, Virginia, at about 6:00 p.m. eastern standard time. The National Weather Service was predicting that the hurricane's eye would be twenty-five miles in diameter and the body would extend fifty-five miles beyond at that time. Storm winds of ninety-five miles per hour and steering winds at twenty miles per hour were predicted at landfall. In the storm's right quadrant, the Delmarva Peninsula would see winds in excess of 115 miles per hour.

OVERCOME OBSTACLES
PORTSMOUTH, VIRGINIA AND DELMARVA PENINSULA
SEPTEMBER 4, 2022

Changing the status quo to make CGSysOps a reality was difficult. Operations centers were traditionally the domain of emergency response, a single place where leaders gathered to handle a crisis. Busy, noisy, and chaotic best described a normal crisis management operations center; everyone came together in one place to make decisions and to mobilize response. CGSysOps was designed to work in much the same way. The key difference was that the place where leaders met was now in the cloud. Social networking systems, tightly integrated web conference systems, BIMSynergy, and rules-based decision-making tools worked together to engage decision makers, wherever they were at the time. Real-time collaboration tools provided emergency management leaders greater situational awareness. Collaboration tools enabled increased interaction with others.

Emergency management had always been a team sport requiring high levels of collaboration. Emergency management was about solving problems. It was about addressing complex security and public safety needs. It was about timely responses, and being right when decisions were made. To achieve these goals, decision-making tools had to be present at all levels. High-level situational awareness required access to information from various sources. As had always been the case, government, emergency management, public safety, and physical security professionals needed to be involved. The new factor was the involvement of many other professionals. As crises had become more complex and unique, the teams had grown in size, and different types of players had been added. Flexibility and adaptability were key.

At 12:00 a.m. eastern standard time, hurricane Edgar's back edge passed Kiptopeke. The storm's eye was now twenty miles in diameter. The body extended an additional fifty miles. The storm was contracting. The track was shifting to 30°, and the storm was moving at twenty-five miles an hour. The hurricanes winds were averaging ninety miles per hour.

CGSysOps enabled Pete to work with data from everywhere. He could understand the hurricane and its effects in a big world situation. Pete zoomed out to see the course and scope of the storm. He zoomed in to analyze both the areas currently affected by the storm surge, and those predicted to be affected. He published his analysis for those in the storm's path, to guide their actions. He zoomed in further to see the damages to the areas where the storm had already passed. He accessed the transportation network, interconnected with the storm effects analysis, set triggers for numbers of people, added the status of significant bridges, such as the Chesapeake Bay Bridge, and created a mash-up that clearly showed the locations of highest risk. This information was directly fed to emergency management leaders so that they could allocate resources appropriately.

Unworkable options were eliminated before the first responders spent time on unproductive tasks. Pete no longer worked in isolation from anything or anyone; his vision of the problem was not limited to the local context. Business requirements directly affected his analysis. He knew where, when, and how decisions affected others. He knew how things impacted on the environment and other resources, usually before the actions required by the decision were completed.

He knew that he was using technology in a predictive mode; he knew about "black swans," that extreme outlier events might occur; he knew that no prediction was guaranteed. He also knew that his decisions were better informed, and more often right than not. No prediction was perfect, but this was as close as you got. When Pete analyzed a situation, his results were repeatable and much more accurate, since he was working with real-world information, not assumptions, guesses, or opinions.

The front edge of the storm hit Crisfield, Maryland, at 2:00 a.m. The storm was moving at twenty miles per hour on a heading of 30°. Winds had dropped to seventy-five miles per hour. The eye was predicted to pass just to the west of town from 4:00 to 5:30 a.m. High tide was predicted to occur at 4:30 a.m. Based on the conditions in the towns south of Crisfield, the storm's surge was predicted to be about nine feet. Mean high water level in Crisfield was at elevation 2.2 feet. A storm surge of 5.8 feet was considered to be a hundred-year event. Much of the land in the town was at an elevation of two to four feet. The whole town could be under seven to nine feet of water.

In dealing with the catastrophic effects of Hurricane Katrina in New Orleans, the Coast Guard had learned how to minimize damage and expedite recovery from storm events. The integrated systems at work in CGSysOps allowed Pete to assess the human and economic consequences in the affected area. He could calculate the effects to local, national, and international interests. Pete had been working since noon the previous day to develop and implement emergency procedures that would ensure continuity of operations and essential public services. He had completed contingency plans for getting commercial activities back in business as soon as possible.

The storm's course had made McCready Hospital in Crisfield into one of Pete's foremost concerns. The system showed the hospital's first floor to be at an elevation of five and a half feet. Only those activities housed above a floor elevation of eleven would not be flooded. The system predicted that the hospital would lose all first floor functions. When

Pete added the wind and wave effects to the hospital's facility condition index, the system predicted near total destruction.

Six hours ago, Pete posted contingency plans for response, assessment of damages, and recovery of the hospital's systems. The first thing that happened was to completely evacuate everyone. The plans provided for the coordination of public and private sector efforts to bring to bear all necessary assets, including support of civilian authorities. The plan clearly defined how personnel should respond to minimize danger to first responders. Treating the injured, minimizing damage, and quickly reconstituting operations were the first priorities. Every effort had to be made to reduce long-term hazards while getting the hospital back in action as soon as possible. The community would need the hospital to anchor the restoration process.

The plan's goal was to protect life, property, and the environment. The first tasks would be to restore order and essential services while covering social, economic, and political structures. In any catastrophe, residents and first responders alike needed to be aware of outside hazards. The system alerted everyone to the possibility of broken water and sewer mains, dangling power lines, and washouts that might weaken roads and bridge structures.

Edgar passed over Salisbury, Maryland, at 3:30 a.m., the winds continuing to blow at seventy-five miles per hour. As the storm moved totally over the Delmarva Peninsula, the track shifted to 50°.

The sensors on Smith Island sensed the eye of the storm starting at 4:00 a.m. Crisfield felt the full impact of the storm's right quadrant. Sensors showed apparent winds of ninety-five miles per hour and a storm surge of 8.9 feet. Everyone in town had been evacuated to at least Princess Anne. Not one person experienced the winds or flooding in Crisfield or Smith Island. There were no casualties in either place.

The storm moved on after wreaking havoc across the Chesapeake Bay region and Delaware. At 5:00 a.m. eastern standard time, September 4, 2022, Hurricane Edgar was over Ocean City, Maryland. The storm was on a heading of 80°, clocking to 60° after hitting the Atlantic Ocean coastline. With winds of seventy-five miles per hour, the storm was picking up speed as it moved back over the Atlantic. As the storm progressed and faded from the Delmarva Peninsula, it became clear that the ability to access and use emergency systems data had enabled many lives to be saved.

Data from the emergency response system had provided live weather feeds and first responder status throughout the storm. First responder management data was one of the first things managed via BIMSynergy. Aircraft and satellite feeds provided near real-time views of the devastated area. Command decisions were made based on accurate information. These systems had worked well. Because of the evacuation, most people came through with flying colors. There were the normal stress-driven heart attacks, and some people got wet because they just had to have their "hurricane party," but, all in all, the population had come through well. The actions of hundreds of first response personnel made the systems work. Thousands of lives had been saved and immeasurable losses had been averted because of their actions.

The town of Crisfield was not so lucky. Since monitoring systems for buildings were not widely in use, planners had trouble accurately predicting the impact on facilities. Little could be done to prepare the town for the massive storm surge. McCready Hospital was damaged extensively. Things were a mess. Most of the hospital's facilities were not built to withstand this storm. Only the shell of the historic part of the hospital survived. The new nursing home and the replacement hospital built in the late 1970s were totally destroyed. Crisfield and the residences surrounding the hospital were leveled.

Hurricane contingency plans and prepositioned responders were getting the recovery started. The Coast Guard and the Federal Emergency Management Agency were conducting maritime damage and risk assessments. Engineers were surveying the condition of bridges and roads, as well as water and sewerage systems. Emergency services staff were responding as soon as the water receded and it was safe to enter the town. Resources were beginning to arrive from all over the East Coast. Working together, the people of Crisfield would rebuild. Recovery would be a long and arduous process.

THE ART OF CHANGE

5. The Tonight Show's Ed McMahon used to introduce "The Amazing Karnak," a comedy skit where host Johnny Carson acted the part of a reader of crystal balls and psychic of the past, present, and future. He answered "secret" questions that were kept "in a sealed mayonnaise jar on Funk & Wagnall's front porch."

No question was too stupid or obscure for an answer. The results were goofy, offbeat, and sometimes even amusing.

Jump ahead forty years.

You're a facility manager in charge of two million square feet of clinic space in seven locations in three New England states. And it's your job to find Funk & Wagnall's front porch. Seriously.

Faster than you can say, "all-knowing seer of the universe," you can search all of your properties and find the "sealed mayonnaise jar."

MORE THAN A CRYSTAL BALL

Elle knew that she needed more than a crystal ball if she were going to position Cork Point to become more competitive. She realized that the enterprise had to adapt to the ever-changing technological advances in the market, the necessary evil of developing, designing, and constructing new space. She needed a way to make decisions, document them for all to see, and then easy ways to track them during the process.

Her board was objective driven and worshipped metrics; it was in their DNA, and they had in the past confronted questions of performance to goals during and at the end of projects. Did the contractor, architect, and consultants perform as agreed? Were budget and schedule goals achieved? Was the project's scope sufficient for its intended use? Unfortunately, the answer was all too often "no."

Her experience in her last hospital also told her that how she and her team performed in the process was critical to their projects' success. Her internal team dramatically affected delivery and outcomes. She could not control her team solely through plugging people into her organizational chart. She needed tools to make the internal processes and intradepartmental communication clear and easily visualized. Having the right people in place was critical to Cork Point's future.

Paralleling the need for metrics and the right people was the need for reliable tools and processes that everyone could easily use and buy into. The tools needed to be flexible enough to let her team customize reports to adapt to changing needs, while standardizing communications and reporting. Cork Point could not afford the duplication and inefficiencies that were overburdening many in the industry. They could not afford a "locked-in" mindset about solutions.

Traditionally, planning, design, construction, and facility management were entirely different tasks in the life cycle of a building. From the perspective of the building owner, separating these tasks often resulted in additional costs and inefficiencies. The traditional project delivery process was fraught with lack of cooperation and imperfect information sharing. Traditional checks and balances no longer ensured outcomes. The industry had become too disruptive and undependable.

Few architects were managing these concerns for their clients. The ones that did used information models to provide improved early decision-making facts to support client needs. Using rules-based tools, collaborative processes, and commercial off-the-shelf technologies, their approach created sustainable solutions for their clients.

Pioneers were producing systems that allowed the use of rules-based systems in the information modeling environment. These systems were rapidly developing and were able to do things that were once only dreams. These savvy architects were starting to capitalize on the bookends of regular practice. They were providing opportunities that occurred outside of the "normal" design process and after construction. Often the opportunities were not planned and came from what could be seen as "downstream" use of the data they generated. These unplanned and unexpected benefits allowed their clients to do more and to take advantage of opportunities that might otherwise never have been possible.

Elle had learned the hard way that capital planning decisions made without clear facts were fraught with peril in any fast-paced environment. With this kind of information model, she could dramatically reduce waste due to pursuing the wrong direction, misallocation of funds, and other decision-making errors. Cork Point and the community could see direct financial and time savings. Helping the community and her staff to implement life cycle information models to improve decision making was likely to create new revenue streams. It would give Cork Point the potential to become more valuable to their clients and the world.

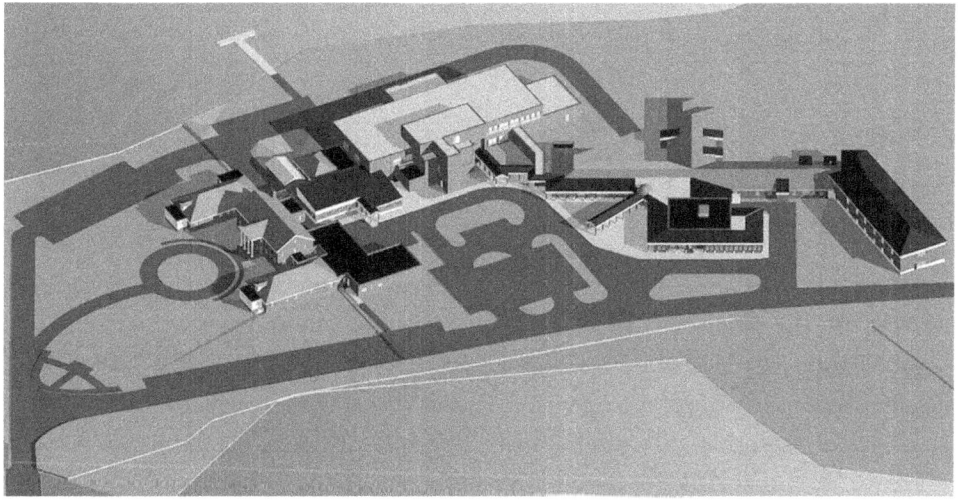

The Little Annemessex River and Daugherty Creek site of what was McCready Hospital. The hospital became the center of Cork Point after Hurricane Edgar. 37° 59' 49" N 75° 51' 10" W

GET IN THE BOX
CORK POINT, CRISFIELD, MARYLAND
JUNE 3, 2024

Elle's last hospital had been the poster child for the command-and-control-based organization. She knew that, at Cork Point, she had to do something else in order to be successful. A tone of openness and a willingness to come to the table with free ideas was the cornerstone. Cork Point had to focus on what their customers wanted. They needed to be able to act and plan on the fly. The organization had to have the tools to make reasonable and effective decisions early in the planning process. It needed to become a culture of collaboration with a "flat" hierarchy that valued the contributions and expertise of all. Cork Point needed to be adept at mainstreaming operations and professional relationships. Everything they did had to be built on trust and respect for colleagues. Team members must be highly collaborative and share risks and rewards equitably.

Follow this tag to learn more about integrated practice at http://4sitesystems.com/iofthestorm/?page_id=888

Collaborative ways of working and integrated practices had become common in many practice settings. Health care, accounting, information technology, and the construction industry embraced these practices, at least in theory. Many of the blog posts and other writings on the Internet addressed how different industries were adapting integrated practices.

As Elle conducted her research, doing due diligence on her Cork Point idea, this was one of the threads that she tracked. After several months of following the integrated practice thread, Elle began to see patterns. The patterns were intriguing and offered insights into where integrated practice was headed. The pattern showed that integrated practice was becoming "stovepiped." After spending time and energy to connect different departments and systems within health care, they still did not get it. The industrial era hierarchal style was difficult to change, especially when one was trying to integrate multiple industries and professions.

Since facilities were so vital to the hospital's success, Elle needed to find a way to make sure that everyone got involved. Her research seemed to show that her medical staff might not be a problem, but she was not so sure about her architects and contractors.

Integrated practice was clearly not created by and was not unique to health care. It was a way to a goal, a process, not an end goal. The patterns seemed to be saying that other industries were actively involved in their own integrated practice implementation, with health care in the lead. Perhaps this was because of the complexity and cost of health care.

It may also have had something to do with privacy issues and the difficulties the physicians encountered in managing their practices in an insurance company-driven business. Whatever the case, Elle needed everyone on her team—health-care professionals, planners, architects, and contractors—to embrace integrated practice. They all had to begin to work like an integrated team.

Connecting all aspects of Cork Point would give the organization the ability to serve the community through technology. Technology would remain in the background, but form the foundation for a people-friendly way of working that valued community and rewarded competence. The process would focus on the most economical solutions to reaching the community's goals—not always the cheapest solution, but always the most cost-effective solution that delivered what was needed, when and where it was needed. The system must never forget that people were the focus, not technology.

To get the most cost-effective solution, Cork Point had to have access to information. The information needed to be managed in ways that kept the data fresh and accurate. Taking this information, making connections between different databases, and then using the data for the benefit of the community was the goal.

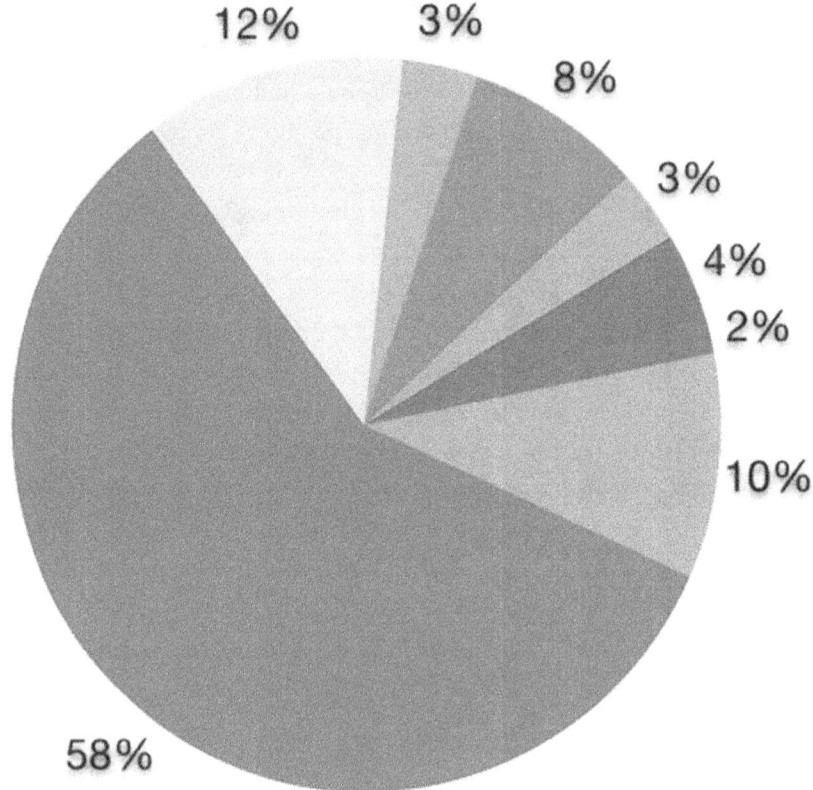

- meditation/religion
- social work/education
- art/music
- coaching/sports
- writing/publishing/IT
- law/general business/accounting
- health/science
- construction industry

Elle decided to track and plot how often the term "integrated practice" turned up each day on the Internet, by profession. After several months of tracking, the results showed that health care and science made up a total of 58 percent of the posts online. Legal, the arts, sports, meditation, social work, education, accounting, writing, and IT accounted for an additional 30 percent. Construction industry alerts accounted for only 12 percent. It was riveting that fully 88 percent of the postings for integrated practice have little or nothing to do with design and construction. From what Elle had been hearing from her architects, their industry was leading this charge. Evidently, their perceptions were not true.

As facilities were planned and built, information models supported integrated management and design-build strategies. Established teams, managed within the virtual enterprise, integrated with the enterprise-wide approach at Cork Point. Proven delivery systems, supported by technology, efficiently delivered projects that integrated with enterprise systems. Capital planning was connected to facility planning, was connected to architectural design, was connected to construction, was connected to business planning, was connected to health-care planning, was connected to facilities management, was connected to operations, was connected to staffing, was connected to medical equipment, was connected to....

In the integrated enterprise, data is more valuable than facilities. By capturing the data in everything we do, we build this value. This value occurs over the life of an asset. With the data, we can be more efficient. We can analyze conditions and react before crisis. We can be better stewards of our world. Because of these facts, we look at everything as an enterprise asset. Projects are limited in duration. They are not long-term or sustainable, unless they are integrated into the enterprise and become assets.

From conception, every asset is modeled. The goal is to, over the life of an asset, achieve virtual parity between the information and the real world. At some point in every asset's life, the information closely follows the reality. At this level, projections and decisions become extremely accurate. At this point one can literally create a project in the computer before fabrication, to see and experience each and every part and activity involved.

It may seem counterintuitive to some, but the process of modeling assets over their life actually saves significant amounts of money, especially when the assets are archived in BIMSynergy. This process is not possible when data is saved on file servers, hard drives as files, or on other storage media. The instant a file is saved, your data begins to rot, and has rapidly diminishing value. All of your work up to that point is effectively wasted. Only by maintaining "live" data do the benefits of asset management actually happen.

Every effort must start somewhere. At Cork Point, we started by defining an asset's needs and building a virtual box that holds all of the parts needed to deliver the required outcomes. The information in these virtual boxes can be monitored and assessed from the time that the idea is formed directly through the operation and maintenance of the asset. The virtual box is, in this case, a scheme in the Onuma System. The virtual box is housed in BIMSynergy.

The box holds many things. The box contains program costs for use in managing enterprise capital resources. As the work progresses, the program costs become the constraint about which outcomes are managed. The box contains the definition of everything known and all decisions made about the asset. Initially, everything is highly conceptual. Most of the information may be the result of the application of rules of thumb and speculation. This is to be expected. By documenting ideas toward your goal, adding those things that are known at the time and allowing the system to measure, analyze, and calculate, you create a framework. The scheme gives you the ability to determine how close you are to solving a problem or filling a need. Most people think that it is easier to make decisions with clear information rather than with anecdote. Early decisions made based on minimal information lead to error and often take projects down the wrong path.

BLANK SLATE

> ...to learn something at first feels like losing something.
> — George Bernard Shaw

After the devastation from Hurricane Edgar in 2022, McCready Hospital decided to rebuild, embracing new ways of delivering health care and supporting the community. The hurricane offered McCready an unparalleled opportunity. The hospital had to be rebuilt, almost from scratch. Federal disaster assistance and community contributions made the hospital's rebirth possible. Open-standard planning tools allowed the community to become involved in defining how the change would occur. Sophisticated communications and marketing enabled the community to understand that continuing to adhere to the traditional approach was no longer viable. There were serious problems with business as usual. The system was no longer working. Once the community understood, they said, "Enough is enough."

After experiencing the same type of extreme weather event that happened in New Orleans with Hurricane Katrina, the community knew that the hospital needed to become more resilient. A hospital that is closed and cannot provide essential medical and public health services in a crisis is not doing its job. The rebuilt hospital needed to move beyond saving lives to improving health while restoring ecosystems and improving the community.

This was an opportunity to start with a blank slate. After years of struggle with traditional medical practice, Dr. Elaina Bagayoko-Smith, Elle to those who knew her, learned what the health-care business could do to physicians and patients alike. Elle overcame the objections of self-serving board of directors members, regulators, and those who could not tolerate change of any type. It helped that health care was in the throes of disruptive decentralization. No longer was the high technology medical center, optimized for disease treatment, the best option. It was now feasible to handle most health-care requirements in low-impact, low-energy settings in the home or community.

It is easy for people to forget that much of what we take for granted now was revolutionary at one time. The way that we live today did not happen by accident. Today's approach came about because creative people applied creative ideas to solve problems. They took risks to achieve results and make the world a better place. Elle and the people of Crisfield were doing the same thing.

As Elle studied the post-WWII years, she learned of the thinking of Buckminster Fuller and Alvin Toffler, who envisioned many of today's sustainable systems. During the same period, Caudill Rowlett Scott and George Heery pioneered processes that became the multidisciplinary design process in health care. Eliyahu Goldratt and others defined systems for managing and controlling complex organizations. By the mid-1980s, commercial software to create what were now known as information models was in productive use. The tools and processes were available.

A strategic vision, systems thinking, and a willingness to change were all that was missing. When Elle looked at the seeds planted in the last half of the twentieth century, she realized that much of what these visionaries theorized was the best way to proceed. Many of their ideas seemed obvious. The ideas informed Elle's approach and provided pointers to "next practices" and implementation strategies. They offered a framework that would allow Elle and the hospital to reverse the declines in productivity that others experienced when building new facilities. By integrating the community, health care, design, construction, and all other parts of the hospital's business, Elle created Cork Point.

Even in this context, the change was not easy. Traditional hospitals were designed to care for the sick. Highly complex procedures and comprehensive inpatient care facilities were no longer the best approach, although the need for those services would never vanish. "Sick care" was not the focus of health care for the future. Acute care services could be handled in more traditional facilities than Cork Point. Cork Point's focus was different. Cork Point was setting the pace for people-centered health care, focused on wellness.

Renewable energy systems and on-site water treatment and storage were two of the strategies embraced in the new Cork Point. Cork Point would become an integrated part of the community. They would sponsor farmers' markets and exercise and wellness programs. They would become the model for moving away from fast food and sedentary lifestyles. Cork Point would be positioned to participate in all aspects of community life.

The change was happening, like it or not. To many, change was a threat. Often, the first response was to resist. The more changes one faced, the more one pushed back. Shifting McCready Hospital from a traditional rural hospital with an attached clinic and nursing facility into a life cycle community support network required change at all levels. Shifting the culture was the biggest challenge for most people to accept. Historically, over 75 percent of cultural change efforts fail. Even with a compelling rationale, dedicated leaders, and high levels of enthusiasm, changes in culture can fail before the transformation reaches its potential. Changing to a sustainable health-care model required more than technology, because cultural change was about people—not about technology.

When people did most work by hand, it was relatively easy to fix problems. As technological innovation accelerated, it became harder and harder to make systemic changes. There were problems of poor execution and poor cost controls. Some recognized that traditional processes were deteriorating. Productivity was declining. Industry studies showed that 30 percent of the resources spent on built environment processes was wasted.

As society began to embrace technology, the speed and magnitude of change increased significantly. Many lacked the resources to respond to the change. Vendors were using tools to advance their self-interests, rather than doing things to serve their clients and the end user. Managers were attempting to use "nonintegrated" communication and collaboration tools to solve the problems, with little success. Systems became more complex than ever before. The sheer number of new products became difficult to understand. Every day it became more difficult to respond to new needs.

In today's world, people have new and unexpected needs. New systems that satisfy these needs are the answer. Systems that allow real-time collaboration, better sharing of facts, and increased community participation are essential. Knowing how to apply and use collaborative technologies to achieve high-performance solutions creates the ultimate sustainable system. A cultural change requires leaders who are passionately committed to growth and excellence.

Cultural change affects everyone. The Internet constantly changes and evolves as people find new needs and uses. The health-care business is much the same. People need to jump in and start using integrated systems to achieve the full potential and to engage the community. The best thing—and maybe the only thing—we can do to prepare ourselves for the future is to learn how to change. And, each of us must lead the way!

HEALTH CARE CHALLENGED

Overcoming health-care issues was a challenge, but Elle was up to it. She found an approach that allowed her to explore options and build systems tailored to community needs. The process engaged everyone and let Elle try out any idea, no matter how silly it might seem, with just a little effort. The people who created the system called it "having virtual train wrecks."

The health-care business had become massive and unwieldy. It lacked the ability to adapt. The problems were too complex, too messy, and too expensive. Many could not afford the care. Hospitals, especially in rural communities, could not get enough medical practitioners. They faced transportation and supply chain problems. Often hospitals were the largest employer in the community, the largest consumer of resources, and one of the most intense users of energy.

The built environment consumes most of our resources. With the planet heating up and fuel becoming ever scarcer, Elle knew that Cork Point must do something now. They had the tools to analyze consequences and change trajectories. The community saw it as their responsibility to promote sustainability not only in design, but across the entire community. They knew that they must take action. There was no time to wait.

Before coming to Cork Point, design and construction were generally far down on Elle's list of priorities. As a physician, facilities were not a significant concern for Elle. Each project posed a new set of problems. Cost overruns, delays, design errors, and shortfalls were all possible disasters from her perspective. The potential for harm to workers or visitors was always there. Each project was a new learning experience.

From a health-care perspective, construction was more of a threat than a benefit. Elle was not in the construction business, she was in the healthcare business, and would rather not have to deal with design and construction problems. New and renovated facilities were needed to remain competitive and to attract both physicians and patients. For the three or four years that a hospital was engaged with creating a new facility, the building seemed to get the top priorities. But that did not make the process any more enjoyable or beneficial to Elle's health-care objectives.

From the perspective of the health-care administrator, Elle would always prefer to invest in the next generation of open MRI or a new linear accelerator. New medical equipment, new services, improved information technology, and electronic medical records could all be used to tell the hospital's story on radio and TV. Building technology was not seen as a good investment. People looking for the best in health care understood the need for medical technology; construction technology did not have the same impact.

Sustainability, aesthetics, integrated project delivery, and building information modeling did not seem serious to those whom Elle represented. They did not engage donors, and generally made a remarkably small effect on the hospital's total budget. Small savings on the hospital's bond rates or a reduction in worker's compensation expenses usually saved much more money than the savings predicted by the architect during the design process, especially from a near-term perspective. That might be changing.

In the late 1970s and early 1980s, the infrastructure to support new diagnostic medical equipment drove health-care facilities. By the mid-1980s, the issue began to move toward health care and consumer needs. The hospital's brand became the driver. Consumer choice and patient-centered care took over in the late 1980s and early 1990s. Then emerged more accountable delivery models. Clinical safety was the driver in the late 1990s. Safer health-care delivery gave way to evidence-based design around the turn of the century. Aligning solutions with strategic outcomes and accountability took hold. Health-care reform brought us productive and effective models of care. Medical knowledge was available to all. Wellness and prevention drove reimbursement. Services focused on best helping patients. Integrated teams spanned the globe.

Follow this tag to learn more about changing healthcare at http://4sitesystems.com/iofthestorm/?page_id=984

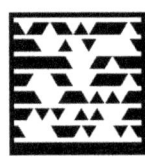

Yet even with this perspective, Elle knew that she needed to look at the overall system differently. People were frustrated and cynical about the future of health care. Hospitals were not optimized for the management of twenty-first-century chronic diseases. Most hospitals were not designed for health promotion or disease prevention. This was beginning to change, yet most hospitals were designed for disease care. The world had changed; so must health care.

HEALTHY SYSTEMS

As Elle and her board explored how to transform the hospital, they saw patterns that highlighted serious issues about how different industries saw and understood business integration. They found that health-care organizations of all kinds (doctors, dentists, and chiropractors especially) were moving to integrated practice technologies. Lawyers, accountants, baseball teams, meditation gurus, social workers, writers, artists, and IT professionals were moving as well. The patterns seemed to show that far fewer architects and contractors were taking the plunge.

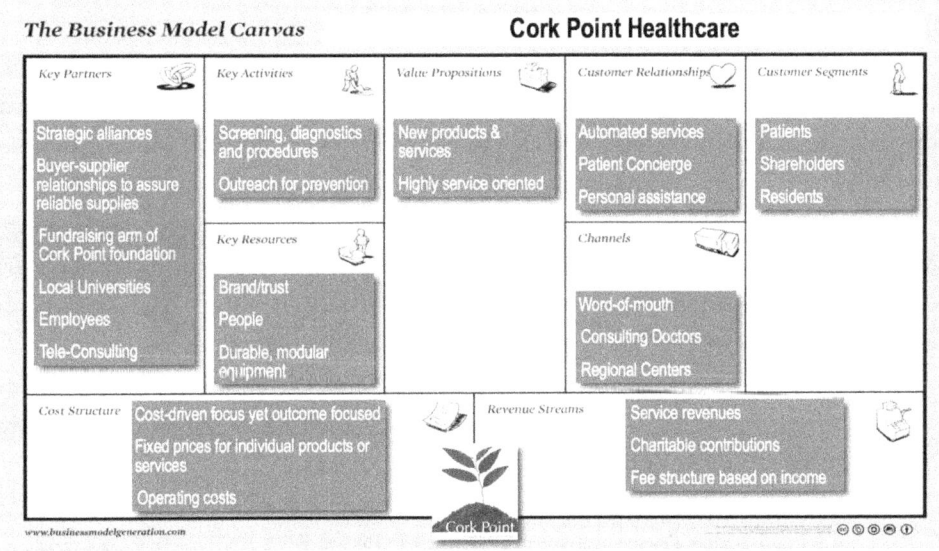

By closely following what was happening in other industries, Elle and Cork Point found their own path toward integrating health care into the community. By defining the rules that would result in the outcomes that they wanted to get, the organization could accommodate change at lightning speed. Elle's team created reliable information designed to get the job done and to reduce errors. Everything was monitored, both actively and passively. They had list-based controls that, much like a pilot's takeoff or landing checklist, assured outcomes. This image is subject to the terms of a Creative Commons, Attribution-Share Alike license from Business Model Canvas, www.businessmodelgeneration.com

Elle had found intriguing overlaps between the systems that were her primary focus and the hospital's capital resources. They were interconnected systems. Elle believed that she could create a more sustainable and flexible organization that did a better job for all concerned—doctors, nurses, and patients—while making the regulators and donors happy at the same time. If health-care professionals embraced integrated practice technology, could Cork Point take things to the next level and integrate everything?

No longer could people look at health care as a separate thing. It was time for the hospital to accept the fact that the world was moving toward decentralized yet integrated systems. The advantages of industrial revolution linear processes had faded. The hospital was now in a society that rewarded choices. Fewer employees created more value and impacted more people. Elle could tell a different story, built around best-of-breed skills focused to meet real needs. The hospital had the opportunity to make an impact far beyond anything they had ever done before.

Health care was in a continuing shift toward consumers as active participants in maintaining and managing their own health on a day-to-day basis. Maintaining health and wellness had become the focus. In the early stages of the shift, procedures moved to clinics and homes, tasks shifted from doctors to nurses and physician's assistants. Initially, lower-cost facilities and lower-paid caregivers made services appear to be more affordable and accessible.

Health-care technology had moved away from a focus at the point of care in the hospital. In the hospital setting, technology sometimes replaced the dialogue between patient and physician. These technologies revealed medical conditions that most consumers could not understand. Physicians took on the role of interpreter.

As health care followed the path of other industries, the shift from a point-of-care clinical approach toward meaningful dialogue between patients and health-care providers was taking place. Management of chronic disease was just one aspect of this emerging two-way dialogue. Reestablishing this conversation while making health-care technology transparent to the process might be the key ingredient to controlling the epidemic of chronic disease. Outpatient services, clinics, and home health care proved themselves in the market. No one could be sure of what would happen next.

They used rules-based controls to configure systems. Visualization and analysis of data combined with decision support tools allowed the team to manage and respond, to boost relationships, associations, and services. Cork Point focused on wellness and prevention services for the healthy and creative low-cost support for those with underlying chronic conditions. At Cork Point, health care was more convenient for caregivers and patients. Through programs in malls, schools, clinics, other public venues, and at home, they developed individual compliance and responsibility.

The BIMSynergy central database provided the underpinnings for the technology that made this all possible. Much of the evaluation and diagnosis that took place in doctors' offices was now carried out by wireless devices to measure blood chemistry, heart function, vital signs, and many other personal medical conditions. The data transmitted by these devices made the monitoring of real-time conditions possible. Doctors could now manage the health status of everyone in the community.

The action took place at many levels. For most, the process was totally transparent; there was no reason for the technology to intrude beyond your receiving an occasional tweet or e-mail. The goal was to make lifestyle choices that would reduce the risk of chronic disease. Where medicines were required, the system optimized and managed them. The system was designed to flag conditions before a disease had advanced to the point where twentieth-century treatment would have even noticed.

Behind the scenes, multiple databases were queried by rules-based systems designed to connect real-time information. Individual genetic profiles, family histories, local conditions, and demographics from those with similar lifestyles meshed together to create personalized support. At this level, health alerts, status reports, and routine monitoring of fitness and wellness would take place.

These databases were continually updated to reflect the latest scientific knowledge. The system allowed the physician to question, analyze, share, and work with volumes of information that would have overwhelmed the most capable of twentieth-century doctors. These rules-based systems, working with data from multiple databases, offered advice and support.

For others, this real-time data supported the dialogue between patient and physician. In most cases, individuals received medical care without having to go to the doctor's office. The hospital had become a place for trauma care, complex surgeries, high-technology imagery, and other highly specialized treatments.

ORGANIZE FOR THE FUTURE

The BIMStorm process was started in order to show people what BIG BIM was all about. As the program matured, BIMStorms began to take on other functions. Some BIMStorms became the format for introducing new technologies and new ways of working. In this format people learned of the possibilities for directly connecting sensor data to information models for better visualization and control. The ability to subscribe to systems created for other uses and the power of information modeling connected to geographic data were also highlighted in this way. Other BIMStorms evolved into design charrettes focusing on particular problems, urban areas, and industry groups. These BIMStorms helped communities realize their options and helped high-tech industries recognize the decision-making power that comes from open standards and true collaboration. Cork Point is a continuation of this possibility. It is a BIMStorm to prepare for enterprise growth and change.

Since 2008, the first step in a BIMStorm has been to identify the requirement or need. The actual event usually takes place over one to two days. Often preparation occurs over one to two weeks prior to the event. This preparation may take many forms. If an existing facility is the subject, building performance evaluation may be started to provide information on current conditions, energy use, and other factors. Planning information is developed both to inform the participants and to identify requirements. Many times this information is in hard-copy form and must be scanned or otherwise entered into the system. Where gaps are observed, data may be re-gathered or verified. This process is much like the standard data collection and mobilization that is required for any planning or design process.

These early stages gain from existing resources such as geographic information systems (GIS) and other as-built data systems. The Onuma System can subscribe to multiple databases simultaneously. The BIMStorm connects to available systems to begin quickly with accurate information. GIS layers often include property lines, building footprints, vegetation, elevations, utilities, and many of the other items that one needs to know when making built environment decisions. Within the system, these layers can be used for tracing to explore relationships, associations, and patterns. The layers can also be imported to provide immediate visualization, analysis, and decision support.

Many other tasks occur as the BIMStorm proceeds. The process is based on making the best possible decision with the information that is available at any time in the process. The process may require little pauses as decision-making information is prepared. The process is not linear. Some people might be analyzing site conditions and utilities based on verified GIS data. At the same time, others could be exploring energy computations in an independent energy analysis program based on exported data. Others might well be creating a framework for visualization. The cost estimators might at the same time extract quantity information and prepare what-if scenarios using a sequence of imports and exports to spreadsheets. The process works at many levels of detail simultaneously. Yet the results of each of these efforts then flows back to the system to support higher levels of decision making over time.

RESHAPE CORK POINT

> "Forewarned is forearmed," still rings true over four hundred years after Miguel de Cervantes wrote the thought.

Reshaping Cork Point would require different methods. Elle needed to harness the creativity of the community to create a powerful new business model. Creativity and collaboration addressed the challenges that Elle faced. People connected like never before in history. As a group, they had the skill sets and passions to solve local problems. They needed a way that would allow them to learn and share in the decision-making process. With such a system, the outcomes would be owned by the community, not just by Cork Point.

Elle was always inquisitive. Her natural curiosity had led her to explore many areas. Often her friends in health care thought she was a little crazy, because to Elle, needlepoint, Tijuana, fishing in the Chesapeake Bay, and the Internet were just as intriguing as medicine. Sometimes she bounced from one thing to another so quickly that hardly anyone could keep up. It was on one of these flights of fancy that Elle learned about the technology that could handle the issues for Cork Point. It was in 2008, when she happened to stumble upon something called a BIMStorm.

The BIMStorm was the instrument that Elle and the people of Crisfield would use to establish and manage the future of Cork Point. To organize the Cork Point BIMStorm, Elle and the community first worked to develop a decision-making framework and captured existing data.

BIMSTORM LOS ANGELES

BIMStorms are proof of concept exercises that allowed people to come together on the Internet to experience the beauty and power of information. BIMStorms were the first exposure than most people had to next-practices in information modeling. Elle found the program while searching on the Internet for information about Tijuana. To this day, she was not altogether clear about why she was searching for information about Tijuana. But, in Tijuana, she found information on the work of a group called familia Corazón. The group was doing marvelous things for the people of Tijuana.

Corazón helped people help themselves. The group was building a home for a Mexican family as part of BIMStorm LAX. One team helped Corazón with planning and coordination for a home to be built by volunteers in one day. To Elle, this seemed like a wonderful use of technology. BIMStorms got directly to the heart of the question: How can technology make people's lives better?

Follow this tag to learn more about familia Corazon at http://corazon.org

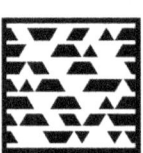

What happened during BIMStorm LAX was almost unbelievable. In twenty-four hours, 133 players in eleven countries created 420 buildings totaling 54,755,153 square feet, or an equivalent of 2.8 million pages of documents. The best part was that zero miles were traveled to gather for the event; it all happened virtually on the Internet. The event's carbon footprint could not have been lower.

Prior to BIMStorms, few knew about building information modeling. Others understood only a small slice of the information model pie. Most felt that an information model had to look like a virtual copy of real life. They expected the highly detailed, visually oriented models that had been popularized in movies and by architects whose main purpose was to highlight the aesthetics. Most could not understand why models in the BIMStorm looked rough and blocky. This was unfortunate, since models in the BIMStorm often contained much richer and more detailed information than the pretty models.

The BIMStorm programs deliver interoperable, data-oriented, and rules-based design solutions that enable rapid decision-making. The system is, in the broadest terms, a planning system. There are few things that cannot be planned within the system. One key element of the system is the ability to make easy connections outside of the system for work that needs to be developed in other tools. The system embraces the idea that no one tool can do all things; many tools are needed to support the life cycle of the environment. By sharing information in ways that everyone can use, the system is a design continuum.

Within the system, people plan, organize, and make decisions. They then send the relevant information out to other tools for further development and analysis. When the development and analysis is done, the other systems send the results back for validation and coordination. This plan-organize-decide-develop-analyze sequence is repeated over and over again throughout the life cycle of the built environment. If there is a planning and decision-making need, the system supports that need. Other tools may claim to be more powerful and complete. The Onuma System's focus is on planning. It is unique.

Hospitals and other facilities with complex needs and relationships benefit from this planning functionality. Health-care planners develop delivery systems, capital needs, and economic forecasts which then proceed directly into design, construction, and space planning. Room data, cost planning and cost control, sustainability, security, energy, and equipment planning all occur within the system. All of these are looked at in context. Tight budgets, complex systems, and health-care business processes share information to enable decisions that accurately represent local needs.

The whole concept was so appealing and comprehensive that Elle made it a point to keep up with other BIMStorms over the years. She followed BuildLondon Live BIMStorm, BuildHong Kong, and both the Oslo and Washington, DC BuildHospital Live. BuildHospital Live was the catalyst that fully opened her eyes to using information modeling to prepare for the future of health care. The creation of BIMSynergy carried the idea much further. In a few years, Elle and her board members will look back and laugh at what things were like when they started the process. By integrating Onuma's model server and its ability to subscribe to data from virtually anywhere with the complex and comprehensive model server capabilities built into BIMSynergy, much was possible. BIMStorms were real, high-performance information models that set enterprise up for integrated decision making, for life.

NATURAL FLOW

Elle designed BIMStorm Cork Point with many goals. At the community level, her goal was to involve everyone. At the organization level, her goal was to integrate Cork Point's business needs with state-of-the-art health-care delivery to better support the community. At the system level, her goal was to promote sustainable and comprehensive strategies for the future of Cork Point and the community. At the facility level, she hoped to make design decisions that connected people with business needs. All were tied to the built environment. BIMStorm Cork Point would become the foundation for a new flexible and adaptable system that responded to people, the environment, and change. The process would go something like this:

First, the core group meets to understand the key resources that will be involved in the process. As the discussion evolves, marketing and promotional concepts are solidified. Without letting people know what is happening and making them feel welcome, none of the rest will be possible. The team also identifies and documents the source data, existing resources, and scheduling issues that must be addressed. The core team's planning is designed to identify and manage the overall process so that as many people as possible can participate, in any way that they feel comfortable.

Communication systems are put in place. Team members shift all of their communications to systems embedded within BIMSynergy. The goal is to connect all communications to the models so that nothing is lost. Team members see clearly that behind-the-scenes communications using e-mail can easily undermine the collaborative process. Transparency and openness are needed for people to fully buy into the process. Where people recognize that a process is driven from a command-and-control perspective, interest wanes and fewer people participate. Over time, a truly collaborative process that allows people to innovate without fear will accomplish much more than any linear command-driven approach. The goal is to create a system that allows people to ask for help, to take risks, and to develop new things without fear. Everything builds around this concept.

At the same time that the core group is planning, others are cataloging and accessing existing knowledge about the Cork Point peninsula, the community, the county, and the region. As much as possible, this information comes from existing geographic information systems connected to BIMSynergy. By subscribing to government and private geographic information resources, BIMSynergy makes property information, topography, water and other natural resources, cultural background, existing facilities, transportation, utility, demographics, and virtually any other public information available to the BIMStorm. As gaps in the data are identified, the group makes arrangements for experts to input the required data. In some cases, this requires scanning and digitizing of hand sketches. Some information, particularly related to existing facilities and historic building resources, must be scanned and imported from standard blueprints and other documents.

Where they are available, the group integrates building information models that their local architects have built in the past. Fortunately, McCready Hospital was modeled at some time in the past. Although the storm destroyed much of the infrastructure, these models provide valuable information about the location of existing structures and historic buildings that may be rebuilt as the process moves forward.

As these planning and data collection processes take place, the second part of the process begins. Marketing and promotion of the big-picture ideas are rolled out in the community and the region. Participation is solicited from all affected people. Facebook, Google+, and every other social networking tool is deployed and actively used to create interest and accept input. The goal is to get people involved, using every tool in Elle's toolbox.

A series of public meetings begins in this phase. These meetings take many forms. Some are fairly traditional open meetings where core team members inform those who attend about what is happening and take questions. These meetings depart from tradition in that the goal is to create a dialogue with participants, rather than convincing them of the Cork Point position. Meetings also occur in community groups such as the Rotary, the Chamber of Commerce, and churches. The goal is to reach as many people as possible. Other meetings are focused on individuals. These meetings are held with prominent people who will then recruit others.

Each of these meetings needs a set of core members. One or more members act as the event manager and moderate the discussion. At the same time, another group operates BIMSynergy to reflect the discussion that takes place during the meeting. When practical, team members work at the meeting site. At other times, this activity is provided from remote sites. Participants are encouraged to provide input to the system using their mobile devices.

The information created is projected so that participants can follow the discussion. As the group explores possibilities, the participants see their ideas pop up instantaneously. A discussion of a new housing development results in an information model of a housing development on the site in question, with costs and other information immediately available. The discussion quickly focuses on people's concerns. The participants become engaged in the process, because they can see that their views are being considered and incorporated into the record. This is not talk to fill the void. This is a discussion to achieve results. And everyone knows it.

Strategic planning, systematic data collection, and collaborative participation were the goals of the first phases of BIMStorm Cork Point. Everything became easier as the team focused on these early tasks. Elle had started the process by creating an environment that gave people the greatest chance of a successful outcome. Everyone knew that there were no guarantees. Everyone also knew that the critical mistakes were all made on the first day. It was essential to begin the process right.

BIMSTORM CORK POINT
CRISFIELD, MARYLAND
APRIL 9 to MAY 6, 2024

Planning for BIMStorm Cork Point had been going on for the better part of a month. If you lived in Somerset County, you knew about the process. You had had more than one chance to have your voice heard. If you had attended a meeting or posted to a social networking site, your input had been recorded, and you knew it. You felt as though you were part of the process. Today, the real effort began.

For BIMStorm Cork Point, Elle planned to use a pretty standard process. By the end of day four, much of what had been talked about in concept would be thought out and organized. People had learned to use the Onuma System so that they could participate. Indications were that as many as two thousand people might add their schemes over the next four days. Another five thousand people had signed up to see progress and make comments.

Three hundred professionals from around the country and the world had signed up to be active participants. Most of these professionals came from the design, engineering, and construction industries. For the first time a significant number were environmental scientists, specialists in social systems, and health-care planners. The scope and possibilities represented by Cork Point had attracted a lot of interest.

BIMSynergy's new systems were also receiving a lot of attention. Since no one else had a fully functional model server utility in place yet, many investors and potential operators were closely following the event. Cloud-based computing had become so prevalent that no one truly paid much attention anymore. Distributed model servers were another matter entirely. It was not every day that a new public service, with potential impact similar to what happened when Thomas Edison began to establish electricity, went live.

Most of the people that were participating in BIMStorm Cork Point did not see the complexity that underpinned the process. They took advantage of the information and graphics to understand the problem. Once people clearly understood the background facts, it became easier for them to provide solutions to problems that they faced. Once the solutions were analyzed, viewed, and validated, the community could reach a consensus for how to proceed.

There were basic rules for how people worked with the system, much as one would not make a fax to Expedia to book an airline reservation. The rules for participating in

BIMStorm Cork Point revolved around collaboration. When communications and information were not accessible to all, collaboration became difficult. Through sharing, transparency, and information in standard formats that all could see and use, the system became a way to understand the reasons behind decisions and thought processes that people used as the decisions were made. These basic concepts make this possible:

This is a digital process. Everything should be documented in digital format using information models. Traditional ways of working, hand sketches, and notes can be used, but they must quickly be scanned and input into the system for all to use.

Work within the system is much as possible. Real-time collaboration with others is essential. Minimize situations where things happen in isolation, disconnected from the system.

Save your work in BIMSynergy. Do not save files as documents in file servers or on other media. The goal is to create a life cycle resource where data remains alive and active. A file on a hard drive, a DVD, or other media is subject to what we call data rot, from the moment it is saved.

Everyone has access to the system. How could you communicate with your friends on Facebook, if some of them were barred from the system?

Manually entered data should be added to the Onuma System. Do not manually enter data in other applications. When working in other systems or software, this manually entered information is transferred as you export data from the system. When working in other applications, import your results regularly. You should avoid going for long periods of time without importing to and exporting from the system. This ongoing work flow between applications results in one spending less time manually coordinating data. The goal is continuity of data in BIMSynergy.

There is no single way to interact with the system.

Some will view information and obtain reports. Others will complete planning and other design tasks. Yet others will enter detailed data manually and through imports from spreadsheets and other databases. Some will require extensive use of the system and others will only reference information. The goal is to let people to work in ways that they are most comfortable, using the tools that they know best. As long as everyone works with the same data in a collaborative process, the BIMStorm will be successful.

Elle made sure that as many people as possible would understand these rules when BIMStorm Cork Point started. Some people jumped right in and became almost overnight experts. Most took a bit longer. No matter how people learned to work with the system, Elle made sure that the resources were available to make it happen. On Day One, people were excited. They were ready to start. They knew that they were part of a life- and community-changing event.

DAY 1...2...3...4...
CRISFIELD, MARYLAND
MAY 7 to 10, 2024

Elle and her core team expected to make a lot of design decisions early. The excitement was building as Elle opened the door to the Crisfield Library at 8 a.m. on BIMStorm Cork Point Day One. Today all of the planning and hard work would come together.

Most of the participants were working remotely. One of the big advantages to this process was that you didn't need a large area where everyone could come together face-to-face. Everyone came together, but it was all virtual. Only a few people were using computers in the library. Elle was here. Joe Krantz, Cork Point's construction manager, was here. A few local residents that still did not have access to high-speed Internet were also scattered around the room.

One of the beauties of the BIMStorm process was that professionals all over the world were also online, ready to support the effort. There were engineers in Sweden, Tokyo, Germany, and Ireland ready to begin analyzing concepts that the community developed. Elle expected that they would provide much of the most sophisticated energy and environmental analysis, in conjunction with University of Maryland environmental scientists.

Designers in Korea, Norway, and Finland were ready to begin the process of validating models. They were also developing time scheduling scenarios. In Buenos Aires, London, Paris, Boston, and New London, Connecticut, graphic design experts were prepared to deliver visualization models as solutions developed. Architects in Milwaukee, Denver, and Chicago were adding their health-care expertise, coordinated by the BIM Delivery Company.

There were teams of emergency response professionals, transportation engineers, cost managers, constructors, social scientists, change management experts, business planners, urban designers, and many other professionals participating. Each group of professionals was supported by a BIMStorm certified expert whose mission was to use their knowledge to where it was needed. Many of the certified experts were already listed in the BIMStorm Hall of Fame.

The Hall of Fame came about in 2015 as the BIMStorm system transitioned from a training program with marketing undertones into full commercial use. Early BIMStorms, such as those in Los Angeles, New Orleans, and Charleston, West Virginia, focused on power and possibilities. Other early BIMStorms, such as those in Boston, Chicago, Rotterdam, Montreal, and Hong Kong, were focused on presenting the opportunities represented by BIG BIM. Commercial BIMStorms designed to support customer needs have been in demand since about 2010. The commercial BIMStorm has been used to describe organizational change, EcoDistricts, major facilities, statewide school systems, and healthcare facilities. Any complex situation with critical needs and resource restrictions benefits from the BIMStorm process. No standard design or planning process is able to respond to wicked problems as well as the BIMStorm.

The fact that experts across the world were involved did not diminish the local efforts. The Crisfield and Princess Anne Chambers of Commerce had their own group, led by an architect from the BIM Delivery Company. Architects and engineers across Delaware, Maryland, and Tidewater Virginia were all dialed into the process.

McCready Hospital's staff had four groups: one was made up of physicians and specialty health-care providers, one came from the elder care center, one was made up of board members and administration staff, and one was made up of facilities and maintenance personnel. These four groups were the only groups in the BIMStorm that were directly supported by paid professionals. In most cases, the professionals that were donating their time to this effort looked at it as a combination of benefits.

At one level, the professionals benefited by experiencing the latest technology first hand. Few of these professional's peers would be so lucky. At another level, the professionals benefited by the recognition and credibility that participation brought. In the past, BIMStorms had won unprecedented recognition both in mainstream media and professional awards. And, perhaps most importantly, the professionals learned much more than they taught in this environment. There is no way to get a faster education on the future of information modeling and collaborative practice than by working in a BIMStorm.

In California and various other locations, the Onuma team was assembled to support the effort. Over the next four days, the team would continue with Cork Point, 24x7. In Pasadena, California, home of Onuma, Inc., it was four o'clock in the morning. In Europe, it was two o'clock in the afternoon. In Tokyo, it was nine o'clock in the evening. Participants quickly learned how to juggle the time zones. The system's ability to foster collaboration across time zones is one of the factors that allows the BIMStorm to produce so much decision-making information so quickly.

As participants in one time zone end the working day, those in other time zones are just beginning. After one group spends the day inputting and resolving an idea, it can be handed off to others for further development while they sleep. In this way, an architect can lay out a building, go home for dinner and a decent night's sleep, and return the next morning to see the energy analysis completed by an environmental engineer in San Diego, the mechanical systems completed by a mechanical engineer in Sweden, and the structural system completed by a structural engineer in Tokyo. This cycle continues throughout the BIMStorm and is repeated by many different teams.

Everybody was ready. Nearly everyone had already started to work by the time that Elle officially opened BIMStorm Cork Point.

CATALYSTS

The planning team seeded the BIMStorm with as much existing information as possible. Participants opened Day One by reviewing the Google Map sketches, Google Earth boundaries, and information from old-fashioned land surveys and U.S. Geodetic Service mapping. Where possible, community goals and criteria had been converted to visual representations that overlaid Google Maps. Background information for health-care and facility staffing needs had been refined so that it was easy for all to follow. For those more fluent with numbers, the spreadsheets and databases were also embedded.

Hurricane Edgar largely destroyed McCready Hospital. For almost two years, the hospital had been supporting the community in makeshift quarters. It had been a struggle, and everyone knew how grave a solution had become. Because of urgency to rebuild, the hospital had already retained a proven management firm. The construction managers were working for the hospital in an agency role. They functioned much like a hospital employee, bringing significant health-care and construction expertise to the process.

Due to the extensive damage and changed conditions wrought by Hurricane Edgar, the planning team devoted a lot of time and energy to condition analysis. They evaluated several site schemes to act as catalysts for the planning process. Until the community and the hospital settled on the final strategic direction for the future, everything and anything could change. The original hospital site, a peninsula bounded on three sides by water, was extremely tight. For years, the hospital suffered and growth was limited as the Chesapeake Bay cleanup programs evolved.

Maryland's Critical Areas laws had been especially restricting, limiting the hospital largely to the building footprint that was appropriate for the 1960s. One of the few positive outcomes from the hurricane could be the fact that much of the surrounding area was no longer occupied. Current environmental regulations were likely to affect people's ability to rebuild. This situation created restrictions. It also offered opportunities. If the BIMStorm, and the international experts, could determine a solution that allowed the hospital to grow organically while dramatically improving water quality and other environmental impacts, it might achieve things that would not have been possible before the hurricane.

DECISIONS

> Many participants... many ways of working... many ideas... many tools... many different work flows.

BIMStorms are organic processes. They depend on those who participate. They evolve so that each BIMStorm takes on a distinctive character. No two are alike. In fact, few people's work flow in a BIMStorm are alike. BIMStorms, much like their namesake brainstorms, meander all about as people's ideas ebb and flow. BIMStorms expose innovative solutions, make possibilities evident, and capitalize on opportunities that emerge. BIMStorms solve problems. BIMStorms are perhaps the only way to create a framework for actually managing wicked problems. Wicked problems have no single solution. What seems like a solution to a wicked problem, exposes a new problem. A wicked problem changes, depending on the people, places, and things focused on the problem.

On Day One, a work flow used by some people for BIMStorm Cork Point might look like this:

First, a spreadsheet is created using a template. The spaces, floor levels, and room sizes for the building under consideration are added to the spreadsheet. With this spreadsheet in hand, it takes sixty seconds to enter into the system, select the studio, add and name the project, add and name a scheme, and set the site location, either through Google Earth import, latitude-longitude, or by a bounding box in the system.

Thirty seconds more and you have imported the spreadsheet to create spaces and floors. You name the building and verify that the spaces in your spreadsheet are actually imported. You have an information model after a total time expenditure of ninety seconds.

Next, you start to lay out spaces. You begin the design process. Space numbering, space areas, and sizes and costs are generated automatically. In five minutes to two hours, depending on the level of difficulty and scope of information you include, you have a completed design concept information model. This model can be exported to other tools for more detailed analysis and further development. The model carries with it not only the data you have added, but also the data the system automatically generates.

Even after exporting your model for action by others in other tools, you continue to add information. When the work by others is done, they will re-import their work and it will automatically update and add to your model, making your model richer and richer each time.

You include details about the site, building, and rooms. At the room level, you add furniture, fixtures, and equipment in both 2-D and 3-D from component lists. You input other building systems data and define space attributes, types, security zones, privacy, and finishes. You add heating, ventilation, and air-conditioning systems to rooms. All while continuing other design tasks.

At any point in the process, you output reports detailing information in the model. These reports are dynamic. As you change the size of a room, everything else changes to reflect the additional square footage. Enlarging the area increases the cost. As you generate different schemes, you can compare your schemes side by side. The comparisons enable you to assess energy, cost, security, sustainability, operations and maintenance costs, and other project data.

In ten to forty-five seconds, your data can be directly exported from the Onuma System in Construction Operations Building Information Exchange (COBie) format for use in operating and maintaining the building you are designing. Since the COBie data is maintained in a multi-tabbed spreadsheet format, an additional ten to forty-five seconds lets you re-inject the data back into the Onuma System after you make changes.

Twenty seconds is all it takes to export your information for other information modeling systems that comply with international standards. When your export is opened in other information modeling systems, they automatically generate models with spaces and furniture. These models contain information that you created in the Onuma System. By retaining the Onuma System information, these models can export the model as it is further developed back into the system. Participants can explore options remarkably quickly using similar work flows.

For those in Crisfield, Day Two started slowly. Yesterday, they explored several options and made a lot of progress. Late last night, as people became tired and went home, it was unclear what might happen with all of their studies. That morning, everyone was excited to see what those in other time zones might have created while Crisfield slept.

Several of the schemes were studied by energy analysts in Europe. Attached to the models was a lot of energy data. Even better, there were a series of energy visualizations showing how the schemes would respond at different times of the year. An urban planner in California and an urban designer in Seattle had added detail to the most promising master plan concepts. The ideas from Seattle were especially intriguing. They focused on many of the environmental issues that would set Cork Point apart, if managed properly. That afternoon, when these planners on the West Coast were back in their offices, Elle planned a working discussion with them to focus on the master plan layout. In the interim, she and her team would examine some other alternatives. By the time they left that evening, Elle hoped that they could choose the preferred site strategy for further development.

Much of the work today would revolve around the evaluation of options. Groups would see the metrics of schemes in context. More schematic buildings would be developed for analysis. Overnight, Elle and the Onuma team had assigned specific tasks to different groups, as the starting point for study at higher levels of detail. By the end of the day, the selected strategy would be shared to all for further development.

The work by the energy analysts in Sweden was of particular interest. Their initial recommendations suggested that, with proper planning, Cork Point had the potential to become a zero energy organization. In fact, it might well be possible that the facility would make more energy than it used.

While the engineers were working on detailed analysis, some architects were refining the blocking and stacking models to develop early thoughts about style, enclosure concepts, and costs. Using this information plus the site conditions that were being developed, they had exported to Google SketchUp to begin the process of visualizing how the project would look. By the next morning, they should have vignettes and sketches that would help people know what was being proposed. Since the goal was to develop people-centered places, their sketches would focus on how the facilities relate to the water, how pedestrian and vehicular transportation works, and the spirit of space. From an urban and architectural design perspective, the goal was to determine the essence of Cork Point.

Planning committee members were on site, supported remotely by health-care consultants in Chicago, Oslo, San Francisco, and Washington, DC. Elle and the health-care consultants had started the process of defining what the new Cork Point organization would look like several months ago. They had spent much of Day One in meetings to reach agreement on both the overall concept and the exact space needs to achieve their goals. Today, they were in the process of converting that whole discussion into spreadsheets using templates. Much of what they wanted to create involved an entirely new direction. Yet, the new direction was founded in many years of health-care precedent. The requirements for many of the services they were defining were well known. The needs for procedure spaces, exam rooms and clinics, surgery and diagnostics, and other spaces were straightforward; the uncertainties arose from volumes and relationships.

Projecting numbers of visits and the spaces and personnel required to support them is difficult, especially when you are moving toward decentralized services supported by technology. The concern is that creating a system based solely on managing wellness may skew the numbers. Yesterday's focus on curing sick people might result in quite different metrics than will a wellness focus. Coupling this with increased use of sensors, analytics designed to identify problems early, and increasing reliance on services delivered directly to people in their homes, historical information may no longer be accurate.

Elle and her team realized the potential problems and were making reasonable estimates of needs. Fortunately, the system gave them the ability to compare several concepts side by side.

First, the group added room names and room sizes to a spreadsheet template, assuming all spaces were on one level. Next, they imported this spreadsheet into the system, giving it a name and adding an executive summary that described the theory behind the scheme. The system created an information model of the spaces and "landed" the spaces in Crisfield. Space relationships and room design were not completed at this time. There was nothing that one could call a floor plan. There were only groups of boxes laid out across the site. Yet, even without formally laying out the boxes to get a floor plan, Elle and her team were provided with decision-making data at this point.

The system already included standard cost data, as well as standards for support spaces such as corridors, elevators, and stairs. Immediately they could see how powerful the idea was and how much it cost. This process was repeated until the group had modeled most of their options. Each option explored different possibilities. Each option allowed the team to evaluate different "what-if" scenarios. As the options developed, the system allowed the team to make direct side-by-side comparisons that feature the schemes' net and gross areas, construction costs, and line-by-line operations and maintenance costs. Using this information, the team eliminated schemes, added new schemes, and finally focused on the preferred solution.

As the team got closer to a preferred solution, hospital designers began to create basic footprints of buildings. The first schemes laid out the room boxes with the entire organization on one level. The team soon found that a one-level solution would never fit on the site. The team quickly reallocated rooms by floor to make multistory buildings. The hospital designers then began the process of laying out the floors. Since they were working over live geographic information system mapping, they received immediate feedback about whether their solutions were appropriate. Working in conjunction with Elle and the health-care planners, the designers created schematic diagrams that directly responded to the program needs assessments. By the end of this exercise, Elle, the planners, and the designers all agreed on the two most responsive solutions. These solutions would be shared for further development.

After an energetic and productive day, the Crisfield team headed for home and a full night's sleep, knowing that others would continue to improve the two schemes. Engineers were already in the process of analyzing foundations and structural systems. Based on the preliminary massing of the two schemes, energy experts were developing zero energy analysis. Architects had exported the schematic layouts to desktop building information modeling systems and were refining the buildings. Overnight, experts worldwide would analyze, develop, and examine how the schemes would go together. By the next morning,

Elle's team would have much more information to work with and would further refine their decisions.

Day Three focused on timely decision making. Project overview presentations began to determine the way forward. Short working sessions filled in gaps. Tomorrow was the time where everything would wrap up. Final decisions would get made tomorrow. Today, Elle must make sure that everything was ready to go.

The output from remote teams seemed to confirm both of the concepts that were shared the previous night. Either scheme could work. Since both had merit and neither had obvious flaws, Elle decided to proceed with both. Tomorrow they would become the basis of a community decision for the future.

Building on the work developed overnight by the architectural teams, the designers were also developing the schematic models. They continued to organize plan layouts and were refining buildings' massing. As the design and massing of buildings progressed, the structural engineers quickly reflected the changes. Several architects worked on building exterior options overnight using desktop bim applications. The architects' solutions had been reimported into the system and were under evaluation.

Construction managers were exporting area and volume data to enable them to develop detailed estimates of cost. Last night the engineers made progress on the design of the structural systems. Structural concrete and steel estimates were also in progress, using quantity data extracted from the models. As detailed cost information was developed, it was added to the system to refine comparisons between schemes.

Throughout the day, the schemes became increasingly real. Structural systems evolved to the point where one could see bolted connections. Building skins included specific materials and fenestration. Urban design concepts integrated transportation systems, landscaping, streetscaping, and lighting. The models included LEED checklists, energy data, and layouts of spaces with furniture.

The last two hours of the day, Elle and the whole team met physically and virtually to consider early master plan concepts. The construction managers conducted a presentation on expected costs and quickly integrated the team's feedback. Overnight the work would continue. The main focus had transitioned toward the next day's public decision-making process.

Day Four started bright, hot, and humid in Crisfield; typical weather for an early spring day on the Eastern Shore.

Much detailed design and documentation remained, yet much of the planning and development concept was finished. Building program development had progressed to a level that traditionally could be called design development. Size projections, schematic layouts, and other conceptual design aspects were well established. Structural estimates were finalized. The building enclosure estimate was finalized. A complete building exterior estimate was completed in less than an hour at two o'clock that morning. The construction managers were done with their program estimate, backed up by design assumptions, preliminary schedules, and a lot of data. Models for the site, roads, adjacent structures, the environment, foundations, and residents had been combined for quick review and analysis.

The team was ready for the final presentation. BIMStorm Cork Point had reached the point where decisions must be made. Elle and her core team led off by reviewing what had happened over the last four days and describing the effort for those attending in person and via the Internet.

Each person that participated contributed a minimal amount of time. Because of the intensity of the effort, the process seemed to some to be overwhelming, but the fact is that most individuals who participated still had time for other normal business tasks even while participating in the BIMStorm. The process leveraged the skills and knowledge of many people. People got a broad perspective and feedback about their ideas. With many involved, the group produced more. With many involved, no individual became a bottleneck for others.

A DENSIFIED CONCEPT — ELLE
CRISFIELD, MARYLAND
MAY 11, 2024

"I am Dr. Elaina Bagayoko-Smith. For those of you that do not know me, I am the hospital administrator for McCready Memorial Hospital. The hospital has decided to embark on a new and more community-focused direction that we call Cork Point. The board of directors and I determined that the best way to begin this endeavor was to embrace community collaboration. We decided to use the tools of today and tomorrow to consider and decide how to proceed.

"As we began the process, we learned about BIMStorms.

"BIMStorms use information models to hone in on the best solutions. They improve decision making, allowing the community and the world to participate. With information models, we felt that we could find new ways of working with the community. The hospital will become more valuable to our patients and to the world. Information models give the hospital the ability to plan for the long term, while doing the right things up front. The success of BIMSynergy Corporation up the road in Marion Station reinforces our belief that this is the future.

"The process is inherently sustainable and allows the hospital to find the most cost-effective ways to work with the community. Rather than defaulting to the lowest-cost solution, the BIMStorm gives us the ability to find the right solution at the lowest reasonable cost, without sacrifice. The process works to eliminate uncertainty and reduce misunderstandings, and will get the new Cork Point off on the right foot.

"Over the last four days, several thousand people have worked to define the new Cork Point. Many of those special people are in this room. Others are connected to this presentation over the Internet. To you, I say, 'Job well done.'

"I am proud of what we have achieved in BIMStorm Cork Point. Let me explain for you what the new Cork Point will be like. After I finish the report, we will have a discussion. There are no limits on what can be discussed. At the end of the discussion, I will take a vote. Each of you has a share in the outcome. Each of you will receive a vote. Whatever is decided will guide Cork Point for years to come.

"First and foremost, Cork Point will be more comprehensive and will provide world-class services that are needed to support growth in Somerset County. There will always be an acute-care hospital at Cork Point. This is the guts of the enterprise. The new hospital will be small and will focus on emergency care and critical support. Other hospital services will be remotely managed. The community will have access to specialists both locally and remotely through robotics and new medical practice paradigms.

"Everything will be monitored and managed based on new rules-based systems. The goal is to use technology as a force multiplier that allows a small, dedicated staff to practice their craft, supported remotely by others. Using the latest technology, we will be able to provide better care at lower cost for more people.

"Specialty care will be a key draw. We will bring the specialist to you without requiring you to travel far from home. New health-care technologies will connect experts to you when and where required.

"Outpatient support is expected to be the leading use by locals. We will make sure that we are the best at outpatient care, no matter what.

"Nursing and elder care will take place in the Life Hub. You will receive a lot of choices at Cork Point. We will have remotely managed cottages located throughout the region. They are always on the water or have distinctive amenities. Most will be within one mile of the main campus. We will manage units as far away as Florence, Italy; near Taos, New Mexico; and on the Boundary Waters in Minnesota.

"The Rehabilitation Center will be available if you need it. It will work closely with the specialty care center and provide a place for those who need more immediate, closer attention.

"The Elder Care Center will have three distinct parts: Assisted Care, Long-Term Care, and Hospice Care. We will be there when you need us.

"Building and managing these facilities will require the efforts of the community, the Cork Point family, and many experts throughout the world. It is a major undertaking. Together we can do it. Together we can create a place that the world will envy and copy."

SUSTAINABLE ASSETS —ELLE

> Computers can figure out all kinds of problems, except the things in the world that just don't add up. —James Magary

The goal is to make Cork Point the best place to live anywhere, and we are excited about it.

In order to become the best place to live, we must use the information that surrounds us. Today, we produce information every time we take action. When we surf the Internet, a record is made of which sites we visit and how long we stay. Our purchasing habits are a known quantity. Everywhere we go, for everything we do, information is being created and stored by someone. Together, we will use this information to do a better job. We must ask, "Who owns the information about me?"

Each of us owns all rights to the data about ourselves. We have the right to use our personal data as we see fit. No one has the right to buy or sell our information without our knowledge and consent. Owning our personal information creates new possibilities and new opportunities. It is these possibilities and opportunities that Cork Point will help each of us to utilize.

Cork Point will allow you to use your information for better decision making. You may want to make any or all of your information available to systems that track your fitness. Spending habits, shopping patterns, lifestyle choices, and environmental conditions to which you may be exposed can be assessed. You will then get immediate feedback on healthy lifestyles and issues that you should consider. You may want to have your physical conditions monitored actively. This will allow our experts to assist you as you go about your daily activities. Your home, your car, your friends, and everything else about your life creates data. You choose how to use information.

When you authorize Cork Point staff and systems to use your information, we will use technology to give you quality services when and where you need them. The organization is designed to respond at high-speed to any issue. In crisis, the system is at its best.

This system is designed to adapt to changing conditions. It can be reconfigured as needed. The system is complex, but the functions are customized to your needs. The complexity is hidden. The experts' job is to manage the complexity. You are presented with the facts that allow you to make decisions about your personal circumstances, without worrying about the underlying complexity.

None of us has a reliable crystal ball. Even with the best of intentions, the best planning, and the most accurate information, things will not be as we predict. No one knows what changes will happen…but with Cork Point's approach, we can accommodate the changes at lightning speed.

The Cork Point system begins with values. We take the long view, even if it affects short-term gains. We minimize waste at all levels—people, production, and resources. When we are efficient, we do a better job. We cannot afford waste.

The system allows us to maximize efficiency, even at low volumes of activity. This allows us to focus on individuals, rather than creating bureaucratic systems that respond to the average and poorly serve either extreme. No longer must you suffer because your needs are not like the needs of the majority.

Technology allows us to create many different services and products quickly and efficiently. The development and production process has been "flattened" by integrated technology. We can now design a service, check how it works online, and focus it on those who require the service. Things go from conception to execution quickly and with quality as the first priority.

The system uses technology and information to empower people. Cork Point thrives on consensus and fast decision making. We value organization and control, but we use technology to help people and make Crisfield a better place to live.

Without educated leaders and people who value lifelong learning, Cork Point would not be possible. The community's success is the true measure of our success. As we share risks, costs, and our knowledge, we make decisions that will affect us all. Cork Point will always be under development. As new buildings go up, existing buildings will need to be renovated. As new programs develop, existing programs will need to be adjusted to the changing community. The organization will always be a work in progress.

KNOWING OURSELVES

Knowing ourselves and understanding how we work is the first step toward working effectively in a collaborative environment. Since the beginning of the industrial age, and especially since the end of World War II, we have usually broken tasks into specialty areas. We have become dependent upon single-subject experts and classification of functions. This resulted in the process breaking down into planning, design, construction, and facility management. In health care, we find radiology, surgery, pediatrics, outpatient surgery, dermatology, and many other specialty departments. Separate tasks and functions have often resulted in additional costs, errors, and inefficiencies. Much time and energy has been spent to integrate different tasks. In both construction and health care, strategies have been developed with the purpose of improving conditions. Some have been successful; most have not.

Implementing change requires an in-depth understanding of our process. Yet change is only partly about process. In many situations and almost all organizations, the success or failure of a change revolves around people. Discussion often revolves around resistance to change. Individuals are usually the principal factor in keeping changes from bearing fruit. People are usually the main obstacle to successful deployment and implementation of changes. Because people are so critical to success, one must first understand the strengths and weaknesses of the people involved in any change.

As the discussions about the new Cork Point began to take shape, Elle began to question everything. She dug into the processes used by others and broke everything down into their smallest components. She looked at the processes and how people worked and reacted in a similar business models. From her explorations, patterns began to emerge. Elle began to examine ways that she could adapt Cork Point to capitalize on the community's strengths and to overcome the community's weaknesses.

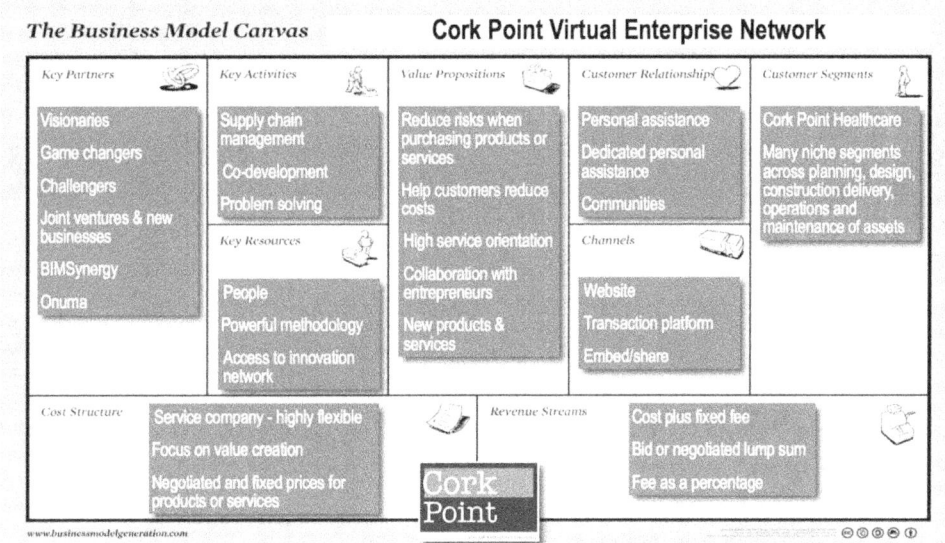

The Cork Point Virtual Enterprise Network was an alliance of individuals and companies coming together to share their knowledge and resources to respond to the needs of Cork Point and the community. Most group members were small, like-minded businesses, pooling complementary expertise to work in a global economy. For most of the members of the alliance, their address was not an obstacle. Most members could be located anywhere in the world, because it was their expertise and attention that was needed, not their physical appearance. Other members, such as Joe's company, Integrated Construction Managers Inc. (ICMI) had on-site staff. A few of the members worked exclusively at Cork Point. This image is subject to the terms of a Creative Commons, Attribution-Share Alike license from Business Model Canvas, www.businessmodelgeneration.com

Elle found many constraints about how McCready Hospital was doing business. In most cases, the constraints were seen as limitations. They imposed restrictions that prevented innovation from occurring.

Organizations can manage performance by managing critical constraints, no matter how complex the system. By understanding the organization's constraints, you build a foundation for success. By tailoring the organization's processes using constraints, you can achieve much more than many would think.

Elle studied the Theory of Constraints (TOC). In 1984, Dr. Eliyahu Goldratt published The Goal, in which he theorized that any business could improve its results through applying scientific methods to resolving organizational problems. Goldratt theorized that each business has a single constraint that limits its performance relative to its goal. Manage the constraint, and the business will overcome obstacles to productivity and become more efficient and responsive. Elle took this straightforward idea and created an organization and a new approach to doing business.

Elle realized how interconnected Cork Point was with the Crisfield community. She decided that Cork Point had to be a leader in providing value beyond their traditional role. Cork Point had to expand the community's perception of the world. They also had to expand their vision of where the organization fit into the built environment. They were moving to a process designed for today—and tomorrow.

Her investigation taught Elle to look at the organization as a system rather than as a hierarchy. For her, the theory explained why list-based controls and agency construction management works in hospitals. It also explained Toyota's phenomenal success and perhaps their subsequent problems. She learned that the Theory of Constraints underpins many of the management approaches that work best in an integrated environment.

Finding the key constraint and deciding how to handle it is essential to your success. It seems almost too easy. But Elle learned to understand that if she tried to control everything, she was not actually managing anything. She needed to focus on Cork Point's limiting constraint.

From the facility's perspective, Elle had come to believe that architects who were not managing constraints created much of the poor documentation, cost overruns, and other problems she had seen in recent years. By not managing constraints, they allowed many of the problems, even with conventional project management controls. From the health-care perspective, the same seemed to be true.

You can control processes by managing constraints. It is a four-step process. The first step is to identify the constraints on your process. Which is most critical? The next step involves deciding how you will use the constraint to improve performance toward your goal. The third is to make the constraint important—give it power by integrating it into your process. The final step is to make the constraint a part of your daily work practice.

Using these four steps, Elle, the board of directors, and staff assessed how the system worked. They identified constraints on the system. They did not look at departments or functions in isolation. They took a holistic view, designed to get comprehensive answers. When the analysis was done, the group identified Cork Point's critical constraint to be costs without compromising needs; followed closely by people.

Costs that support what is needed, no more no less, and people were the constraints that would be managed as Cork Point moved forward. They would be the focus of the organization's attention. They would be the priority as initial decisions were made. They would be integrated into the DNA of the new Cork Point.

BALL GAMES AND BOWLING LEAGUES

Virtual Enterprise Network

Cork Point's process revolves around national groups of firms that work cooperatively to achieve dramatic improvements in the built environment. These firms produce more sustainable and reliable outcomes that support fair value to all. They are progressive, cross-disciplinary organizations and achieve benefits through systems that provide rules, standards, and relationships designed to deliver superior results. The groups empower firms of any size to work big, anywhere.

Cork Point systems are built around principles that convey information rather than simply giving orders. Everyone looks for threats and opportunities, knowing that they are accountable. They are working transparently. They are able to communicate instantly using any and all tools. The Cork Point system trusts people as partners and values the skills and capabilities of both internal and external communities. Cork Point teams include all project stakeholders, guided by principles of real collaboration, open information sharing, shared risks and rewards, just-in-time decision making, and the use of the latest technology. With integrated practices, they expand their value throughout the entire facility life cycle.

The people who created the groups knew that people have established social organizations for ten thousand years. From clans to countries, from early Mesoamerican ballgames to bowling leagues, people have always come together because they share values, have common needs, and have agreed upon a community strategy. The founders of the groups that support Cork Point share the risks and rewards of their endeavor. Realizing that technology was evolving faster than people, they have retooled their corporate cultures to catch up and take advantage of the workhorse created by the Internet, cloud computing, and BIMSynergy.

Because of its alignment with these groups, Cork Point is able to capitalize on strengths such as personal service and quick response. The groups have the versatility to become whatever Cork Point needs, wherever and whenever they need it. Often working like boutique organizations, they bring large-firm tools, resources, and networks with them to Cork Point. The groups can turn on a dime. They bring the best of the best to bear to solve problems, no matter how large or how small.

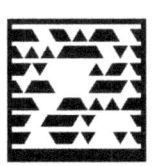

You can use the tag to read more about Virtual Enterprise networks at http://4sitesystems.com/ iofthestorm/?page_id=820

The groups have the ability to mobilize quickly with just the right information and just the right team. They advocate transparent ways of working, have a moveable leadership system, and can adjust their teams to any assignment. Whatever processes they bring to bear on an asset, they use technology and work processes to hold down costs, manage risk and uncertainty, and eliminate—not just reduce—haggling and lawsuits. They know that their success has less to do with the actual process than it does with how the parties share risk in a binding agreement designed to deliver sustainable results.

WORK BEGINS

Members of the virtual enterprise provide a central control to manage the data and information models. Managing this information used to take a long time and expend a lot of staff resources. Now the effort is a matter of a few experienced and dedicated people working with BIMSynergy. These people monitor the data in ways that allow them to detect anomalies and catch errors. No system is perfect; all systems need checks and balances. That is one of the things that the virtual enterprise network provides.

Cork Point, the virtual enterprise network, and BIMSynergy are designed around the fact that no one is perfect. Because of this fact, these systems use rules-based processes and aggressively minimize repetitive inputs. If something can be input once and reused many times, that is what is done. They know that every time something is manually input, it doubles the chance of an error. Minimizing manual inputs and maximizing inputs from devices such as sensors are just two strategies for minimizing error. The systems' philosophy is based around the concept of "fail fast and move on."

...Blink.... Screw up.... Blink.... Fix the screw up.... Blink.... Move on.

The system consciously allows for the act of being wrong. Rather than an error being fatal, an error becomes annoying and something expected. In some areas, errors must be held as close to zero as possible. In these cases, the system relies on checklists and standard operating procedures with proven outcomes. The pilot of a Boeing 747 has checklists for prior to departure, prior to landing, and for almost every other situation. Health-care professionals at Cork Point have much the same. The system recognizes that this level of critical control is not appropriate in most cases.

Innovation and discovery of new ways is stifled if people are obsessed with being right all of the time. Innovating requires people to try new things. Trying new things will result in errors. The system is open to being wrong, when appropriate, and as much as can be afforded. This does not mean that the system accepts sloppy work or errors for errors' sake. As professionals, people are expected to balance their explorations with the realities.

As Integrated Construction Managers began to pull the pieces together to enable Cork Point to be implemented, they focused on organizing the members of the network. During Elle's explorations over the last couple of months, the members had been selected for their expertise and skills. Extensive discussions had been held to make sure that everyone understood and committed to the process. Multiple trust-building sessions had also taken place. Everyone understood the rules.

Agreements were in place. Everyone signed nondisclosure agreements and the virtual enterprise charter. Those with current responsibilities also completed contracts for their work. Accounting systems were in place. Funds were available to support early needs. Somerset County Economic Development and the BIMSynergy Corporation were underwriting much of the early cost, in anticipation of the future value. From the perspective of the virtual enterprise, the BIMStorm was a final dress rehearsal. The program let the group try out collaboration, mentoring, and many of the other traits that would be critical to the future. As a group, they passed with flying colors.

Both the individual and corporate competency database in BIMSynergy had been completed for all involved parties. As Joe Krantz began to evaluate how teams would be structured, this data would be invaluable. The ability to judge who had what skills and what resources was essential.

ENTERPRISE ZEN

Joseph Krantz (Joe) was the on-site built environment representative of the Cork Point Virtual Enterprise Network. Joe used BIMSynergy and information models to coordinate development as Cork Point moved forward. One of Joe's first tasks was to work to create a master schedule. Joe's master schedule was tied to the central enterprise schedule that allowed Elle to stay on top of development at all times.

The BIMSynergy network enhanced the group's skills and resources. Elle felt that the virtual enterprise gave Cork Point a number of advantages. As a group, they could respond much faster and more responsively than any large corporation with the equivalent personnel. The level of internal bureaucracy and impediments to progress were almost nonexistent in the group. Since most of the group was made up of small entrepreneurial enterprises or individuals, their focus was on innovation and doing the best possible work. They saw their success as tied to making their clients successful. They were flexible and understood how to use appropriate technology to keep costs down, productivity high, and excellence foremost.

The factors that made the group successful closely match those that drove many recent innovations. They knew and used technology appropriately. Complicated systems were generally not the answer. Easy access, sharing, and open communications underpinned everything they did. They understood how to run a network of entrepreneurs and experts, and they took management and control seriously. They knew that the group must have agreed-upon standards and means of governing the network. Without an agreed-upon and formalized structure, the network would fail.

Members understood the difference between cooperation and collaboration. They had invested the time and resources to establish effective working relationships. They had agreed upon decision-making processes and how to resolve internal conflicts. The system handled problems as they occurred and added or removed members as needed. Within the group, everyone understood the roles that others played. Roles might change over time and as needs dictated. There was no single leader, and leadership transitioned from one member to another as needed. Some members were expert at finding and integrating resources to mold the team to customer needs. Some members were skilled at identifying opportunities and allocating members to capitalize on them. Some members were adept at keeping track of money, time, and resources to get the work done, while building trust and accountability. Each of these was critical to the group's success.

Elle was pragmatic about the virtual enterprise network at Cork Point. From her perspective, the group just needed to get her projects done.

During BIMStorm Cork Point, the members served to help others in the development of the master plan. They brought their expertise to bear to add decision-making information that Elle and the community required. They demonstrated to the community the value of their expertise. Most of the members were well known to Elle and her board of directors before the BIMStorm. As Elle monitored earlier BIMStorms, she saw the kind of support these people could provide. Those asked to be part of the virtual enterprise were selected for their knowledge and ability to collaborate. Their success in BIMStorms was also a factor.

The virtual enterprise network would remain as a separate entity as the new Cork Point facilities moved forward. The appropriate parts of the group would become a permanent operational management company as Cork Point moved into occupancy and use.

As Elle built her team at Cork Point and found the people to become part of Cork Point's virtual enterprise, she looked for dedicated individuals, people with a high level of self-awareness who were committed to an open process and a movable leadership structure. She wanted people who understood where she was headed and had the abilities and long-range vision to "get it." They had to be capable of coordinating multiple activities at the same time.

People with vision were Elle's first priority. Systems thinkers, people who embrace change, innovators, and risk takers are the standard. Cork Point is about people in the community; those who work here must be servants of the people and stewards of the environment. They must be prepared to be teachers, mentors, coaches, and lifelong learners. They must have vision and be prepared to help the community build their dream.

Cork Point is the future of integration. Not only design and construction integration. Not only health-care integration. Cork Point ties together all of the things that make the community a better, safer, and healthier place to live.

At Cork Point, you find systems for what you need when you need them. You have to access to specialists from everywhere via robotics and remote technology. Integrated teams get you access to international experts. Cork Point sets the pace in today's world. It undoubtedly is the Zen masters meet Star Wars type stuff.

FOCUS

As Joe organized the team to begin the process, others focused on beginning the process of defining the projects. They knew and understood the long-term issues and the need for everything to occur in an information model. They realized that each of the projects they were defining were only a small piece of the overall enterprise. Their pieces must harmonize with the whole, but they must also stand on their own.

They were using time-tested procedures and philosophies designed to provide the most reliable starting point for the future.

The BIMStorm Cork Point concepts contained significant amounts of information. The selected solution included cost analysis for each building and the entire site. The concept was fairly well developed, yet much of the information remained at the rule-of-thumb level. Site costs, in particular, were made up of a series of professional guesses. The guesses came from those knowledgeable in the components included, and were based on system areas and volumes. Building costs were based on industry averages for different levels of quality. The averages were modified by the location, dates, and other factors.

Compared to any traditional planning and design process, the information was quite accurate. To a layman, it would compare to what one might expect after a month's concerted effort in an architect's office. From the architect's office, the information would come with significant disclaimers. Based on what usually happened in the last half of the twentieth century and the first fifteen years of the twenty-first century, the information might be as much as 300 percent wrong. For Cork Point, that was not nearly good enough. Cork Point's goal was to be exactly on budget and on time with minimal conflict.

Information modeling is only one part of what will enable us to achieve this goal. Individuals with mastery and a proven method are truly what make it possible. When Elle and Cork Point chose to embrace the Theory of Constraints, the Onuma System, and BIMSynergy, they committed to new ways of thinking. Some aspects of the change they had seen in operation for many years as they worked with agency construction managers. Other aspects were significant departures in how one looks at the world. Cloud-based information models, real-time collaboration, and business transparency are revolutionary. Integrating these new ways of thinking is a complex task with significant upside benefit.

The Theory of Constraints suggests that the enterprise question everything to find the constraint that limits its potential. By asking questions, you expand your views. How do I decide what to accomplish? Can I improve how I manage projects? If I constrain a system, will it affect the quality of the outcome? What constraints can I use to manage my process more effectively?

As Elle and her board of directors explored questions such as this, they identified cost and people as the primary constraints on their process. They came to believe that managing cost constraints to get what they need, at the proper quality level, was the most significant change that they could make to help people. By managing the cost constraint throughout their processes, they could improve how they interacted with the community.

You can follow this tag to more information about the Theory of Constraints at http://4sitesystems.com/iofthestorm/?page_id=1318

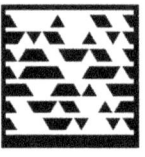

WHAT CONTRACTORS FACE

In the building industry, contractors are faced with a catch-22. They face an expectation that they need to use information models. This expectation has made modeling a requirement for most large projects. In some markets, the modeling requirement has made a limited set of modeling processes a commodity service that is delivered at wildly varying levels of quality. In an effort to protect their self-interests, some constructors agree to these requirements, having no real idea of how to deliver on their promise. Next, they face increasing demands to move data into the facilities operation and management system via such tools as COBie. This creates a confusing and complex interface that needs industry action. Currently, commissioning requirements, legacy facilities management tools, and highly stovepiped resource management systems all contribute to a confusing situation that must be resolved to achieve the long-term benefits from information models. False expectations, poor compliance, and outright fraud are the result.

Elle recognized the impact of technology on a fragmented industry. For some reason, the industry as a whole did not seem to believe that the remedy would not come from technology alone, it was a business and people issue. The issue was about the way that people work and how to get things done. Elle knew that at Cork Point they must understand the big picture and become nimble enough to respond to change. Technology might be a key to curing the fragmentation, but other things were much more serious.

One critical decision facing Elle was the structure of the delivery team. The virtual enterprise network gave her many options. Since the system was designed for collaboration and integrated working practices, many of the traditional reasons for selecting one methodology over another might not apply. Whatever method was chosen, the network would work collaboratively with Cork Point to create pain share/gain share relationships. Elle's board of directors was adamant that contracting relationships be resolved prior to proceeding. They also required that agreements be clearly understandable and enforceable. They expected that Elle and her team would be able to put the process in context and justify the costs, benefits, and work efforts. Multiple options were under scrutiny because of this requirement.

With the right value system in a perfect world, any delivery method could deliver superb outcomes: outcomes where all share equally in the risks and rewards; outcomes where the constructor is paid for the work completed, with a reasonable profit; outcomes where the owner pays fairly for what was delivered, nothing more and nothing less. This is the way that most of us would like to think that design and construction works. Unfortunately, it is rarely so.

> Delivery methods, such as design-bid-build, design-build, construction management at risk, agency construction management, and integrated project delivery, are someone's idea of how to most closely achieve a perfect project. The sad truth is that none of them actually achieves these goals. Some come closer than others. Some may have worked once upon a time, and are no longer effective. It is not too hard to understand the basic differences between these options. The subtleties and complexities are more difficult.
>
> Each option would be molded to involve collaborative work processes. Because of the necessity to build upon traditional delivery methods, each of the options would achieve this goal a bit differently. Some were, at their core, not collaborative at all. Some were relatively easy to convert. Each of the options required Cork Point management and control at a different level. Each imposed a slightly different cost structure.

Each required a separate investment from Cork Point in time and money. Each option had been used widely for many years. As Elle evaluated her options, she knew that the process needed to foster collaboration, transparency, and shared information. Each must be understood in that context.

The first option involved Cork Point assigning full responsibility for project delivery to a developer. In this option, Cork Point would monitor the developer's progress and participate throughout. The developer would be responsible for all activities required to provide a complete project. The developer would hire a general contractor. At project completion, Cork Point would retain the option of operating and managing the facility themselves or retaining the developer and leasing the project. This was Cork Point's most expensive total cost option, adding about fifteen percent over the lowest-cost option. The fees and markups for the developer accounted for much of the added cost. Cork Point staff involvement and personnel cost was low, at about 3 percent, in this option. Design-bid-build was perhaps the most traditional option. It allocated liability between Cork Point, the architect, and the general contractor. This option was arguably the most difficult to restructure to be collaborative and integrated. Case law and established standards of care were clear in this option. Unfortunately, adding technology to design-bid-build has been shown to result in conflict and people working at cross-purposes. The effort required to overcome these issues is significant. Some find this to be counter intuitive, believing that design-bid-build offers the only way to be sure of the lowest possible price. This belief has been shown repeatedly to be false.

Design-bid-build has long held favor in the government world and for public bidding. It would seem as though this is the best way to assure everyone that you are getting the best price for your project. For many years, the truth has been much different. This method has produced more sub-par quality work, more lawsuits, and lower productivity than any of the other options. In this day and age, design-bid-build is almost a promise of unplanned change orders and litigation. In fact, many agencies budget believing that litigation is coming from day one. This option added about 4 percent over the lowest-cost option. Cork Point's direct costs were a total of about 29 percent in this option.

Next was design-build. This option placed responsibility for all design and construction operations on the design-builder. Cork Point would bear the cost of fees, financing, legal, and accounting. Design-build has become increasingly popular over the last thirty years. This method can deliver on its promise of a single-point responsibility. In many situations, this single-point responsibility has led to compromised design solutions and shoddy workmanship. These issues are generally local. Local contractors, styling themselves as design-builders, offer prices too low, based on imperfect design documentation. They then drive quality to the bottom to deliver.

Recently, processes where the owner retains designers to create documents that become the standard of the design-builder's performance have become more prevalent. This approach has been proven to overcome many of the quality issues. As a hybrid approach where the designer would develop information models for design-builder use, this method could achieve many of the benefits that Cork Point sought. Outcomes would depend on good intentions and ethical behavior. Substantial opportunities would still exist for participants to create benefits for themselves while harming others, without anyone actually knowing what occurred. This option added about 5 percent over the lowest-cost option. Cork Point direct costs were approximately 16 percent of the total cost.

Construction management at risk was the fourth option. This option could also be called developer-entity construction management, since responsibility for the entire project is similar to the first option. The key difference is that usually a large general contracting firm would act as the developer in this option, eliminating one layer of organization and associated costs. Construction management at risk is favored by many for large projects. In this method, the construction manager has control, much as in the design-build method. The construction manager supports the owner, while retaining responsibility for delivering the design support and construction. Cork Point would contract with a single entity and a single surety bond could be provided.

After experiencing the construction management at risk choice in other hospitals, Elle realized that a surety bond or any other warranty did not add integrated delivery benefits. In her experience, construction management at risk retained many of the fundamental flaws associated with the traditional design-bid-build approach to the process. The construction manager usually did not hold contracts with the architect and engineers, who worked in an advisory role to the owner. Usually the construction manager was required to bid the trades and then consult with the owner and award trade construction packages. Once past this point, the construction manager at risk assumed full construction liability.

On the surface, the construction manager at risk offers an improved model of single point of responsibility. The reality can be quite different. As design progresses and construction starts, the construction manager at risk is no longer required to share financial details. Suddenly, detailed negotiations with trade contractors, the actual value to the owner of change orders, and the cost of project support staff become an issue. Even with a guaranteed maximum price, the owner is often harmed. Savings that should accrue to the owner too often accrue to the construction manager at risk. The construction manager at risk, in strict compliance with the contract, has too many opportunities to enhance project outcomes to his or her company's benefit. This option added approximately 1 percent over the lowest-cost option. Since costs flowed through a developer entity, Cork Point management costs were minimized.

Integrated project delivery is seen to be the way to correct these issues. Integrated project delivery offers incredible possibilities. Much energy has been spent to determine how integrated project delivery works and how relationships should be structured. Collaboration, information sharing, openness, and transparency are essential to the process. Sharing risk and reward is a worthy goal. The problem with integrated project delivery is that, in most cases, it departs from procurement standards. Many find abandoning the traditional checks and balances between owner, designer, and constructor to be difficult. A small number of owners have been willing to take the risk, yet lack of legal precedents and a significant early-stage investment in time and money to negotiate collaborative agreements continues to make integrated project delivery a goal that is rarely reached.

Agency construction management was the last and arguably the lowest-cost option under consideration. Cork Point would become the contracting entity between all parties, assisted by the construction manager. The agency construction manager would not hold any contracts. All contracts would be directly with the owner. This would require that the owner be a direct party to many more agreements than in most of the other methods. Contracts and surety bonds would be managed by the agency construction manager in the owner's interest. Since the agency construction manager was not the contracted entity, he or she would include the requirement for surety bonds to come from the project's trade contractors. The construction manager would manage costs in Cork Point's interest to ensure that payments to contractors occurred at a pace that minimized risk of default. Since costs would be managed by the construction manager, Cork Point's additional management costs would be minimal.

Agency construction managers work as an extension to an owner's staff. They are the owner's agent. In this role, the successful construction manager becomes the advocate for the owner's needs. Since the agency construction manager does not hold any contracts, the ability to create windfall profit opportunities is limited. In their role as the owner's agent, the construction manager has little reason to keep information close. Short of integrated project delivery, agency construction management offers the most transparent and collaborative strategy for project delivery. The contractual underpinnings of this method lead to an open and free exchange between all parties. With a construction manager acting as a trusted advisor to the owner and a design team contractually obligated to share and collaborate, agency construction management offers a significant step toward integrated project delivery. Combining information modeling, model servers, and proven agency construction management techniques creates a system that balances traditional delivery with state-of-the-art technology to do better work.

STUDY

Planning is essential for the successful completion of any project. Choosing the appropriate delivery method and tailoring it to achieve your goals is a critical first step. At their best, projects move forward using delivery systems that motivate people to use their energy and skill to develop new and marvelous things. Any collaborative process requires the active participation of others. Leadership moves around, knowledge takes center stage, and shared risk and reward govern. That is what happens when you use an information model-based approach. People study and freely trade off new technologies and traditional tools as needed to do the best job possible. They share risks and rewards.

Sharing risks and rewards is a terrific goal. But if used as nothing more than mantras, shared risks and rewards have no more value than any other words. Clear and easy ways to monitor progress, manage outcomes, assign responsibility, identify errors, and assign credit and rewards are needed. Without such a system, shared risks and rewards become subject to gaming, positioning, and manipulation, all things that threaten collaboration.

Using the concept models developed in the BIMStorm, all Cork Point projects linked directly to the core controls embedded in BIMSynergy. The information model was used for resolving conflicting information virtually so that money and time were not lost. As projects progressed, Cork Point's recognition and reward system compensated people for collaborative behavior tied to productivity and outcomes. Using agency construction management techniques enhanced by information models and BIMSynergy, Elle and Cork Point had the information that they needed to plan and determine how to proceed.

As Elle and her board of directors studied the methods available for managing the construction at Cork Point, they found that managing cost as a constraint had worked effectively for more than thirty years. They only had to ask any successful agency construction manager or hospital that used agency construction managers to get an earful.

Key to Elle's understanding of how to control costs as a constraint was her understanding of what makes agency construction managers so successful in hospitals and schools. She deconstructed how agency construction managers work. To get a broader perspective, she also looked at how design-builders, at-risk construction managers, and general contractors work. She wanted to know the benefits and issues associated with each of their systems.

She found that the groundwork laid by early adopters of agency construction management, such as George Heery, Caudill Rowlett Scott, and CM Associates, took on new significance when viewed in the context of integrating practice and early decision making. These professionals pretty much created the profession of construction management. They sought to remedy the same issues that concerned Cork Point today. By identifying problems early, in a client-centered manner, they changed how projects had been delivered over the past thirty years. They improved results for many owners. By controlling risks, costs, and time, they developed improved project outcomes for those who embraced the process. They did this without much technology. They knew nothing of information models and at best used early forms of spreadsheets to achieve their results.

As a group, these early practitioners of agency construction management had received little recognition among the buzz about building information modeling. For many decades, their approach may have been the only bright spot in the ever-declining productivity of the industry. Their methods closely paralleled the cost and schedule management strategy that works best in integrated projects.

Elle saw many parallels between the work of these early adopters and the construction industry's approach to enterprise information modeling. Few understand the scope and breadth of the integration required by the enterprise. Few can see the vast possibilities. Most become entangled in arguments about software. Far too many offer solutions that work best for their own self-interests, often masking harm to their clients. Most clients cannot understand the subtleties and opt for the obvious feel-good solutions, missing the real benefit. As industries embrace information modeling and integrated processes, many new horizons open up; as do opportunities for deception.

MANAGE COSTS

The pace of change, design challenges, and economic complexity increase the opportunities for catastrophic errors of judgment. Projects that are over budget, late, and not fit for the intended use are symptoms of the problem. Solutions that are focused on solving problems quickly and economically to guide those who make critical project decisions are rare. Cork Point was one of the rare exceptions.

At Cork Point, initial planning decisions were made based on real-world facts. Everyone understood that even with facts, early decisions were but projections and speculation. Because of this, early decisions were not static. They grew and changed as work moved forward. These early decisions became the standard upon which everyone's success was measured. Cork Point's systems were built around the fact that good early decisions, implemented correctly, lead to better outcomes and an improved ability to capitalize on opportunities.

Elle learned that, when building information models are tied to real-world data, they can support local needs and concerns. Building information models can hone in on the optimal business, planning, and design solutions. The largest opportunities from models developed before what many considered the "normal" design process and after construction. Capitalizing on these bookends of traditional design and construction let Cork Point plan for tomorrow.

When Elle started her research, most model-based systems were driven by detailed design and construction needs only. These systems focused on what could be seen as the middle of the market, often ignoring planning, forecasting, development, portfolio management, property management, operations, and real estate. They accelerated processes and decisions; they reduced trade conflicts, highlighted scheduling, and improved the efficiency. Few products and processes capitalized on the information model's ability to support business decision making.

For Cork Point, Elle searched for and found technology designed to help owners with the process from beginning to end. Costs were managed within the information model, based on time-tested agency construction management techniques enhanced by technology.

Analysis and evaluation of early concepts affects outcomes. Elle and her board of directors believed that early decisions affected the bottom lines of everyone involved in every project. Cork Point staff, constructors, designers, fabricators, and the community all received benefits from the process. To some, the benefits were not obvious and easy to obtain. Architects particularly bristled and had to adjust their approach. Many architects' approach traditionally revolves around early decision making based almost exclusively on broad concepts and narrative representation. In a process where the earliest sketches include analysis and decision-making metrics, everyone soon learns that transparency and collaboration rule.

With Cork Point's approach, everyone knew how the direction they were taking would impact on the environment and other resources. They knew that when they analyzed an aspect of an asset, the results were repeatable and accurate, since they were working with real-world information, not assumptions, guesses, or opinions. They imposed constraints, and the unworkable options were eliminated before they spent time on unproductive tracks.

THOUGHT AND DEVELOPMENT

Decisions are captured. You know the lay of the land. You organize the work of the virtual team by making everyone's efforts transparent and open. You quickly study concepts and research design variations. You begin to formulate solutions. Concepts are resolved using simulations that allow you to select sites and fine-tune preliminary design and programming decisions. You verify the location and project needs. Step by step you detail spaces and equipment and implant information for future use.

At every step in the process, you create program estimating cost controls. If an area gets larger or the building grows, you see the effect on the costs. You overlay basic scheduling to allow time-based planning. Scheduling, energy, and LEED assessments occur at the same time. You validate the numbers of stories and the quantity, type, and size of spaces, and classify space usage. As the level of detail increases, the design is compared to the programmed area. Others extract data and begin to develop building elements using tools designed for this purpose.

As people worked in BIMStorm Cork Point, they did all of these things and more. They began the process of defining the project.

The BIMStorm defined Cork Point at various levels of detail. At its most broad, the structure and strategy of how Cork Point works in the community and world was defined. At its most detailed, the arrangement and description of health-care treatment spaces were completed. Between these extremes were individual projects and things that had to be implemented to make Elle's vision a reality. As Cork Point moved forward, several processes took place simultaneously. Teams worked to achieve a synchronized whole. The approaches used by these teams had many things in common, whether the teams were focusing on business processes, health-care delivery, or design and construction. Information models and BIMSynergy underpinned and supported each of them.

The primary focus was on management of costs and scope while maintaining Cork Point's quality goals. Ultimately, estimating, value engineering, procurement, and delivery occurred within the scope of the overall budget and the budget for each effort. The enterprise master budget and individual project budgets came from the solution identified in BIMStorm Cork Point. One team was focused on validating the accuracy of these budgets and negotiating with funding sources. Cork Point's virtual enterprise network was developing project teams tailored to each requirement. A master plan that accurately reflected community needs, financial resources, and the right team were all essential ingredients for success at Cork Point.

Regular virtual and face-to-face meetings carried over from the BIMStorm process. As Cork Point moved into the implementation process, these meetings became mandatory events for all team members. Everyone understood that the projects' and their personal success at Cork Point would be measured by the standards that were created in those early stages of development. Major standards were clear and used collaborative work processes.

VALIDATION

The scheme selected from the BIMStorm included crucial information about the new Cork Point. Some of this information was correct, some was based on rules of thumb, and some was speculative. In each case, the quality of the information was made evident by the Onuma System. Now the team began the process of adding the data needed. They improved upon those items that were uncertain. Compared to the normal planning and design process, what was achieved in the BIMStorm seems incredible. In four days, several months of work were completed. Four days were not sufficient to complete everything; more had to be done.

The BIMStorm leveraged collaboration and work of the many. In whole, the process allowed the group to visualize and test to eliminate the train wrecks. The group quickly focused on preferred solutions. Preferred solutions may not always be ideal solutions. Things change as more details are added and decision points are reached. The process requires that key decisions be validated after completion of significant development efforts. At Cork Point, this approach was seen as getting as much information as possible into the box that defined a project or work effort and then verifying why the information was added, where it came from, and how accurate it was.

The validation process begins with the executive summaries for project description and other project parameters. The space types, sizes, and other parameters are revisited. Everything about the space program is brought into question by a team separate from those who created the space program. Sustainability and LEED checklists are either created or and verified.

Site locations are fine-tuned. Since BIMStorm Cork Point was connected to Somerset County's GIS server through BIMSynergy, site checks were limited to adjusting setbacks and site features. In places where the GIS data is either skimpy or nonexistent, this effort might well involve retaining an expert surveyor to document the site. Connecting GIS to the models both simplifies and accelerates site validation.

A conceptual master schedule, overlaying budget and funding considerations, is also reviewed. Quality assumptions are added to the model. These items form the backbone of the validation. They become a vital component for future evaluation against standards. Are the concrete slabs completed on time? What is the status of the project contingency? Does this piece of millwork achieve the quality level that we established? Can our maintenance people change this pump, if it is broken?

While these details are under consideration and development, the designers are also at work. During the validation process, it is essential that the project's architectural design be developed to a level where spaces are properly laid out. The character and external treatment are conceived. The goal is to create a conceptual solution that contains all of the components required to deliver this project. The designer must realize that this is the driving factor. This conceptual solution may not be the final design direction; this solution is intended to establish the scope and quantities to support more accurate estimating and budgeting. Design work is completed either within the BIMSynergy, or imported to determine compliance with project requirements.

At this point, Elle and the management team reviewed project information to verify that the effort was on track and within the agreed-upon scope. Based upon the information coming from the BIMStorm, supplemented by this additional information, more detailed cost evaluations began. These evaluations took into account the assumptions made to date and anticipated local resources.

Knowledgeable professionals determine the parts necessary for a complete project. Costs up to this point have come from parametric cost data and published cost databases, combined with quantity information from the system. A generalized estimate of costs offers a significant benefit to early decision making and analysis. Without expert input, significant gaps can result.

The process takes current assumptions and adds professional knowledge about all of the other things necessary to define the container that holds all of the parts needed to make this a successful project. New assumptions are documented within the system. Value engineering ideas challenge current assumptions. Input from other team members creates changes to define the project.

Program, quality, schedule, and contingency assumptions are documented. Cost standards and unit prices are adjusted to reflect existing conditions or to provide for market conditions. If costs vary from the original budget, changes are identified to give decision makers options for adjustment. Based on the space program, financing, schedule, assumptions, and the concept design, the costs are documented within the system for review and approval by the leadership team.

The leadership team reviews the validated information and makes decisions about how to move forward. Their decisions may require the team to modify the project's scope or design concept. Any item can change. When significant issues are identified, they may require that the entire project return to the beginning for reconsideration. As new information surfaces and more details are created, the decisions might need to be revisited.

After changes were made and the validated project was ready to move forward, the leadership team decided how best to proceed in Cork Point's interest. Once their decisions had been made and documented within the system, the project budget was fixed. With a fixed budget, the project was monitored against the contingency, until completion. Less contingency meant that costs had increased. Higher contingency meant that costs had decreased. Elle and her team monitored the status of the project's contingency. Changes to the project contingency would affect project decisions.

DEVELOP

Once the project had been validated, and the budget had been fixed, the process moved into the detailed design and coordination. Scope, project assumptions, and tactics had been documented and agreed upon. The project's budget had been set. The team moved into this phase with a rich set of backup documentation and significant constraints. The project team had been formed. Now was the time for the team to take all of this information and create the solution that would be constructed. Design team members included Cork Point staff, architects, engineers, constructors, and fabricators in various disciplines.

Traditionally teams such as this worked pretty sequentially. The architect developed the design, allocating space as he or she felt was needed. Once the design reached the point where the architect was satisfied, backgrounds were given to the engineers to add their work. Constructors and fabricators rarely became involved until design work was finished. Detailed coordination of the work often occurred only during construction.

At Cork Point, things are different. Now the whole team collaborates on the process from the beginning. By training and temperament, the architect functions more like an orchestra conductor than like a general. The architect's ability to synthesize the work of all the others is what produces the best results. The expertise and knowledge of each member is valued. Working as a collaborative team, the detailed design begins to emerge. The process is not linear. The architectural designer exports spaces and values from the system to a desktop 3-D visualization application and develops the project's look and feel. At the same time, the mechanical engineer exports the spaces and begins to determine heating and cooling loads. The architect and the structural engineer engage in conversations about steel versus concrete. The structural engineer plugs the architect's concept into her system, and provides the architect with a fast analysis of the difference. At the same time, the architect models the floor height deviation possible from using concrete instead of steel.

The architect opens the variations in her desktop building information modeling system, adds the spaces and space data from BIMSynergy, and creates two possible solutions, one with the concrete structure and one with a steel frame. She refines the spaces without losing the system data. This is truly no problem, because the only requirement is to keep room names and room numbers that were automatically generated. She models several options for the exterior skin and roof system. She quickly arrives at a preferred approach. The preferred approach for each of the two solutions is then reimported into the system. The desktop building information model is also captured in BIMSynergy.

At this point, things seriously take off. The team now has a framework for adding systems and detailed analysis. Each of the specialists exports or opens the model, using whatever tools he or she needs to do the job. The structural engineer opens the model and the system computes the loads and stresses. The system creates an automatic solution for the engineer's consideration and development. The mechanical engineer exports the model. Since the model includes location information and walls, windows, doors and roofs, the system automatically computes heating and cooling loads and suggests how systems should be zoned. The engineer uses this information within a third system to compute carbon footprint, energy use, and recommendations for sustainable system types. Fuel and alternative system analysis is completed at the same time. The window/wall specialist exports the model to a specialty solution that tries thousands of alternatives for how to best and most economically enclose the building.

While this is happening, other people continue to add detail. One person is inputting interior finishes, walls, floors, and ceilings. Another is adding furniture, fixtures, and equipment. At this stage, these items are placed in rooms much as you would expect from a moving company. Everything is in the room but nothing is laid out properly yet. The detailed layouts will come later. As ceilings and windows develop, the electrical engineer working with the lighting specialist begins the lighting analysis. They make initial fixture selections, post suggestions for window review relocations and size changes, and analyze energy use to focus on the proper lighting types.

Everyone is in such close communication, enhanced by modeling systems and BIMSynergy. Tasks happen concurrently. In rare cases, tasks occur sequentially. Iteration and adjustment are expected. When things move this fast, everything moves around. The days where the mechanical engineer waited on the architect, who waited on the structural engineer, who waited on the civil engineer, who waited on the surveyor, who waited on the owner, who waited on the bank are no more. Almost everything happens in real time.

At appropriate times during the process, everyone submits their work for review. At that time, the models are put together into a master-model. Rules-based automated systems identify variations from the requirements and highlight conflicts. At the same time, progress and changes are reviewed with the leadership team. This review is more of a formality and a requirement, since the leadership team is able to lurk in the background and follow everything that is happening at any time. They know what is developing.

This is the time for revisiting assumptions. Cost parameters are adjusted to create check estimates. Traditionally this has been the time when value engineering was used to force projects to budget. Value engineering in this mode was usually neither a value, nor engineering. With the highly collaborative process now used at Cork Point, value engineering occurs all the time. Designers no longer work in isolation; they receive direct and immediate feedback from those who must implement the design. Fabricators and constructors' input is valued and occurs at the place and time of most benefit. As the check estimate develops, the team works together to find solutions, should estimated costs vary significantly from the budget.

After pausing to take a breath and assess where the project stands, the team resumes their work. Depending on the need, project detail increases or the team repeats the process. The process invites the team to test-fit program functions, design features, and disaster recovery. Flexibility and the ability to test-fit solutions were critical. The ability to quickly evaluate and discard unworkable solutions let the team move quickly. Cork Point could not afford anything less than an optimized process as they were rebuilding. The process gave the team the ability to produce projects of any type without sacrifice, even in one-off situations.

ASSESS IN MANY WAYS

Assess the detailed design in many ways. Fulfilling peoples' need for beauty and functional space is the first level. Assess from the architectural perspective. Aesthetic merit, space definition, proportion, scale, organization, context, social response, integrity, and many other factors come into play. There are many other areas that get assessed and monitored for projects at Cork Point. Cost as a constraint, benefit to the community, environmental response, and life cycle sustainability are just four of the factors assessed.

Assessments take place in many ways. At the most human level, assessments take the form of personal opinions based on your view of the world. Is a beautiful? Do I like this space? Can I work here? Can I live here? Other assessments are automated based on rules. Rules-based assessments use systems that allow Cork Point to describe a requirement in BIMSynergy. The rules checker in BIMSynergy looks at a model and determines how well the model complies with the rule.

The space must comply with the most current version of the life safety code. The rules checker finds three dead-end corridors that do not comply with life safety requirements.

All floors must be three feet above the Hurricane Edgar surge level. The rules checker finds one two-bedroom cottage to be located eight inches too low.

No building system may penetrate the space used by another system. A steel beam cannot penetrate an air-conditioning duct. The rules checker looks at the first models submitted by team members and finds fifty conflicts.

Each mechanical device must perform a set of predetermined tasks. An air handling unit must deliver 30 ft.³ per minute of air at 62°F. A sensor measures the output from the air handling unit and reports the values to BIMSynergy. The values are compared to the requirement and the area in the model served by the air handling unit changes color depending up on whether too much, too little, or just enough air at the proper temperature is flowing. An alert is sent to the maintenance staff if the values are out of the proper range.

There are also assessments that combine automated systems with human interaction to visualize areas requiring further analysis. The approved solution includes building space requirements. Each space must have specific characteristics. Size, height, types, and amount of conditioning and other characteristics are defined. As the team develops solutions, the solutions return to the system for side-by-side comparison and review for compliance. Where characteristics have changed as a design develops, the logic behind the change is also evaluated and either accepted or rejected.

DELIVER THE PRODUCT

The process repeats until the models are done to a level that can be used for fabrication and installation. A high proportion of the work at Cork Point is fabricated off-site, using these models. A minimal amount of this work is ever printed onto paper. There is no longer a need. Everyone in the system is able to open and use the models to coordinate their efforts. The models do not rely on desktop software or hardware and can be accessed, visualized, and understood anywhere that an Internet connection exists. Where more complex and accurate information is needed, that is also available. Detailed models at high complexity are maintained on BIMSynergy systems, convenient for anyone who needs them. The idea is to make the simplest and most easily accessible form of information available to anyone who needs it. The complexity is still there, but if you don't require the complex format, why be burdened by it?

Management of cost and other project constraints never stops. One of the major advantages of BIMSynergy is that anything that occurs can automatically be assessed and understood against a predefined rule. Because of this, every change and every extra generates a report. The information reported may take the form of "everything is as expected." Often change reports are telling us that something is incorrect or that something needs to be reevaluated.

Automated change reports and system updated cost analysis only go so far. Intervention by experts is still required. The construction manager continues the cost control process during bidding, negotiations, and any buyout process that occurs at Cork Point. As the models pass through validation and detailed design, units of work and contracting strategy are developed and added to the models. As a team, units of work are broken down to achieve the greatest benefit for Cork Point, while assuring that all participants are successful. Combining each scope of work produces a complete package that when fabricated and installed will result in a complete project. As negotiations occur, the construction manager maintains a running analysis of where each scope stands relative to its individual budget. As a whole, the units of work must achieve the budget, or the project returns to detailed design for correction.

Team members are expected to work to improve Cork Point. Team members expect the same in reverse. Because of this, most units of work are negotiated and supplied by team members. In some cases, procurement from companies outside of the group is needed. As units of work are identified and resolved, decisions related to procurement and contracting are made. Before bidding or negotiations, the construction manager prepares a list of qualified bidders for each unit of work under consideration. These bidders are given access to the model. Team members work to clarify needs, identify procedures, and to make adjustments that may be required.

Team members and outside companies realize that the master model is the measure of performance. The requirements included in the master model determine what must be built, where it must be located, at what time it must be installed, and everything else about the project. Each fabricator and supplier signs a contract acknowledging these facts and accepting responsibility for their units of work within the model. The system is highly collaborative. Multiple checks and balances exist in the process, but mistakes still happen. Since the master model represents the entire project in detail, each constructor assumes responsibility for installation in conformance with the model. When work occurs that is not in accord with the model, the constructor who varied from the models' requirements automatically assumes responsibility.

Before Elle finalizes any work product or authorizes construction, negotiated and proposed costs are reconciled against the work scopes and estimates prepared by the construction manager. This reconciliation helps to ensure that pricing errors do not affect the project. The process is designed to identify costs and quantities that are either too high or too low that may result in incorrect contract amounts, or subsequent failure of a supplier. Since Cork Point's approach is collaborative, everyone works toward pricing that will provide the quality required without over- or underpaying for the work. Everything is a win-win exchange. The team is not served by any party taking advantage of another's mistake.

At times, the reconciliation identifies costs and quantities that exceed the budget. When this occurs, the construction manager consults the team to assess cost-reduction alternatives. The value of these alternatives is then determined. The construction manager then reviews the reconciled pricing, performance capabilities, and alternatives with Elle and her management team. At this point, the final "go/no go" decision takes place. No work is awarded that increases the established budget without first pursuing every possible approach for reducing cost. Elle and her team arrive at their decision understanding clearly where they stand.

At this stage, Elle's team has created highly detailed digital models that will guide the construction, operations, business simulations, and planning for the life of Cork Point. The model stores and links to built environment and business data in a series of BIMSynergy database files. The models are true archives of existing conditions, planned work, and future dreams. The archive is live. It will build up over time. As Cork Point moves forward, the archived data will become more and more useful. Cork Point's data is more valuable than the facility itself.

As projects move into construction and become assets of Cork Point, several things happen. The models allow the constructors to manage progress in real time. Coordinating the work becomes an automated process. Models are combined into a central master model that highlights and documents interferences and problems that might cause delays or added costs. This is all linked to provide Elle and the construction manager almost real-time control of costs. As things change, they are immediately reflected on the dashboard of the project's contingency. Visualization of costs is only one metric that the project dashboard in the upper right-hand part of Elle's screen shows. Each metric has a trigger point. Should the trigger point be exceeded, the metric turns red and alerts the right people that something needs to happen.

Sometimes, the correction is no more complicated than resetting a switch. Other times, the remedy requires research and a new way forward. The goal is to learn of an issue before the problem progresses to the point where it requires carrying out of work, extension of time, or additional cost. It is clearly more expensive to change after pouring the concrete than when the designer is first conceiving the slab layout. The greatest benefits come from tweaking processes to take advantage of this simple fact.

Much record keeping and site verification has been eliminated. Projects use sensors, tags, and nanodust to track almost everything. Now when you walk into a room with a model-enabled device, the model knows where you are and can show you anything and everything about the space. Mundane markups and error lists are things of the past. Everything is tracked and monitored. Commissioning projects for end use is a snap and happens throughout the process. No longer must you finish a project and independently figure out how to make building systems work. Now everything is validated and functioning as it happens.

SEAMLESS

Everyone who works at Cork Point understands that the underlying complexity is designed to make the user's experience as easy as possible. The goal is to let people make the critical decisions, without burdening them with the complexities that can be handled by technology and experts. Without the people who live here and use the facilities, what would be the point? Cork Point is a lovely place that lets everyone take advantage of the community and local environment, while tapping the world when needed.

The data that make Cork Point possible would overwhelm almost anyone. Without systems that manage the data, few would be able to take advantage of the benefits. If residents were required to sort through sensor data and maintenance logs in order to figure out how to optimize their energy bill, few would be successful. Most would set the thermostat at the level that seems comfortable, would leave everything running at all times, and would complain when the bills arrived. Technology has changed the world. Technology has even changed how people react to the world.

We all have to become more versatile and capable. Most people know that we have to adjust faster. We must process information faster. Cork Point is designed to help people with the change. As change has accelerated everything in the built environment, Cork Point has worked out ways to manage the complexities, to expose the simplicities, to engage the community.

A year once seemed like a long time. Now a year happens in a relative instant. Decision making must be optimized when things happen this fast. The complexities must remain in the background. Items needing decisions and action must go to the front. People make too many errors when they are overwhelmed. Forecasts must be made with better, more focused information than before. We must be more flexible and must plan with longer horizons. Otherwise, the errors and disastrous decisions that characterized the late twentieth and early twenty-first century will continue.

For many years, only a small fraction of the population has understood that files, once created, are out-of-date the moment that they are stored on a file server. Most have created their proprietary format models, gotten the direct benefit, and either did not care or did not know about the longer-term issues. As professionals convinced people of the value of information modeling, some people started to see the disconnect between the file-based information models and the life cycle benefits that should happen. Savvy individuals were able to recognize that file-based models are little better than outdated blueprints. Project documentation may have improved. There may have been fewer interferences between ductwork and steel. But the fact that information models are life cycle assets seemed to be a foreign concept. The fact that most information created in the last thirty years is no longer accurate or available is not widely understood. The fact that many of the models created in the last twenty years have little or no life cycle value has escaped most professionals in the industry. As a society, we can no longer afford this waste.

The two-dimensional process used to create and document projects for millennia had little long-term value; not because of an inherent lack of value, but because of paper copies, ignorance, and faulty processes. Print documents stored in a cabinet in a basement, only to be accessed when a problem occurred, had little value. The same can be said for most of the three-dimensional models created since the 1980s. This lost data resulted in costly and inefficiently managed buildings.

At Cork Point, we create furniture, equipment, and materials in an object database and link them to almost any inventory and procurement program. Existing manufacturer data is linked and used in the same manner. Suppliers then use this centralized information to enable automatic installation coordination. When changes occur over a product's life, the changes directly reflect throughout the system. Products include sensors that interface with the models, allowing immediate management control of their functions.

Cork Point requires that their information modeling tools support open standards and connect to distributed systems through web services. Because of this, many solutions for intelligent and automated systems become available. Automated site systems are just one example. The structural engineer adds a steel beam to the model. The steel beam carries all the properties of the genuine product and is located in geographic space. The fabricator connects the model to his or her computer-assisted manufacturing system that cuts, drills, and coats the beam as specified. The beam is also tagged. Sensors are added. From the time the fabrication begins until the beam is installed, it will be monitored and tracked, connected to the model. The beam is loaded onto the truck and scheduled to arrive at the site at precisely the time that the crane is available to raise it in place. The riggers and steelworkers are ready with the proper tools when the beam arrives. The beam swings into place. The steelworkers install the correct bolts with the right washers and nuts and torque them in place as directed by the model. The engineer receives confirmation that the beam, as installed, complies with the requirements. Operations and maintenance information associated with the beam's coatings and connections link to the facility management database. The project cost accounting system is told by the model that the work is in place, and funds are distributed to the fabricator, the trucking company, and the installer. Elle's dashboard for completion inches up as another piece of work is done.

Along with standard management controls comes a high level of off-site prefabrication. In fact, over 85 percent of all materials are designed and detailed virtually and then cut and assembled using computer-aided manufacturing in the shops of Cork Point's suppliers and fabricators. Since the model is accurate and complete, materials arrive on site, are tagged electronically to their location and schedule, and just plug in at the right time. The process requires a balance of resources and technology to be successful.

When the resources needed to carry out a goal exceed the resources available, we can find ourselves in big trouble. We sometimes forget this classic equation. Our resources become disconnected from our goal. When a goal is set, and the resources required to deliver on the goal are open-ended or unknown, people's opinions, rather than facts, often guide decisions. One person may value the goal higher than another and spend more resources to achieve the goal. Another may see the goal as irrelevant and withhold resources. Information models connected to real-time data show people the facts. They connect the facts to goals. Outcomes become more predictable as personal opinions are reduced. Results are more likely to match the goal that is set. Achieving this balance requires more than technology. It requires people to work together with the technology.

If we step back, look at the character traits of those successful at Cork Point, and compare them to the character traits that would mean the most to the traditional process, there are serious misalignments. The traditional process is much like an assembly line, getting high volume from a large contingent of semiskilled laborers. The traditional approach relies on cooperation; others involved pick up the slack. A fully integrated process requires something more. People collaborate. They maximize their knowledge and productivity, using tools that enable them to make rapid decisions based on facts. Working together, asking for help when needed, admitting, accepting, and correcting mistakes, and proactively working in the organization's long-term best interest are the traits that make people successful.

CONNECTED FUTURE

Organizations have facilities to accommodate people, processes, and equipment. They have facilities staff to make sure that buildings remain in operation and systems work properly. Beyond that, most organizations' interest in facilities ends. Historically, facilities and facility staffs were treated as necessary evils by most organizations. Facilities were a line item in the budget. They fought for funding much like any other overhead account. Facilities were rarely seen as strategic assets.

As overhead, facilities and facility staff did not contribute to the bottom line or to the organization's mission. Compared to a program that created income or a department that delivered on the core mission, facilities had little value. Because of this, facilities suffered from deferred maintenance, were often the first place for cuts, and were low in the organizational structure. When times got tough, maintenance suffered. Facility personnel lost their jobs. Facility management software delivered services in predefined ways. Rare was the group that would invest in these complex and expensive systems, since their failure rate approached 80 percent. Integrated systems and information changed this dynamic.

Facilities are organizational assets. They have strategic value. Facilities can improve mission outcomes. When organizations begin to realize that facilities are capital assets that contribute to an organization's bottom line and mission, things change dramatically. This is not a new concept. Major organizations, such as the Coast Guard, have long championed this idea. Hospitals design facilities to establish their brand and engage patients. Hospital facilities house medical technology and patients. Health-care facilities are designed to attract new staff and set the organization apart from the crowd in a highly competitive world. People at Cork Point knew and understood this concept.

Facility managers work behind the scenes. They support electrical, mechanical, and other building systems that people need to perform their jobs. The facility manager's mission is difficult, especially when mission-critical information is not accessible or is missing. Managing repairs, maintenance, and operations for multi-building campuses is a highly specialized task. Managing dozens or hundreds of buildings can be a nightmare of tiny, interconnected decisions. That's why information models and BIMSynergy are used to integrate planning, design, construction, and everything else about the enterprise.

Cork Point teams began to develop operations and maintenance information during the first concepts. Over time, this information became richer and richer, so that when construction ended the facility managers were able to take over seamlessly from the constructors. One day, carpenters were hanging doors. Painters were painting walls. Thermostats were being installed. The next day, the locksmith was cutting new keys for Dr. Bagayoko-Smith's office. The paint crew was touching up walls damaged when the construction managers moved out of their temporary space. The mechanical supervisor was on her computer setting schedules for air-conditioning systems in the Emergency Department. The plumbing supervisor was studying the model to locate the sewer cleanout for the toilet the nurses on 3C had already managed to clog up.

Operations and maintenance is not a technology issue; it is a business issue. The goal is to respond quickly and to eliminate unnecessary tasks that add no value. The Cork Point facilities department plays a strategic role. They keep things humming, and quietly optimize operations throughout the organization. They respond before problems occur. If not, they react quickly, knowing the solution. They use technology to help them to do this, but it is about people collaborating and taking pride in their work. They understand what they do and know how best to do it. Much of what they do is based on dynamic, "what-if" planning designed to keep the facility operating at peak performance.

Elle knew that she could change things in ways that increase the organization's likelihood of future success. She can create processes that reduce future problems. The alternative is to continue as before, creating the design in a partial vacuum, disconnected from construction, and leaving Cork Point to bear the cost of the corrections. By allowing constraints to continue to manage the organization, rather than becoming proactive, Elle would relinquish her responsibility to tradition. Poor documentation, cost overruns, and late delivery would once again be the norm. By putting aside her fears and concerns and embracing the broader issues, Elle is using technology to improve outcomes and provide better value.

Clinging blindly to the old ways is no longer the best solution. Technology gives Cork Point the opportunity to forecast with better data. If frees the organization to respond quickly. It allows Elle to study change with detail. It provides information to explain new ideas.

When Cork Point's process started, many people took for granted things that were once revolutionary, while at the same time refusing to consider anything new. Yesterday's revolutions did not happen by accident. They came about because creative people applied creative ideas to solve problems. They took risks to achieve results and make the world a better place.

SIMPLE INFORMATION

> Everything should be made as simple as possible, but not simpler.
> —Albert Einstein

The Internet has become the focus of much that we do. The medium constantly changes and evolves as people find new needs and uses. People jump in and start using the tools and networks, and by spreading information have altered how we look at our world. Social networks, e-commerce, polling, news, entertainment, and much more make it so that we can quickly find ourselves buried in details. The Internet has affected how we live, work, and play.

It may not be possible to understand the extent to which information impacts upon our lives. Information can be overwhelming. The speed that things change can transcend our ability to adapt. Yet, adapt we must. Realizing the need for better ways to understand and use information is the first step.

In some industries, remarkable strides have been made in tailoring the information to people's needs. The travel industry is an excellent example. Internet-based tools such as Expedia give people the information that they need to make decisions, while keeping the complexity at arm's length. Expedia does not ask you to determine how much fuel to put in the plane or to schedule the crew. You tell Expedia where and when you want to travel. It then asks you to select your flights and seat preference. The system then takes your credit card information, completes the transaction, and issues tickets. The goal is a straightforward transaction.

There are many similar tools and processes that come from the Internet. Behind the scenes is highly complex data. The data supports easy decision making by users via browsers. People connect with little regard for where they live, where they work, or where the data resides.

The system revolves around sharing information and collaboration to accomplish things. Some of the things seem unimportant. Others achieve significant results and are extremely valuable. The results come from clearly understanding the complex data that is available and creating tools that allow people to take advantage of the data without needing advanced degrees or knowledge of computer science.

There are many ways to interact with complex data. Industries have long used data to enable computer-aided manufacturing, just-in-time processes, and other integrated ways of working. Shipbuilding, aviation, and the automotive business rely on complex data and complicated tools for many of their processes. Normally, consumer issues are factored in by experts, and end users are involved only as products go to sales. The disconnect between the production and use of products has been seen by some as an inefficiency that should be corrected. These industries are working to better integrate users in order to achieve greater efficiency. They explore concepts such as mass customization to provide the end user greater choice while reducing the need for inventory.

These users of complex data have at least three things in common.

First, they usually focus on specific industry needs. They may use data in integrated ways, but the use is focused on one particular field. Generally, the data remains within a single business group or organization.

As these industries use complex data, they have experts or trained staff to create and use the data. Sophisticated industrial processes take advantage of model servers and other complex technologies that require the involvement of specialists trained in their use. A database manager organizes and maintains the database. A computer-aided design and manufacturing specialist works to support robotics on the plant floor via the model server. At each level, staff members are educated or trained to do things with company data. The companies have the resources to hire and formally train people to use their systems.

Sensors and monitoring are the final common theme. Sensors and controls are significant factors in industrial efficiency. Sensors are critical to assembly lines and production processes. Everything that can be measured is measured. Since the days when Henry Ford first created his assembly line, this has been so. In this environment, sensors exist for a specific purpose. They direct products down line A, rather than line B. They close valves. Step-by-step, they do things in predictable ways.

Things are not so predictable in the built environment. Creating systems that will work in this environment is not easy. It is not possible to teach everyone how to work with the complexity. The built environment is too messy. It touches and connects too many things in our world. Focusing on one area, one subset, one industry, or one process is not viable. Closed and tightly managed systems cannot, even with the best of intentions, handle this level of complexity. Solutions may learn from industry, yet industry solutions do not resolve built environment issues or needs. The Internet, and the systems that it has enabled, offers solutions.

The Internet relies on people interacting with information in straightforward ways. Information on the Internet can be re-purposed for new and unplanned uses. Data can be captured for one particular application and later some or all of it can be extracted for other uses. That is what makes the Internet so powerful and all-reaching.

Data about the soda that you bought yesterday at a convenience store can tell your local grocery store of your preference. When the data shows a predefined number of local people that choose your brand, the system tells the grocery store to carry it on their shelves. Your purchasing habits affect the availability of a product. Transactions that produce potentially usable data happen all the time and all around us. Finding, analyzing, and using data for new and unplanned purposes are the keys to better managing the built environment.

CORK POINT
CRISFIELD, MARYLAND
MAY 5, 2026

> On a group of theories one can found a school; but on a group of values one can found a culture, a civilization, a new way of living together among men.
> —Ignazio Silone

At Cork Point, you will find a cozy new waterfront home on Crisfield's Tangier Sound with modern health care. It is a new community for senior citizens and others requiring medical care, and their spouses or housemates. Cork Point offers all of the conventional medical services, and much more. The Boardwalk, a three-star dining room, a movie theatre, the bike paths, and a health spa combine with the natural attractions of bird watching, fishing, crabbing, boating, and hunting to provide a stimulating environment. Here, you stay healthy through exercise activities, regular health monitoring, socializing, and active living. You will find a home, and amenities to make life pretty enjoyable. West Memorial Medical Center, the Sunset Assisted Living Center, and the Selma George Nursing Home are all within easy walking distance of your door. If you need it, you can have in-home assisted-living care such as therapy or help getting dressed, bathing, or taking medication. If you face the challenge of illness, no other place provides the dignity of private residential living combined with such a rich range of health services.

Picture yourself reading or relaxing on your screened porch. The only noise is the gulls squabbling overhead. You are watching the sun setting in front of you over Tangier Sound. This morning you walked into town, drank coffee, and solved the world's problems with some locals at Gordon's. The pace of life is slow, the people are friendly, the weather is mild, and you caught the flounder this afternoon. The churches are small, and the sermons are short. This is pleasant living on the Chesapeake Bay, state of Maryland, Somerset

County, city of Crisfield, Cork Point. The big businesses are farming, crabbing, and oystering. It is country here, but within thirty minutes, you find eighteen golf courses, a minor league baseball team, two universities, a symphony orchestra, an airport, a world-class zoo, and shopping malls. A few minutes farther lie Ocean City, the ponies and wildlife of Assateague Island, and the Atlantic. The Cork Point transport vans will take you wherever you want to go, including the big city—provided you find a compelling reason to leave your porch.

Betsy is the concierge, a fancy title for the person who organizes everything. She gets us where we want to go, finds what we want to buy, settles arguments, plays bridge better than most, and can sometimes be talked into a cold beer after work in the summertime. We go fishing anytime we want, and that is often.

Betsy gets the boat, and some of the locals to come along. The fishing gets people talking, and you make some new friends. Betsy plans the menus with the chef, David. Some people here cook, some do not. You can take your meals at the Boathouse with fancier food, beer, and wine, if you want them; the Cork Tree Cafeteria with casual, faster, cheaper, and probably healthier food; or you can walk downtown and get a world-class crab cake sandwich 363 days of the year. If you are too tired to cook and do not want to go out, there's room service. You can order from the Boathouse or the Cafeteria. The second floor of the Boathouse has economical guest rooms for when friends or family stay over. They've got antique furniture, cable TV, comfortable beds, and a lovely view of the creek.

Most of us here use the maid service. Once a day, once a week: you decide. You deserve a few luxuries. About half of the residents here need some help. Some people need help with their bath or getting dressed. Others need daily attention for medication or therapy. You can use as little or as much as you need right at home.

The staff still makes house calls. Food, maid service, nursing care: you just pay for what you use. In addition, if you have a problem, you talk to Betsy, and it gets fixed. You will enjoy the cottages and apartment suites. They are a comfortable, efficient place to call home. The cottages offer more personal space, warmed by a fireplace, with a complete kitchen, a roomy master bedroom, and a smaller guest room or den. The bathroom and the entire cottage (and the apartments) are wheelchair accessible, inside and out. You get a nurse's call button in every room and the security of immediate medical assistance.

In the apartments, you get either more space or less; it depends how you look at it. The L-shaped floor plan gives a couple ample space, with a roomy bedroom, bath, studio kitchen, and smaller living room…complete with sunsets. Your private space is smaller than in a cottage, but you share a large living room with other residents of your floor. You will love the fireplace and big-screen television room (you have never seen football this big…in high definition). You also have a library, a craft/workshop area, and room enough to enjoy solitude when desired.

The residents are a mixture of locals and folks from the city, which makes life entertaining. Imagine a liberal Boston Democrat talking politics with a Crisfielder. (They get along just fine.) At Cork Point, one spouse might need or will need health care. Apartment living is more communal and supportive. Healthy and ill spouses can continue to live together...and healthy spouses can continue to have a life, secure that their loved one is safe and well attended.

When it comes right down to it, Cork Point is for lovers...or maybe best friends. You can live together longer here. They designed the cottages and apartments for independent living with some help...as much as possible. You have West Memorial Medical for health maintenance and emergency care. You do not want to think about moving your partner to an assisted-care facility or a nursing home, but most of us will have to face that decision sometime. When the time comes when one of you needs more help, you can choose to move on to the Sunset House, our assisted-living home, or to the Selma George Nursing Home. Both are on the Cork Point campus, a short walk from your door.

You probably want to know about our doctors, nurses, and staff. They are good. They are from all over the world and board certified in the specialties. One other thing: Crisfielders live to be pretty old, late eighties or early nineties. That could be because of small-town life, the salt air, and the sunsets...or because they've got decent doctors.

Making Cork Point work takes a lot of outstanding people, but it also takes systems that make it possible for them to thrive. Elle and her team created the system with the help of ideas that came from the music and software industries. Using virtual enterprise concepts, they have created a system that is flexible, quick to respond, and adaptable to new needs. Why wait?

COMMON SENSE MULTIPLIED BY TECHNOLOGY

6. The Deepwater Horizon disaster might well have destroyed the Gulf Coast ecosystem. Only with a massive effort was the disaster avoided. People can once again travel to Destin Beach in Florida. They can suntan on the whitest sand in the world and swim without getting a mouthful of toxic goop. The mission of the Network for Sustainable Decisions is to make the same thing happen for the Chesapeake Bay.

Less than twenty years ago, the Chesapeake Bay attracted millions of tourists to Maryland and Virginia each year. For decades, the bay supported fishing, crabbing, swimming, boating, and sailing, in what became known as the "Land of Pleasant Living."

In the twenty years either side of the new millennium, strident, polarized groups spent so much time fighting and arguing that they had no time or energy left for fixing the problems. Hard-headed, old-tech manufacturers and self-absorbed people were harming the bay without thinking. Years of battles, disjointed regulations, and overuse allowed many bay grasses and oysters that historically kept the bay clean to be killed off. Urban manufacturers used their political clout to keep the public looking at the wrong things. Few people truly understood the problem, or the fact that groups on both sides of the argument were manipulating the public to achieve their own goals.

In the second decade of the twenty-first century, the bay reached a point where the natural systems could no longer overcome the external pressures. The bay was at a tipping point. Either the bay would become a dead sea or everyone would start to work together to repair the damage. Scientists believed that there was time to fix the problems. The Network for Sustainable Decisions was created to change the social and environmental conditions to enable recovery.

The Network for Sustainable Decisions, headquartered in Princess Anne, MD is responsible for managing the clean-up of the Chesapeake Bay. 38° 12' 5" N 75° 41' 19" W

We are headquartered in Princess Anne, the county seat of Somerset County. Princess Anne was founded in 1733 at the head of the Manokin River and is home to the University of Maryland Eastern Shore. The area's rich cultural heritage, and its central place on the Chesapeake Bay, made the hamlet an ideal location for managing the bay recovery process. We were close to the water, far from outside influences, and technologically well connected. BIMSynergy was located just down the road in Westover.

Sandy Kim was the virtual enterprise manager, charged with orchestrating the process. Think of her as a symphony conductor with a model server as her baton. She knew that people have remarkably short memories when it comes to environmental disaster. Even before the mess in the Gulf of Mexico back in 2010, there have been environmental problems. To this day, she remembered the lessons that her grandparents taught about the Dust Bowl and the problems we bring on ourselves and how hard it is to improve conditions. Sandy was passionate about her work and realistic enough to know that the recovery will take decades, even with everyone pulling together.

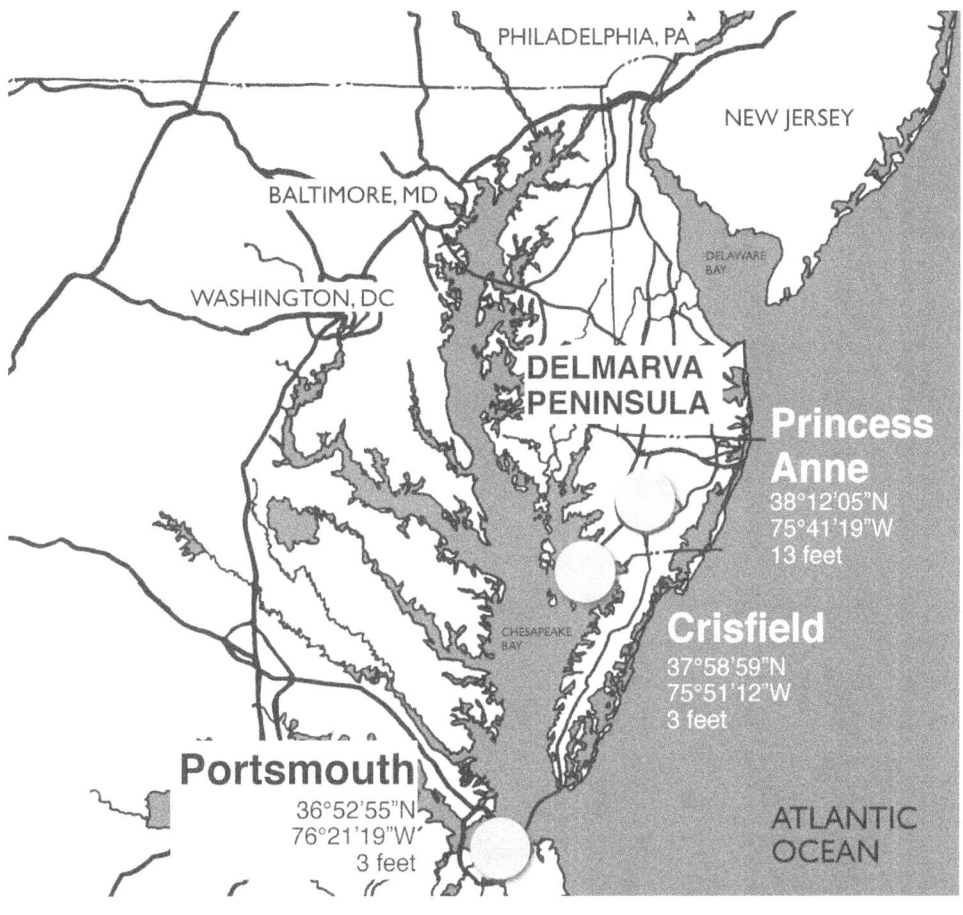

Saving the Chesapeake Bay is a wicked problem. The complexity of the systems that interconnect in this ecosystem is overwhelming. Gaining a comprehensive view of all the issues is difficult. Reaching a consensus amongst the wildly divergent stakeholders may never be possible. Conditions go from grave to worse as every effort achieves mixed result.

THE BAY IS ALIVE

> The best time to plant an oak tree was twenty-five years ago. The second best time is today.
> —James Carvillee

Sandy and her friends turned heads. You could find her with three or four of her friends every Wednesday night racing Amber Waves on the Choptank River. They were the only boat with an all-woman crew at the yacht club. Sometimes they won, most times they lost, but they always had a terrific time, especially when they kicked back after the race at Jimmie and Sook's Raw Bar and Grill.

She had moved to the area so that she could sail her Bill Shaw-designed Pearson Flyer. Amber Waves was a one-design racer, but she was quite roomy down below, with her eleven-foot beam. Sandy figured that anchoring out with a couple friends, about a mile up the Wye East River on Granary Creek, was just about heaven. Granary Creek was her idea of how the entire Chesapeake Bay should be: quiet, rural, and with few boats, especially in the spring and fall. Nothing was better than waking up in the morning, sticking your head out of the main hatch, and looking up at a pair of bald eagles sitting on the dead tree overlooking your boat. Granary Creek was one of the few truly wild and undeveloped anchorages left on the bay.

On hot summer nights, her favorite anchorage was on Dymer Creek flowing into Fleets Bay on the Northern Neck of Virginia. Riding gently at anchor behind uninhabited Grog Island as darkness fell took Sandy back to the days of John Smith and Pocahontas. Moonlight laid a path to the horizon. The sandy beach glowed. The Osprey nest on red bouy number six was barely visible as darkness fell. Not much was left of Grog Island these days. The winter storms washed more of the island away every year. Soon it would be only a shoal and one of Sandy's treasured memories.

The bay is a living thing. It was Sandy's fondest hope that her work could bring the bay back to health and preserve this magnificent resource. There were few places where you could experience the Chesapeake Bay as it probably once was. La Trappe Creek on the Choptank River was one of the few places where Sandy ever experienced crystal-clear water on the bay. The delightful anchorage behind the long sandbar that extended from Martin Point at the entrance to the creek was one of the few places where this sometimes occurred. Clear water on the bay was always a surprise, especially as the oysters and bay grasses had died off.

For Sandy, La Trappe Creek was a dichotomy. The creek was a lovely place to anchor and enjoy the day. Yet, in the early morning, one dared not swim in La Trappe Creek, because many boats allowed the sewerage from their heads to pump overboard into the creek. Why would people who have the most to gain from a healthy bay do something like that?

Amber Waves on a close reach on the Chesapeake Bay near Point Lookout, MD. 38° 1' 26" N 76° 14' 18" W

NINETEEN SEVENTIES

In the 1970s, we learned that the Chesapeake Bay contained marine dead zones. In these zones, the water was so depleted of oxygen that no life existed. Massive fish kills were a result. Today, the dead zones are larger. The dead zones are responsible for the death of thousands of tons of shellfish and worms each year. The Chesapeake Bay food chain is at risk. The famed blue crab is at risk of losing its primary food source.

Enormous algae blooms are part of what cause these dead zones. Runoff from agriculture and industrial plants throughout the watershed contribute to the algae blooms. Many of the pollution sources that affect the bay lie upstream on tributaries far from the bay itself. Many lie in the drainage area of the Susquehanna River. The Susquehanna flows from New York, through Pennsylvania and Maryland before emptying into the Chesapeake Bay. Natural gas development using hydraulic fracturing, mining, sewage pollution, development, and poor planning all contribute to the pollution of the Susquehanna. The river has long been considered one of America's most endangered rivers. Year after year, concerns are raised that the river will reach the tipping point, and never recover.

Storm water runoff from Maryland and Virginia communities increases the problem. Efforts to reduce runoff and limit use of fertilizer have either failed or achieved marginal results. Although communities retrofit storm drains, require the installation of rain gardens, and try many other solutions, pollution continues to be flushed into the bay.

Fed by phosphorus and nitrogen that enters the watershed from human activities, alga prevents sunlight from reaching the bottom of the bay as it grows. The alga removes oxygen from the water when it dies and decomposes. The amount of new building construction and substantial increases in pavement increase the rates of soil erosion and runoff, adding sediments to the bay's waters, further blocking sunlight. Much of the Chesapeake Bay's bottom has become a muddy wasteland.

Eelgrass and other bay grasses have declined as the sunlight and nutrients required for their health have been compromised. It was estimated that when Europeans first colonized the Chesapeake region, oysters in the bay could filter the entire bay in 3.3 days. By 1988, it was estimated that the oysters took 325 days to filter the bay's waters. It has been many years since the Chesapeake Bay's oyster population could filter the water in the bay in less than a year. Pollution from all sources must be managed, over many years, to change this dynamic.

Sandy was fortunate to experience a day with clear water on La Trappe Creek. Almost everywhere in the Chesapeake Bay area the water is now so cloudy that one loses sight of one's feet before wading to one's knees. Many traditional swimming areas are off-limits.

The levels of fecal coliform and other pollutants make swimming in these areas unsafe. Overharvesting of oysters, crabs, and several species of fish, pollution, sedimentation, and diseases such as Dermo and MSX have devastated the livelihood of an entire industry. Without dramatic changes by all of those that impact on the Chesapeake Bay watershed, the bay will soon become a dead sea.

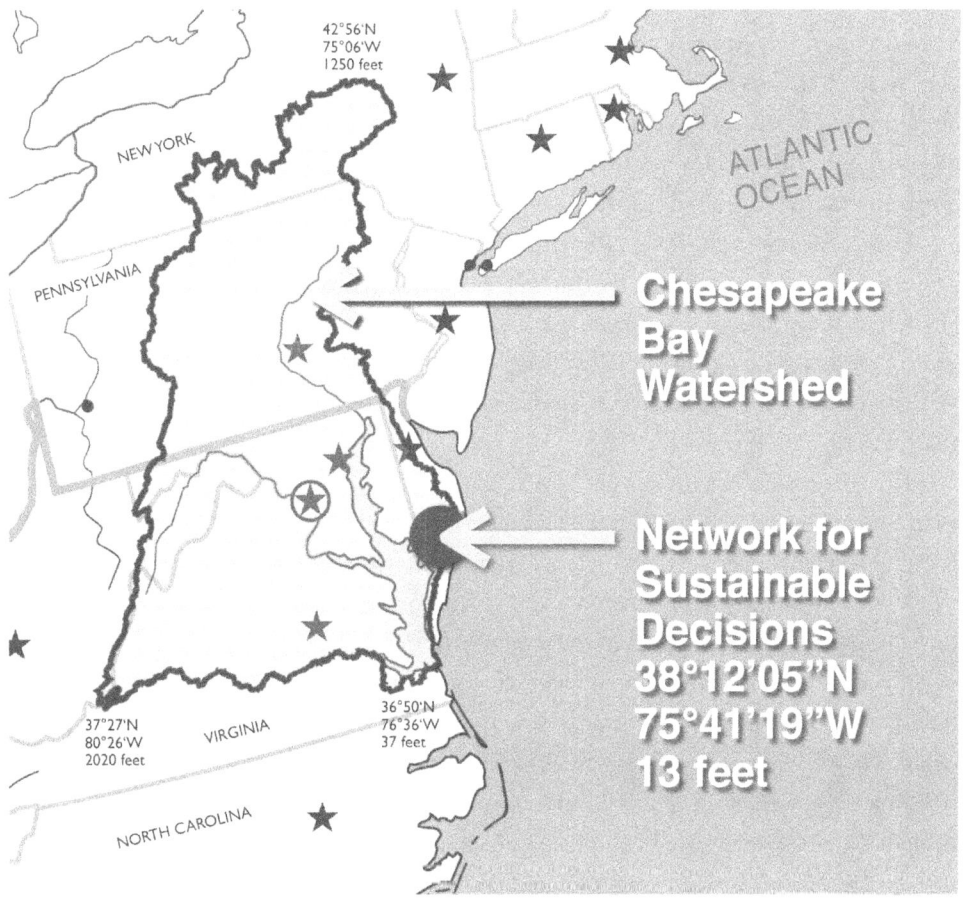

Everyone must understand that the things they do ultimately affect their world. Sometimes it seems like everyone is talking about sustainability, green products and environmental stewardship. Everyone wants to be sure that we make the world a better place for our children and grandchildren. Talk about sustainability and the environment is cheap. What we truly need is action. In the days when people solved significant social issues and flew to the moon, smart people worked together to solve the problems they faced. Today, the problems are different. Resources are limited. Yet we still need to solve the problems.

TURN OF THE CENTURY

At the turn of the twenty-first century, Leadership in Energy and Environmental Design (LEED) requirements resulted in codifying what can be described as a "touchy-feely," politically correct environmentalism. The standards were fraught with requirements that rewarded solutions based on anecdote and feelings about sustainability, rather than focusing on proven and verified solutions. This approach may have been required from a marketing, advertising, or technology perspective. Reports of LEED-rated buildings operating less efficiently than comparable buildings without ratings served no one.

Hysterical representations of environmental issues in the early twenty-first century created confusion and conflict. Fortunately, people stepped up and created systems where environmental decisions are made based on factual information. Today we have an integrated sensor and management network that lets us fully monitor environmental processes worldwide. Knowing the results of our decisions has saved a lot of money and is improving the environment everywhere.

It is estimated that 30 percent of all systems are included in the program. The plan is to extend this by 8 percent every five years until we reach a level of about 65 percent coverage, which is seen as the theoretical maximum. It is believed that there will always be places that do not lend themselves to this level of control.

The biggest success story is in the monitoring and control of homes. Gone are the days when people got a statement from their electric company and wondered how they could have possibly used that much power. Now they know moment by moment what they are using. They can adjust their consumption patterns to reduce costs.

In a pre-information-model LEED process, projects were designed and implemented using what were believed to be sustainable concepts. The lack of validated design data tied to a feedback loop capable of reporting on the results and benefits of installed systems resulted in a disconnected process. The process was not inherently sustainable. In fact, LEED created a stovepiped system masquerading as sustainability. As a building was operated, there was little or no connection to the design data. Limited analysis to ensure that the design was functioning as planned was available.

You can now use the data management and analysis tools integral to the information modeling process to make environmental and sustainability decisions with facts tied to your project and site. Systems can then be monitored and adjusted to match the basis of your decisions or to provide feedback for improvements the next time.

As the designer creates project solutions, he or she can receive immediate feedback for a wide range of metrics—everything from energy use, to environmental consideration, to transportation access, to the client's ability to pay for the building come into play.

As the project is built, each component is integrated into the information model. The model directly ties to a sensor network to provide in-use data for analysis and monitoring. As the project is completed, these systems and this information allow the project to be managed to achieve sustainability goals.

Declines in productivity, wasteful processes, and inefficient operations are prevalent in the built environment. Construction is valued at about $5 trillion per year. A hundred million people work in the industry. The industry is responsible for about 10 percent of the world's gross domestic product. Half of the world's resources and 40 percent of the world's energy are consumed in the construction industry.

Did you realize that the construction industry is the only industry in the United States that has steadily declined in productivity since the introduction of the computer? Did you realize that the industry as a whole is 45 percent more wasteful than other industries? Did you realize that, for every dollar spent for construction, we only get ten cents of value? When you buy other manufactured goods, your dollar buys sixty-two cents of value. Something has to change, because something is seriously wrong.

If we could reduce waste in the construction industry to the same level as other industries achieve, could we save the 2.25 trillion dollars per year that make up the difference? Could we reduce industry's pressure on resources and energy? Could we be more sustainable?

Many believe that the answer to all three questions is yes. Information modeling, distributed model servers, the Internet of Things, and new ways of working are seen as the tools that will make the changes happen. We can no longer continue business as usual, or business as usual with new software, if we are to achieve these results. Integration requires that we learn how to manage change.

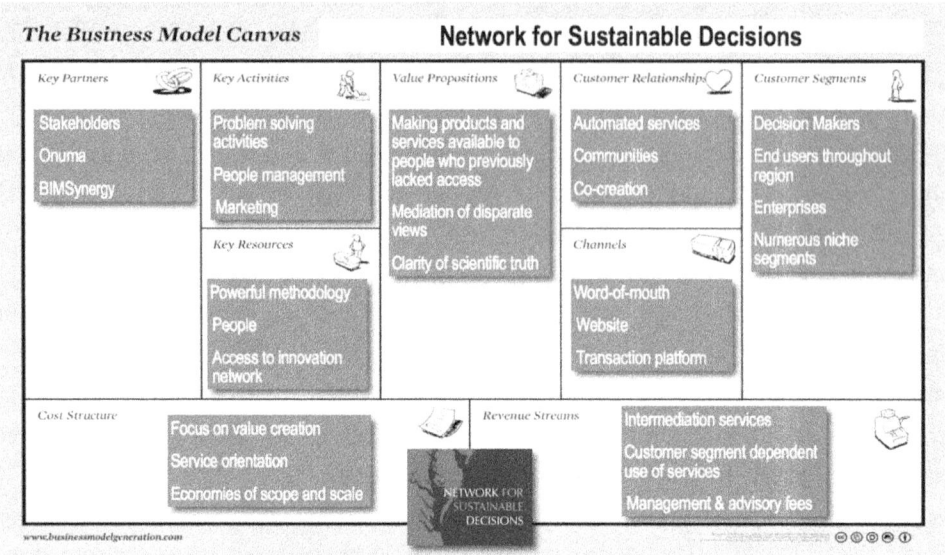

The Network for Sustainable Decisions is tasked with moderating, managing, and implementing integrated processes throughout the region. The group has the power and resources required to integrate systems into the BIMSynergy system to promote real-time facts about the things that affect the bay. The group's mandate extends into all aspects of the built environment. Agriculture, industry, housing, government services, tourism, fisheries, and every other group that impacts the bay will be measured, monitored, and managed. The group's mandate requires that this process occur using state-of-the-art collaborative technologies. This cannot and will not become a government-imposed task. This image is subject to the terms of a Creative Commons, Attribution-Share Alike license from Business Model Canvas, www.businessmodelgeneration.com

BE MORE

As the Environmental Protection Agency, the states of Maryland, Virginia, Delaware, Pennsylvania, and New York, and the region's environmental organizations met to establish the Network for Sustainable Decisions, there were many questions asked. Much argument and heated discussion revolved around two questions: Can the Chesapeake Bay be salvaged? And, if it can be salvaged, how can we, as a group, make that happen? The Chesapeake Bay summit participants eventually said yes to the first question. The ultimate answer to the second question was the Network for Sustainable Decisions.

The process will provide the people who affect the bay's ecosystem the facts and tools that they need to fix the problems. No one believes that this process will be easy or inexpensive. The burden will be shared by all, equitably. Using systems that provide repeatable, fact-based assessments, the group's processes will identify those with the greatest environmental debt, so that their systems can be corrected efficiently. The group's system will become a clearinghouse and decision-making support structure to advocate fact-based and scientifically validated decision making. The goal is to reduce opinion- and anecdote-based solutions, which do not solve problems and often create conflict and confusion.

Most know that it is unsustainable for our debts to grow faster than our income. Yet, in the years leading up to the Great Recession and the Wall Street Bailout, thousands (millions?) of us went against this simple rule, only to suffer the consequences. Today, people are subtler and less prone to spend money no matter what the long-term costs. But are people aware and ready to apply the lessons learned to the built environment? That is what the Network for Sustainable Decisions was designed to find out.

Scientists claim that our environmental debts are growing faster than our ability to recover from them. Are we making the same mistakes in the built environment that we made with housing and the economy? If the environment crashed tomorrow, could we recover? These are the questions that must be answered. Assuming that the answers are yes, now is the time to make the changes required to pay off our environmental debts—before we are overwhelmed by them.

Some solutions will be painless, requiring minimal effort. Many of these solutions are well researched. We know how to apply them. Other solutions will require massive change to how we live, work, and play. Little is totally new. Simply providing people with better early information makes it easier than ever before for them to see future possibilities. Technology allows us to draw more people in the solution while giving us greater confidence that we are doing the right thing. We have the tools and resources to change things for the better. We can correct the problems that are rapidly turning the Chesapeake Bay into a wasteland.

Using analysis that integrates with information modeling, we can now make environmental and sustainability decisions with real-time facts. As the designer creates, he or she receives immediate feedback for everything from energy, to costs, to an assessment of the client's ability to pay for the project. As the constructor builds, each part is first integrated virtually, then connected via robotics, geo-location, and other technology to BIMSynergy and the built environment. The work is now tied to the sensor grid. Work-in-place, costs, payments, and operations items are all fully integrated. The handover of both the building and the data are seamless. The final product is tied into the system and optimized for life. The decisions that people make as they change the built environment include creating systems that protect the Chesapeake Bay. The systems repair the damages, as well.

The Network for Sustainable Decisions leads the way to achieve this future. Real-time facts, sensor networks, and technology are only a small part of the solution. The larger parts of the solution come from society and people. The solution requires that we change how we live, how we think, and how we operate. Cultural change is up to us—it is not about technology.

The Internet constantly changes and evolves as we find new needs and uses. Jump in and start using the information that surrounds us to find solutions. Front-load the decision-making process. By linking business processes with facilities and the world, we can improve early decision making to support the full spectrum of the built world. People can make more reliable decisions as early as possible in the process. Rules-based tools, collaborative processes, and commercial-off-the-shelf technologies make this possible. Knowing how to apply and use collaborative modeling technologies on high-performance design and construction to create the ultimate green buildings is but one of the outcomes. These are the things that the Network for Sustainable Decisions makes available. The convergence of information modeling and the sustainability ethic offers an opportunity to engage in solutions in a richer way. There is true value to individuals and to communities. This convergence offers people the best opportunity in decades to reassert their value to society.

The Network for Sustainable Decisions helps people synthesize information and manage complex processes at an extremely high level. The group's processes encourage just-in-time decision making, eliminate duplication, and make the appropriate information available. Decisions flow directly to the process of creating solutions and become the basis for improved management as projects move from planning, to design, to construction, and ultimately to operations. Decisions made within this system are directly linked to middle-market modeling tools, geographic information systems, and a wide range of analysis and design tools.

Tools are as uncomplicated as they can be; the complexities occur behind the scenes. Homeowners are able to understand and manage their impact on the environment. Retailers are able to make a profit, selling products that are sustainable and provide positive environmental outcomes. Farmers are able to manage their farms and increase crop yields while improving the Chesapeake Bay. Industrial users are able to integrate their processes to make them as efficient and environmentally sensitive as possible. Municipalities are able to handle the runoff from their streets to manage water quality. In all cases, the Network for Sustainable Decisions assists, supports, and guides to achieve a healthy Chesapeake Bay.

INHERENT SUSTAINABILITY

Much of the work done using virtual building technology and building information modeling prior to 2015 was completed, stored on file servers, and quickly became irrelevant. Valuable data existed within many of these models, yet the information was difficult to retrieve and use. In most cases, the information was lost. At best, the information became static and required updating prior to future uses. Once design and construction was completed, users did not have the software, hardware, or training to enable them to access these models. The models were not sustainable assets. They were little more than large and difficult-to-use static files. The models may have saved time and money for the designer and constructor, but for the life cycle uses that make up the majority of the benefits from information models, the files were little better than printing on paper. This was the situation that BIMSynergy was created to overcome.

It is now easier to manage the built environment. Models are still created using complex desktop software. Design and construction continue to take advantage of the benefits that come from these models. Enhanced visualization, code and conflict checking, schedule and implementation coordination, and cost control are critical to these phases. Desktop software remains the best way to handle this level of complexity. BIMSynergy makes the entire data structure of these models available. In most cases, the information that is needed for a specific task or activity is available in real time. Critical data is maintained so that it can be accessed when needed over the asset's life. The benefits come from easily accessible information, when and where people need data. People see the benefits. They save money and achieve better results.

Traditional or desktop modeling processes did not provide this capability. BIMSynergy project databases are designed to anticipate and manage future alterations. Facility and operations data give facility managers the information needed to do their jobs. The facility management database gives leaders the information needed to make better decisions and to maximize the returns from their assets. Downstream users see immediate benefits from the information.

Looking back on the early twenty-first-century use of technology in the built environment, we wonder how so many could have been so misinformed. Few understood the breadth and depth of the changes that were happening around them. Few understood that many of the technological innovations were little more than highly sophisticated continuations of outmoded ways of working. Developers tweaked file-based storage systems thinking that that would solve the problems. "Cloud" resources were available, yet most developers merely adapted legacy systems to work without local servers, sub-optimizing the benefits. Many believed that by purchasing desktop information modeling tools and becoming proficient in their use, they were contributing to a better future. Many became strong and vocal advocates of their way of working being the solution. More often than not, this evangelism added to the confusion and delayed the move toward sustainable and integrated systems. Positioning for personal advantage, selling more software and projects while cloaked in a veil of false sustainability fooled too many, for too long. Too many professed experts and bim gurus unwittingly impeded progress.

At the same time, other forces were developing solutions to problems with a more distributed and cloud-based focus. This group of people better understood the data-centric nature of the cloud. Geographic information experts were beginning to consider what they called Geo-design. Geo-design was the intersection of geographic information systems and building-oriented design tools to better visualize and analyze geographic data. One could say that this approach sought to integrate building design with geographic scale design to create a built environment solution, coming at it from the GIS side rather than the architectural side. Geographic information systems can be seen as focusing on the "what-exists." Building design can be seen as focusing on the "what-will-be." Geo-design was working to combine the two.

Geographic information systems are at their best when managing global infrastructure. For many years, these systems have been used to document and manage existing infrastructure. In most cases, the systems focused on urban and regional-scale existing conditions for things like roads, sewers, airports, forests, and mapping. Systems such as Bing and Google Earth are the result of geographic information.

Federal, municipal, and other large clients worldwide have used geographic information systems to underpin their planning efforts for many years. These efforts have been quite successful when working at urban scale or larger. As some users sought to extend these efforts to manage the intricate detail required for buildings, geographic information systems were stretched to their limits. Geographic information systems work best outside of the building footprint, and building information models work best within the building. The ideal scenario seems to be an integration of the two. In either case, the goal is better long-term management and operations of the built environment.

At the same time that Geo-design began to develop, others were exploring solutions tied directly to energy and sensors. Data was becoming ubiquitous in systems throughout our world. There was agreement that access to information and the ability to transform spatial data into action were key factors to moving forward. Finding innovative ways to access and use this data received much attention. Connecting suppliers with consumers to manage power and information flows to control utilization and pricing was one piece of the puzzle. The smart grid, the Web Wide World, and the Internet of Things became topics of thousands of web logs and hundreds of conferences, all exploring how to optimize energy distribution and use. Computer and networking manufacturers, leading energy utilities, and automation companies began to focus on the intersection of energy, controls, and sensors, with the stated goal of a better future. Significant discussions occurred over many years as these key industries debated how best to go into the future. The missing component in this discussion was the information model.

The power structure revolved around legacy organizations seeking how to move into the future. These organizations saw that the world was changing. As a group these companies owned significant proprietary resources that they did not wish to abandon. Their purpose seemed to be to maintain the profitability of their proprietary solutions while managing the changes to their benefit. Moderating this focus to reach consensus among these groups, while at the same time guarding the common good, is why so much discussion and time was required and so little got done. Only when new organizations began to offer solutions, built around open standards and information models, did the problems get resolved. The large, legacy organizations found themselves in the position of having to embrace interoperability and open standards, or losing to the new players.

Nimble, young, and highly creative people were working on this issue. They were students of history. They understood how large organizations often become dinosaurs and die off after radical change occurs. They were working to find ways to get the data that people needed—on time and in formats that would get responses in real time—for anything that was connected to sensors. These people were interested in the large companies' proprietary solutions only to the extent that they produced usable and actionable data. They believed that open standards and readily available technology would allow people to see and use data from anywhere. Once data became available, and solutions were created to analyze and act on the information, much was possible.

By way of example: The crew closest to a situation is dispatched by an automated system when a problem is sensed in a piece of equipment. If the crew or the system determines that the solution to the problem requires expert assistance, the expert is alerted automatically and directly connected to the crew—without manual intervention.

This example only touches the surface of the possibilities. With real-time data flowing from sensors, there are millions of such opportunities. The challenge is in managing and using the data throughout the ecosystem. Sensors are all around us. They have long been a part of our lives whether we knew it or not. Air conditioning and heating systems include sensors to measure and control airflow, pump speeds, outside air, humidity, and many other factors. Your room thermostat is a sensor. Sensors are common in many home appliances. Your car contains sensors and much of the diagnostics that occur when you take it to your mechanic come from these devices. Industry uses sensors. Government uses sensors. Agriculture uses sensors. Sensors have become part of everything we do. Managing the built environment is easier with sensors that tell us what is happening, notify us of a crisis, and give us information that we can use to make better decisions.

Geo-design, sensor networks, and information models are three of the technologies and processes that allow a more sophisticated and fact-based approach to managing the built environment. Integrating these and many other processes is what BIMSynergy is all about. The Network for Sustainable Decisions uses the information to understand and manage the cleanup of the bay. Making bay cleanup information available to all in simple, easy-to-understand forms that support individual action is the key.

Geographic information systems, sensor networks, information models, model servers, and many other technologies enable the Network for Sustainable Decisions to bring the information to people, wherever and whenever it is needed. We cannot relinquish responsibility to any of these systems. We must make decisions. Without these systems things will continue to fall through the cracks and we will continue to miss critical issues. We cannot hand off key early decisions to others, hoping for the best. We must pay attention to the details from beginning to end.

Some are concerned that this sensor system will allow knowledge to be captured and used to "take control" of our world, the Orwellian vision of sensing and monitoring. The opposite is closer to reality. Captured knowledge and rules-based systems will not "take control" of our world. These systems give us facts to make better decisions. They help us to find solutions to the problems in the built environment. They improve communications and outcomes.

NEW WAYS

> Alone we can do so little; together we can do so much.   —Helen Keller

Processes in the built environment must start to use data in different ways that combine the work of other industries and the Internet. Solutions will come as ways are found to better use existing information while building and capturing information that historically vanishes from built environment processes. In most built environment processes, data is created, lost, and created again, time after time. The costs of this lost and recreated data are enormous. Society can no longer afford these costs; the losses are not sustainable. An architect is hired to design and document a new building. When her work is complete, she transforms her electronic information into paper, which is then handed to a contractor. The contractor then converts the paper into spreadsheets, production schedules, and other electronic forms. Each time a new player steps into the process, the work of the previous player is archived and lost, and must be re-created as the work moves forward.

Transforming an idea or paper sketch to electronic media is forward motion. The reverse is waste. Yet, these wasteful processes underpin nearly everything that has taken place in the industry since the advent of computers. Statistics show that the construction industry lags far behind in using data to streamline operations.

The construction industry operates differently from other industries. It has long relied on one-offs. Each project is individually designed, hand built, and debugged as the process proceeds. The process that occurs in other industries of prototyping a product, finding and eliminating the flaws, and then producing thousands of copies rarely occurs in the construction industry. Processes more closely align with the freeform social patterns that exist in the Internet then the linear processes that characterize other industries. In order to be successful in a world of data, industry processes must change to incorporate integration that connects people, places, and knowledge to achieve true mass customization. The goal is to create a sustainable world, not merely a sustainable construction industry. That is what information modeling and BIMStorms are all about.

Information models are both technology and an entirely new way of looking at the built environment. In this context, they offer virtually unlimited opportunities. With information models, you can provide essential information remarkably early in the life cycle of assets to increase certainty of outcomes. Information models significantly increase feasible options and the quality of decision making.

BIMStorms are social design and planning processes geared to show individuals and organizations the tools and processes that make information modeling work. BIMStorms are easily accessible and affordable ways for most people to experience the power of model servers, real-time collaboration, and integrated processes. Cloud-based technologies and improved processes enable normal people from all walks of life to participate.

Volunteers in Tijuana use geographic information system and information modeling technology to build complete homes in one day, all managed from across the country in real time. Residents of a small town see their ideas pop up in three dimensions right before their eyes, with all the facts they need to make educated decisions. Teams of designers across the globe act in unison to create entire metropolitan areas in twenty-four hours—with results that previously took months or years—all with zero travel costs. A ship queries the facilities decision framework and the captain can immediately know the conditions of every port in cruising range, schedule repairs, book hotels, and take care of almost everything else that happens in the transition from sea to shore. A community defines and creates public/private development collaborations in environmentally critical estuaries. Homeowners focus on using information models and sustainable development tools to optimize urban development in a New Orleans neighborhood devastated by Hurricane Katrina. The goal is to engage people in large-scale decision making, while providing the small-scale details they need to decide. This requires that we build knowledge step by step, over time.

The Onuma System is a tool that enables one to build this step-by-step knowledge—fast. This occurs within a cloud computing environment. In the system, work takes place with a life cycle view of the built environment. People capitalize on both information models and geographic information systems, moving from a broader view to detail and back, as their approach requires.

Flying in from orbit you first see your project at the world level. Your project always knows its location in the world. At ten thousand feet, you see the site and understand your project in its community or regional context. From this view high in space, you see a tag for Pete's office in Cincinnati, with seventy-six buildings of 64,526 square feet.

At five hundred feet, you see the structures and begin to see spaces and space relationships in the context of your facility. At this, site view, you see utilities and each building individually.

At twenty feet, you see your space with furniture and equipment. At this, structure view, you see the geolocation of anything in the building, the energy use, space use, circulation, and more.

Zooming in further, to the room view, you see Pete's chair, Pete's avatar, the carpet in his office with a link to its source and type, other furniture, and equipment.

Follow some basic rules to interact with others in this environment. Much as one cannot send a fax to Expedia to make an airline reservation, and it is not possible to use paper and pencil to send an e-mail, the Onuma System and BIMStorms have similar rules. Georeference everything. Focus on sharing and collaboration. Consider systems and think non-linearly. Link to everyone and everything. Understand that you are working with built environment assets, not merely projects. Keep things as simple as possible and use the most effective tool for each task.

You are not required to have a server or specialized software to work with the data. Information models and integrated processes support your ability to build community consensus, validate needs, and promote sustainable, cost-effective solutions. You can use examples from other projects to demonstrate the power and possibilities in order to communicate your ideas. You maximize early-stage decision-making effectiveness.

Because the processes are not linear, there is no best way to interact in the Onuma System or in BIMStorms. Some work from their office next door. Some work in group environments surrounded by digital projection and online collaboration tools. Some work on the other side of the world in isolation. Others work closely with you from anywhere in the world. Everyone works together, on the issues and assets that are the subject of your exploration. The goal is to have all users collaborating with the same information regardless of their task or tools that they use. Information coming from whatever media is quickly and efficiently converted to information models. Participants begin in the way that they are most comfortable. Hand sketching, digital sketching, bubble diagrams, mind maps, Google Maps overlays, and most other methods feed to the process. The idea is to keep things uncomplicated. Even a formatted spreadsheet that lists the room name, the floor level, and the size of the space quickly becomes an information model. You work in real time as much as possible. You capture your decisions in the system to make your ideas and reasoning accessible to everyone.

OVERCOME FEAR
CHESAPEAKE REGION
FEBRUARY 2 to MARCH 9, 2026

BIMStorms were selected as the tool for modeling and managing the bay cleanup process. The management of the Network for Sustainable Decisions plans a series of interconnecting BIMStorms to integrate each of the affected constituencies into the process. Knowing that the bay cleanup is a wicked problem, the goal is to create a series of highly flexible solutions that satisfy the needs each constituency while protecting the interests of the many. Rather than creating a set-piece master plan, the BIMStorms will stay active for many years. Initial concepts may change as needed, and may never become fixed, although individual tasks will by necessity require solutions that can be built. When complete, each of these solutions will roll back into the system, adding data and evolving into a healthy Chesapeake Bay.

One of the first BIMStorms that Sandy had to conduct focused on agriculture. After tourism, vegetable and grain farming, mass poultry production, and seafood are the economic engines of the Delmarva Peninsula. Much of the land immediately against the Chesapeake Bay and its tributaries is farmed. Tidewater Virginia, Maryland's Western Shore, and Pennsylvania up the Rappahannock River all contribute to the agricultural richness of the area. Adding this farm richness to the complexity of the entire BIMStorm program would make it easy to misunderstand the purpose and goals of the process. It is easy for people to "blow smoke"—making it difficult for smart people to understand what is actually happening. Bad information adds confusion. Communications suffer. It is hard to figure out the best approach. These confusions can result in people turning their backs on the process or fighting the results. Because of this, the BIMStorm Chesapeake Agriculture was not only first in the series, it might have been the most critical in the series.

Much of Sandy's early work was focused on overcoming the fear that farmers felt about others planning what to do with their property. The political system had scapegoated farmers at every turn. In most cases, farmers had led the charge to make changes that improve the bay watershed. As a group, they realized that they needed to evolve their farming practices. No one is ever perfect. They were quietly husbanding the environment long before many of the current impacts even existed. They were willing to change, but they wanted fair and even distribution of the pains and gains that would be required.

The farming community is much like others when confronted by new technologies. They face similar fears and concerns. Farmers are, better than most, used to living and working with complexity. They know that they can plant seed at the proper time, nurture the young plants, manage moisture, and do everything else right, and still experience a crop failure. There are always things outside of their control. Farmers strive for perfection. They work to stay ahead of the curve, because if they do not, serious things will not get done. They respond by holding their cards close, because they become afraid of taking risks. Every planting season they face the same risks that got them in trouble before.

Land is often their principal asset. They fear for their property rights—with good reason, since society requires them to put everything they value on the line with every crop. When something goes wrong, they are often an easy target. They are first to be scrutinized by the environmentalists. They are first to be sued when they use farming practices that have been proven for millennia. They are regulated, nearly out of existence, while they watch industry dump pollution into the bay every day. They have a lot to lose.

Fortunately, the BIMStorm process offers them a way to a solution. But it also offers confusion. Sandy and her team would be responsible for clearing the confusion and making sure that everyone had the opportunity to participate. Since BIMStorm Chesapeake Agriculture was first in an interlocking set of BIMStorms designed to assess and find ways forward for the Chesapeake Bay, much was expected. This BIMStorm would set the tone with those most affected by where the process would lead.

Following BIMStorm Chesapeake Agriculture there would be ten additional BIMStorms, each focusing on a critical aspect of the bay's recovery. The final BIMStorm, BIMStorm Chesapeake Restore & Governance, would join them together and coordinate the process of reaching a consensus direction and formal agreement in the region.

CONVERGENCE

> The process does not occur within some "matrix" in which we have been embedded. The action takes place through mobile devices, browsers, and millions of connections that surround us. The process is only partially technology. The greater part is people understanding when and how to access the technology to get things done right.

Your path may lead to a building, a room, or something else. Anything in the built environment is along one of the paths. The paths can be virtual as well, since transactions, goals, processes, energy, web pages, business decisions, and almost anything else contribute to the background and understanding of the environment.

The kilowatt-hour reading from your electric meter can be converted into a real-time carbon footprint analysis, for the last week, the last hour, or the last minute. You visualize the results as numbers, or graphs, or imagery overlaying the three-dimensional model of your home. Analysis results come from tiny apps that interact with you and your systems. Using advanced imagery plus sensing plus information, you get certainty of understanding and outcomes.

The system is not just a data repository. It facilitates interaction. It facilitates mash-ups and visualizations. The system responds to both the physical and the digital. Smart buildings, intelligent cities, and informed environments supported by ad hoc networks make these systems become ubiquitous. They are so widespread that imagining their uses is difficult.

Architects design buildings with real-time constraints on the context, available funds, and many other factors. Decisions directly inform the process to minimize inefficiencies. Constructors fabricate buildings with integrated teams whose output compares favorably with other industries. Real-time information enables them to change their behavior and move past the fragmentation and disconnected processes of the past.

Facility managers manage buildings, neighborhoods, and cities using continuous post-occupancy controls to ensure that things operate as designed. Sensor data support smart services so that facilities and energy are used efficiently. Networked electricity metering enables users to compare and contrast usage and strategies for conservation. Buildings talk to and learn from each other. Buildings share information on energy consumption, occupancy, and resources, adjusting to threats and changing conditions. When a tornado or hurricane is near, the network broadcasts alerts, secures buildings, and prepares to respond.

Sensors throughout the hidden and underappreciated infrastructure that keeps the built environment working are part of the system. They watch roads and bridges for safety and efficiency. They monitor and control water systems to ensure a healthy and plentiful supply of fresh water. They monitor wastewater pumps, piping, and treatment facilities for proper operation and to catch problems before failure. Sensors watch electrical and communications systems, eliminate waste, and balance loads.

The system enables farmers to be more efficient and better stewards of the environment. Sensors enable sustainable planting practices, environmentally friendly poultry production, and improved productivity. Food production is monitored and tagged so that quality and safety can be traced from field to consumer.

The digital and physical worlds have converged. As the distinction between the physical and digital faded, systems became easier to use and focused on people's specific need for information. Technology and people's behaviors evolved. People became more aware and fluent as the technology became less obtuse.

The scale of the systems required to satisfy this real-time convergence was a problem. Large-scale mass collaborations, such as the BIMStorm, created an ecosystem of ad hoc connected environments. Outdated ways of working are replaced with a plethora of services and business models geared to an integrated and fact-based built world. Integrated decision making, management of resources as assets, and sustainable development are the watchwords of this new world.

MASSES OF DATA

The system enables people to track, compare, manage, and visualize the data. The scope of the knowledge that is captured throughout every day is staggering. As the technology matured in the early twenty-first century, we reached a point where fully 30 percent of all processes throughout the Chesapeake Bay region are monitored and managed with a constellation of integrated sensors. The sensor data flows through BIMSynergy systems and is visualized and managed in tools such as the Onuma System.

Since the turn of the century, people have been wrestling with the opportunities and challenges. Masses of data, so large and complicated that most of it was unusable, were stored across the world. Organizations found themselves to be overwhelmed with information. Health-care organizations generated massive amounts of information so fast that most of it was lost or misfiled. Government agencies generated enormous stores of data, using everything from spreadsheets to relational databases. The information in their files led to confusion and inefficiency. Commercial organizations accumulated data on their customers, generating pervasive spam and other waste. Organizations mined the data and used it for their benefit. In the first decade, it became clear that only those highly trained and conversant with the technology could take advantage of the data. Those connected with the systems found cheap and easy-to-use data. The rest of us found our data taken by others and unavailable, in proprietary and tightly controlled systems. Some argued that open data would level the playing field to allow everyone to take advantage of the benefits that come from electronic information.

Some means needed to be found to "level the playing field." A multi-class system, giving power to the technologically adept, was not sufficient. Ordinary people also needed to see what was available and how to use the information to their benefit. All needed affordable and easy-to-use access. Transparency and equal access only come with easy-to-understand and -use interfaces. The intersection of wireless sensor networks, the cloud, model servers, and information models creates such a system and allows each of us to benefit from the data.

There will always be a place for experts. Behind the scenes, the complexity still exists. For the rest of us, access and use of the data is focused on making just the necessary information available, when and where it is needed.

There was much discussion about who owns this data. In many cases, people did not know what they had or how it could be used. People started to ask questions. Who owns the data that I leave behind? Do the companies collecting the data own the information? Or do I own my own information? Is information about when and where I buy something, of value? When I make a telephone call, or buy a book online, or get a new credit card, shouldn't I own my own information?

At the same time, property owners and their architects had similar discussions. Who owns the information model that the architect is creating for the new project? How do we separate the designer's intellectual property from the data about the owner's new building? Is there long-term value in the model or the data about the building? Ultimately, a consensus was reached that information about data is essential, and the creator of that data should be the ultimate owner.

Automation systems, sensor networks, and smart buildings produce significant amounts of personal information. Adding this information to an individual's web browsing history, credit card histories, calling patterns, travel histories, and other transaction records represents a significant opportunity. As the owner of this personal data, an individual can find ways to produce benefits that save time and money and create new opportunities. This personal data offers customer awareness, allowing companies to focus their offerings like never before. The data creates opportunities for optimizing systems to improve the built environment, tailoring facilities, services, and utilities to the actual needs of the consumer.

BIMSTORM CHESAPEAKE AGRICULTURE
CHESAPEAKE BAY REGION
MARCH 12, 2026

At 10 a.m. eastern daylight time, Sandy officially kicked off BIMstorm Chesapeake Agriculture. The kickoff was soft and unassuming. Sandy and her team sat in front of their computers in Westover, Maryland. There was no fuss and no one had to travel to the event. The BIMStorm Chesapeake process was actually a zero carbon event. Over 12,500 people sat through the training sessions and attended the opening webinars. The decision to publicize and promote the event seemed to be paying off.

Sandy had spent the last month visiting anyone and everyone to tell the story. She had been on television five times, quoted in the paper too many times to count, and eaten more rubbery chicken than she could remember. At this point, the farming community knew that if they stepped up and did the right thing by participating, that brilliant things would follow. They could make the benefits happen. They did not have to tell the world about it; they just had to do it. Sandy found that once they learned how they could help, farmers became advocates for the process. Many of them were still not quite sure about how it was happening, but the early signs looked terrific.

As Sandy met with community organizations and spoke to farmers, it became clear that some people would not participate. Some people farm much as their parents, grandparents, and great-grandparents did. They plant, pray, and harvest. Outcomes are predetermined by God or the work of others. Their approach is a bit naïve in today's world. They have ceded their responsibility to learn and understand. These are the farmers who are moving off the land or failing year after year. Fortunately, most do not follow this pattern. Most modern farmers are professionals, learning, growing, and understanding how the systems that they manage work. They ask questions. They consider outcomes. They are always working to improve. The professional farmer is into metrics and management. They embrace new ways of working that increase their yields and reduce their risks. State-of-the-art farming methods are nothing new to them. These are the farmers that BIMStorm Chesapeake Agriculture was created to help.

The BIMStorm process takes place at various levels simultaneously. Many groups are working concurrently on the process. Groups share information. They do not need to work on the same parts of the problem or task. One group may be focusing on highly detailed analysis, while another group explores regional-scale master planning issues. All groups work with the same information repository, accessing and working with the data that they need for their particular application. The following is one of the many threads that are taking place concurrently.

By 10:08 a.m., groups from around the Chesapeake Bay area had started to input background information. People understood that those with different perspectives must input data about their positions. The level of transparency made it difficult for a group to stand outside the process and protest. Not every idea would resonate; yet every idea needed to be considered. As data developed, some ideas would form the "train wrecks" that the process seeks, exposing the weaknesses and faults for all to see. The next couple of hours would see the background material becoming more and more complete. Patterns were beginning to emerge. Agriculture experts in Iowa, Nebraska, California, Washington State, Europe, Australia, and New Zealand were monitoring the inputs and beginning to ask questions of the local teams.

By noon, discussions had started to focus on the fact that much of the farming acreage in the Chesapeake Bay region abuts on bay tributaries. Much of the runoff from this acreage in Maryland and Virginia had been managed for some time. Based on the currently available statistics, a relatively small percentage of crops in the region were farmed using the full range of sustainable farming practices. On many levels, sustainable practices geared toward improving soils seemed an obvious process. Farmers have learned that, by transitioning their fields to sustainable practices, they can effectively drought-proof their land. The process also helps to deal with climate change. By sequestering carbon in soils and improving soil quality, they improve water retention and make their land more environmentally beneficial. The process takes effort, knowledge, technology, and capital. The issue holding many back in the Chesapeake region appeared to be that the process takes as long as six years. During that time, the farmer would be subject to increased costs. In the transition time, a cold and wet spring could make it difficult to get the seeds germinated and growing. Until the soil was fully restored, the farmer's risk increased, in a business that already had a high risk. Ways were needed to reduce the farmers' risks enabling them to see the long-term view.

POSSIBLE SOLUTIONS

By 1:30 p.m., possible solutions were beginning to pop up in the system. As the information continued to build, there began to be threads of similar stories from across the land. Farmers in the Midwest were inputting information about their experiences with geographic information systems and sustainable soils. Several of these farmers had bought in early to the concept of never-till or continuous no-till and felt that similar solutions would work here. No-till farming had been around for over fifty years, but the combination with cover crops and controlled wheel traffic took this environmentally beneficial use to a new level. Several groups within the BIMStorm participants were forming with the purpose of finding ways to help local farmers as they made the transition.

Farms that embrace continuous no-till practices are minimizing wheel traffic with the intent of disturbing the soil ecosystem as little as possible. The farmer uses gentle herbicides to control weeds rather than mechanically tearing them from the ground. Soils maintain active populations of earthworms and other beneficial organisms and a stable, vigorous microbial community. Seeds are drilled in and fertilizers are knifed in to minimize soil damage. The process saves fuel and allows farmers to work their fields much quicker after heavy rainfalls than with conventional methods. The system can sequester one metric ton of carbon dioxide per year per acre of soil, resulting in the farm receiving carbon offsets. The system has enormous long-term efficiency potential and is a terrific tool for climate change management and Chesapeake Bay recovery.

One team identified a serious drawback with the system. The system has a tendency to build up disease organisms, just as it builds up valuable organisms. Farmers have found a couple of notable approaches to overcome this tendency. One approach is the use of broad-spectrum fungicides, largely on corn and soybean acreage. These fungicides add to the cost of producing a high-yielding crop. Continuous no-till generally offsets the costs with increased seed fertility. Seed companies provide the other approach. Companies have continually improved yield potential and stress tolerance. Using advanced biotechnological systems, the companies can track the key genes and traits of seeds. Seed can also be treated to protect young plants in the critical first weeks of development from fungi, insects, and nematodes. In most cases, these chemicals total less than three ounces per acre and are less toxic than table salt.

By 4 p.m., farmers throughout the region had learned how to input the status of their fields, facilities, and equipment. Up until this point, much of the information had come from public sources. Geographic information system layers made information on property lines and ownership, soils, slopes, access, drainage areas, and much more accessible. Public records and yield information from chemical companies and seed distributors were also available in some cases. For the first time, individuals had now added their specific information. Details about local site conditions, issues about fields, and other details known only to the farmer had now been added to the process. The addition of this information allowed the teams to assess patterns of development and soils patterns. Opportunities began to emerge at the scale of the individual farmer's field.

Taking a long-term view of the land was always part and parcel of being a farmer. Since the mid-1950s, this has been changing. As production methods have evolved, seeds and tools have become better and agriculture has moved from small farms to large-scale operations. Fewer and fewer farmers own their land. A high percentage rent much or all of their land. A farmer who rents the land would be foolish to make a long-term investment in the future growing potential of land that might next year be farmed by someone else. We must handle this situation if sustainable methods are to take hold. New ways of relating to the land were needed. The landowner needed to understand the importance of sustainable practices, and to require the process, no matter who holds the lease. The farmer making the transition needs to be rewarded for the hard work and costs associated with sustainable practices put in place.

By 5 p.m., a pattern of farms that directly abutted waterways was taking shape. Fields were now identified, classified, and categorized. Current soil states and sustainable potential were highlighted. The discussion had shifted toward programs that would make improvements occur in these areas as soon as possible. For the first time, significant numbers of people saw the value in having easily accessible information housed in a dependable repository. Farmers were now able to see detail about their fields, integrated in one place. They were beginning to realize that it was no longer necessary to make a trip to the courthouse for title information, a trip to the seed supply for planting patterns, and a trip to the extension agent to review soil conditions. These pieces of information and much more were now in the information model and accessible with the proper permissions.

By 6 p.m., a layered picture was emerging. The concept appeared at regional level as bands of color, representing how critical each area was to the solution. Red bands typically abutted a bay tributary. Because of the information input by local farmers, the information was unusually accurate. As one zoomed in, the layers broke into clumps of color that identified individual fields and in most cases clearly identified parts of fields. Farmers used geographic information to optimize their methods based on how critical an area was to bay recovery. Interconnected systems offered farmers endless possibilities. By embracing new farming practices, they created an environment with essentially no erosion and extremely low ground and surface water contamination. The system was highly energy efficient and had a net negative carbon footprint. Their fields supported high levels of biodiversity above and belowground. Their fields were highly productive in dry years.

By about 7 p.m. eastern time, many of local farmers had left the process for the day. Experts in other parts of the world continued to improve the concepts that had emerged during the day. A group of experts representing chemical suppliers, seed developers, lawyers, and agricultural specialists began to draft a set of layered agreements to enable the changes being considered. The experts had identified that the largest barriers to widespread adoption were the risks during the transition and leasing issues. All needed to realize that the practice of cover cropping, controlled wheel traffic, no-till, and precision-fertilization benefited us all. The agreements focused on equitably sharing both the pain and the gains that would emerge as the changes moved forward. The processes relied on communication, information, and the need for support through farm policy.

Other experts were modeling how the layered implementations would perform over time. Their simulations assessed the impacts over the six-year period required for the transition to sustainable practices. They were also modeling the net effect on such things as market pricing, subsidies, and impact on local economies. The overlap between technology and people was affecting how things happened in all industries, throughout the built environment. The pressure came from technology redefining how people work. In agriculture, the pressure comes from the land and how people relate to the environment. Legal requirements defining how people interact were one factor. Attitudes, learning styles, and ability to change were others. At their core, these factors are about people and how they interrelate with each other. In this context, technology was an enabler and a force multiplier that increased the uncertainty and doubt. Technology moves us into the realm of the new and unknown, giving us the tools to make more informed decisions about our future.

SUSTAINABLE PRACTICES

The need to adapt to sustainable practices, as soon as possible, has emerged as issue number one.

Farmers in other areas of the United States are beginning to input information about their experiences. Farming, our most traditional industry, is arguably one area that cloud-based technology will have the greatest impact. Management and planting systems using microelectromechanical system sensors (MEMS) and mobile communications networks are available to all farmers. Where labor-intensive nonautomated systems required the farmer to collect the sensor data, we now have automated sensors that allow the farmer to sit at home, in the office, or on his or her tractor to retrieve information. Temperature, humidity, soil moisture, pH level, and macro nutrients are collected in the field using sensors. Crops get the nutrients they need in the correct amounts based on the sensor data. Wheel steering, precision planting, and variable-rate fertilization optimize the work flow and minimize environmental impact. Sensors, information models, geographic information systems, model servers, and other data repositories are creating a network for planning and control of the farm. Tying this system to the equipment and people to get the work done in the fields lets farmers realize the true benefits. One farmer in Iowa tells an account of his sister's farm.

No one was actually driving the tractor. Beth was in the cab listening to music and working on the planting projection for the next field. The tractor and the fertilizer-planter were both controlled by a guidance system called real-time kinematics (RTK). RTK used geographic information systems and a carrier signal from towers to auto-steer Beth's tractor and attachments. Beth had started using this approach when the family converted the fields to sustainable practices and began precision planting and controlled wheel traffic about five years ago. These days, much of her field was never compressed by the weight of equipment. By not compressing the soil, Beth's family farm qualified for carbon offset credits. She had dramatically lowered her field's release of nitrous oxide. Controlled wheel traffic pretty much paid for the RTK system by itself.

When you ride along with Beth, you notice that, as the tractor moves down the row, you don't see much if any actual soil. Brown plant residue covers the entire surface of the field. Last year's crop residue and last winter's cover crop combine to create this trash cover. The plants growing on this land feed the soil every day of the year, not just when Beth is growing a cash crop. The trash cover also blocks evaporation. Beth saves more of the snowmelt and rain that falls on the field. The plant matter on the surface goes beyond reducing evaporation. This continuous no-till farming approach treats the soil as a delicate, living system.

Beth was keeping an eye on the computer display as the fertilizer rate was adjusted according to the field's yield history and soil maps. Fertilizer was being knifed in at just the right distance below the seeds so that the developing roots would most efficiently absorb it. This precision, variable-rate fertilization significantly reduced the nitrates that leached into the groundwater from Beth's fields and further reduced nitrous oxide emissions. Beth's family and the neighbors drank well water from beneath this field. It was good to know that remarkably few nitrates were leaching into the aquifer.

Last week it had rained hard for two days. Nearly everything was flooded. The fields where farmers drought-proofed their soils captured virtually all of the water with no erosion or runoff. These fields had been reclaimed. The soil was excellent. The fields did not contribute pollutants to local streams from fertilizer or pesticide runoff. No-till, cover cropping, ever-increasing organic matter, and wheel traffic practices made these undisturbed soils like a sponge, storing the water that they got. They did even better in a drought than traditional methods. The prior year there had been a severe drought. Beth's fields did dramatically better than those of her neighbors, producing yields above the national average. Other farmers were amazed by the high yields she got using sustainable farming methods while others had a significant drought stress loss.

INTERLOCKING BIMSTORMS
CHESAPEAKE BAY REGION
MARCH 26 to OCTOBER 15, 2026

BIMStorm Chesapeake Fisheries & Aquaculture would focus on the fishing, crabbing, and shellfish industries that have long been a staple of the region. The BIMStorm Chesapeake Environment would focus on sustainability and environmental policy, giving those concerned with energy, greenhouse gases, and other conservation issues a forum. BIMStorm Chesapeake Air & Water would build on the previous BIMStorms while focusing on drinking and industrial water resources, wastewater, and storm water. Biological nitrogen removal, storm water remediation, and aquifer protection are but a few of the issues this BIMStorm would handle.

Next came a series of BIMStorms focused on infrastructure. BIMStorm Chesapeake Infrastructure would lead off, followed closely by BIMStorm Chesapeake Utilities and BIMStorm Chesapeake Transportation. Participants in these BIMStorms would primarily focus on roads, public transportation, significant regional utilities, and the other manufactured systems that support life in the region.

BIMStorm Chesapeake Industry and BIMStorm Chesapeake Housing would look at regional growth patterns and zoning. Studies in these BIMStorms would analyze current development patterns and look for opportunities for improvements that would better support the recovery efforts. Much of the area had been industrialized for many years. These industries had contributed significantly to the problems with the Chesapeake Bay. Mining, hydraulic fracturing for natural gas, and abandoned industrial sites throughout the watershed would become a key theme in BIMStorm Chesapeake Industry. Those pollution sources, often far from the Chesapeake Bay itself, had long been a substantial contributor to the problem. Industrial pollution sources offered one of the largest potentials for correction, although they would require significant resources to clean up.

BIMStorm Chesapeake Housing would tackle another significant issue with the region's ability to recover the Chesapeake Bay. There had been a number of initiatives in the region aimed at consolidating residential development and moving residential development from sensitive areas adjacent to the bay and its tributaries. Maryland's Smart Growth Initiative, the Chesapeake Bay Critical Areas Program, and others had made inroads in finding solutions. None of these programs had been quite successful, in part because of the fact that they imposed requirements on one state alone, allowing others to continue as usual or to make sometimes conflicting standards. A goal of BIMStorm Chesapeake

Housing was to change this paradigm. Only by coordinating local requirements to achieve compliance throughout the watershed would real change happen.

Emergency services professionals usually found themselves in the role of planning for how to respond to local emergency services needs long after the designers and planners were done. Often they found themselves shoehorning required facilities into locations that might have been handled much better, had they been involved in a meaningful way at the beginning. BIMStorm Chesapeake Safety & Response would feature the ability of current technology to enable emergency services planning to switch from a reactive to a proactive model, where needs were overlaid as the designers and planners were creating solutions. Best of all, this approach would bring national experts to the table to make the process happen quickly in an extremely economical way. The process would highlight real solutions for even small urban areas and allow emergency services professionals to experience the state of the art in integrated planning.

The Chesapeake Bay recovery would take many years. Much growth would occur in the process. It was essential that emergency services planners find the most economical and effective solution to handle each step of the way. The BIMStorm Chesapeake Safety & Response process offered significant advantages to emergency services personnel who participated. They were able to determine emergency services delivery needs from in-progress design and planning. They could also visually assess critical and high-risk areas as they would evolve over time. Emergency planners could create phased-in and integrated emergency services delivery plans tied to community planning goals. While this took place, they could extract equipment and personnel requirements for each phase of the process to optimize for capital and operational cost and capital needs. They made an "engine" that allows for future flexibility and changing planned futures.

As design and planning teams created solutions and the area adapted to the changes required by the bay recovery, BIMStorm Chesapeake Safety & Response teams would be able to assess the ebb and flow of support needs. Data from each of the BIMStorms would be generated to allow the team to assess critical needs (population densities, population types, criticality of functions/building types, changes to access patterns, etc.) at any point in time. From this data and the emerging design concepts, the BIMStorm Chesapeake Safety & Response team would relocate emergency services equipment, staffing, and facilities. They built timelines for facility design and construction and developed budgets. Provisional plans were created to respond to growth. At the same time, the BIMStorm Chesapeake Safety & Response team recommendations would flow back to the other BIMStorm teams to develop their concepts.

The last two BIMStorms focused on broad, regional-scale planning, design, and governance issues. BIMStorm Chesapeake Communities would deal with the issues specific to the cities and towns in the region. Teams began to resolve the full range of issues that affected the Chesapeake Bay. This BIMStorm required the teams to move across many levels of detail as they explored possibilities throughout the region. At one level of detail, teams assessed greenways, transportation systems, and changes to zoning patterns. At another level, teams zoomed in to evaluate and develop solutions for individual structures that anchored the larger opportunities. In some cases, a team would propose solutions to localized problems. Using the full potential of geographic information systems, information models, and BIMSynergy, teams would create options that best fit the millions of interrelated issues in the region. As possible directions emerged, the teams' work would be reviewed, analyzed, and commented on by thousands of people monitoring progress. As options emerged, the team would model them to find the points of failure, make corrections, and present the results for comment. Options deemed to be acceptable to the largest group of participants moved forward for further consideration.

BIMStorm Chesapeake was not a project. It was a work in progress that would evolve over time. The final, official effort was BIMStorm Chesapeake Restore & Governance. Each of the BIMStorms had added data to the system at that point. It was the capstone, which integrated all of the individual BIMStorms to create a master information model. In this BIMStorm, the work from all other BIMStorms was evaluated. Options were assessed. Priorities began to be assigned. The goal was to reach a consensus for next steps, priorities, and the way to recovery. Now that the issues were "on the table," participants in the region could debate the merits of each option and arrive at a direction. The process was highly representative, relying on the "wisdom of crowds" concept. Each participant had a voice in the decisions. Residents of Maryland, Virginia, Pennsylvania, the District of Columbia, New York, West Virginia, and Delaware all participated.

Political, community, organizational, and Network for Sustainable Decisions leaders, had, after much debate, agreed to accept the outcomes. Rather than reverting to the closely guarded and professionally produced efforts from the past, all had realized that this was a situation where crowd-sourced solutions might be the only solutions. The process was democracy in action. The process was quite open and straightforward enough for all to participate. Results appeared in real time. Everyone's interests were actually represented. Not everyone would be totally satisfied with every solution, for that is human nature, but no one would be able to claim that their thoughts were not considered. Because of this, politicians' ability to control with the purse strings was limited. Like any other citizen, each politician had the ability and the right to advocate for those things that he or she believed needed to happen. Beyond that, their ability to push the system toward stagnation or lack of progress was limited.

VISUALIZE

We live in a world of devices that sense the things around us and report their findings to support our decisions. In isolation, these devices are useful, but they have limits. As a network, visualized and managed in an information model, the possibilities are endless.

The thermostat senses the room's temperature to turn your furnace off and on as required. With the addition of a clock, the thermostat can be matched to your schedule, to reduce the temperature when you are away from home, saving you money. This level of connected sensors can be purchased at any home improvement store. As your thermostat is connected to other systems, larger benefits begin to emerge. When your setback thermostat is connected to other sensors in your home, the data takes on new power. With a browser, you can arrange fuel deliveries from your oil supplier. You can increase or lower the heat while sitting on a lounge chair at the beach. Your utility company can use your information to manage their systems to optimize loads and reduce costs. When systems malfunction, support can be ordered automatically. You can make your energy use patterns available to receive individual services, if you choose. You can visualize patterns of energy use and make adjustments, saving money. All based on your preferences, not someone else telling you what to do. The data from this one thermostat can influence outcomes in ways that we cannot now predict. Think of what is possible when sensors connected and managed through the cloud take hold.

The cloud-hosted sensor system is made up of millions of devices, each connected to other devices. The sensory input from the network combines to produce accurate, complete, and reliable information. The network is highly adaptive and capable of monitoring physical and environmental conditions and much more. Temperature, pressure, sound, vibration, patterns, pollutants, and movement are only a few of the things the sensors in the network can monitor.

The sensor data is combined with historical data, best practice knowledge, environmental reality, and human input to assist decision making. By filtering, aggregating, and making inferences, we collect information that is relevant, less expensive, and of higher quality than ever before. The sensor nodes are intelligent. One can think of them as little, highly focused computers. Each is as basic or as complex as required for the job that it must perform. Each includes a communication device. Radio transceivers, Wi-Fi, and optical devices are a few of the possibilities. Each includes a processing unit to interface with the sensory devices. Each includes a power source such as a battery, an energy-harvesting system, or a wired power system. And each includes sensors, cameras, or microelectromechanical devices required for collecting data or doing something.

Most are wireless and self-managed. They are designed for long-range communications, low power consumption, and ease of use. Depending upon the complexity of the tasks that the sensor node must complete, the device can be as large as a desktop computer or much smaller. They are reliable. Costs vary depending on the complexity and sophistication of the device. Tiny sensor nodes or "motes" can be the size of the end of your thumb, the size of a grain of sand, or smaller. Microscopic motes became commercially available in 2018, and are now used widely.

Most people do not think of these devices as computers. Often they are networked versions of devices that we all know. The devices may look different or be extremely small. They are still thermostats, humidistats, door sensors, motion detectors, and other common devices, yet they are modular, "system-on-a-chip" devices that allow integration with existing or new devices. By adding computing capabilities to these devices, we are able to expand their use. These devices can do more than sense the water temperature in the distribution system. They can alert someone as water begins to freeze, so that action can be taken. Devices have long been able to take pictures of the congested intersection. Now they can also identify patterns that might indicate a problem. These devices can monitor the load on the electric grid and notify remote operators as the loads exceed the capacity. As a system, these devices transfer technology into places that were once hard to visualize or control. Sensors, smart grid networks, RFID tags, 3G/4G wireless networks, smart phones, and tablets are transforming ordinary objects in the physical world into "smart" devices.

These devices create a mesh that connects to cloud servers that organize the details. This distributed system makes the information widely available and increases the system's reliability. As data comes from sensors throughout the built environment and is managed in BIMSynergy, we are able to monitor and control devices through web browsers. At the server level, data is fused together and made available for use by all. The data, integrated with information models, enables high-performance visualization. This visualization works both ways. We can use the information to help us make decisions, and we can send data back to the devices to control things connected to them.

Some of the benefits are not new. People have used sensor technology for many years. Now the technology is available to us all. In our homes, we can turn lights and appliances on and off remotely, while capturing the costs or savings. Our browser displays our electric meter and energy use. We manage our movies, music, and communications systems. Smart systems turn on the lights when we need them. Advanced climate control optimizes our costs and comfort. Systems monitor our safety and security, recognizing patterns that may be problems and calling for help when needed. Sensors are embedded in most of the things that surround us. They connect through BIMSynergy. We use the information all the time.

Around the Chesapeake region, sensors monitor air pollution. Wireless sensors are located strategically in areas where there are risks of hazardous gases. Wireless sensors control temperature and humidity levels inside commercial buildings. When temperatures and humidity rise above a set threshold, the system triggers air conditioning and dehumidification. When ventilation falls below a specified amount, vents open, fans turn on, and outdoor air is added. When the inside temperature and the outside temperature reach predefined levels, the boiler fires to heat water in preparation for a future demand for heat. All of these events are visualized in BIMSynergy.

As the temperature changes from too cold to comfortable to too hot, the visuals change from blue to green to red. A message is sent to the building operator letting him or her know that the area is overheating and that an electric heater needs maintenance.

Information comes from many sources and moves from device to device, maintaining and building functionality as the data moves through the system. We connect with smart, electronic, open source devices and software that wirelessly connect sensors of any type, through the cloud. The devices themselves do not matter. The data is synchronized and massaged in the cloud. We are free to access information from anywhere, using any browser. The cloud is the center of everything—our data, our applications, and our models. The data is safe and readily available. Computing devices are actually tools. We are no longer held hostage to complex desktop systems, or software that can only talk to itself.

WIRELESS SENSORS

Industry uses sensors in almost every activity. Where industry comes together with the public, sensors and remotely monitored controls manage sales. Health care, telecommunications, buildings, retail, transportation, and every other business and social activity use sensors. Cameras see movement and through pattern recognition are able to monitor space and activity. Sensors detect events, report them through the model server, and then take action. The action might be to turn off a fan, send an e-mail, dispatch a person, or append the data to a record for future analysis.

To complete these actions, we must understand the meaning of our data. The data must become actionable intelligence that can be analyzed to find patterns of interest to control systems and get things done.

What can one do with a value of 96.70? Is it 96.7 degrees Fahrenheit or centigrade? Or could it be kilowatt hours or miles per hour? Or maybe it is dollars or euros? Or pounds of steel? Unless one knows the units of measurement, the data has little value. Not much can be done without the units. The units (and similar information about data) are called metadata.

The units are not enough by themselves. Without knowing the location of the 96.7, we do not know where to use the information. Much of the data that was collected before the first decade of the twenty-first century lacked location information. Without knowing where a piece of data comes from, someone must locate it in space every time it is used—an extraordinarily labor-intensive process. That is why, with billions of points of data, only an extremely small percentage became actionable.

The ability to locate a data point and to convey the units underpins our ability to create a fusion of wireless sensor networks. Location-based systems with clearly identifiable metadata make many of today's systems possible.

Sam Steen, the steel fabricator, accessed his account on BIMSynergy. Yesterday, Joe Krantz, the construction manager, signed off on the purchase order for the framing steel for the new care center at Cork Point. With the purchase order were the details Sam needed to connect to the project's building information model. Sam's password linked him directly to the structural steel objects and requirements. He noticed that the steel members were geo-tagged. They included radio frequency identification (RFID) data points. He opened the model in his system and began the process of producing the first beam, Beam A4. The whole process was automated.

Sam's mission was to keep an eye on things and make sure that the shop didn't run into any problems. The steel for the job was dispatched from the mill minutes after Joe pushed the send button for the purchase order. The mill attached RFID tags and the beam was loaded on the truck so that it came off first at the plant. Beam A4 was scheduled to arrive the next morning at 8:15 a.m. The beam must have already been on the truck, because a notice had just popped up on the model. The truck had gone through the toll plaza on Delaware Route 1 two minutes ago. The crew in the plant should not have any problem with this beam. They should have it prepped and ready to ship out to the project by 3:35 p.m. From the time the beam arrived, until the steelworkers swung it into the air and it was bolted in place at the job site the next day, every action was planned and would be verified.

Sam's shop was a mixture of old-fashioned tools and automated assembly equipment. Most of the work was now completed by computer-aided manufacturing systems and robots. These systems connected to the design tools used by structural engineers and to management and control tools used by builders. Wireless sensors in the plant also monitored the machinery for condition-based maintenance. A few short years ago, before wireless sensor networks were readily available, this level of equipment management was not possible. Wired systems could not economically keep up with how the equipment was used. Inaccessible locations, machines that changed often, hazardous areas, and movable equipment are now easily managed with wireless sensors.

The plant's wireless sensor network was tied into the company's information model. Sam could visualize the sensor data in real time to control the maintenance systems. Since the plant was located near the Choptank River, all types of other sensors were also connected. The entire site was closely monitored. Rainwater runoff, utility use, storm water quality, and all kinds of other environmental systems were monitored by the sensor network. The Network for Sustainable Decisions kept close tabs on Sam's business and just about everything else in the Chesapeake Bay watershed.

The group has found almost limitless opportunities to use wireless sensors to aid in the bay recovery effort. Wastewater is tightly controlled. The days where sewage treatment plants over-boarded excess sewerage into streams, are no more.

Wells and piped and surface water are also monitored, measured, and controlled.

These days, wireless sensor networks for farms are common. Everything from equipment operations to irrigation automation is measured and controlled by sensors. Farms now have sensors to monitor runoff and to help the farmers plan crops and manage their use of water and additives.

Nearly every structure in the area includes wireless sensors. Not only buildings, but infrastructure such as bridges, tunnels, roads, underground piping, and transmission lines. The days of actual site visits, just to see if there were problems, are behind us. The sensors tell us as problems develop, so that corrective measures can take place before failure.

Homes use smart meters that allow homeowners to become active managers of their environments. No longer must they rely on knowing their energy use once a month, when their bill arrives. Now they have immediate information on how they are doing and can adapt as needed. All devices, from thermostats to personal computers, home networks, and mobile devices, speak exactly the same language—the web services language. With web services, they directly connect their devices to the model server without any intermediaries, conversions, or manipulation…it just works.

AMONG NODES

With BIMSynergy, we can share information, much like one would share videos on YouTube or Vimeo. Using the data, we can monitor and share real-time built environment information from sensors that link in the cloud. As the interface with platforms such as Pachube, the Lavelle Energy's Virtual Realtime Information System, and the Onuma System, BIMSynergy gives us the ability to handle millions of bits of data every day coming from hundreds of thousands of individuals, companies, and places around the world. It is an open ecosystem, expanding, contracting, and adjusting as required. The ecosystem lets us share data and build communities, much as we do in social networks.

BIMSynergy is but one node among many. These nodes act together and separately to capture data from remote sensors and to transmit data to remote actuators. They watch anything in the built environment. Homes, commercial buildings, transportation hubs, hotels, hospitals, seaports, and parks are a small sampling of the places in this ecosystem. Spontaneous and unplanned connections are common in this environment. Everything is interconnected and interrelated, and one never knows how information may be reused for new and unexpected benefits.

Arbitrary and capricious methods for assessing operating risk and costs are no longer needed or reasonable. Wireless sensors allow an accurate assessment of driving habits and hazardous behaviors, making insurance underwriting more accurate and unbiased.

Follow this tag to learn more about real-time data at http://4sitesystems.com/iofthestorm/?page_id=897

No longer must you purchase things that you rarely use. Wireless devices enable companies to lease capital-intensive equipment such as cars and aircraft by the hour. Car-sharing firms such as Zipcar, I-GO, and WeCar capitalize on the fact that cars can be managed. Their use can be metered, so that people no longer need to purchase them.

Similar programs have existed for many years in the aircraft industry. It is common for users of aircraft to rent planes by the hour and engines by the time that they run. Through sensors and continuous operation assessment, owners of the equipment control maintenance and schedule engine changes. Charging for the use of this expensive equipment works to the benefit of both the seller and the buyer.

Using sensors for commercial benefit is only a small part of the equation. Communities are developing around devices and data collection systems. Within these communities, people connect electricity meters, weather systems, air quality monitors, water quality monitors, building management systems, biosensors, and much more.

At Cork Point, the laboratory uses testing equipment that senses when the device produces usable data and charges accordingly. Much of the equipment throughout the system is rented this way. Costs to the hospital are directly connected to community needs. Charges to the community are fine-tuned, based on behaviors and patterns of use. Sensors give everyone better information, improving pricing. They ensure that essential goods and services are available.

Around the Chesapeake Bay, the sensor network achieves many things. The conditions of the Chesapeake Bay Bridge near Annapolis and the Chesapeake Bridge-Tunnel near Norfolk are monitored and assessed. No one wants to repeat the mistakes that happened during Hurricane Edgar. The Network for Sustainable Decisions uses sensors to focus attention on citizens who negatively impact upon the bay recovery effort. Sensors allow them to determine charges and to assign responsibility for pollution events. By monitoring the runoff from industrial users, they are able to punish those doing harm to the bay and to reward those that are doing well. Their sensors and the algorithms they use even let them reward improving compliance, when appropriate.

The programs of the Network for Sustainable Decisions have enabled a number of smart growth initiatives to succeed. As the group's programs move toward fact-based discussions based on real data, they can predict the density of people in urbanized areas, anywhere and anytime. They are able to focus people on improving their environments, rather than focusing on sensors and isolated programs. In the past, programs took place out of context, focused on one group or another. Farmers were targeted for nitrogen runoff from their fields, while communities' sewage treatment facilities dumped raw sewage into rivers. Homeowners were targeted for fertilizing their lawns, while industrial plants in urban areas flushed chemicals down storm sewers. Ethical developers could not afford to build, while others were allowed to install infrastructure for McMansions.

Insight into how people were actually behaving and how their behaviors could be modified was needed. Sensor data and information mined from other activities was analyzed with algorithms designed to uncover the truth about what was occurring. This gave the Network for Sustainable Decisions the facts that they needed to achieve their goal.

DATA COMES FROM EVERYWHERE

Sensor data comes from almost anywhere and can be used by virtually anyone. Certainly there are limits, although, in most cases, the limits are limits of imagination. The data from sensors tells us what happened and what is happening. The data gives us the facts and can be recombined and analyzed. Information models are designed fiction. They are virtual representations of the world we live in—or they are virtual representations of possibilities.

The cloud is a name for the Internet, as fixed hardware and software become irrelevant. Information on the cloud can be accessed from anywhere by any device. Combining sensor data with information models in the cloud creates opportunities and possibilities.

We can extract information about the universe and make it publicly available. We can track or inventory any public or private vehicle, vessel, or object. We can follow the history of things and compare them to other similar things. We can track pollution and climate data by area of the city or region of the bay and make the material available for general purposes. We can observe how communities work to inform the design process. Games can use sensors to allow interaction between players or to respond to real-world conditions.

Sensor tags can automatically deliver information about those things we want to know. Sensors and web services combine to create mash-ups that quickly solve problems. Clothing and footwear can include sensors to let people interact with those around them. Websites can respond to sensor feeds, changing dynamically. A web page connected to tsunami sensors can send warnings to all who subscribe, when target conditions are exceeded.

Real-time data from actual sensors can be visualized to advance understanding of current conditions. An avatar of your office can pop up to suggest that you open the window rather than allowing the air conditioning to cool the space, as the temperature becomes too hot. By sensing indoor and outdoor temperatures and humidity and comparing them to psychometric charts, the system chooses the optimal combination of mechanical and natural ventilation and cooling. The sensors and algorithms allow you be an active participant in informed conservation.

Devices can connect, or talk, to each other and share real-time data that can be used to activate other devices or make better decisions. Mobile gadgets can use sensor data to help the user understand nearby opportunities. Networked objects such as appliances and lamps can respond to each other and engage other data systems. Communities can connect systems to allocate resources, monitor power, and optimize systems. Data from government operations can be shared publicly without compromising security. Building management systems can share energy use and temperature data. These systems can validate user compliance, purchasing, and public disclosure requirements.

Sensor data can create an information model to support design or other facility operations. Real-time sensor links embedded in information models can support continuous maintenance and management so that things always functions as designed. Real-world sensors can change virtual environments such as Second Life, and virtual-world sensors can affect real-world environments. Home automation devices and sensors let you manage and respond to your particular situation. Sensors connected to your electric meter track usage over time. Sensor data can be embedded in your website, used to determine your real-time carbon footprint, and can monitor your efforts toward a net zero energy lifestyle.

Throughout the built environment, sensors and network devices send and receive information that can be used to the benefit of all.

INTELLIGENT BUILDINGS

In the past, buildings operated as islands of consumption, with few constraints on their energy use. Energy suppliers also operated in isolation, charging tariff rates that included instantaneous peak demand charges. Demand charges isolated a single peak of energy use over a month. They also isolated events. Building owners' budgets faced ever-increasing energy costs. Operating costs for users and suppliers continually escalated. The cost of energy continued to grow. Pricing moved toward dynamic models that could change every fifteen minutes. New systems, new ways of working, and new technologies added to the pressure.

Disconnected systems created confusion. Misinformation and the lack of easy solutions kept building owners from minimizing peak demand, even though in many cases, limiting demand would pay off in days or weeks; few investments have such short returns. Because of the business and technology pressures, energy awareness began to build. More people became aware of the need to manage energy use. As awareness increased, people began to change their energy habits using technology.

Few buildings operated more efficiently just because they included intelligent features. Proprietary control systems were applied in ways that limited their effectiveness. Open standards and free exchanges of decision-making information often did not exist. Existing buildings rarely functioned as designed. Air distribution and comfort were not optimized to save energy. Building automation systems were capable of collecting millions of bits of information and making them available, yet most were viewed as static installations.

Sensor contractors installed devices, verified that information was flowing, set up parameters, billed for their work, and were seen no more. Vendors installed products to care for the obvious needs and returned when someone complained, usually on a cost plus fee basis. Owners and property managers were held in a contractual headlock that allowed building automation vendors to obtain fees at every opportunity, without actually solving the problems at hand. Custom protocols blocked devices from communicating with existing systems, locking in vendors and blocking competition. Major vendors gamed the market to deny future work to others. Low bids locked buildings into long-term maintenance requirements worth much more than the initial installation.

Few owners saw building automation vendors as providing satisfactory value. Alternatives to proprietary approaches were found. These solutions empower people to handle building energy management in ways that avoid the stranglehold that traditional vendors had on building energy management. Managing energy in buildings requires the integration of things that have traditionally not been considered together. A holistic approach that integrates technology and systems, real-time information and people, suppliers and end-users, and much more was needed. Now companies use open standards to devise better methods for converting raw building data into actionable information.

Integration has long been the holy grail of building communications. By reducing our dependence on proprietary protocols, we reduce the need for specialized training. Where custom protocols drive costs up, open standards drive costs down. Building users can now help to manage their own energy use. Social network-inspired solutions have changed how people interact with buildings. Building information is shared. Property owners, building managers, and occupants communicate using systems much like Google+. In the past, perhaps the facility manager interacted with building data. Now, energy use in building operations is everyone's interest.

All know how their world works. Information is filtered so that it is relevant for the recipient's need. The days of storytelling- and belief-driven energy plans are behind us. These days building energy plans go far beyond platitudes and "reducing our carbon footprint." Each building has a tailored energy plan that evolves over time. The system is created using a variety of crowd sourcing technologies. Users are involved in the process whenever possible. At the same time, processes that can be automated are automated. Every user has at least a basic understanding of the plan. Buildings at this level are able to become fully grid-aware and part of the BIMSynergy network. By including everyone in the mix, it becomes easier to optimize how the building functions. The building becomes an intelligent ecosystem, rather than an island.

The intelligent building becomes a node on the smart grid. Advanced energy metering and timely information about how people use energy allow the network to be optimized to the benefit of all.

Existing schools were first to make the transition to this intelligent ecosystem. Real-time energy management systems capable of starting small, with immediate results and easy payback, enable the switch. These low-cost and open-source systems enable schools to connect to virtually anything, using web services. Their expansion potential is almost limitless. They are capable of handling near real-time information flow from thousands of buildings simultaneously. They can start small and grow to match a school district's needs and resources.

These open-source systems allow students and faculty to see energy, space use, and operating data. They can click to zoom and learn the details. They can see thousands of buildings in near real time. School leaders can receive dynamic energy pricing. The system automatically takes appropriate measures. Dynamic information updates in near real time, and is viewable on mobile devices, browsers, and Google Earth.

One can connect to temperature and humidity sensors, cameras, security devices, and the Internet of Things. Data is displayed in many ways. At the simplest, real-time predefined graphs represent the sensor data. This data can actively change the colors of spaces as preset thresholds are achieved. As a space moves from too cool to too hot, the space changes from blue, to orange, and finally to red. The changes occur dynamically across buildings and spaces to provide quick visual indication of conditions. In any two-dimensional or three-dimensional view, the user can manage energy, space use, lights on (or off), surveillance, and many other details. All are accurate within the information model.

No longer is the building information model only a design and construction tool. Building information models have now evolved into tools that model any data. Dynamically linked to sensors, other cloud-based information, and endless analysis and visualization tools, these information models are reliable and rapidly scalable platforms for power monitoring, building automation, and smart microgrid energy management. They bring real-time decision-making facts, anytime and anywhere there is an Internet connection. Much as you do with Expedia and Google Earth, with open-standard sensors and information models you see energy data in a real-world context and make real-time decisions.

Humans respond to visual information. Tables of data are uninteresting and difficult to understand. You see and understand things better in information models than you do with flat representation. You manage data best in real time. Cloud-based information models are contextual tools that let you visualize and manage data from sensors and remote devices.

PATH FORWARD

The World Wide Web has always been about connections; connections between people, places, and things. Originally, connections focused on documents. Over time, the focus evolved toward search and retrieval of information and social connections. The meaning of things became critical. The scale and extent of connections grew. IBM proposed the Internet of Things, geospatial experts proposed the Internet of Places, and others discussed the Web Wide World. The union of decentralized systems implied by these proposals made it possible for mankind to manage wicked problems.

Early in the twenty-first century, it became clear that fragmentation and stovepipes must be eliminated. Fragmented documents and disconnected processes restricted growth and productivity. The construction industry remained mired in complexity and fragmentation. Construction-related interoperability became an international competitive tool, creating new and subtler disconnects between people. Established organizations and experts actively worked to oppose the transfer of new paradigms from the Internet into the industry, while scrambling to find ways to make individual profits from the cloud.

The industry's most forward-thinking people found themselves mired in the last-generation computing paradigm. Those with long records of supporting interoperability and open standards found that they were working toward outcomes that were too complex and too disconnected from the synthesis of systems that was developing. Holding to traditional standards and evolving information standards such as Industry Foundation Classes was not getting the job done. Too much time was passing, and too little progress was taking place. The industry as a whole had embraced information modeling as an inevitable next step.

Information modeling, geospatial resources, real-time sensors, business metrics, and crowd source information fuse together to create a unified vision of our world, a connected world that supports better decisions with real-time data from natural and man-made sources, to live, work, and play sustainably. Planning, design, and construction combine to increase productivity and provide a long-term solution to global problems. Integrated systems using tools that work much like Expedia, Facebook, and Google align the built environment with the rest of the world.

The world is a blend of the digital and the physical. In this world, technology is invisible. Each of us uses and creates information as we move through this world. Little planning goes into how and what information we produce, because the system is flexible. The system does not expect us to plan each step forward. Everything happens in the context of dynamic frames of reference not possible when we focused on projects, devices, sensors, or individual objects. Rather than becoming engulfed in virtual worlds, as some science fiction writers have described, we participate in the physical world enabled by virtual connections.

Readily available data support decisions, resulting in better decisions. We take a step; the implications are reflected in the data. We decide to take another step. The new implications are shown. The process continues through every activity. We see immediately when we are stepping off of the correct path. We understand the implications when we consider alternatives.

We do the things that need to be done, tapping into the data to inform our decisions as we move forward. Most activities are commonplace. We do them by rote. Yet, much of what we do informs or creates innovation. Decisions requiring leaps of faith or intuition are made knowing that we have covered the known issues.

As Expedia became popular, people learned that when they needed an airline or hotel they could directly manage their reservation on the site. Few transactions went awry. Nearly every transaction solved a need. The same level of reliability and even greater availability come from the combination of technologies in the built environment. When you need the information, it is there, in forms that complement decision making and let you choose your way ahead.

CHANGE AND ADAPT

> If I'd asked my customers what they wanted, they would have said a faster horse.
> —Henry Ford

Under Sandy Kim's leadership, the Network for Sustainable Decisions was the first to use interconnecting BIMStorms to plan and manage a significant wicked problem. The group recognized the fact that returning the Chesapeake Bay to health would involve millions of people, thousands of organizations, and too many opinions to consider. Only by working with a system that made information readily available, in ways that people needed, could the process move forward. Isolated programs that did not respond to stakeholders with different outlooks and needs usually failed. Federal and state mandates showed slight results at best. BIMStorms connected people. By empowering people to make decisions, trusting in the wisdom of crowds, the Network for Sustainable Decisions has overcome many of these issues.

In the six years since BIMSynergy was created, integrated systems in the cloud have gradually emerged as critical systems in the built environment. Growth has been slow and steady, led by visionary organizations such as the Coast Guard. Now, the system is being used to its full potential as the twelve BIMStorm Chesapeake programs unfold. BIMSynergy is the system's linchpin. The system allows people across the region to use their energy and skill for the greater good.

In 2008, BIMStorm Los Angeles offered many their first glimpse of what BIG BIM is all about. In twenty-four hours, teams with 130 members from around the world created over four hundred building information models. People from around the world collaborated in real time with information models and many open-standards software applications. The event was such an extreme example of the change that BIMStorm Los Angeles was described as the "Woodstock" of building information modeling. It was a glimpse of information modeling on steroids. It was a watershed event that opened the eyes of the world to the possibilities of information modeling. Just like the world of music was changed forever by Woodstock, the built environment was changing faster than we realized at the time. Today, we look back and laugh at what things were like when BIMStorms started.

Early BIMStorms were intended to give people a clear idea of where the technology was heading, making it easier for people to plan their personal transformation to a more integrated and collaborative world than in the past. These BIMStorms let people roll up their sleeves and experience real information modeling in ways that were straightforward and cost-effective. They were zero carbon events; since everything happened in the cloud, no one had to travel to take part. They did not require a significant time or money investment.

They happened in a rush. Typically they took place in one to three days, in total. In that short period of time, extraordinary things happened—all because everyone was simply working in an integrated environment. There was little wasted effort. People worked within their expertise. Those with design skills devised creative concepts. Those with estimating and planning talents applied those talents to the concepts. Specialists input their knowledge. At the end of the event, incredible things emerged. Often the results mirrored several months' efforts with traditional design and planning processes.

BIMStorms symbolize change and adaptation. They link business and lifestyle to facilities and the built environment. Over the last twenty plus years, they have evolved. The first BIMStorms involved architects, engineers, and those in facility leadership positions. Quickly they transitioned to encompass wider design and industry participation. Beginning in BIMStorm LAX, there were glimpses of things to come. Rules-driven systems, business metrics, integrated decision support, and building information modeling in the cloud were always a part of the BIMStorm. Support for familia Corazon in Tijuana, urban planning in Rotterdam, and green roofs in London crept into the process. The first evolution involved communities.

The BIMStorm in Charleston West Virginia was first to focus on extending the concept to the general public. Organized as a series of public meetings, an on-site and a remote team captured community issues and used the tools to engage the public. In a typical session, a downtown resident expressed the need for housing at the confluence of the Elk and Kanawha Rivers. The remote group would then, in near real time, create and display housing solutions in the location under consideration.

Enabling the public to see their ideas immediately reflected in Google Earth, with massing, areas, costs, and other material, was extremely powerful. People left the process knowing that their ideas were understood and reflected in the ultimate solution. The evolution of the BIMStorm to support community involvement continued in BIMStorm Chesapeake.

The next evolution involved community service and disaster recovery. The earthquake in Haiti and the tsunami in Japan were both the subject of BIMStorms focused on the recovery process. After Hurricane Katrina, BIMStorm New Orleans looked at emergency services, integrating geographical information system data to support urban planning and new downtown structures. BIMStorms' ability to engage people locally with experts anywhere in the world offered significant benefits in the disaster recovery process. This evolution, much like everything that had gone before, offered glimpses of more things to come as the cloud and web services began to blossom. The Onuma System and BIMStorms became drivers in the movement toward what some called Geo-design.

With Geo-design, the ideas detailed by visionaries such as Ian McHarg and Buckminster Fuller began to come to pass, as building information modeling in the cloud and geographic information began to unite. As the complexity of the built environment increased, this alignment resulted in better solutions. Decisions were made earlier in the process, with more accurate and reliable data. No longer did each area of technology need to operate in isolation. Multiple technologies and knowledge domains could be integrated to the benefit of all.

The ability to interact with all systems and all areas of the built environment became the highest and best use of the Onuma System. Ecology, energy, facilities management, and sustainability were the domains of this evolutionary step. The system was by this point probably best described as middleware and lightweight model server technology. The system became a central hub, supported by internal design and planning tools. At the simplest level, concepts could be created for export to desktop systems for further development. After changes were made, the desktop solutions could be reimported into the system.

The system became the starting point for further development. By archiving the existing built environment data, such as plans, utility information, and virtually any research that can be imagined, the system was a repository for the background information needed to seed complex design processes. In Washington, DC, the capital city's first EcoDistrict used the Onuma System to capture the documentation, site analysis, energy and environmental data, and much more to inform further development. As an offshoot of this project, examples of the subsequent progress became apparent. Real-time sensor data and live device control emerged. The Onuma System and BIMStorms have gotten more refined and elegant; yet at this point all the components for the future were in place.

Familia Corazon volunteers build a home in Tijuana, Mexico as part of BIMStorm LAX. 32° 29' N 117° 5' 1" W

The system meets present needs without jeopardizing the ability of future generations to meet their needs. The system depends on people's motivation, willingness to cooperate, and teamwork. It focuses on people and their needs, not on technology. The system is sustainable and impacts everything in our world.

BIMStorm Chesapeake is taking advantage of all of the systems capabilities. By breaking the BIMStorm down into functional components, the Network for Sustainable Decisions lets all participate. The process focuses on agriculture, fisheries, aquaculture, the environment, air, water, infrastructure, utilities, transportation, industry, housing, safety, emergency response, communities, restoration, and governance in the future. Without this wide range of involvement, a many-layered solution that can actually solve the problems is unlikely to develop.

Integrating the built environment into community programs and individual action accelerates the recovery. Communities move away from conventional models of development toward sustainable development, so that urban and natural environments work in harmony. The process allows people to contribute and know that their voices are heard. The days of planners opening a forum for the express purpose of taking nominal public input are no more. When you provide input in a BIMStorm, you know that you are heard. Your material may not be immediately reflected in the final direction and may, in fact, be rejected out of hand, but everyone is heard. Knowing that the best ideas can come from anywhere, the process works to involve everyone.

Expertise and experience are celebrated in the BIMStorm. International and local experts communicate, examine, and propose solutions. There is little reason for experts to keep their opinions close, for all are welcome. The process is transparent. Trust is given to those who create solutions and work to solve problems. Many teams focus on the problems, from a global perspective. As the BIMStorm focuses in on possible solutions, the experts also focus their inputs. Since the process is working with open-standard and interoperable data, the experts can quickly extract the information they need for research using basic or highly sophisticated tools, at any stage.

Background data resides in the system and comes from distributed sources. Sensor data flows from across the region, to BIMSynergy and to those participating in the BIMStorm. The data is complete. It is collected and presented in ways that allow participants to make informed decisions. The data allows them to understand current performance, to set targets, and to develop recommendations for performance. Energy, access and accessibility, air quality, emissions, water, climate, functioning and obsolete industrial zones, habitat and ecosystems, and community vitality are just some of the things monitored and reported by sensors into BIMSynergy. As BIMStorm Chesapeake progresses, these sensors, the devices they control, and the BIMSynergy data repository will become the backbone of standards and tools that enable Sandy and the Network for Sustainable Decisions to manage the ongoing process.

The relationships between the bay and the surrounding area will change. The dead zones, key fisheries, and other problems will be corrected only as we manage the remote impacts, improve agriculture and land use, guide tourism, and restore the region's ecological health. The layered Chesapeake BIMStorms are identifying where and how to intervene to impact energy, water, and the ecosystem. As the BIMStorms turn everyone in the region toward the true issues, the effects and solutions become clearer. Environmental stewardship tied to integrated strategies for managing both man-made and natural systems begins to improve the quality of people's lives in meaningful ways. People begin to take responsibility for themselves and for future generations. The Chesapeake Bay may never return to the days when skipjacks were everywhere. But we can learn to use only what we need and no more, and become stewards of the region.

END GAME

7.

Looming on the horizon is a time when we can no longer sustain our society or ourselves. We must learn to embrace technology and develop new ways of working that enhance our collective ability to create a more sustainable world. New processes enabled by technology create new opportunities. Managing the information that surrounds us lets us remove the mundane to focus on better design. In the process, we become better stewards of our world.

This book is not about which software product is best for you. It is not about buying a new computer system. This book is about the ins and outs of changing to make information work for you.

Let's face it: resources are limited and you need to use them more effectively. Today's technology enables you to make earlier decisions based on more complete and accurate information. This book provides the information that you need to learn how the integration of technology with the built world can change things. Integrating technology does not require you to throw away all of your proven tools and experiences. It does require you to look at them differently. It requires you to separate the things that should be kept from those that should be replaced.

We live in a world that is complex, confusing, and difficult to tie into neat packages. The people who work and live in this world run the full gamut, from the poorest of the poor, marginalized in every conceivable way, to casual labor working with little autonomy, to highly trained and experienced experts who create new and exciting things every day. The built environment touches on and affects each one of us, every day. It defines our world.

Estimates show that 46 percent of global resources go to the built environment. We currently are not using these resources efficiently. Our current ways of doing business are not sustainable. In fact, productivity has been in steady decline since the advent of computers. We spend too much and get too little for our investment in the built environment. We must change how things work in the built environment. We must stand up and demand changes. We can afford nothing less.

The construction industry as a whole must become technology literate. Technologies such as building information modeling, integrated project delivery, and integrated decision making enable us to create a better world. The "comprehensive anticipatory design science" first described by Buckminster Fuller is within our reach. Technology has caught up with the theory.

Figuring out how to integrate technology into the industry is a gargantuan task. The industry is so widespread and includes so many players that it is hard to wrap it into a tidy package. It is so diverse that it touches everything in our lives. It is difficult to describe, and when a problem is difficult to describe, it is hard to solve.

Finding solutions to problems within this complex system has always been difficult. Architects and other professionals have made incremental changes, trying to solve individual problems. Their improvements have tended to focus on one group or one client area. At times, these solutions filtered through the industry. Prior to building information modeling and integrated technologies arriving on the scene, few groups even attempted to find genuine solutions to the larger problems.

When people did most of the work by hand, it was relatively easy to fix problems. As people have adopted increasingly technological innovations, it has become harder and harder to make systemic repairs. Today, the industry faces problems of poor execution, poor cost controls, and the recognition that traditional processes are deteriorating.

For many, information modeling seems like another software solution. In this context, it is difficult to accept change. The benefits seem minor.... It is just another software package, right? It can be difficult to see how information technology will serve you personally. It is hard to see a clear path to success. Done right, information models, sensors, web-enabled devices, geographic information, and all of the other web-based tools can change everyone's life for the better. The plan has been to show you a glimpse of what it might mean to you right now.

TARGET-RICH ENVIRONMENT

Finding scenarios that illustrate the power and complexity of the model server is not difficult. A soldier might say that it's a target-rich environment.

The first scenario touched on how the Coast Guard uses the system across their entire organization. We highlighted their use of the model server to support decision making and emergency response. The question was: "Can the Coast Guard use the technology to achieve more with fewer resources?" Terrorists, budgets, people, boats, and weather all played into the scenario. To the Coast Guard, technology is a force multiplier.

The next scenario revolved around the rapidly growing medical facilities at Cork Point. At Cork Point, BIMSynergy and BIMStorms support the entire enterprise. In a health-care environment where every dollar is critical, closely integrated processes support fact-based decisions in all areas. Expansion programs, change management, leadership, magic tricks, and a storm helped to demonstrate how Cork Point uses the technology. The people at Cork Point manage their assets, not just their projects.

Finally, we concluded by looking at the Network for Sustainable Decisions as they led the cleanup of the Chesapeake Bay region. Pollution, urban growth, agriculture, and a host of preexisting conditions created the problem. Model servers, information, and new ways of working and thinking will fix the problem. Real-time sensors, early planning, toxic goop, crowd sourcing and sailboats all figured into this scenario.

The BIMSynergy framework is the foundation of this book. It describes tools and processes designed to handle the data that seeds the entire continuum. Decisions made using the system are directly exported to middle-market tools, geographic information systems, and a wide range of analysis and design tools. The focus of the tools and processes are the larger world issues that will sustain the world for our children. BIMSynergy provides improved early decision-making imagery and information to support the built world.

For many, the system represented by BIMSynergy will look like another software solution. In fact, it is both a technology and an entirely new way of looking at the built world. The goal is to create truly sustainable solutions.

Many of the opportunities are exploited and defined by major architects, contractors, software developers, and vendors. They are on the front lines of changes that will rival the disruptions that large companies are experiencing in the music, publishing, and automotive industries. Rapidly evolving technology, social networks, new ways of communicating, and economic conditions all work to make the normal processes fail. As large companies struggle to maintain their positions in this new world, it seems like a modern version of "the Wild West." One hears about the failures—the late and over-budget projects, the lawsuits and the conflict. Decision makers find themselves in the role of mediating between a confusing host of options. They find themselves embroiled in philosophical discussions that easily lead down the wrong path. Were things only complicated, solutions could be mapped out. Unfortunately, things are complex. The problems are often "wicked," and "solutions" only lead to further problems.

BIMSynergy envisions a solution to the problems. The solution requires that we rethink how we interact with the built environment. Large and small companies can no longer continue business as usual, thinking that by buying "this new information modeling software" that the problems will miraculously go away. Working effectively and achieving success in a world based on information will need real change.

COULD IT BE TEN YEARS SINCE WE OPENED BIMSYNERGY?
MARION STATION, MARYLAND
OCTOBER 15, 2030

It is hard to believe the changes that have happened in those ten years. We were only open two years when the world came crashing down around our ears. The Coast Guard Base down in Portsmouth was attacked. Right behind that was the storm that destroyed Crisfield. It seems incredible looking back on it, but BIMSynergy handled the data flow for both of those events. There were glitches, but all in all we did a terrific job. So good, in fact, that the facility received a Presidential Citation.

BIMSynergy is pretty well established as one of the preeminent Fusion Hubs on the East Coast. In the early days, Fusion Hubs were called SMART Connexion Servers, but that changed in about 2023. For some reason, the concept of data fusion caught on, and the server systems all over the world came to be known as Fusion Hubs. The idea of a central hub that acts to organize and massage data from everywhere is well established.

As a system, the Fusion Hubs are as robust and ubiquitous as we hoped when we were doing our initial planning. Information models, geographic information systems, sensors, devices, financial systems, and much more are linked together through the Fusion Hubs. In the Fusion Hubs, we have verifiable, build-once-and-use-anywhere digital models at multiple levels of detail. The information is valid, repeatable, and handles the vast majority of situations.

One of our better ideas was to keep the whole thing cloud-based and open-standards compliant.

The ultimate goal in most people's mind is still to host the highly detailed virtual model created during design and construction… the virtual model as an exact simulation of the physical. The easy-to-use and fully interoperable model hosted in a reliable cloud-based model server remains elusive. This goal may become reality in another ten years, but there remain many hurdles to overcome.

Even today much of the construction industry has difficulty supporting common standards. Standards organizations and the building information modeling software industry have always been slow to respond to the power of the Internet and cloud-computing. These standards are slow to emerge and often significantly lag other information technology standards and protocols. When standards are released, we embrace them, but they are usually at least two years behind the curve. If we waited for this set of standards to mature, nothing would happen. Fortunately, Internet standards organizations are fast to market. People take advantage of this fact as they use cloud-computing and data fusion.

There are problems with both the desktop and cloud versions of many legacy systems. The old-line developers continue to produce proprietary building information software and model servers that rely on programming interfaces and various data interchange standards to work with other software. These systems are pretty capable, but have a project focus and rely on the power of desktop hardware. These solutions are complex, and require significant expertise to operate. Large organizations still believe these systems to be core business tools. BIMSynergy hosts these solutions where possible.

Most software systems still do not play well with others. Competitive pressures and positioning for sales could be the problem. When you look at the first principles that are the foundation of these systems, there are more systemic problems. Parts of these systems can integrate well with others; it is a matter of following naming conventions and other standards. In many other cases, however, the way these systems work is not compatible with the way other systems work.

We have come to believe that conceptual differences are the key to why interoperability is an elusive concept. Because of this, we focus on connecting the key data points, while allowing the systems to be used independently of each other. This creates a situation where users can take advantage of the rich features of these systems, while supporting the life cycle of things in the built environment. Fortunately, the Onuma System continues to be a potent coordinator, interfacing with a wide range of software and sensors. The system has become the lightweight interface to the complex and feature-rich tools to manage the data.

In the last six years, we have learned many lessons. Some compelling lessons changed how we work. Without feedback we cannot grow.

Everything must be simple to learn and easy to use. If the system is not easy to use, few will use it. Integrating systems must also be easy. If your sensors, geographic information, applications, maintenance system, and other tools cannot be integrated easily, what's the point?

Open standards are the only way to go. The world does not stand still, even for an instant. We cannot keep our ideas close. By innovating…by creating…by shipping and sharing, we move forward. Those who do not move forward fail.

New systems require people to make leaps of faith. The potential gain from innovating in all things is difficult to assess at the beginning.

The incremental cost of tools is irrelevant. The cloud-computing and BIMSynergy-based systems are inexpensive when compared to buying full-featured desktop systems. Cloud-based tools enable us to manage the vast majority of built environment systems, economically and efficiently.

The ability to visualize information should not be underestimated. Data visualization can be a quality check to highlight errors and make self-correcting mechanisms.

The world is a messy place, complex and infinitely changeable. Our teams must be like living systems, adapting and fluid. We start small and fragile, growing stronger as we move forward. Individual knowledge and the power of teams intersect to do tremendous things.

AFTER THE BOMBS

The six weeks after the terrorist attack on Portsmouth in 2022 were intense. People died. People were injured. Three cutters were severely disabled. Buildings were destroyed and damaged. Docks were out of commission. And everyone was in shock.

Designed to be blast-proof, the CGSysOps facility suffered only minor damage. Pete Jarvi and the crew in CGSysOps were stunned, but okay. Immediately after the first response, they were tasked with figuring out how to make the repairs and get the base back in operation, better than before.

Admiral Kosinski and Pete's boss, Gary Boyle, brought people together using BIMStorm technologies and Coast Guard expert systems. CGSysOps staff managed the process in conjunction with Norfolk's Facilities Design and Construction Center staff and BIMSynergy experts. Coast Guard subject matter experts from Base Support Unit Portsmouth and Coast Guard Headquarters in Washington, DC, acted as liaisons for missing stakeholders. Architects, engineers, and contractors with recent experience on Coast Guard projects provided input from the beginning. Ultimately, the integrated project team members implemented the solutions. Even with the weight of the attack on their shoulders, in just six weeks they managed to sort out the physical mess.

BIMSynergy enabled Pete and his team to assess and achieve optimal solutions. Much of the background work was simplified because of the building information models, geographic information system data, and sensor grid in place throughout the base. Base Support Unit Portsmouth and BIMSynergy had detailed up-to-the-moment as-built and as-operating information for the entire facility. Only cleanup and demolition had to be verified and documented.

The information and tools enabled the team to arrive at design concepts that met all Coast Guard standards and guidelines quickly and efficiently. In some cases, rapid planning systems enabled the team to turn around the detailed design in as little as two days. BIMSynergy created the required documentation and submittals to support the team working on solutions and not focusing on paperwork.

The most remarkable thing was when the Commandant went before the Joint House and Senate committee only five weeks after the attack. She was able to lay out such a clear and compelling case that the politicians gave her the money to get the job done, right then and there. That may have been the first time that DC politicians truly saw the potential of BIMSynergy and information modeling.

The House and Senate members in attendance came away understanding the opportunities for applying the technology to achieve unprecedented community-based approaches to disaster recovery, crime, and emergency response…using new technologies, rather than trying to patch the mistakes of the last generation. The challenges to public safety were continuing to grow. These new capabilities offered effective ways to make public systems more connected, more efficient, and smarter.

For the first time, a significant group of leaders understood the transformational possibilities. Instead of responding after the fact, BIMSynergy and information models gave them the ability to analyze, anticipate, and actually work to prevent problems before they became problems. They saw smart systems that capture data from millions of interconnected systems, processes, devices, and objects. The systems then identify patterns, visualize decision-making information, and take action in real time. Data plus analytics plus advanced visualization equals certainty and improved public response.

It seems like that was the tipping point for Congress stopping the logjams in their system. For the first time, they saw a presentation with clear and present data…no hype, no guesses, and no fluff…just facts designed to help them decide. Things have been much better in DC since then. The stupid decisions and petty bickering sure eased up when their world became fact-based.

Two weeks after the politicians approved the funds, building started. In six months, Portsmouth was back…better than ever.

It took an extra couple of months to rebuild the cutters, but the USCGC Nestor managed to fill the gap during that time. She had a little help from some other commands, but the integrated systems managed the transition with flying colors.

CORK POINT IS HAPPENING

Without BIMSynergy, Cork Point could have never structured the deals they have all over the world with local hospitals to support what they call their "cottages." I am looking forward to the end of the year, when Samantha and I are heading to the Tuscan hills to live in a villa that Cork Point manages outside of Florence.

Just the other day, I was eating lunch at the Olde Crisfield Crabhouse with Elle from the hospital. The crab cakes were as good as always, and you cannot beat the view out the Little Annemessex River.

Elle was getting second-by-second updates on her iStorm6 of all the vital things happening over at Cork Point. They are managing most of the health-care systems in the region. Her job is enormous. There is no way that she could keep up without systems that reduce the clutter and kept her up to speed on the critical facts.

Cork Point's success came from figuring out how to make health care into a real system. Elle and her board decided it was time to stop the endless debate and to figure out how to connect providing health care to insurers, to employers, to patients, and to the community. They figured out how to reduce the duplication in handoff by tapping into the enormous wells of health-care information in the health-care world. Applying advanced analytics using BIMSynergy, Cork Point has dramatically improved outcomes for the people they serve.

The result is better connections, better information, and faster, more detailed analysis. When these things come together, you start to have an integrated system. Integrated systems let people leverage their abilities to do more. Every element in the Cork Point system is connected. The connections create new and innovative opportunities. Lower costs, higher-quality health care, and a healthier community are the results. Data is all around us. Cork Point's systems are making information available when and where we need it, in ways that are easy to understand and apply, to focus their services on you, the patient.

Cork Point's approach centers on the patient and the community. Each patient can access a tailored collaborative care team. Paper records are a matter of the past, reducing errors and improving efficiency. Since the patient owns his or her information, the patient retains control and decision-making authority. Some people felt that this level of computerization would eliminate the human from the process. What they found at Cork Point was just the opposite.

The integrated approach allows Cork Point patients enormous flexibility. They can tap into health-care services throughout the community, the region, and the world, knowing that their current and most up-to-date records will be there for the doctor. Even when you're far from home, you are not treated as a number or research project. Your doctor, anywhere in the world, delivers highly personalized attention. Your information guarantees individualized treatment.

Doctors, insurers, and patients seamlessly share the data. Each has tailored analytic tools and visualization capabilities to use the information to best advantage. In the Cork Point system, the inefficiencies and errors due to disconnected procedures do not exist. Nothing touched by humans is perfect. Yet Cork Point's approach enables smarter decisions and delivery of higher-quality care; all because information is managed to create actionable knowledge.

The coolest part of the lunch was when Elle showed me how her new toy could project a 3-D hologram. It reminded me of when I was a kid and went to the first Star Wars movie. It was just like when Princess Leia loaded the Death Star plans into R2-D2 so that the Rebel Alliance could plan how to launch an attack.

Elle has just about the same level of detail and clarity. Too cool!

THE BAY IS ON ITS WAY

In the days before BIMStorm Chesapeake, Sandy was fortunate to experience a day with clear water on La Trappe Creek. Much of the bay was a dead zone. The water throughout the bay was so obscure that you could not see the bottom in water six inches deep.

People discounted long-term solutions to the problems. Only quick and easy half-measures could move forward. Time was running out. The federal government, state governments, and many others thought they controlled the problem, but the truth was that there was no central authority capable of reaching solutions. Those trying to solve the problems were the ones creating the problems.

The choice to link with as many people as possible turned out to be a home run. Crowd sourcing truly works, especially when supported by the proper technology. By making those affected by the problems into active participants, we were able to find common ground. If we had gone into this in the traditional way, this would have been another in a long line of well-intentioned failures. There is no way that putting the problem in the hands of a few people or pitting those with opposing views against each other could have worked. In the first case, no set of authorities and experts has the perspective needed to tackle the range of problem. The second situation would have done nothing more than create more conflict. The opposing groups would have continued to fight with each other just as they had for years.

Today we have the facts needed to restore the bay. We know where people's values are in conflict. We actively focus on resolving the ideological and cultural constraints that stymied earlier efforts. Political and financial constraints are becoming balanced. Facts and transparency are overcoming the logical fallacies and half-truths. The ambiguity and uncertainty are gone. People have a clear picture of the consequences of their action or inaction. Change is in the air.

The BIMStorm Chesapeake process took two years to complete. Planning and organizing twelve interconnected BIMStorms took lots of effort…but it was worth it. Reaching a shared understanding and commitment to solve the problems was time-consuming. Communicating what was happening, collecting data, and organizing programs to educate people about how to join took most of the time.

People have started to implement the concepts and solutions. They now believe that the Chesapeake Bay's problems are all connected. Most problems are symptoms of other problems. People understand that each problem is unique, and with this in mind, they are able to create interconnected solutions. Flexible systems are the way forward. They optimize for the best solution, taking into account the impacts on everything else.

Things are changing. The bay is recovering.

Four years is a remarkably short time to correct the mistakes of many generations. Overcoming regional impacts from the Susquehanna River is a significant challenge. Many of the pollution sources from the Susquehanna are extremely disconnected from the bay. It is difficult to change people's behavior when they are so removed from the problem. Fortunately, the BIMStorms have dramatically increased general awareness of the problems and solutions. Even people in Pennsylvania and New York know about the problems and are helping with the process.

Much has happened in the four years since BIMStorm Chesapeake Agriculture was completed. People have become engaged in the recovery. People have become involved in making the corrections needed to save the bay. People know how we got to where we were and how we can improve. The bay is on its way to health.

Farm families and the agricultural community have proven to be our most active participants. Significant numbers of farms in the region are now converting to sustainable practices. The newspapers project that 80 percent of the acreage in the watershed is now in the process of being converted. Major programs are underway to fully sensor every farm in the region. These programs are being underwritten by chemical and seed companies, supplemented by state and local government. The data and models that came from BIMStorm Chesapeake Agriculture have been fully linked into the central Chesapeake Bay Model Server, hosted at BIMSynergy.

The best thing to come from BIMStorm Chesapeake Fishing & Aquaculture may have been the dialogue and fact-based discussions that took place between watermen, the Department of Natural Resources, and the University of Maryland's Center for Environmental Science. The level of expertise and support that has come out of the program is astounding. The common sense and "eyes on the water" experience of the watermen, the hands-on experience of the aquaculturists, and the knowledge of the scientists are all coming together to find innovative ways to improve the bay.

Every BIMStorm has had similar results. Communities are coming together with developers to focus on transportation, infrastructure, housing, safety, and security. Industrial and business organizations are retooling their operations to become better environmental stewards. In Pennsylvania, there are significant efforts to resolve the mining and legacy industrial problems that have plagued the Susquehanna River for generations. Environmentalists and government agencies are working together with the Network for Sustainable Decisions to manage the entire effort.

The bay is finally on the path to full recovery. Just the other day, Sandy crewed on her friend Bob's Comet 111 out of Cambridge for a Wednesday night race. As usual, they came in third. But winning was not point; having fun with friends, getting a little fresh air, and then kicking back in La Trappe Creek was.

For the first time in twenty years, the water in La Trappe was clear. Sandy could see all the way to the bottom. She had been hearing stories about the improved water quality from the scientists at Horn Point Lab for a while. But, until she saw how clear the water was in La Trappe, she did not quite believe them. The bay is truly coming back....

INTERTWINED WORLD

People have been trying forever to understand the impacts of technology on society. The World Wide Web would have seemed like science fiction in the 1970s. In that era, pioneers envisioned or invented many of the technologies that make information models and an interconnected world possible. Visionaries such as R. Buckminster Fuller and Alvin Toffler foretold many of the issues that we are working to handle today. Much of what Fuller and Toffler envisioned is now possible.

To many people, the Internet of Things…Internet of Places…Web Wide World, may sound like science fiction. Imagine how the Internet and cloud computing work today and extend that to the physical world. Tomorrow, all buildings, things inside buildings, people, and business needs will be connected through the common interface of the built environment. The concept of a world where data and the Internet touch everything that we do is close at hand. The systems and processes are here today. They are not science fiction.

As the Internet evolved, it shifted from being a place to "view" information, to a place for creating your personal information and collaborating with others. The Internet is about you being in control. YouTube turned TV viewers into producers of content. Facebook and Twitter changed how you interacted with your social networks. Not long ago, few imagined a world of Google Earth, Google+, and Expedia. The Internet changed everything about our personal and business lives.

Today, if you are not connected to the Internet, you are no longer relevant. Google, Expedia, and Amazon have revolutionized how we interact with the world. Yet, even in this new "flat" world, many have not changed how they manage and deliver their services. There are incredible savings and efficiencies to be had by those who embrace change and think differently to take advantage of this new world.

Tomorrow, the connections will be more robust and all-encompassing. The three intertwining design futures in this book illustrate a few of the possibilities, but they are only a tiny sliver of the reality. Available tools and processes let us remove the disconnected practices and inefficiencies of the past to make the world better for us all. The Internet is bigger than information models, and it has the infrastructure to make BIG Data and BIG BIM a part of everything we do.

The core design future that flows through this book describes technology that allows people to manage complex information in the built environment. The BIMSynergy Corporation provides the backbone to maintain consistent, shareable, and reliable information needed to get the job done. The creation of BIMSynergy shows how a small and poor county can pull together to take advantage of today's technology.

Embracing short development cycles, the county became a world leader in the management of information to support the built environment. The BIMSynergy Corporation is just one of the public utility businesses that fulfills this requirement across the world. With systems and processes such as this design future describes, we for the first time in history can have a safe, verifiable, and accessible repository for the digital assets that help us to define and manage our real-world assets. The central design future forms the foundation for the three scenarios that use the information to improve our world.

The United States Coast Guard uses information tied to their operational processes to keep us safe and secure.

Information enables the Coast Guard to fulfill this mission in a world of ever-increasing complexity and danger. In this design future, you met Pete Jarvi, a BIM manager and your guide to how information is used to create certainty of outcomes.

Cork Point is a forward-thinking enterprise, faced with all of today's health-care and business issues.

Cork Point uses the intelligence of the crowd connected to information to redesign health-care delivery. They capitalize on peoples' passions. They use new technology and ways of working to let people use their art to create a better world. Dr. Elle Smith, hospital administrator, showed you how a health-care organization can use information to nurture and support the community, in a world of economic and regulatory constraints.

The Network for Sustainable Decisions is restoring a Chesapeake Bay in crisis.

The Network for Sustainable Decisions is tasked with creating the system that lets everyone actively participate in the revival of the Chesapeake Bay, while managing the interests of all. The group uses BIMStorms, ubiquitous data, virtual collaboration, and bioteaming in innovative ways to overcome the super wicked problems faced by the Chesapeake Bay watershed. Sandy Kim, a virtual enterprise manager, led you through the issues and a few of the opportunities for managing environmental recovery using live data, collaborative systems, and rule-based controls.

Managing information more efficiently allows people to interact with the world and increases information's value. Information is the currency of today's world. As our society becomes more complex and interrelated, we cannot continue to manage through traditional methods. The lines between the domains of architects, contractors, geographers, and everyone else are fading. Individuals are competing with the largest corporations. Technology and communications continue to compress our world.

Today we buy something from our "local" computer store and they deliver it to our door from the other side of the world, in what seems like the blink of an eye. We live in a world where the old ways of living, working, and playing are fading away, to be replaced by something new. Everywhere we turn, people are embracing information to become more connected and relevant.

DESIGN FUTURES

This book offers design futures for how society can take advantage of new and emerging technology to create a better, more sustainable world for our children. Today's technology lets us to talk to each other in ways that enable positive change. Technology allows each of us to make decisions about the things that affect us personally. Technology is leveling the field for everyone. No longer must we rely on experts talking at us as we find solutions to today's most vexing problems. We can all participate directly in the decisions, with real data, to get greater certainty of outcomes.

When we started *BIG BIM little bim* in 2005, people looked at the built environment differently. There were well-televised battles about whether we faced a global energy and environmental crisis. Financial markets were escalating as though investor confidence and price increases would last forever. Toyota was number one. There was little talk of systemic change. Business was thriving. Few understood the power and opportunities that technology could make possible. Few had a vision for how to move forward. But people were starting to understand that change was coming, whether they liked it or not.

Now, things are much different. A vision for the future remains elusive. We know that we must improve our energy and environmental sustainability. Green design and geographic and building information are beginning to intersect. We are slowly recovering from the financial crash, although too many are still out of work. Toyota's image is tarnished. Many are embracing new tools, and the cloud is becoming ubiquitous. Some are reaping financial benefits from the low-hanging fruit, and modeling is rapidly becoming a commodity. Complexity has changed the nature of the game.

Awareness of new technology in the environment, such as building information modeling (BIM) and integrated practices, has come a long way in a short time. These tools, coupled with owner demands for better, faster, less-costly projects and processes that are more effective, are driving change. There are significant barriers to improving processes in the built environment. Some of the barriers are due to ignorance…people do not know what they do not know. Some are due to inertia…people have a hard time changing to new ways of doing things. Some are due to self-interest…people are looking out for "number one." Some of the barriers are slowing the change, and others are undermining the benefits to society.

In this cycle of rapid acceptance, information modeling has become the "next new thing" and an important part of many people's plan for the future. Awareness of the technology's impact on society and the advantages to the public are lagging behind.

Decisions made without clear facts are fraught with risk in today's fast-paced environment. The pace of change, environmental challenges, energy uncertainty, and financial complexity work to increase the potential for catastrophic errors of judgment. Problem projects that are over budget, late, and not fit for their intended use are all symptoms of the problem. Adapting to an environment rife with waste offers opportunities for efficiencies, new products, and new ways of working that will make our world a better place for us all.

The built environment consumes most of our fossil fuels. With the world heating up and fuel becoming ever scarcer, we must do something now. We have the tools to analyze consequences and change trajectories. It is our responsibility to promote sustainability not only in design, but throughout our world. We must take action. There is no time to wait.

APPENDIX

Cedar Island Marsh near Coast Guard Station Crisfield, MD, 37° 58' 27" N 75° 51' 16" W

GLOSSARY

2D
Analogous to painting or hand drafting. The architect's equivalent to word-processing. 2D computer graphics deal primarily with geometric entities (points, lines, planes, etc.). Blueprints, construction documents and anything output (or drawn on) paper are 2D.

3D
Analogous to sculpture. Prior to computers, architects manually constructed perspectives and physical (cardboard, Foamcore, balsa) models to represent a project's design concepts. Today computers have automated concept visualization. These 3D graphics can be exported to rapid prototyping systems to create physical models. 3D computer graphics rely on much of the same programming as 2D computer graphics.

3.5D
3D with the addition of limited object technology (minimal object intelligence and not integrating NCS, NBIMS or IFC) or, 3D with implied movement (Ken Burns effects, trees blown by wind, moving people, etc.). This is definitely not BIM, no matter what you are told.

4D
Building Information Model with the addition of time (virtual building model with scheduling).

5D
Building Information Model with time and construction information additions (virtual building model with cost and project management).

Adhocracy
Adhocracy is a type of organization that operates in opposite fashion to a bureaucracy. The term was first popularized in 1970 by Alvin Toffler. Adhocracy is "any form of organization that cuts across normal bureaucratic lines to capture opportunities, solve problems, and get results" —Robert H. Waterman, Jr.

aecXML
Architecture/Engineering/Construction-oriented Extensible Markup Language. Internet-oriented data structure for representing information used in BIM.

Agency Construction Management
Delivery process where a construction professional organization is retained to exclusively support the owner, acting in the owner's interests at every stage of the project. The owner, with the assistance of the construction manager retains separate entities for design and construction.

API
An application programming interface (API) is a set of rules that enable software programs to communicate with each other and to facilitate their interaction. An API can be seen as the means by which two software programs talk to each other and share information.

Beyond Information Models
Uses currently available technologies and couples them with proven business management techniques to achieve integrated practice results—today, efficiently, and economically. Beyond Information Models firms have changed their working practices, methods, and behaviors to better support their clients. They practice "small is the new big" and achieve significant practice improvements.

BIG BIM
BIG BIM is like the personal computer once it is fully networked and fully integrated with the internet and has become a Web3.0 appliance. Using an accounting and tax software example, you access your tax information in a central database that someone else maintains. When Congress passes a new law, it is integrated immediately. You now have immediate access to the latest versions of everything. When you try to input illegal or illogical information you know it immediately. You add your information; standardized processes verify it and it is integrated with the central repository, where the system reacts in standardized ways, depending on the need.

In the design and construction context, you are working globally. You no longer work in isolation from anything or anyone. You integrate data from everywhere to understand what you are doing in a big world context. No longer is your context limited to the surrounding buildings or the neighborhood. Your client's business requirements directly affect your design. Now you know how a decision affects the bottom lines of the designer, the fabricator and the owner, before that are memorialized. You know how the direction that you are taking impacts on the environment and other resources. When you analyze your design, your results are repeatable and much more accurate since you are working with real-world information—not assumptions, guesses or opinions. You set constraints to control your work. Unworkable options are eliminated before you spend time on unproductive tasks.

Data and information are king. With BIG BIM your data is fed from a central repository that archives everything. The repository links information that once could not be linked. The data in the repository is shareable, interoperable and grows over time to encompass everything about an asset (as opposed to a building or a road or any other individual thing.) The data is invaluable. You can create or manipulate the data using an almost unlimited set of tools. It is truly sustainable and makes our world a better, more efficient place to live, work and play. Everything from Google Earth™ to spreadsheets to modeling software can be used by anyone that wants to interact with our world.

BIMStorm

BIMstorms demonstrate the power of faster and better communication, fuller stakeholder participation and, up-to-date...real-time information. Information models and Integrated Process data grows over time...allowing the management of facilities from beginning to end... without recreating the data at every step. The programs better align project needs, scope and budgets using BIM and Integrated Processes.

The BIMstorm leverages collaboration and work of the many. In whole, the process allows the group to visualize and test to eliminate the train wrecks before they occur. People quickly focus on preferred solutions based on significantly more data than in traditional processes. Adjustments are quickly made as more detail is added and decision points are reached. The process requires that key decisions be validated after completion of significant development efforts. This approach is seen as rapidly and comprehensively defining a project or work effort and then verifying why the information was added, where it came from and how accurate it is.

BIM Washing

There are significant barriers to improving processes in the built environment. Some of the barriers are due to ignorance...people do not know what they do not know. Some are due to inertia...people have a hard time changing to new ways of doing things. Some are due to self-interest...people are looking out for "number one". Some of the barriers are slowing the change and others are undermining the benefits to society. As people 'paint' the changes with their version of whitewash to confuse, confound and create personal advantage, BIM Washing takes place. Refer to - http://www.bimthinkspace.com/2011/06/episode-16-understanding-bim-wash.html

BIMXML
Describes building data (sites, buildings, floors, spaces, and equipment and their attributes) in a simplified spatial building model (extruded shapes and spaces) for BIM collaboration. This XML Schema was developed as an alternative to full scale IFC models to simplify data exchanges between various AEC applications and to connect Building Information Models through Web Services. Refer to - http://bimxml.com/

Building Information Model
1. To manage project information including data creation and the iterative process of exchanging data through the built environment value network: BIM includes processes by which the right information is made available to the right person at the right time. BIM adds intelligence to project data to allow data to be interpreted correctly removing attribution errors and assumptions. Or...
2. To create or work with a single archive where every item is described once: Graphical representations drawings and non-graphical documents—specifications, schedules, and other data are included. Changes are made to any item in one place and changes flow through the system. Or...
3. To represent physical and functional characteristics of an asset digitally in a reliable archive of asset information, from conception onward: without open standards and a focus on shared data, it is proprietary, not interoperable and not BIM.

    The acronym BIM (Building Information Modeling) was coined in early 2002 to describe virtual design, construction, and facilities management. BIM processes revolve around virtual models that make it possible to share information throughout the entire building industry. These virtual models are embedded with data which, when shared among design team members, greatly reduces errors and improves facilities. BIM offers owners the ability to become more efficient and effective by linking their business processes with their facilities. The federal government has predicted savings of over $15.8 billion annually from integrated processes. Projects today save 5-12% when BIM is properly used.

buildingSMART Alliance
The mission of the buidingSMART Alliance (a council of the US National Institute of Building Sciences) is to - Improve all aspects of the facility and infrastructure lifecycle by promoting collaboration, technology, integrated practices and open standards.

buildingSMART International Ltd
Renamed from the International Alliance for Interoperability. Subset of the International Standards Organization (ISO), charged with developing standards for standardizing how software represents data.

Business Model Canvas

Pre-formatted strategic management tool for developing and presenting new and existing business models based on nine building blocks of business conceptualization. Originally proposed by Alexander Osterwalder based on his work on the Business Model Ontology, the Canvas is a single, clearly understandable approach to business planning beyond the traditional business plan document. The Canvas includes descriptions of: Infrastructure broken down into Key Activities, Key Resources and Partner Networks; the Value Proposition; Customers broken down by Segments, Channels and Relationships and; Finances broken down into Cost Structure and Revenue Streams.

CAD Object

These objects are symbols and 3D representations that are static (line work with little or no intelligence). These objects are "instance-based," i.e., each use requires a new "instance" of the object, tailored to the specific situation. This approach requires a significant library of objects (i.e., one object for each size of window, another for each type of window and another for window detail). This approach results in significant storage and file size requirements to store repetitive and unconnected information.

Cloud Computing

Cloud computing is Internet-based computing that enables users and systems to share resources, software, and information on demand, much like the electric grid. In a cloud-computing environment, users are not required to have complex, powerful or expensive local hardware, since many of the processor intensive tasks handled in the 'cloud.' Refer to - en.wikipedia.org/wiki/Cloud_computing

Complicated tasks

Difficult to understand, but have an understood set of rules. If you follow the rules, step-by-step, you can solve complicated problems. Quadratic equations and building Boeing-747s are complicated tasks, but if you know the rules they can be completed successfully.

Complexity

Do not follow the same pattern as complicated tasks. One does not know where things are heading until other things happen. Things are likely to happen, about which you have no knowledge or control over. The unknowns and uncertainties that characterize complex tasks make them difficult to solve with traditional tools. With real-world experience, you can prepare for the known, unknowns that happen in complex situations. Other things are outside of your control. It is the things you don't know, that you don't know that make complex tasks so difficult to resolve. Farming is an example of a complex task. Many things can be planned; the farmer can choose the right time to plant, can use the land properly, but weather, pests, and all of the other things that cannot be controlled make the difference between success and failure.

Construction Management

Delivery practice using a construction consultant that provides design and construction advice. The owner retains design and construction services separately.

Construction Management at risk

Delivery process that delivers projects within a Guaranteed Maximum Price (GMP) in most cases. The construction manager acts as consultant to the owner in early project phases and becomes the equivalent of a general contractor during the construction phase.

Design/Bid/Build

Delivery process where an owner hold separate contracts with separate entities for design and construction. In today's environment, this is considered to be the "traditional" method for procuring design and construction services.

Design/Build

A construction method where the same company has contractual responsibility for design, construction and delivery of the project.

Design Fiction

"Design fiction has emerged as a pre-eminent tool for designing, challenging and understanding speculative future realities. However, design fiction aims to make the extraordinary ordinary. It merges the elastic creativity of science fiction with everyday matter of fact reality. Furthermore, in using current media conventions as a way to express ideas about the future, design fiction is able to twist reality and trick us into accepting the fantastic as possibility.

This process seems to afford us a moment in which we can reframe our expectations of reality. Consequently, it alters our conditional assumptions and stories we are using to define our future"… —Dr. Stuart Candy

"Design Fiction is making things that tell stories. It's like science-fiction in that the stories bring into focus certain matters-of-concern, such as how life is lived, questioning how technology is used and its implications, speculating bout the course of events; all of the unique abilities of science-fiction to incite imagination-filling conversations about alternative futures." —Jullian Bleeker, Near Future Laboratory

First-Order tools and techniques

First order tools and techniques simply follow the rules and focus on doing-things-the-right-way. They are the foundation for expertise and process compliance. Scheduling software is a first-order tool.

First Principles

Basic principles include the assumptions and basic knowledge that are the foundation for any other undertaking or activity. Math first-principles are called axioms or postulates. First-principles ground the texts, arguments, ideas, and themes that underpin society and are fundamental to the design and implementation of tools, processes and solutions in the built environment. Without understanding the principles behind things, responsible and reflective action is difficult or impossible.

GDL

Geometric Description Language. A scriptable language for programming intelligent objects using a fraction of memory of other modeled objects. A GDL object can store 3D information (geometry, appearance, surface, material, quantity, construction, etc.), 2D information (plan representation, minimal space requirements, labels, etc.), and property information (serial numbers, price, dealer information, URL, and any other kind of database information). Multiple instances of the same object but with different appearance, material, size, etc. are kept together in one object. GDL is especially important as the Internet emerges as the best communication platform for the building industry.

Georeference

Refers to exactly locating something in the virtual world, via coordinate systems. Georeferenced buildings are tied to established coordinate systems such that they can be rapidly located in their proper place and time. Latitude, longitude, and elevation are three of the possible coordinate systems for referencing a location. Georeferencing allows for high-level studies of relationships, causes, and effects in a real-world context.

Hyperbolic discounting

Preference for a reward that comes first. The value of later rewards are discounted, often rapidly discounting value due to delay, no matter the time involved. A reflection of a "I want it now" bias and a strong tendency toward inconsistent choices when considering future situations.

IDM
Information Delivery Manual is a document-mapping building processes, identifying results and describing actions required within process.

IFC
Industry Foundation Classes. IFCs define how "things" such as structure, doors, walls, and fans (as well as abstract concepts such as space, organization, information exchange, and process) should be described so that different software packages can use the same information.

ifcXML
One of the hundreds of XML based textual data formats. Defined by ISO 10303-28 "STEP-XML". Derived from the neutral and open Industry Foundation Class object-based file format. This format is suitable for interoperability with XML tools and exchanging partial building model

Information Model
General term for shareable, organized models of things that represent the relationships, concepts, rules, operations and other parts of things. Can represent an individual component or highly complex systems. Can be focused on buildings (Building Information Models), business processes, software engineering, data, semantics and many other things.

Infrastructure as a Service (IaaS)
Infrastructure-as-a-service (IaaS), is the category of cloud computing that refers to Web-based access to storage and computing power on the cloud.

Integrated Practice
Uses early contribution of knowledge through utilization of new technologies, allowing people in all industries to realize their highest potentials. Uses information and improved business process in a collaborative environment. With integrated practice, people increase the value they provide throughout the life cycle of any endeavor.

Healthcare is becoming integrated, as are most other aspects of modern life. The next great step for integrated practice is cross-disciplinary integrated practice. By example: design and construction become integrated with healthcare to deliver optimized services and support and creating built environment systems that are more economical, less wasteful and more beneficial to society.

Integration

The introduction of working practices, methods and behaviors create a culture in which individuals and organizations are able to work together efficiently and effectively.

Internet of Things

A world in which real-world objects are networked and may locate, identify and interact with people and each other. The Internet of Things (also known as the Internet of Objects) refers to the networked interconnection of everyday objects in a self-configuring wireless network of sensors whose purpose would be to interconnect all things... Also called the Web Wide World.

Intelligent Object

These Building Components can behave smart, i.e., they can adapt to changing conditions. The user can easily customize them through an interface. These objects are "rules-based," i.e., they incorporate rules that define how the object adapts to other objects, database calls, and user input parameters. Because of the "rules base," each object can represent an entire subset of an entity, i.e., one window object can represent an manufacturer's entire window line and can generate all 2D, 3D, details, finishes, shapes, and profiles. This results in significant decreases in the space required to store the equivalent information and results in very small files.

little bim

...little bim is like computing {circa 1987} before the internet. Networks {LANs} were not in widespread use. Using tax software as an example, you improve how you prepare your return and simplify the computations. You depend on software that you have loaded on your machine. You do not really know whether the databases included are up to date. You probably do not even know that there are databases behind what you see. You load new versions of the software as they are sent to you. You share files with your accountant via sneakernet or paper. You print out and mail your return.

In the design and construction context you replace AutoCad with Revit/Archicad/Bentley/etc... on your personal computer. You leverage your work product, but the improvements are largely internal to your office and your projects. In this mode, bim is really just regular computer-aided-drafting on steroids. You model your project. Perhaps you run simulation software, but you run it locally. You get all the benefits of real 3D CADD and then some. This is the mode where most people start to become virtual building proficient and what most people understand as BIM today. In this mode, people worry about what software they should use.

...little bim is also like computing [circa 1996] connected to a good local network and starting to transition to full internet connectivity. Taking the tax software example one step further, you now have centralized files from last year and you share the tax schedules with your accountant, so that more eyes are available to pick up mistakes. Your accountant takes your data and checks it for you. You either print out and mail your return or try e-filing.

In the design and construction context you are now beginning to do more collaboration. Now you can share information within a larger context. Data still comes to the network in a package, but more information is centralized and shared among your closely connected associates. You are closely linked to software and the data embedded in these tools. If you are the architect, ideally your engineers are on the same network. You begin to be able to do real conflict checking, cost modeling and process simulation. You have many of the benefits, but it is still mostly an internal, project-by-project oriented exercise that gives big benefits. This is the mode where most of the people talking about BIM right now are working toward. In this mode, people worry about what software they should use and are just beginning to figure out that they really need to change how they do business.

Mashable Software Fluency

Mashable fluency is the ability, skill or possibly, a self-perceived ability to interconnect software and hardware tools in order to solve problems in new ways. People that are mashable software fluent understand how software is built and deployed in the interconnected world of social networks, web services and APIs. They are seen as facile in the use of new of technology with a minimum of training and support. Those with a deep understanding of the open, malleable, interconnected application sets that make up today's cloud computing environment, and can leverage functional components and data from many sources to add value and create whole new kinds of software and solutions.

Microsoft Tag

Barcodes connect people with information, entertainment, and interactive experiences in the digital world. In mobile tagging, the barcode is what connects a physical object (a book) to a digital experience on a smartphone (a web link, video or detailed information). A 2D barcode like a Microsoft Tag adds a new dimension to books, making them more engaging and interactive. There are three types of barcodes:

1. Traditional barcodes provide basic product information using the linear barcodes such as you have seen on products for many years. Some services use mobile apps to scan these barcodes and display data such as prices, descriptions, and user reviews.

2. Quick Response (QR) codes are open-source with a variety of formats and reader apps. This old-style 2D barcode contains the entire message in the code, so online access isn't needed to decode it, but the barcode size varies depending on the amount of encoded data.
3. Microsoft Tags takes mobile tagging to the next level, offering more flexibility both in the barcode design and content behind it. Because Tags are linked to data stored on a server, they deliver a more robust experience and update the content can happen at any time without having to change the Tag.

Model Server

Model servers allow centralized storage of IFC information models allowing them to be accessed and modified via the Internet. Model servers are a critical element in the long-term management of building information that will be hosted, added to, and manipulated by a large audience over a building's life cycle. The IFC-based model server is a virtual building archive, is possibly the most innovative technical approach to the future of BIM.

Mote

A mote is a sensor node in a wireless network that is capable of performing some processing, gathering sensory information and communicating with other connected nodes in the network.

Multi-file approach

Multi-file systems use loosely coupled collections of drawings, each representing a portion of the complete model. These drawings are connected through various mechanisms to generate additional views of the building, reports, and schedules. Issues include the complexity of managing this loosely coupled collection of drawings and the opportunity for errors if the user manipulates the individual files outside the drawing management capabilities.

NBIMS

National BIM Standard. Standard for how information is presented via BIM, currently under development with the cooperation of the AIA, CSI, and NIBS. The National CAD Standard will become a subset of NBIMS upon completion.

NCS

National CAD Standard. Graphic standard for how information is presented via CAD systems, developed with the cooperation of the AIA, CSI, and NIBS.

Net Zero

Things that are Net Zero are self-sustaining and require not outside energy source. A Net Zero Building, is a building with zero net energy consumption and zero carbon emissions annually.

NIBS

National Institute of Building Sciences. Organization supporting NCS and the IAI in the United States.

Object Oriented

A computer program may be seen as a collection of programs (objects) that act on each other. Each object can receive messages, process data, and send messages to other objects. Objects can be viewed as independent little machines or actors with a distinct role or responsibility.

Parametric

Objects that reflect real-world behaviors and attributes. A parametric model is aware of the characteristics of components and the interactions between them. It maintains consistent relationships between elements as the model is manipulated. For example, in a parametric building model, if the pitch of the roof is changed, the walls automatically follow the revised roofline.

Platform as a Service (PaaS)

PaaS delivers hardware and software as a service without the cost and complexity of buying and managing and provisioning hosting capabilities. PaaS provides all of the facilities required to support the complete life cycle of building and delivering web applications and services entirely via the Internet. Model servers can be seen as PaaS or SaaS support.

Prototype

A working model used to test design concepts, impacts, and ideas quickly prior, to physical implementation. Integral part of a system design process created to reduce risks and costs. Can be developed incrementally so that each prototype is influenced by previous prototypes to resolve deficiencies, refine the design or increase understanding. When a prototype is developed to a level that meets project goals, it is ready for construction.

Software as a Service (SaaS)

SaaS provides software applications as a hosted service that is accessed via the internet. The Onuma System is a Software as a Service application.

Second-Order techniques
Use first order tools and higher level skills to adapt, modify and improvise to focus on doing-the-right-thing. They are targeted on achieving the end-goal. Google+ and the Onuma System are second-order tools.

Single model approach
Revolves around a single, logical, consistent database for all information associated with the building. The building design is represented in a single virtual building that captures everything known about the asset. From this database, all project visualizations, analysis and management information can be extracted.

Super-wicked problems
Wicked problems that include the added attributes of: 1) Time is running out, 2) No central authority has control or responsibility for the problem, 3) Those seeking to solve the problem are causing the problem and, 4) A strong tendency toward hyperbolic discounting of future costs and impacts.

Tame problems
Well defined with a straightforward problem statement. They can be complicated. You know when you have reached a solution. The solution is either right or wrong. You solve most tame problems using similar methods and the results can be tested to determine whether it works or not. Most of the project management tools that we use today are designed for tame problems. The ability to solve tame problems is a part of professional development and is a step toward mastery. Tools for managing tame problems can be called first-order tools.

Value network
The Value Network adds an extra dimension to the concept of Value Chains. Value networks represent the complexity, collaboration, and interrelationships of today's organizations and environment. Value Chains are linear and Value Networks are three-dimensional.

Web Services
A Web service is a method of communication between two electronic devices to support interoperable machine-to-machine interaction over a network, such as the Internet.
Traditional enterprises have popularized the use of web services via XML using Simple Object Access Protocol (SOAP) standards in many JAVA and .Net frameworks. An alternative approach, Web APIs have moved away from SOAP based services towards Representational State Transfer based communications (REST) services that do not require XML, SOAP, or other API definitions. Web APIs allow the combination of multiple Web services into new applications known as mashups.

Wicked problems

Wicked problems usually involve significant numbers of people changing their behavior and mindsets. A wicked problem is a moving target. When you think you have solved a wicked problem, usually all that you have done is to identify a new problem. Even defining a wicked problem is in itself a wicked problem. Wicked problems do not have a stopping point. There is no test of solutions to wicked problems. Rather than "right or wrong," a wicked problem can usually only be described by "better or worse." Every wicked problem is essentially unique and is often a manifestation of another problem.

Writeboard

Collaborative Web-based text development system that allows for editing, version control and change comparisons.

Definitions are compiled from a variety of sources including: Wikipedia, technology vendors, NIST, NBIMS, and others.

TIMELINE

http://interactivetimeline.com/391/makers-of-the-environment/

CHARACTERS

Pyotr Ivanovich Jarvi (Pete)

BIM Manager—US Coast Guard CGSysOps—Portsmouth, VA.

Age - Born June 15, 1976

Job - BIM Manager. He drives his 2014 Honda Civic to the Portsmouth to his job in at CGSysOps.

Ethnicity - Mother Ivana Borisovna, Russian met and married Pete's father in Helsinki. Father Jon Jarvi, Finnish. Parents emigrated to USA (NYC) in 1974 and settled in Wilkes Barre, PA.

Appearance - Pete is 6-4 blond, blue eyed and looks Nordic.

Residence - Pete lives in a brick colonial revival home at 694 Beacon Drive, Norfolk, VA.

Pets - Pete has a 2 year old Chesapeake Retriever , Missy that he is teaching to retrieve.

Religion - Pete is a staunch Lutheran and attends the Bethany Lutheran Church near Mt. Vernon.

Hobbies - Pete races his J24 that he keeps in the Paradise Marina in Deale, MD..Pete belongs to a gun club near Cambridge, MD and in the Fall and Winter, hunts Canadian Geese, near the Blackwater Refuge.

Single or married? - Married - Wife (Melanie).

Children? - Two kids Thomas (5) and Cindy (9).

Temperament - Theories which cannot be made to work are quickly discarded.

- Pete is able to tell you almost immediately whether he can help you, and if so, how
- Pete knows what he knows, and perhaps what is more important, he knows what he doesn't know
- Pete can hardly rest until he has things settled, decided, and set
- To Pete everything is negotiable... Anything is possible for Pete
- Pete is unsparing of both himself and the others on the project
- Pete has a seemingly endless capacity for improving upon anything that takes his interest
- Pete is one of the most open-minded of all people that he knows
- Pete is not at all eager to take command of projects or groups, preferring to stay in the background until others demonstrate their inability to lead

Favorite Color - Teal Blue, the color of his high school football jersey.

Friends - Pete races his sailboat every Wednesday evening with a three of his old college buddies.

- Will Thomas, a carpenter with New Home Construction has know Pete since third grade.
- Bob Smith, an engineer with Data Solutions met Pete at Rodney Scout Camp when they were 15.
- Frank Thompson a high school English teacher meet Pete at a frat party at Penn.

Favorite foods - A Pittsburg Style ribeye steak and baked potato with the works is Pete's kind of feast.

Pete's favorite thing in the world is a Crab Feast at the Red Roost near Salisbury, MD.

Drinking patterns - Pete got away from keggers in his twenties, but he still likes a few St. Pauli's with his crabs and who could resist a fine Bordeaux with a steak from Ruth's Chris?

Phobias - Pete does not like snakes, and breaks out in a cold sweat when he encounters even small snakes.

Faults - Pete spends every waking moment online. Pete sweats the details or, at times, omits them..Pete is known to take it upon himself to implement critical decisions without consulting their supervisors or coworkers.

Something hated? - Pete hates raw fish, Indian Food and Mexican food, in that order. He's a meat, potatoes and steamed crabs kind of guy. Pete hates people that don't pull their weight, obstruct forward movement or sabotage projects.

Secrets? - Pete has learned to simulate some degree of surface conformism to mask his inherent unconventionality.

Strong memories? - Just before he was 18, Pete became an Eagle Scout. To this day he gets warm feelings when he remembers his parents awarding the honor.

Any illnesses? - Pete is healthy as a horse, but has started to worry about his blood pressure and cholesterol now that he has kids.

Nervous gestures? - Pete taps his foot with impatience when people are slow or attending to what he sees as 'touchy feelie' things.

Sleep patterns - Pete goes to be late and gets up early. He doesn't seem to need much sleep, though he has been known to sleep in on Father's Day.

Elaina Bagayoko-Smith (Dr. B or Elle), MD, PhD
Hospital Administrator—Cork Point Healthcare—Crisfield, MD

Age - Born March 16, 1955. Known as Dr. B or Elle to those that know her well.

Job - Hospital Administrator. She is a FACPE (Fellow of the American College of Physician Executives).

- Cork Point Healthcare and Cork Point Virtual Enterprise Network.
- Elle has a 2 mile commute in her plug-in electric car to the Park-and-Ride and then a 30 minute commute on the light rail to the hospital each day.
- Elle's started building her specialized knowledge systems at an early age.
- Elle's desk is always immaculate.

Ethnicity - Mother Nikki Jones, raised in Columbus, OH. Father, Andrew Bagayoko raised in Mali. Emigrated to the US in 1949. Parents met, married and lived in Cincinnati, OH.

Appearance - Elle is tall and stately with a flawless, medium complexion. She is always impeccably dressed and coiffured. She projects a aura of power and assurance.

Residence - Elle lives in a restored stone farmhouse on 18 secluded acres near Marion Station, MD.

Pets - Elle lives on a working farm. They have chickens, goats, sheep and cows. There are even a few cats around to handle the mice. But, no pets.

Religion - Elle and her husband attend St Francis Episcopal Church near Chance, MD.

Hobbies - When Elle has free time, she does needlepoint and reads romance novels.

Single or married? - Her husband Efram Smith raises Guernsey's and is a leader in the local slow food movement.

Children? - Elle and Efram have two grown sons, Eric (26) a broker in Valley Forge, PA and Samuel (28) an architect in Philadelphia. Neither son is married and there are no grandkids.

Temperament - Elle isn't a Type A Personality, she is an A++.

- Elle is alert to the consequences of applying new ideas or positions.
- Elle has a very strong will.
- Elle is more self-confident than almost anyone else.
- Elle has intuitive abilities and a willingness to "work at" a relationship.
- Elle is an idea person.

- Elle sees what might be and says, "Why not?!"
- Elle enjoys developing unique solutions to complex problems.
- Elle is capable of caring deeply for others.
- Elle applies (often ruthlessly) the criterion "Does it work?" to everything from their own research efforts to the prevailing social norms.

Favorite color - Wild Blue Yonder, a smoky blue that reminds her of her husband's eyes.

Friends - Elle has a small circle of close friends.

- Elle attends Needlepoint Guild meetings to see her friend Susan about once a month.
- Elle helps her friend Joan to administer her churches Sunday School program.
- Elle has lunch with her medical school roommate Tracy about once a month a their old hangout near U Penn.

Favorite foods - Elle fancies herself to be a gourmet cook. On a lark between college and medical school she spent a year at the Cordon Bleu in Paris and never looked back.

Elle loves fresh food, local wines and traditional Pennsylvania Dutch food.

Drinking patterns - Elle restricts herself to club soda with a lime at the many cocktail parties that she attends as the hospital's representative. When Elle drinks she prefers Dirty Martinis, Beaujolais and Frascatis. Elle developed her taste for Frascati on her many trips to visit her art dealer friend in Florence over the years.

Phobias - Elle's fears failure and is compulsive about managing risk. Elle approaches reality as she would a giant chess board, always seeking strategies that have a high payoff, and always devising contingency plans in case of error or adversity. And, in no particular order: Doctors, Reimbursement, Competition, Regulatory bodies, Nurses, Patient safety and liability, Patients, Technology, Big donors and Foundations, Public relations, marketing, catastrophes and malpractice.

Faults - The knowledge and self-confidence which makes Elle so successful in other areas can suddenly abandon or mislead her in interpersonal situations. Organizational structure and operational procedures are never arbitrary, never set in concrete, but are quite malleable and can be changed, improved, streamlined.

Something hated? - Elle hates rigid attitudes those that cannot work toward a better future.

Secrets? - Elle was found to be legally responsible for a series of bad business decisions at resulted in harm to patients at the hospital where she had her first administrative job.

Paying the costs and overcoming the bad press took her years and she hopes that the issue will not continue to haunt her.

Strong memories? - When Elle was almost 14, Apollo landed on the moon. She and her father spent every waking hour for months before and after the landing studying, talking about and watching the event. To this day, it is one of fondest memories of her father.

Any illnesses? - In 2012 Elle had a breast cancer scare. A lumpectomy and a series of radiation treatments handled the problem and has had no further issues.

Nervous gestures? - Elle tends to pick at her cuticles when deep in thought.

Sleep patterns? - Between her obligations at the hospital, the farm and her other commitments, Elle never gets enough sleep.

Sandra Maria Kim (Sandy) PE, MVE (Professional Engineer, Master of Value Engineering)

Age - Born Oct 2, 1991 in Taos, NM. Know by all as Sandy.

Job - Virtual Enterprise Manager—Network for Sustainable Decisions—Princess Anne, MD.

Ethnicity - Latina/Korean. Mother Inez Maria from Juarez, Mexico. Father Thomas Kim, 2nd generation Korean who grew up in California.

Appearance - Small, dusky complexion with an oriental cast. Long dark mane of fine hair. Favors grays with bold accents, hates those that affect the current 'basic black' look.

Residence - Lives in a second floor, one bedroom condominium at 2368 Orchard Lane, Dover, DE with a view of the shuttles landing at Dover Air Force Base. Fortunately, she can do most of her work virtually. Besides, she travels more than she stays home.

Pets - 4 year Persian Longhair named Snark.

Religion - Raised Catholic and went to Catholic Girls School in Taos, but now toying with the New Scientologists.

Hobbies - Who has time for hobbies? Sandra is trying to make sense of so much data, that it's a 24x7 job.

Single or married? - Sandy tried that once and once is more than enough.

Children? - Are you kidding? Sandy manages to get away a couple of hours a week to meet with her 'little sister" at Fifer Middle School. She started to volunteer for Big Brothers Big Sisters right after she moved to Dover in 2015.

Temperament - Sandra is able to formulate coherent and comprehensive contingency plans.

- Sandra is a natural brainstormer, always open and aggressively seeking new ideas.
- Sandy can be quite ruthless in implementing effective ideas, seldom counting personal cost, in terms of time and energy.
- Sandy has the unusual trait of a combination of imagination and reliability.
- Sandy is ever perceiving inner pattern-forms and using real-world materials to use them.
- Sandy tends to be scrupulous and evenhanded about recognizing the individual contributions that have gone into a project, and to have a gift for seizing opportunities which others might not even notice.
- Sandy has an unusual independence of mind, freeing her from the constraints of authority, convention, or sentiment for its own sake.
- Sandy's self-confidence is sometimes mistaken for simple arrogance by the less decisive.
- No idea is too far-fetched to be entertained-if it is useful.
- Sandy is inclined to take charge of whatever is going on.

Favorite color - Forest Green, color of the plants she is working to bring back.

Friends - She sneaks away one week a year to hang out at her friend Wanda' house at Rehobeth Beach and always gets sunburned. Sandra is single, but has a fling now and again. Sandra power walks every day with her best friend Jodi.

Favorite foods - Sandy loves tradition Korean food, just like her Mom used to make. When you add green chili chicken enchiladas chased with New Mexico sopapillas, she is in heaven. She drinks at least six large lattes each with four extra shots each day.

Drinking patterns - Sandy learned in high school that she has a very low tolerance for alcohol. She has a Dos XX or a glass of chardonnay every so often, but rarely gets buzzed.

Phobias - Sandy cannot stand bugs, mice or anything else in her personal space. She has been known to go nuts over a tiny spider climbing up the wall in her condo.

Faults - "I've made up my mind, don't confuse me with the facts" could well have been said by Sandy on a mission

Sandy tends to have little patience and less understanding of such things as small talk and flirtation.

Something hated? - Anyone considered to be "slacking," including superiors, will lose Sandy's respect -- and will generally be made aware of this.

Secrets - When Sandy was 19, she went to Padre Island supposedly with her college room mates. Unbeknownst to her parents she spent the whole week in a hotel in Galveston with a dreamy Italian Count. She still has not told her Mom.

Strong memories? - The fears and memories from the terror attack on the Twin Towers in NYC when Sandy was 10 still resonate. Now she uses every bit of data at her disposal to make sure such attacks never happen again.

Any illnesses? - Last year Sandy's dermatologist found a small cancerous mole on her cheek. With a quick genetic test and a tailored ointment for a couple of weeks, the cancer was cured.

Nervous gestures? - When Sandy is very nervous, she pops her knuckles.

Sleep patterns - Sandy seems to never need sleep. 4-6 hours of sleep a night seems to be enough. She is online close to 24x7.

Joe Kranz, PE (Professional Engineer)
CM Project Manager and On-site lead for the team's construction Manager, Integrated Construction Managers Inc. (ICMI)—Cork Point Virtual Enterprise Network—Crisfield, MD

Rear Admiral Elmo Kosinki
CG Information Champion—In command of CG Portsmouth when terrorist attack begin—Portsmouth, VA

George Thomas
County Development Manager—Creator and driving force behind Somerset County's move into the model server business—BIMSynergy Corporation, Princess Anne and Marion, MD

Jim Krauss, PE (Professional Engineer)
Facilities Engineer—US Coast Guard Facilities Command in Anchorage, AK

Gary Boyle, PhD Information Dynamics
Information Director (Pete Jarvi's boss)—US Coast Guard CGSysOps—Portsmouth, VA

Fred Boyd, AIA (American Institute of Architects)
BIM Manager—US Coast Guard CGSysOps—Portsmouth, VA

Terrance Connor, AIA (American Institute of Architects)
Architect and Project Manager—BIM Delivery Company—Salisbury, MD

Sam Steen
Framing steel Fabricator for the new Care Center at Cork Point—Sparrows Point, MDBIBLIOGRAPHY

Recommended reading for those who want more information on the subject:

Alexander, Christopher et al., A Patten Language. NY: Oxford University Press, 1977, ISBN 0-19-501919-9.

Branko Kolarevic (Ed.), Architecture in the Digital Age – Design and Manufacturing, Taylor & Francis; New Ed edition (August 4, 2005).

Caudill, William Wayne. Architecture by Team. NY: Van Nost Reinhold, 1971.

Cheng, Renee, Questioning the Role of BIM in Architectural Education, AEC Bytes Viewpoint #26, July 6, 2006.

Cohen, Michael; March, James; Olsen, Johan, A Garbage Can Model of Organizational Choice, Administrative Science Quarterly 17, JSTOR 2392088, 1972

Cotts, David and Lee, Michael. The Facility Management Handbook. American Management Association, NY, 1992, ISBN 0-8144-0117-1.

Dettmer, H. William. Goldratt's Theory of Constraints: A Systems Approach to Continuous Improvement, NY: Asq Quality Press, 1997.

Eastman, Chuck, Teicholz, Paul, Sacks, Rafael, ListonKathleen, BIM Handbook: A Guide to Building Information Modeling for Owners, Managers, Wiley

Elvin, George. Integrated Practice in Architecture: Mastering Design-Build, Fast-Track, and Building Information Modeling. Hoboken, NJ: Wiley, 2007.

Feldmann, Clarence G. The Practical Guide to Business Process Reengineering Using IDEF0. NY: Dorset House, 1998, ISBN 0-932633-37-4.

Forsberg, Kevin; Mooz, Hal, and Cotterman, Howard. Visualizing Project Management: Models and Frameworks for Mastering Complex Systems. Hoboken, NJ: John Wiley & Son, 2005.

Friedman,Thomas L. The World is Flat: A brief history of the twenty-first century. NY: Farrar, Straus and Giroux, 2005, ISBN 978-0-374-29279-9.

Fuller, R. Buckminster. Operating Manual for Spaceship Earth. Carbondale, IL: Southern Illinois University Press, 1969, ISBN 671-78902-3, Lib of Congress 69-15323.

Fuller, R. Buckminster. Intuition: Metaphysical Mosaic. Garden City, NY: Anchor Press/Doubleday, 1973, ISBN 0-385-01244-6, Lib of Congress 72-182837.

Fuller, R. Buckminster. Buckminster Fuller: Anthology for the New Millennium. NY: St. Martin's Press, 2001.

Fuller, R. Buckminster. Critical Path, NY: St. Martin's Griffin, 1982.

Gallaher, Michael P.; O'Connor, Alan C.; Dettbarn, John L. Jr.; and Gilday, Linda T. Cost Analysis of Inadequate Interoperability in the U.S. Capital Facilities Industry. U.S. Department of Commerce Technology Administration, National Institute of Standards and Technology, Advanced Technology Program Information Technology and Electronics Office, Gaithersburg, MD 20899, August 2004, NIST GCR 04-867, Under Contract SB1341-02-C-0066.

Gladwell, Malcolm. The Tipping Point: How Little Things Can Make a Difference. NY: Back Bay Books, 2000, ISBN 978-0-316-31696-5.

Goldratt, Eliyahu M. What is this thing called Theory of Constraints and how should it be implemented. Toronto, North River Press, 1990, ISBN 0-88427-166-8.

Hatch, Alden, Buckminster Fuller, At Home in the Universe. NY: Crown Publishers Inc, 1974, Lib of Congress 73-91509.

Heery, George T. Time, Cost and Architecture. NY: Mcgraw-Hill, 1975, ISBN 0-07-027815-6.

Hino, Satoshi, and Jeffrey K. (Fwd) Liker. Inside the Mind of Toyota: Management Principles for Enduring Growth. Portland: Productivity Press, 2005.

Koch, Richard. The 80/20 Principle: The Art of Achieving More with Less. NY: Bantam, 1998.

Kunz, John and Gilligan, Brian. 2007 Value from VDC / BIM Use survey, Center for Integrated Facility Engineering (CIFE) at Stanford University, 2007.

IfcWiki-open portal for information about Industry Foundation Classes (IFC), List of certified software and Free tools that support IFC.

Jantsch, John. Duct Tape Marketing, Thomas Nelson Inc. Nashville, TN: 2006, ISBN 978-0-7852-2100-5.

Jossey-Bass. Business Leadership: a Jossey-Bass reader, Jossey-Bass, San Francisco, CA, 2003, ISBN 0-7879-6441-7.

Kieran, Stephen, and James Timberlake. Refabricating Architecture: How Manufacturing Methodologies are Poised to Transform Building Construction. New York: McGraw-Hill Professional, 2003.

Kotter. John P. Leading Change, Boston: Harvard Business School Press, 1996, ISBN 0-87584-747-1.

Kymmell, Willem. Building Information Modeling (BIM). New York: McGraw-Hill Professional, 2007.

Liker, Jeffrey K., and James M. Morgan. The Toyota Product Development System: Integrating People, Process and Technology. Portland: Productivity Press, 2006.

Liker, Jeffrey. The Toyota Way, McGraw-Hill, NY, 2004, ISBN 0-07-139231-9.

McKenzie, Ronald and Schoumacher, Bruce. Successful Business Plans for Architects, McGraw Hill, NY, 1992, ISBN 0-07-045654-2.

Nisbett, Richard E. and Ross, Lee. The Person and the Situation. Philadelphia: Temple University Press, 1991.

Ritchey, Tom; Wicked Problems: Structuring Social Messes with Morphological Analysis, Swedish Morphological Society, 2007.

Rittel, Horst, and Melvin Webber; Dilemmas in a General Theory of Planning, Policy Sciences, Vol. 4, Elsevier Scientific Publishing Company, Inc., Amsterdam, 1973

Rogers, Everett. Diffusion of Innovations. NY: New York Free Press, 1995.

Roundtable, The Construction Users, WP 1202 Collaboration, <u>Integrated Information and the Project Life Cycle in Building Design, Construction and Operation</u>, pub Aug 2004 and <u>WP 1003 Construction Strategy: Optimizing the Construction Process</u>, pub 2005, 4100 Executive Park Drive Cincinnati, OH

Smith, Ryan, <u>Prefab Architecture: A Guide to Modular Design and Construction</u>, Wiley; 1 edition (December 14, 2010)

Toffler, Alvin. <u>The Futurists</u>, NY: Random House, 1972, ISBN 0-394-31713-0, Lib of Congress 70-39770.

Toffler, Alvin. <u>The Eco-Spasm Report</u>. NY: Bantam Books, Feb 1975.

Toffler, Alvin. <u>Future Shock</u>. NY: Bantam Books, 1970.

Toffler, Alvin. <u>The Third Wave</u>. NY: Bantam, 1984.

Wilfrid, Thomas Nelson , <u>The Garbage Can Model reopened: Toward improved modeling of decision-making in higher education</u>, dissertations available from ProQuest, paper AAI9026670, 1990

ABOUT THE AUTHOR

Finith E. Jernigan, is an internationally recognized architect, educator, author and publisher. An expert in integrated practice using information model technology and next business practices, he has received unprecedented press recognition for teaching people how to use information modeling tools, including Google Earth, in new ways that help save money...and help make money.

Finith's award winning first book, *BIG BIM little bim* – The Practical Approach to Building Information Modeling – Integrated Practice Done the Right Way! is recognized as a clearly written and highly beneficial guide to making money from easy-to-use information modeling software and the dramatic business processes improvements information models allow. His no-nonsense descriptions of complex concepts made *BIG BIM little bim* directly applicable to building industry business processes that increase effectiveness of building design, construction and operation. Properly informed designers, contractors, operators and users achieve substantial costs reductions that save energy, reduce waste, increase the efficiency of material use and other benefits. With more than 40 percent of the world's resources focused on building construction and operation, many industry leaders predict that effective use of information models will help fight global climate change.

Finith uses proven systems and technology in new ways to help people everywhere move toward a more sustainable and integrated world. He teaches how to adopt and use a more integrated mode of work and life that streamlines processes, improves visualization, and achieves superior results during design, construction and beyond.

ACKNOWLEDGEMENTS

My special thanks to Professor Emeritus Bob Smith of Tall Trees Lab, Hugh Livingston of Interface Design Engineering Systems Inc., James Salmon, Attorney-at-Law, John Stebbins of Digital Vision Automation, Joost Wijnen of Oadis Open BIM, Professor Tamara McCuen of the University of Oklahoma, Chuck Brands of Green Build Energy Inc. and Deke Smith Executive Director of the buildingSMART Alliance.

I have not attempted to cite all the authorities and sources consulted in preparation of this book. To do so would require more space than is available. The list would include federal government agencies, AIA chapters, clients, libraries, institutions, and many individuals. I would like to acknowledge the following individuals for their special contributions; without their input, advice, and feedback, this book would have never happened.

My most special thanks and all my love to Beth. Without her support, none of this would be possible.

CONTRIBUTORS

Kevin Connolly, AIA, of Milwaukee contributed to the content of *BIG BIM little bim* and I have built upon his work in this book. Mr. Connolly is president of Connolly Architects and founder of the Triglyph Architectural Organization and Capital Facility Industry Information Works (CWIIW). Triglyph was one of the first collaborative groups designed to leverage architects' abilities within the information model environment. CWIIW works within capital facility teams to facilitate the flow of information across the development process.

Kimon Onuma, FAIA, president of Onuma Inc. of Pasadena, CA both contributed to the content of *BIG BIM little bim* and provided additional content for this book. Mr. Onuma is a thought leader in the information modeling world. His conception of the Object Genome, organizing the objects that underpin information modeling technology, has helped many understand the complexity and power of the process. His BIMStorms are giving hundreds the opportunity to work with BIG BIM concepts for the first time. Mr. Onuma won the 2007 American Institute of Architects BIM award for the US Coast Guard Web-Enabled BIM Projects and the 2007 FIATECH CETI award for the Sector Command Planning System for the US Coast Guard. My architecture and planning firm, Design Atlantic Ltd worked on both of these projects with Onuma.

DISCLAIMERS

This book explores possible futures for the built environment. It is sold with the understanding that the publisher and author are not engaged in rendering legal, insurance, or accounting services. If you require legal or other expert assistance, you should seek the services of a competent professional. Materials and processes discussed in this book may appear to disclose proprietary or confidential information. All such items are readily available in the public realm.

We have made every effort to make this book as complete and accurate as possible. There may be mistakes, both typographical and in content. The purpose of this book is to educate and entertain. Quotations used in this book remain the intellectual property of their originators. We do not assert any claim of copyright for individual quotations. By quoting authors, we do not in any way mean to imply their endorsement or approval of our concepts. To the best of our knowledge, all quotes included here fall under the fair use or public domain guidelines of copyright law in the United States. The author and 4Site Press shall have neither liability nor responsibility to any person or entity with respect to any loss or damage caused, or alleged to have been caused, directly or indirectly, by the information contained in this book.

It would be presumptuous to assume that this book is all-inclusive. There are many other ways to do a book like this. There are as many options as there are people in the built environment. This is one path to helping people learn about the changes that are happening in the built world. This book does not reprint everything that is available to those learning about the new tools and processes that are changing how we look at our world. Instead, it complements, amplifies, and supplements other texts. We urge you to read all the available material, learn as much as possible about new ways of managing, new tools and new opportunities. Tailor the resources to your individual requirements. For more information, look to the many resources linked to the book via tags throughout.

WHAT OTHERS HAVE SAID ABOUT BIG BIM little bim AND MAKERS OF THE ENVIRONMENT

Finith's approach to the highly dispersed subject of information management builds on the style he initiated in *BIG BIM little bim*, yet with in a much more ambitious context. His position is now firmly set as one of the foremost authors of modern information management techniques. His natural grasp of what is really important in Building Information Management (sic), and this work's fictional approach to the enigma of design information management helps the reader understand the implications of action and inaction from the human perspective. Instead of a work of dry technical theories, Finith manages to exemplify concepts clearly and with real application. Finith has a wealth of knowledge to share and shares it very well. In fact the "almost reality" style is so well written and so close to what we could, and should, be doing with our information models, that I was wondering if I'd missed out on some major changes in the industry. At least with this book, you'll be in a strong position to play catch-up.

BIG BIM little bim is, simply put, the most accurate description of how to BIM that we have at this point in time. In broad terms it breaks down the concept of Building Information Modeling into "bim" (lowercase) as software modeling tools and "BIM" (uppercase) as the integrated design and exchange of project data - Building Information Management. You cannot achieve BIM with bim alone. In fact you can be using bim and be as far away from BIM as you were with CAD.—Nigel Davies – AECO Expert, Director Evolve Consultancy

---

The buildingSMART Alliance in North America is working the BIG BIM issue and I believe that it is a very rich environment for significant transformation in the way we do business. Finith has done our industry a great service in pointing out this very concept. I heartily recommend this book be part of your mandatory reading.—Dana K. "Deke" Smith, FAIA, is known as the father of the U.S. National CAD Standard and, is currently executive director of the buildingSMART Alliance and, working to establish a BIM Standard to help improve adoption of the powerful BIM tool set.

"Masters of the Environment" combines ways for personally working out the richly latent opportunities of Cloud based technologies. It reminds me of the best parts of Douglas Adam's "Hitchhiker's Guide to the Universe", and Peter Schwartz's "Art of the Long View" - a guide and a roadmap that can be used today to think about key future dimensions of data and model based solutions beyond the engineering and economic dimensions too often used in scenarios. Adam's humorous work has evolved significantly into book, movie, and TV forms, shaping attitudes and perspectives, while Schwartz's procedural methodology evolved into thousands of consulting and public reports shaping corporate Fortune 500 firm's thinking and behavior.

It is easy to recognize leaders and decision makers trying to shape their "Built Environment" in siloed energy, water, disaster management, transportation, information systems domains who will strongly benefit from exercising with this book. Yes – the term "exercising" is appropriate. Finith's book is like an electric workbench to exercise their general ideas in the Time Line and the Narrative Table of Contents into more integrated and coherent projects that can be implemented to evolve successfully within an organization's culture.

Finith's earlier book, *BIG BIM little bim* clarified the frequent confusion between an industry standard technology for managing building data on the one hand, and the processes and culture for making decisions within informal social networks.

"A Fool with a sophisticated information modeling tool is still a Fool" - This fact is not always readily apparent at the start of a large project. Understanding how to working within a specific domain within a specific organization around specific problems is the essence of a great case study. Being able to extract management principles that can be cogently reused over time in defined categories of situations is the essence of a guidebook. Being able to assemble guidebooks and requisite knowledge from each of the primary built environment domains is the essence of a knowledge-based Model Server.

An Information Model within a Book is a powerful collaborative tool as long as the larger cultures and turf conflicts are facilitated at the appropriate levels. This is a challenge addressed by "Makers of the Environment" that has yet to be well described elsewhere, and thus remains a "Wicked Problem" in our world today.

However, what is meant by a "Wicked Problem"? Interestingly, Finith calls the first "Book" of seven "Wicked Problems in our World." The solutions for problems that refuse to be categorized are much more cultural than technical, and political solutions are seldom appreciated in the long run unless we have stuffiest data and the means to keep informed wisely. But, maybe this is exactly his point?—Bob Smith, Ph.D., Professor Emeritus at the California State University, Chair of the Green Energy Committee of the City of Huntington Beach, CA. Environmental Board and involved with the National Institute of Building Sciences and the Ontology Forum's work in Building Service Modeling.

As someone who co-founded and built a 20-person architectural general practice, and then moved to the client side of the table, this is a book I would urge any client to read. Although at first impression the author is talking to design consultants, it would also be particularly useful for facility managers and other client executives.—Gerald Davis, IFMA Fellow, ASTM Fellow, AIA, CFM President, International Centre for Facilities, Inc.

———————————————————————

A wonderful book that balances the dream of BIM in the future with the cold real world facts of the profession. It addresses many of the frustrations and peeves I've developed over the last 4 years and formalizes many of the solutions I've stumbled upon. Very inspiring and very practical at the same time.—Kell Pollard, Associate AIA, LEED AP, at Bender Associates Architect

———————————————————————

Finith is a true pioneer in this arena, having practiced what he preaches in *BIG BIM little bim* for years. This book will help you connect the dots in your minds eye between planning, design, construction, operations and maintenance and will show you the difference between thinking of electronic design - i.e. little bim - and thinking of smart buildings and smart infrastructure generally. If you don't own it buy it.—James Salmon, President of Collaborative Construction and Founder at Collaborative BIM Advocates

QUICK ORDER FORM

We recommend the purchase of physical books from either Createspace (www.createspace.com) or Amazon (www.amazon.com). Electronic copies can be purchased at Amazon, Smashwords, the Apple Store, Barnes & Noble, Sony, Kobo and numerous other online outlets. Contact 4Site Press for quantities greater than five copies.

Email orders: fulfillment@4sitesystems.com

Postal orders: 4Site Press, 130 East Main Street, Salisbury, MD 21801-5038, USA

Please send the following books, disks, or reports:

BIG BIM little bim: The Practical Approach to Building Information Modeling - Integrated Practice Done the Right Way! Second Edition

(softcover. ISBN 978-0-9795699-2-0) $29.95 USD   Quantity _____

Path to Certainty: A BIM Chronology

(softcover. ISBN 978-0-9795699-3-7) $19.95 USD   Quantity _____

Makers of the Environment: Building Resilience into Our World, One Model at a Time. BIM of the Book about Information!

(softcover. ISBN 978-0-9795699-6-8) $34.95 USD   Quantity _____

Please send more FREE information on:

_____ Consulting _____ Speaking/Seminars _____ Mailing Lists

Name: _____

Address: _____

City: _____ State: _____ Zip: _____

Telephone: _____

Email address: _____

Credit card

VISA _____ MasterCard _____ Security code _____

Card number _____

Sales tax: Please add 7% for products shipped to Maryland addresses. Shipping and handling in the US is $9.00 for the first and $6.00 for each additional book. International shipping and handling is estimated to be: $16.00 for the first and $9.00 for each additional book.

www.ingramcontent.com/pod-product-compliance
Lightning Source LLC
Chambersburg PA
CBHW080724230426
43665CB00020B/2605